Killing Machines

What causes a Western democratic leader to stop even feigning to value the law of war? Unlike past US presidents, who at least paid lip service to the law of armed conflict, Donald Trump has openly flouted it: pardoning war criminals, denigrating the Geneva Conventions, praising torture, and discarding military norms of restraint. This gripping account depicts how Trump has upended assumptions about America's outward commitment to the law of war, exposing the conditions that make such defiance possible. Drawing on in-depth case studies and original survey analysis, Thomas Gift explains how Trump has relied on right-wing media and allies in Congress to attack the law of war – not in the shadows, but in broad daylight. *Killing Machines* cautions that Trump's approach is not an aberration – it's a playbook other leaders could follow. This title is also available as Open Access on Cambridge Core.

THOMAS GIFT is Associate Professor and founding Director of the Centre on U.S. Politics at University College London. He has published extensively in top scholarly journals, authored popular articles for outlets such as the *Wall Street Journal*, *Washington Post*, and *Newsweek*, and is a frequent contributor to major media venues including the *BBC*, *CNN*, and *Bloomberg*. He has held fellowships and visiting appointments at Harvard, Yale, Stanford, Notre Dame, Oxford, and LSE.

Killing Machines

Trump, the Law of War, and the Future of Military Impunity

THOMAS GIFT
University College London

Shaftesbury Road, Cambridge CB2 8EA, United Kingdom

One Liberty Plaza, 20th Floor, New York, NY 10006, USA

477 Williamstown Road, Port Melbourne, VIC 3207, Australia

314–321, 3rd Floor, Plot 3, Splendor Forum, Jasola District Centre, New Delhi – 110025, India

103 Penang Road, #05–06/07, Visioncrest Commercial, Singapore 238467

Cambridge University Press is part of Cambridge University Press & Assessment, a department of the University of Cambridge.

We share the University's mission to contribute to society through the pursuit of education, learning and research at the highest international levels of excellence.

www.cambridge.org
Information on this title: www.cambridge.org/9781009675888

DOI: 10.1017/9781009675901

© Thomas Gift 2026

This publication is in copyright. Subject to statutory exception and to the provisions of relevant collective licensing agreements, with the exception of the Creative Commons version the link for which is provided below, no reproduction of any part may take place without the written permission of Cambridge University Press & Assessment.

An online version of this work is published at doi.org/10.1017/9781009675901 under a Creative Commons Open Access license CC-BY-NC 4.0 which permits re-use, distribution and reproduction in any medium for non-commercial purposes providing appropriate credit to the original work is given and any changes made are indicated. To view a copy of this license visit https://creativecommons.org/licenses/by-nc/4.0

When citing this work, please include a reference to the DOI 10.1017/9781009675901

First published 2026

A catalogue record for this publication is available from the British Library

A Cataloging-in-Publication data record for this book is available from the Library of Congress

ISBN 978-1-009-67591-8 Hardback
ISBN 978-1-009-67588-8 Paperback

Cambridge University Press & Assessment has no responsibility for the persistence or accuracy of URLs for external or third-party internet websites referred to in this publication and does not guarantee that any content on such websites is, or will remain, accurate or appropriate.

For EU product safety concerns, contact us at Calle de José Abascal, 56, 1°, 28003 Madrid, Spain, or email eugpsr@cambridge.org

Contents

List of Figures	*page* vii
List of Tables	viii
Acknowledgments	ix

1	The Impunity Presidency		1
	1.1	Why It Matters for Research	9
	1.2	Why It Matters for Policy and Governance	12
	1.3	But Is Trump a "War Criminal"?	15
	1.4	A Challenge to the IHL Consensus	19
	1.5	Case Selection: Trump	22
	1.6	Preview of the Argument	31
2	Means		34
	2.1	War Crime Clemencies	37
		Fox News	38
		GOP Allies on Capitol Hill	50
	2.2	Additional Examples of IT Synchronization	59
3	Motive		71
	3.1	"Law and Order" and Moral Foundations	75
		In-group Loyalty	75
		Authority	82
		Purity	89
	3.2	Survey of Attitudes toward War Crimes	96
		Support for Exonerating Crimes	98
		Support for Challenges to IHL	101
		Impunity Coalition Activation	108
4	Opportunity		127
	4.1	Norm Socialization and Ideological Subcultures	129
	4.2	The Impunity Coalition's Influence over the Military	130
		Trump	130

		Fox News	134
		GOP Allies on Capitol Hill	138
	4.3	Rise of Far-Right Extremism in the Military	142
	4.4	Illustrative Case: Storming of the U.S. Capitol	151
		Role of Current and Former Military Members	152
		Means	156
		Motive	160
		Opportunity	164
5		Impunity Here to Stay	168
	5.1	Trends in Conservative Media	169
	5.2	Trends among GOP Allies on Capitol Hill	175
	5.3	Other Political Pressures	178
		Lobbyist Organizations	179
		Troops Granted Clemency	184
	5.4	Impunity Synergies	192
6		Trumpism and the Future of Impunity	200
	6.1	Practical Takeaways	200
	6.2	Can Anything Stop Impunity at the Source?	207
		Nonbinding Methods	207
		Pushback from Moderate Republicans	209
		Critiques from Conservative Intellectual Circles	211
		"Guerrilla Sabotage"	213
		Cabinet Resistance	214
		"Self-Policing" by Other Western Leaders	216
		UN Resolutions	217
		Binding Methods	219
		Executive Order	220
		Accession to ICC Jurisdiction	221
		Impeachment	222
		Domestic Prosecution	224
		Global Prosecution	226
		Reforming the Insurrectionist Act	227
	6.3	The End of IHL?	228
	6.4	Why Trump 2.0 Could Be Worse for IHL	249
	6.5	Where to Go from Here	256

Index 260

Figures

3.1	Distributions of MFT values, by ideology	*page* 98
3.2a	Support for exoneration from the law, by ideology	100
3.2b	Support for exoneration from the law, by MFT values	100
3.3a	Support for using maximum firepower (control), by ideology	103
3.3b	Support for using maximum firepower, by ideology	104
3.3c	Support for using maximum firepower, by MFT values	105
3.4a	Support for disregarding the Geneva Conventions (control), by ideology	107
3.4b	Support for disregarding the Geneva Conventions, by ideology	108
3.4c	Support for disregarding the Geneva Conventions, by MFT values	109
3.5a	Support for use of waterboarding (control), by ideology	112
3.5b	Support for use of waterboarding, by ideology	113
3.5c	Support for use of waterboarding, by MFT values	113
3.5d	Support for use of waterboarding (Trump + Fox News treatment vs. control), combining MFT values	114

Tables

1.1	Presidential quotes regarding the law of war	*page* 27
3.1	Support for exoneration from the law, by ideology	99
3.2	Support for using maximum firepower, by ideology	102
3.3	Support for disregarding the Geneva Conventions, by ideology	106
3.4	Support for use of waterboarding, by ideology	111
3.5	Free-response answers to waterboarding question, by MFT values and ideology	115
3.A.1	Summary statistics for survey respondents	119
3.A.2	Support for exoneration from the law, by MFT values	120
3.A.3	Support for using maximum firepower, by MFT values	121
3.A.4	Support for disregarding the Geneva Conventions, by MFT values	123
3.A.5	Support for use of waterboarding, by MFT values	125

Acknowledgments

This book is the product of many individuals who, both professionally and personally, supported me during the writing of this manuscript.

It goes without saying that this volume would not have been possible without my friend and colleague Andrew M. Bell, who was instrumental in the brainstorming and crafting of this book. Andrew, who I first met in graduate school and has been a collaborator and supporter ever since, provided invaluable insights and feedback throughout the writing process, and it is to him that I owe the greatest intellectual debt. A very early version of this project was presented with Andrew at the 2023 U.S. Army War College Civil-Military Relations Center conference.

I am especially grateful to all my colleagues at the University College London (UCL) Department of Political Science and UCL's Centre on U.S. Politics. This includes, most of all, Julie Norman, Jeffrey Howard, Jennifer Hudson, Jonathan Monten, Michael Plouffe, Christian Schuster, and Lisa Vanhala. At UCL, I was also fortunate to have several tremendous research assistants who worked on this volume, including Anna Brierley, Rob Davidson, Dioni Ellinikaki, Victoria Krueger, Madigan Ruch, and Zoey Weisman.

I was lucky to have several fellowships that granted me an academic home and time to work on this book. I appreciate Terry Moe for enabling me to spend a term at Stanford's Political Science Department at the outset of writing this volume. I am also grateful to Adam Smith, who provided a fellowship at Oxford's Rothermere American Institute. I am also thankful to Greg Huber for arranging a fellowship at Yale's Center for the Study of American Politics.

Numerous professors and teachers helped inspire my interest in political science, and in ways both obvious and not, are reflected in this book. At Duke, this includes Erik Wibbels, Pablo Beramendi, David Soskice, and Mike Munger. At Washington and Lee, I was fortunate to learn from teacher-scholars, especially Art Goldsmith, Tyler

Dickovick, Jim Casey, and Tim Diette. I am further indebted to my former adviser Paul E. Peterson at Harvard, and frequent coauthor Carlos X. Lastra-Anadon at IE University.

This book also benefited immensely from the comments of anonymous referees who pushed me to clarify my thesis, which improved the text in myriad ways. The long journey from early drafts through to a completed monograph would not have been possible without them. At Cambridge, editor John Haslam was extremely generous in shepherding this book through the review process. Carrie Parkinson was especially helpful in compiling all the technical aspects of the manuscript, and Anjali Kumari did an outstanding job copyediting. I am also thankful to Kate McIntosh for her work on the book's index.

Most of all, personally, I have been fortunate to be surrounded by incredible family, friends, and loved ones who offered unwavering encouragement during the writing of this volume. Special thanks goes to my mother, Mary Finucane, who has always been my greatest role model and has been beside me throughout the good and bad of life.

Thanks to my father, Tom Gift III, and stepfather, Mike Finucane. Thanks also to my siblings, Amber Gift, Daniel Finucane, John Finucane, and Robert Finucane. A special thank you to my friends, including especially Chris Lauderman, Neil Sheaffer, Chris Tutor, and Shane Wilson.

Finally, a note to say that I wrote this book during a time of great personal challenge and grief. For those who have battled difficult illnesses, know that things can get better. This book is dedicated to everyone who is enduring trying times and believes that there is light at the end.

1 | *The Impunity Presidency*

"We train our boys to be killing machines, then prosecute them when they kill!"[1] thundered Donald Trump, who, despite being known for his shocking statements, still managed to rattle the Pentagon with his foreboding tweet. The comments, posted on October 12, 2019, came just weeks before Trump would do what critics deemed unconscionable: offer clemency to three U.S. servicemembers charged or convicted of war crimes.[2] In the view of many experts, Trump's actions constituted among the most conspicuous, and egregious, rejections of the law of war by a modern American president. The backlash was scathing. The *New York Times* asked whether the laws of war were "history."[3] Trump has "ushered in the death of decency," decried one legal analyst.[4]

What sparked such uproar was not just Trump's bluster. It was his scorn for the law of war itself. Even gruesome details of the atrocities failed to give Trump pause. Chief Petty Officer Eddie Gallagher, who fellow Navy SEALs called "freaking evil," had been charged with slitting an Iraqi teenager's throat and convicted of taking a photo with the

---

[1] https://twitter.com/realDonaldTrump/status/1183016899589955584?lang=en
[2] Philipps, Dave. Nov. 22, 2019. "Trump Clears Three Service Members in War Crimes Cases." *New York Times.* www.nytimes.com/2019/11/15/us/trump-pardons.html
[3] Philipps, Dave. Nov. 16, 2019. "Trump's Pardons for Servicemen Raise Fears That Laws of War Are History." *New York Times.* www.nytimes.com/2019/11/16/us/trump-pardon-military.html
[4] Brennan, David. Dec. 12, 2023. "Trump Has Ushered in the 'Death of Decency', Former Federal Prosecutor Says after President Meets with Disgraced Navy SEAL." *Newsweek.* www.newsweek.com/donald-trump-ushered-death-decency-federal-prosecutor-president-meets-disgraced-navy-seal-1478775#:~:text=Glenn%20Kirschner%2C%20a%20former%20federal,"Our%20government%20is%20unrecognizable."&text=Trump%20has%20taken%20pride%20in,and%20convicted%20of%20war%20crimes

corpse.[5] Army 1st Lt. Clint Lorance had been jailed for murdering two civilians in Afghanistan.[6] And Special Forces Maj. Mathew Golsteyn faced charges for the cold-blooded killing of an unarmed Afghan detainee.[7] Neither were the clemencies an anomaly. Earlier in 2019, Trump had pardoned Army 1st Lt. Michael Behenna, found guilty of murdering an Iraqi prisoner.[8] In 2020, Trump would also pardon four mercenaries sentenced for the deaths of fourteen Iraqi civilians.[9]

By the standards of his office, Trump's assaults on America's military justice system are unprecedented. But they are even more alarming when viewed against the backdrop of other brazen threats to upend norms of restraint within the U.S. military.[10] Consider that, as either a candidate or president, Trump has denounced the Geneva Conventions as "the problem"[11] and "out of date,"[12] pledged to bring back "a hell of a lot worse than waterboarding,"[13] advocated the killing of civilians,[14] promoted the widespread loosening of military rules

[5] Dec. 28, 2019. "Edward Gallagher: Navy Seals Called Platoon Leader 'freaking evil.'" *BBC*. www.bbc.co.uk/news/world-us-canada-50931195
[6] Tan, Michelle. Jan. 12, 2015. "Hero or Murderer? Soldiers Divided in 1LT Lorance Case." *Army Times*. www.armytimes.com/news/your-army/2015/01/12/hero-or-murderer-soldiers-divided-in-1lt-lorance-case/
[7] Lee, Carol E. and Courtney Kube. Dec. 13, 2018. "Green Beret Charged with Murdering Afghan Man." *NBC News*. www.nbcnews.com/news/military/green-beret-charged-murdering-afghan-man-n947586
[8] Zaveri, Milhir. May 6, 2019. "Trump Pardons Ex-Army Soldier Convicted of Killing Iraqi Man." *New York Times*. www.nytimes.com/2019/05/06/us/trump-pardon-michael-behenna.html
[9] Wamsley, Laurel. Dec. 23, 2020. "Shock and Dismay after Trump Pardons Blackwater Guards Who Killed 14 Iraqi Civilians." *NPR*. www.npr.org/2020/12/23/949679837/shock-and-dismay-after-trump-pardons-blackwater-guards-who-killed-14-iraqi-civil
[10] Neumann, Peter R. 2019. *Bluster: Donald Trump's War on Terror*. Oxford: Oxford University Press.
[11] Schreckinger, Ben. Mar. 30, 2016. "Trump Calls Geneva Conventions 'The Problem.'" *POLITICO*. www.politico.com/blogs/2016-gop-primary-live-updates-and-results/2016/03/donald-trump-geneva-conventions-221394
[12] Benen, Steve. July 27, 2016. "Trump Sees Geneva Conventions as 'out of date'" *MSNBC*. www.msnbc.com/rachel-maddow-show/trump-sees-geneva-conventions-out-date-msna882881
[13] McCarthy, Tom. Feb. 7, 2016. "Donald Trump: I'd Bring Back 'A Hell of a Lot Worse than Waterboarding'." *Guardian*. www.theguardian.com/us-news/2016/feb/06/donald-trump-waterboarding-republican-debate-torture
[14] Hains, Tim. Dec. 2, 2015. "Trump: Islamic State Is Our No. 1 Threat." *Real Clear Politics*. www.realclearpolitics.com/video/2015/12/02/trump_isis_is_our_1_threat_--_we_cant_be_fighting_everybody_at_the_same_time.html

The Impunity Presidency 3

of engagement,[15] praised torture,[16] and even endorsed dipping bullets in pig's blood, considered impure in the Muslim religion, to intimidate Islamic terrorists.[17] Trump has not just criticized specific rules for combat. He has discarded them as obsolete.

Trump's expressed contempt for international law does not stop there. He has attacked global laws on state sovereignty and the use of force, urging America to "fight fire with fire!"[18] Trump has threatened to bomb cultural sites,[19] proposed pillaging Middle Eastern oil fields for profit,[20] and lambasted the need to fight "politically correct" wars[21] while terrorists "chopp[ed] off heads."[22] Media headlines have screamed, "Endorsing Apparent War Crimes, Trump Abandons All Subtlety"[23] and "Donald Trump Says He'd Force U.S. Military to Commit War Crimes."[24] For decades, observers had seen great powers

---

[15] Cooper, Helene. Apr. 5, 2017. "Trump Gives Military New Freedom. But with That Comes Danger." *New York Times*. www.nytimes.com/2017/04/05/us/politics/rules-of-engagement-military-force-mattis.html

[16] Feb. 17, 2016. "Donald Trump: Torture Works." *Fox News*. www.youtube.com/watch?v=Kpj3pp10wD8

[17] Embury-Dennis, Tom. Mar. 19, 2019. "Trump Tells Fake Story about US General Slaughtering 49 Muslims Using Bullets Dipped in Pig's Blood, in Resurfaced Video." *Independent*. www.independent.co.uk/news/world/americas/us-politics/trump-muslims-general-pershing-pigs-blood-video-a8829676.html

[18] Jan. 26, 2017. "TRANSCRIPT: ABC News Anchor David Muir Interviews President Trump." *ABC News*. https://abcnews.go.com/Politics/transcript-abc-news-anchor-david-muir-interviews-president/story?id=45047602

[19] https://twitter.com/realDonaldTrump/status/1213593974679769093

[20] Borger, Julian. Sept. 21, 2016. "Trump's Plan to Seize Iraq's Oil: 'It's Not Stealing, We're Reimbursing Ourselves'." *Guardian*. www.theguardian.com/us-news/2016/sep/21/donald-trump-iraq-war-oil-strategy-seizure-isis

[21] Bump, Philip. Jan. 6, 2020. "Trump's Insistence on Proving His Toughness Is in Open Conflict with America's Actual Strength." *Washington Post*. www.washingtonpost.com/politics/2020/01/06/trumps-insistence-proving-his-toughness-is-open-conflict-with-americas-actual-strength/

[22] Hains, Tim. Nov. 23, 2015. "Trump: ISIS Is Chopping Off Heads and We Worry about Waterboarding." *Real Clear Politics*. www.realclearpolitics.com/video/2015/11/23/trump_isis_is_chopping_off_heads_and_we_worry_about_waterboarding.html

[23] Benen, Steve. Jan. 6, 2020. "Endorsing Apparent War Crimes, Trump Abandons All Subtlety." *MSNBC*. www.msnbc.com/rachel-maddow-show/maddowblog/endorsing-apparent-war-crimes-trump-abandons-all-subtlety-n1114976

[24] Morton, Victor. Mar. 3, 2016. "Donald Trump Says He'd Force U.S. Military to Commit War Crimes." *Washington Times*. www.washingtontimes.com/news/2016/mar/3/donald-trump-says-hed-force-us-military-commit-war/

coalesce outwardly around a set of rules designed to check the use of military force. Trump has proven that there is nothing inevitable about this equilibrium.

Trump now returns to office with an apparent mandate from voters, flanked by a Republican-controlled Congress. The main lobbyist for Trump's war crime clemencies, former Fox News anchor Pete Hegseth, has taken the helm as Secretary of Defense – a man who in 2024 declared that "[o]ur boys should not fight by the rules written by dignified men in mahogany rooms eighty years ago."[25] Mathew Golsteyn, who was granted clemency by Trump, celebrated the unorthodox appointment, saying that the military would no longer be "lions led by morally bankrupt sheep."[26] When Trump left the White House the first time, the risk of an impunity agenda emerging within the U.S. military was considerable. Now with him back in office, the risk seems inevitable.

How did we get here, and how will events play out? Put simply, that is what this book tries to answer. It is about a leader, Trump, who has not just strained the law of war in private, but dismissed the law's very validity, blatantly and unrepentantly, in the open. To date, nearly all analysis on the law of war in Western democracies, including the U.S., has assumed that leaders would pay at least nominal respect to the law's principles.[27] Even President George W. Bush, the modern American leader most castigated for ignoring the law of war, was known for vigorously trying to justify his post-9/11 "war on terror" in legalistic terms. Despite regularly testing, and at times clearly violating, the Geneva Conventions, Western leaders have long paid lip service to their basic strictures.

This book, by contrast, examines a radical departure from that norm – a democratic leader who has dropped even the veneer of caring about the law of war. It explores how Trump's defiance shatters

---

[25] Hegseth, P. 2024. *The War on Warriors: Behind the Betrayal of the Men Who Keep Us Free*. Fox News Books, p. 181.
[26] Ryan, Missy, Dan Lamothe, John Hudson, and Alex Horton. Nov. 12, 2024. "Pete Hegseth Has Said Exactly How He Will Shake Up the Pentagon." *Washington Post*. www.washingtonpost.com/national-security/2024/11/12/pete-hegseth-trump-defense-secretary/
[27] However, see: Travern, David. 2021. *Law and Sentiment in International Politics: Ethics, Emotions, and the Evolution of the Laws of War*. Cambridge: Cambridge University Press.

the long-held assumption, ingrained in the years following the signing of the Geneva Conventions in 1949, that Western democratic leaders will show public respect for international humanitarian law (IHL), the main corpus of law governing military conduct globally.[28] As the Trump case illustrates, even outward deference for the laws that guide warfare is fragile. The idea that flagrantly denigrating the law of war is no longer off-limits marks a crucial shift. It calls into question decades of presumptions about the normative influence of the global order regulating conflict.

This book examines the causes of Trump's overt challenges to IHL, but its analytic aim is broader. It attempts to advance a generalizable theory of when Western leaders may abdicate not their private, but their public-facing responsibilities to pay respect to the law of war. It makes a conditional case for this susceptibility. Drawing on in-depth case studies of Trump's war crime clemencies during his first term and original survey evidence from the U.S. public, this volume explains the conditions under which Western leaders may behave in ways outwardly hostile to the Geneva Conventions. Specifically, it answers three main puzzles: *What gives Western democratic leaders the (1) means, (2) motive, and (3) opportunity to overtly challenge the law of war?*

Regarding *means*, this book addresses how Western leaders can overcome a litany of executive constraints that, on the surface, appear to safeguard the law of war. "Structuralist" theories suggest that democratic leaders should be unable to maintain public support while driving through state and bureaucratic veto points that subvert IHL. By comparison, this book draws on studies of collective mobilization[29]

---

[28] For an overview of IHL, when it applies, and its underlying ethical basis, see: Bohrer, Ziv, Janina Dill, and Helen Duffy. 2020. *Law Applicable to Armed Conflict*. Cambridge: Cambridge University Press. Crawford, Emily and Alison Pert. 2024. *International Humanitarian Law*. Cambridge: Cambridge University Press. Dill, Janina. 2015. *Legitimate Targets: Social Construction, International Law and US Bombing*. Cambridge: Cambridge University Press. Frowe, Helen and Seth Lazar. 2018. *The Oxford Handbook of Ethics of War*. Oxford: Oxford University Press. Rudolphy, Marcela Prieto. 2023. *The Morality of the Laws of War: War, Law, and Murder*. Oxford: Oxford University Press. Solis, Gary D. 2012. *The Law of Armed Conflict: International Humanitarian Law in War*, 3rd ed. Cambridge: Cambridge University Press.

[29] Medina, Luis Fernando. 2013. "The Analytical Foundations of Collective Action Theory: A Survey of Some Recent Development." *Annual Review of Political Science* 16(1): 259–283. Olson, Mancur. 1965. *The Logic of*

to show how leaders, as political entrepreneurs,[30] can marshal allies to consolidate power while disregarding the law of war. The explanation resembles a substantial scholarship on democratic backsliding, where would-be authoritarians undercut institutions by relying on ideologically aligned partners both inside and outside of government.[31]

Next, concerning *motive*, this book grapples with why democratic leaders may possess an incentive to blatantly disrespect IHL even when voters profess to value law and order. "Domestic audience cost" theories indicate that no natural electorate exists in democracies for explicitly challenging the law of war. Yet mounting research shows that citizens are often willing to trade off between an ethical aversion to contravening IHL and other priorities, such as achieving military advantage.[32] This volume adds to that scholarship by tracing

---

Collective Action: Public Goods and the Theory of Groups. Cambridge, MA: Harvard University Press. Ostrom, Elinor. 2009. "Collective Action Theory." In Boix, Carles and Susan C. Stokes, eds. *The Oxford Handbook of Comparative Politics*. Oxford: Oxford University Press.

[30] Moe, Terry M. 1988. *The Organization of Interests: Incentives and the Internal Dynamics of Political Interest Groups*. Chicago: University of Chicago Press. North, Douglass Cecil. 1990. *Institutions, Institutional Change, and Economic Performance: The Political Economy of Institutions and Decisions*. New York: Cambridge University Press. Riker, William H. 1986. *The Art of Political Manipulation*. New Haven: Yale University Press.

[31] Diamond, Larry. 2021. "Democratic Regression in Comparative Perspective: Scope, Methods, and Causes." *Democratization* 28(1): 22–42. Haggard, Stephan and Robert Kaufman. 2021. *Backsliding: Democratic Regress in the Contemporary World*. Cambridge: Cambridge University Press. Haemin Jee, Hans Lueders, and Rachel Myrick. 2022. "Towards a Unified Approach to Research on Democratic Backsliding." *Democratization* 29(4): 754–767. Norris, Pippa. 2017. "Is Western Democracy Backsliding? Diagnosing the Risks." HKS Working Paper No. RWP17-012. www.hks.harvard.edu/publications/western-democracy-backsliding-diagnosing-risks/. Przeworski, Adam. 2019. *Crises of Democracy*. Cambridge: Cambridge University Press. Waldner, David and Ellen Lust. 2018. "Unwelcome Change: Coming to Terms with Democratic Backsliding." *Annual Review of Political Science* 21: 93–113.

[32] Carpenter, Charli, Alexander H. Montgomery, and Alexandria Nylen. 2020. "Breaking Bad? How Survey Experiments Prime Americans for War Crimes." *Perspectives on Politics* 19(3): 912–924. Chilton, Adam S. 2015. "The Laws of War and Public Opinion: An Experimental Study." *Journal of Institutional and Theoretical Economics* 171(1): 181–201. Gelpi, Christopher, Peter D. Feaver, and Jason Reifler. 2009. *Paying the Human Costs of War: American Public Opinion and Casualties in Military Conflicts*. Princeton: Princeton University Press. Hatz, Sophia. 2021. "What Shapes Public Support for Torture, and Among Whom?" *Human Rights Quarterly* 43(4): 683–698.

how ideology correlates with the foundational moral values of voters, which can yield public support for overt challenges to the law of war. It further reveals how elites can activate these preferences through selective, top-down messaging.

Last, regarding *opportunity*, this book addresses how democratic leaders can exploit political openings even in militaries that purport to prioritize IHL in their official doctrines and training. "Socialization" theories tend to assume that respect for IHL is deeply embedded in the cultures of professionalized, Western militaries. However, growing research indicates that these norms of restraint are often uneven within armed organizations.[33] Leveraging studies that highlight political polarization in the U.S. military,[34] this volume explains how pockets of ideological extremism can, even if isolated, back overt rejections of IHL. Amid civil-military relations that offer a permissive climate for partisan activation, leaders may manipulate this environment for office-seeking ends.

Liberman, Peter. 2006. "An Eye for an Eye: Public Support for War Against Evildoers." *International Organization* 60(3): 687–722. Sagan, Scott D., Benjamin A. Valentino, Charli Carpenter, and Alexander H. Montgomery. 2020. "Does the Noncombatant Immunity Norm Have Stopping Power? A Debate." *International Security* 45(2): 170–186. Wallace, Geoffrey P.R. 2013. "International Law and Public Attitudes toward Torture: An Experimental Study." *International Organization* 67(1): 105–140.

[33] Bell, Andrew. 2021. "Combatant Socialization and Norms of Restraint: Examining Officer Training at the US Military Academy and Army ROTC." *Journal of Peace Research* 59(2): 130–196. Bell, Andrew M., Thomas Gift, and Jonathan Monten. 2022. "The Moral Foundations of Restraint: Partisanship, Military Training, and Norms of Civilian Protection." *Journal of Peace Research* 59(5): 694–709. Stephens, Dale. 2019. "Roots of Restraint in War: The Capacities and Limits of Law and the Critical Role of Social Agency in Ameliorating Violence in Armed Conflict." *Journal of International Humanitarian Legal Studies* 10(1): 58–75.

[34] Feaver, Peter D. and Richard H. Kohn, eds. 2001. *Soldiers and Civilians: The Civil-Military Gap and American National Security*. Cambridge, MA: MIT Press. Holsti, Ole. 2001–2002. "Politicization of the United States Military: Crisis or Tempest in a Teapot?" *International Journal* 57(1): 1–18. Liebert, Hugh, and James Golby. 2017. "Midlife Crisis? The All-Volunteer Force at 40." *Armed Forces and Society* 43(1): 115–138. Robinson, Michael A. 2023. *Dangerous Instrument: Political Polarization and US Civil-Military Relations*. Oxford: Oxford University Press. Urben, Heidi A. 2014. "Wearing Politics on Their Sleeves? Levels of Political Activism of Active Duty Army Officers." *Armed Forces and Society* 40(3): 568–591. Urben, Heidi A. 2021. *Party, Politics, and the Post-9/11 Army*. New York: Cambria Press.

This book's thesis closely parallels a broader phenomenon ascribed to Trump, and increasingly, other Western leaders[35] – that of assaulting seemingly sacrosanct laws and norms not "in the shadows," but "in the daylight."[36] In the past, allegations of U.S. military violations of IHL tended to spotlight scandals like abuse at Central Intelligence Agency (CIA) "black sites"[37] or cover-ups of misdirected drone strikes.[38] However, a defining feature of Trump's reign has been that, in everything from trying to overturn an election[39] to explicit race-baiting,[40] Trump has made few attempts to conceal wrongdoing. In a comparable way, Trump has applied this method to attack IHL overtly. Even if most democratic leaders will not follow suit, Trump's tactics constitute a new, if potentially devastating, blueprint.

At the broadest level, this book underscores the centrality of a leader's professed values in upholding the law of war in advanced, Western democracies. It concludes that Trump's record should prompt, if not a reversal in how experts think about the proclivity of democracies to succumb to disrespect of IHL, at least greater awareness of the dangers. If Trump can openly challenge the law of war in the U.S., an unlikely case, other Western democracies may also be at risk. Trump may uniquely personify a democratic leader eager to prey on vulnerabilities that result in direct, sustained strains to IHL. However,

---

[35] Faiola, Anthony. May 19, 2016. "Meet the Donald Trumps of Europe." *Washington Post.* www.washingtonpost.com/news/worldviews/wp/2016/05/19/meet-the-donald-trumps-of-europe/

[36] Baker, Peter and Susan Glasser. 2022. *The Divider: Trump in the White House, 2017–2021.* New York: Doubleday. Frum, David. 2020. *Trumpocalypse: Restoring American Democracy.* New York: Harper. Klaas, Brian. Jan. 14, 2020. "After Three Years of Trump, We've Lost Our Ability to Be Shocked." *Washington Post.* www.washingtonpost.com/opinions/2020/01/14/after-three-years-trump-weve-lost-our-ability-be-shocked/

[37] Mudd, Philip. 2019. *Black Site: The CIA in the Post-9/11 World.* New York: Liveright.

[38] Khan, Azmat. Dec. 18, 2021. "Hidden Pentagon Records Reveal Patterns of Failure in Deadly Airstrikes." *New York Times.* www.nytimes.com/interactive/2021/12/18/us/airstrikes-pentagon-records-civilian-deaths.html

[39] Bump, Philip. Aug. 2, 2023. "The Alleged Trump Crime That We All Saw." *Washington Post.* www.washingtonpost.com/politics/2023/08/02/trump-indictment-doj-jan6/

[40] Cassidy, John. July 15, 2019. "Trump's Overt Racism Is Uniting Democrats and Unnerving Some Republicans." *New Yorker.* www.newyorker.com/news/our-columnists/trumps-overt-racism-is-uniting-democrats-and-unnerving-some-republicans

assuming that similar conditions will not emerge elsewhere clings too strongly to the hope that the post-1949 Geneva Conventions world is "different" from the past.

1.1 Why It Matters for Research

Trump's overt disrespect for IHL "matters." It matters for scholarship because the central topic of when leaders publicly uphold or reject IHL speaks to a largely understudied question in international politics and law. While a rich literature exists on what binds regimes to IHL, the bulk of this research centers on the related, but separate, question of compliance: whether nations refuse to torture, intentionally kill civilians, or commit other heinous acts in war.[41] Studies mostly take for granted that leaders will uphold "parchment guarantees," basic declarations of rights and protections intended to engender dignity amid political violence. These aspirations set the norms, or "rules of the game," within which militaries operate, deploy force, and project power.[42]

The lack of systematic research into how Western leaders publicly treat the law of war may be partially attributable to the difficulty of operationalization. Public statements and acts that severely breach norms are subjective, rare, and difficult to quantify in large-N, cross-country analyses. However, likely more significant is the prevailing belief that major international arrangements such as the law of war exhibit inertia. Political scientists and legal scholars often assume "path dependency," where global actors and institutions "lock in"

---

[41] Kriger, Heikie. 2015. *Inducing Compliance with International Humanitarian Law: Lessons from the African Great Lakes Region*. Cambridge: Cambridge University Press. Simmons, Beth. 2010. "Treaty Compliance and Violation." *Annual Review of Political Science* 13(1): 273–296. Stubbins-Bates, Elizabeth. 2025. *A Framework for Compliance in International Humanitarian Law*. London: Bloomsbury. Watkin, Kenneth. 2016. *Fighting at the Legal Boundaries: Controlling the Use of Force in Contemporary Conflicts*. New York: Oxford University Press.

[42] Hayashi, Nobuo. *Military Necessity: The Art, Morality, and Law of War*. Cambridge: Cambridge University Press. Lazar, Seth and Helen Frowe, eds. 2018. *The Oxford Handbook of Ethics of War*. New York: Oxford University Press. Lucas, Jr. George R. 2016. *Military Ethics: What Everyone Needs to Know*. New York: Oxford University Press. North, Douglass A. 1990. *Institutions, Institutional Change and Economic Performance*. New York: Cambridge University Press.

over time.[43] For example, legal academic Mark A. Pollack summarizes that the "dominant view of most IR and legal scholars" is that "international institutions enjoy substantial robustness."[44] This consensus has largely extended to the Geneva Conventions.

Since at least the signing of the Geneva Conventions in 1949, scholars have broadly expressed confidence that party states would not stray too far, at least publicly, from their formal commitments to embrace IHL. For instance, researchers Matthew Evangelista and Nina Tannewald are hardly alone in referring to the "widespread acceptance of the Geneva Conventions norms in principle."[45] Sociologist Sidney Tarrow has likewise observed the phenomenon of global leaders feeling the need to "pay … lip service to the Geneva Conventions" even when violating the rules in private.[46] Gerald Draper wrote decades ago that "[t]here can be seen the strong impression that it is a bad thing to be discovered, *flagrante delicto*, violating the Law of War."[47]

Even among experts who are skeptical that Western leaders will publicly commit to IHL, the presumption has been that any deviation would be short-lived. Legal scholar Harold Koh, for instance, has suggested that "bold public acts of resistance" and "high opportunity costs, and international realpolitik realities" rein in leaders from ignoring international law.[48] The expectation is that efforts to upend IHL would be met with the same self-correcting mechanisms that have fortified the Geneva Conventions for more than a half-century. Because global compacts are harder to create than to maintain, once created, they are likely to prove robust.[49] The conjecture has been that

---

[43] Pierson, Paul. 2000. "Increasing Returns, Path Dependence, and the Study of Politics." *American Political Science Review* 94(2): 251–267.

[44] Pollack, Mark A. 2023. "Trump as a Change Agent in International Law: Ends, Means, and Legacies." In Krisch, Nico and Ezgi Yildiz, eds. *The Many Paths of Change in International Law*. Oxford: Oxford University Press.

[45] Tannewald, Nina. 2017. "Assessing the Effects and Effectiveness of the Geneva Conventions." In Evangelista, Matthew and Nina Tannewald, eds. *Do the Geneva Conventions Matter?* New York: Oxford University Press.

[46] Tarrow, Sidney. 2015. "War and Social Movements." *Emerging Trends in the Social and Behavioral Sciences*.

[47] Draper, Gerald I.A. 1965. "Rules Governing the Conduct of Hostilities – The Law of War and Their Enforcement." *International Law Issue* 18(3): 22–45.

[48] Koh, Harold. 2017. "The Trump Administration and International Law." *Washburn Law Journal* 56: 413–469.

[49] Keohane, Robert O. 1984. *After Hegemony*. Princeton: Princeton University Press.

outward respect for IHL would be especially durable where leaders are subject to democratic constraints.

Like extensive research linking democracies to an international "zone of law" generally,[50] the idea that democracies are in fact more embracing of IHL has elicited considerable attention.[51] Many studies point to democracies having better IHL adherence records, such as being more apt to ratify IHL principles,[52] to support the International Criminal Court (ICC),[53] to take fewer civilian casualties,[54] and to perpetrate fewer mass killings in counterinsurgencies.[55] Other scholarship, however, has disputed this claim.[56] Yet according to most scholars, democracies always revert to holding the law of war in high regard publicly. As political scientist James Morrow has explained,

---

[50] Simmons, Beth A. 1998. "Compliance with International Agreements." *Annual Review of Political Science* 1: 75–93.

[51] Ginsburg, Tom. 2021. *Democracies and International Law*. Cambridge: Cambridge University Press. Ginsburg, Tom. 2022. "Democracies and International Law: An Update." *Chicago Journal of International Law* 23(1): 1–26. Tannenwald, Nina. 2017. "Assessing the Effects and Effectiveness of the Geneva Conventions." In Evangelista, Matthew and Nina Tannenwald, eds. *Do the Geneva Conventions Matter?* New York: Oxford University Press.

[52] Morrow, James D. 2007. "Why Do States Follow the Laws of War." *American Political Science Review* 101(3): 559–572.

[53] Chapman, Terrence L. and Stephen Chaudoin. 2013. "Ratification Patterns and the International Criminal Court." *International Studies Quarterly* 57(2): 400–409. Meernik, James and Jamie Shairick. 2011. "Promoting International Humanitarian Law: Strong States and the Ratification of the ICC Treaty." *International Area Studies Review* 14(2): 23–48. Simmons, Beth and Allison Danner. 2010. "Credible Commitments and the International Criminal Court." *International Organization* 64(2): 225–256.

[54] Valentino, Benjamin A., Paul K. Huth, and Sarah E. Croco. "Bear Any Burden? How Democracies Minimize the Costs of War." *Journal of Politics* 72(2): 528–544.

[55] Valentino, Benjamin, Paul Huth, and Dylan Balch-Lindsay. 2004. "'Draining the Sea': Mass Killing and Guerrilla Warfare." *International Organization* 58(2): 375–407.

[56] Conrad, Courtenay R., Daniel W. Hill, Jr., and Will H. Moore. 2018. "Torture and the Limits of Democratic Institutions." *Journal of Peace Research* 55(1): 3–17. Downes, Alexander. 2007. "Restraint or Propellant? Democracy and Civilian Fatalities in Interstate Wars." *Journal of Conflict Resolution* 51(6): 872–904. Downes, Alexander. 2008. *Targeting Civilians in War*. Ithaca: Cornell University Press. Valentino, Benjamin, Paul Huth, and Sarah Croco. 2011. "Covenants without the Sword International Law and the Protection of Civilians in Times of War." *World Politics* 58(3): 339–377. Rejali, Darius. 2009. *Torture and Democracy*. Princeton: Princeton University Press.

even when democratic leaders breach IHL, "they do not do so in clear violation of their legal obligations and commonly offer a legal justification to cover their acts."[57]

The Trump case, however, deviates sharply from this pattern. No other modern Western leader has so clearly and consistently displayed contempt for IHL publicly. Democracies are not free from leaders who violate the Geneva Conventions in secret, or under the guise of compliance. Yet as political scientist David Forsyth has written, appeals to the universal values of the law of war have long been heralded as a symbol of "responsible statehood."[58] At a minimum, Trump's failure to respect IHL in public raises the questions of why and how Trump disrupted a steady-state that had lasted for more than seventy years since the establishment of the Geneva Conventions. It equally prompts reflection about whether other Western democracies will endure similar breakdowns.

1.2 Why It Matters for Policy and Governance

Beyond the scholarly literature, this volume sheds light on crucial policy and governance challenges regarding IHL. This is because Trump's refusal to pay even lip service to IHL is not just a continuation, or gradual ramping up, of past efforts to ignore the law of war. It is something new. When prior democratic executives have overstepped the limits or spirit of IHL, they have rarely, if ever, failed to rationalize their behavior as legal. What Trump did – openly and directly flout the law of armed conflict – constituted a different threat to its foundations. If even advanced democracies cannot agree to protect dignity in war, then the architecture on which the global system of governing conflict is built loses purpose. It makes noncompliance more likely and gives others license to dismiss its values.

Since Trump first entered office in 2017, major global conflicts have already pointed to potential signs of weakening public deference

---

[57] Morrow, James D. 2016. "Atrocity, Policy, and the Laws of War: What Does Political Science Have to Say to Law?" In Kontorovich, Eugene and Francesco Parisi, eds. *Economic Analysis of International Law*. Cheltenham, UK: Edward Elgar.

[58] Forsythe, David. 1999. "1949 and 1999: Making the Geneva Conventions Relevant after the Cold War." *Revue Internationale de la Croix-Rouge/International Review of the Red Cross* 81(834): 265–276.

1.2 Why It Matters for Policy and Governance 13

to IHL, albeit outside the West. In Israel's war against Hamas, for example, several high-ranking Israeli state officials, including Prime Minister Benjamin Netanyahu,[59] have made pronouncements explicitly downplaying IHL's importance.[60] In Ukraine, Russian President Vladimir Putin has openly declared his contempt for laws governing state sovereignty and military norms of restraint.[61] The same year that Trump issued his first war crime clemencies in 2019, an analysis by a major humanitarian organization called the global rise of war crimes "the new normal."[62] At the end of Trump's first administration, the United Nations (UN) High Commissioner for Human Rights warned of "a heightened risk of atrocity crimes" escalating across the world.[63]

Even off the battlefield, Trump's military impunity agenda has manifested in indelible, if often underappreciated ways. Within America, it was reflected, at least tangentially, on January 6, 2023, when disproportionate numbers of the military community along with other Trump supporters ransacked the U.S. Capitol.[64] This included some

---

[59] Egan, Lauren. Dec. 12, 2023. "Biden Says Netanyahu 'Has to Change,' Accuses Israel of 'Indiscriminate Bombing.'" *POLITICO*. www.politico.com/news/2023/12/12/biden-says-netanyahu-has-to-change-00131399

[60] Brawn, Steph. Jan. 4, 2024. "LBC: Israeli Ambassador to UK Says EVERY Gaza Building Is a Target.'" *The National*. www.thenational.scot/news/24026946.lbc-israeli-ambassador-uk-says-every-gaza-building-target/ / Goldenberg, Tia. Jan. 18, 2023. "Harsh Israeli Rhetoric against Palestinians Becomes Central to South Africa's Genocide Case." *Associated Press*. apnews.com/article/israel-palestinians-south-africa-genocide-hate-speech-97a9e4a84a3a6bebeddfb80f8a030724 / McGreal, Chris. Oct. 16, 2023. "The Language Being Used to Describe Palestinians Is Genocidal." *Guardian*. www.theguardian.com/commentisfree/2023/oct/16/the-language-being-used-to-describe-palestinians-is-genocidal / Da Silva, Chantal. 2023. Nov. 13. "'Nakba 2023': Israel Right-wing Ministers' Comments Add Fuel to Palestinian Fears." *NBC News*. www.nbcnews.com/news/world/gaza-nakba-israels-far-right-palestinian-fears-hamas-war-rcna123909

[61] Kramer, Andrew E. and Marc Santora. Oct. 20, 2022. "At Mass Grave Site in Ukraine's Northeast, a Sign of Occupation's Toll." *New York Times*. www.nytimes.com/2022/09/16/world/europe/ukraine-graves-russia.html

[62] Stauffer, Brian. 2019. "Atrocities as the New Normal." Human Rights Watch. www.hrw.org/world-report/2019/country-chapters/global-2

[63] Borger, Julian. Dec. 8, 2023. "World Faces 'Heightened Risk' of Mass Atrocities Due to Global Inaction." *Guardian*. www.theguardian.com/law/2023/dec/08/un-and-us-efforts-to-stop-mass-atrocities-have-waned-activists-warn

[64] Sidner, Sara, Anna-Maja Rappard, and Marshall Cohen. Feb. 4, 2021. "Disproportionate Number of Current and Former Military Personnel Arrested in Capitol Attack, CNN Analysis Shows." *CNN*. https://edition.cnn.com/2021/01/31/us/capitol-riot-arrests-active-military-veterans-sch/index.html

of the most notorious figures from the carnage, such as Navy veteran Jacob Anthony Chansley, the "QAnon shaman,"[65] and Air Force veteran Ashley Babbit, who was shot and killed by police.[66] As Trump whipped up his supporters for combat,[67] current and ex-servicemembers responded to his "marching orders" by attacking the seat of U.S. democracy. The crisis confirmed Trump's ability to provoke unconstrained violence among a military population.

Such examples mark what could be a turning point. The developing world has always been rife with blatant breaches IHL. In recent years, endorsements of gross human rights violations have continued unabated in states such as Myanmar,[68] Burkina Faso,[69] Syria,[70] and Sudan.[71] However, in the Trump era, what has the potential to be different is leaders of major powers overtly disregarding commitments to IHL. This is most concerning for nations that purport to be part of the global community, where standards for upholding IHL have traditionally been higher, and which bear primary responsibility for enforcing international laws. Maintaining respect for the law of war is not automatic. It requires sustaining the conditions that uphold its principles.

[65] Ziezulewicz, Geoff. Jan. 11, 2021. "'QAnon Shaman' Charged with Storming the Capitol Is a Navy Veteran." *Navy Times*. www.navytimes.com/news/your-navy/2021/01/12/qanon-shaman-charged-with-storming-the-capitol-is-a-navy-veteran/

[66] Barry, Ellen, Nicholas Bogel-Burroughs, and Dave Philipps. Jan. 7, 2021. "Woman Killed in Capitol Embraced Trump and QAnon." *New York Times*. www.nytimes.com/2021/01/08/us/who-was-ashli-babbitt.html

[67] Savage, Charlie. Jan. 10, 2021. "Incitement to Riot? What Trump Told Supporters Before Mob Stormed Capitol." *New York Times*. www.nytimes.com/2021/01/10/us/trump-speech-riot.html

[68] Aug. 8, 2023. "'Dramatic Increase' in Myanmar War Crimes, UN Probe Finds." *Al Jazeera*. www.aljazeera.com/news/2023/8/8/dramatic-increase-in-myanmar-war-crimes-un-probe-finds

[69] Ahmed, Kaamil. Jun 20, 2023. "War Crimes Surge in Burkina Faso, the World's 'Most Neglected Crisis." *Guardian*. www.theguardian.com/global-development/2023/jun/30/war-crimes-surge-army-islamist-militants-burkina-faso-worlds-most-neglected-crisis

[70] Simons, Marlise. Nov. 15, 2023. "French Judges Issue Warrant for Assad in Syria War Crimes Case." *New York Times*. www.nytimes.com/2023/11/15/world/middleeast/bashar-al-assad-syria-war-crimes.html

[71] Nichols, Michelle. Jan. 29, 2024. "ICC Prosecutor Believes Warring Parties Committing War Crimes in Darfur." *Reuters*. www.reuters.com/world/africa/icc-prosecutor-believes-warring-parties-committing-war-crimes-darfur-2024-01-29/

For policymakers and practitioners, countering an agenda outwardly hostile to IHL involves mitigating its downstream consequences. Western militaries, civilian governments, and humanitarian organizations engaged in security reform all have a role to play. However, for defenders of the Geneva Conventions, the Trump case also highlights the need to stop maliciousness at its source. This requires broader strategies to raise the political costs for Western leaders who openly challenge IHL and to deter or punish bad behavior. As Trump's impunity agenda shows, both domestic and international accountability mechanisms are currently lacking. Understanding why and what can or cannot be done about it is a theme to which this book will return.

1.3 But Is Trump a "War Criminal"?

It is worth clarifying that this book focuses predominantly on the politics of Western leaders publicly challenging IHL – the combination of interests and institutions that enables Trump's norm-breaking behavior. While it delves into international law, and specifically war crimes, it does not adjudicate whether Trump is technically a "war criminal." Much prior work has been done on when challenges to the law of war cross over into clear-cut violations, how courts judge the illegality of military conduct, and the extent to which U.S. presidents are bound by international law generally, and the law of war specifically.[72] Although legal experts have addressed these questions in relation to both Trump and other U.S. commanders-in-chief,[73] resolving them is beyond the scope here.

---

[72] Bradley, Curtis A. and Jack L. Goldsmith. 1997. "Customary International Law as Federal Common Law: A Critique of the Modern Position." *Harvard Law Review* 110(4): 815–876. Breyer, Stephen. 2015. *The Court and the World: American Law and the New Global Realities*. New York: Penguin. Koh, Harold Hongju. 2017. "International Law as Part of Our Law." *American Journal of International Law* 98(1): 43–57.

[73] Bellinger III, John B. 2019. "The Trump Administration's Approach to International Law and Courts: Are We Seeing a Turn for the Worse?" *Case Western Reserve Journal of International Law* 51(1): 7–27. Goldsmith, Jack Landman and Mercer, Shannon. 2019. "International Law and Institutions in the Trump Era." German Yearbook of International Law, 2019, Forthcoming, Available at SSRN: https://ssrn.com/abstract=3324582. Koh, Harold Hongju. 2019. *The Trump Administration and International Law*. Oxford: Oxford University Press.

This distinction is important because it speaks to the crux of the thesis. Trump's public indignation at the legitimacy of IHL is important irrespective of whether he has technically committed "war crimes." This mirrors assessments of the unprecedented nature of Trump's attacks on U.S. institutions, including core tenets of democracy, such as electoral integrity and peaceful leadership transitions.[74] While the strict legality of Trump's undermining of these tenets is debatable, his dismantling of executive norms within the U.S. is indisputable. The outcome of the 2024 election and the vacating of federal charges against him do not change the fact that Trump is unique in publicly attacking the norms of the presidency. The same is true for Trump's public attacks on the law of war.

This is not to imply that no compelling case can be made that Trump is guilty of war crimes. Accusations that Trump has violated the law of war have been forcefully levied by a number of human rights lawyers, academics, national security experts, public officials, and policy analysts. Moreover, countless popular accounts have detailed Trump's aggressive affronts to IHL and labeled him a literal war criminal. For instance, journalist Adam Serwer has denounced Trump as a "war-crimes enthusiast," insisting that "[t]his is not an exaggeration, a mischaracterization, or a misrepresentation."[75] Writer Andrew Sullivan has chastised Trump as "the war crime president."[76] A prominent war historian has accused Trump of lording over a "war-crimes presidency."[77]

Many popular indictments of Trump use the term "war criminal" in a nontechnical way. However, such assessments may not be unfounded, particularly in the case of his military clemencies.

---

[74] Howell, William G., and Terry M. Moe. 2020. *Presidents, Populism, and the Crisis of Democracy*. Chicago: University of Chicago Press. Jacobs, Lawrence R. 2002. *Democracy under Fire: Donald Trump and the Breaking of American History*. New York: Oxford University Press. Peters, Jeremy W. 2022. *How Republicans Lost Their Party and Got Everything They Ever Wanted*. New York: Penguin Random House.

[75] Serwer, Adam. Nov. 27, 2019. "The War-Crimes President." *Atlantic*. www.theatlantic.com/ideas/archive/2019/11/trump-war-crimes/602731/

[76] Sullivan, Andrew. Jan. 10, 2020. "Donald Trump Is the War Crimes President." *New York Magazine*. https://nymag.com/intelligencer/2020/01/andrew-sullivan-donald-trump-is-the-war-crimes-president.html

[77] Beorn, Waitman Wade. Nov. 27, 2019. "The War-Crimes Presidency." *The New Republic*. https://newrepublic.com/article/155857/war-crimes-presidency

1.3 But Is Trump a "War Criminal"?

While most analysts agree that Trump's interventions did not breach U.S. law,[78] considerable attention has focused on whether they violated the IHL principle of "command responsibility."[79] The legal precept, embodied in the Geneva Conventions, requires military heads to ensure accountability in preventing or penalizing war crimes. It stipulates that even if leaders do not personally "pull the trigger," they can still be held criminally culpable. Liability requires that leaders have authority over an armed group, know about a future or past criminal act, and neglect to stop it or to exact punishment.

Many experts contend that one or more of Trump's war crime clemencies meet these thresholds for guilt. For example, Jelena Aparac of the UN has stated categorically that several of Trump's pardons "violate U.S. obligations under international law."[80] Gabor Rona, former international legal director of Human Rights First, has claimed that some of Trump's pardons "may, in fact, themselves constitute war crimes."[81] Yet there is no consensus on the issue. Although in most cases the application of the command responsibility principle tends to be clear, the unique fact patterns of Trump's clemencies are not conducive to a blanket verdict. As law professor Stuart Ford has concluded, "Trump ... probably committed at least one war crime and possibly several."[82] However, multiple questions emerge.

One is whether Trump's commutations actually prevented reasonable punishment for the offenders. Although Trump did preempt Mathew Golsteyn's trial, others had already served substantial

---

[78] Maurer, Dan. "War Crime Clemency: The President's Self-(Defeating) Pardon." *Maryland Law Review* 82(3): 581–669.
[79] Finucane, Brian. 2021. "U.S. Recognition of a Commander's Duty to Punish War Crimes." Stockholm Center for International Law. Rona, Gabor. Dec. 24, 2020. "Can a Pardon Be a War Crime?: When Pardons Themselves Violate the Laws of War." *Just Security*. www.justsecurity.org/64288/can-a-pardon-be-a-war-crime-when-pardons-themselves-violate-the-laws-of-war/
[80] Ernst, Jonathan. Dec. 30, 2020. "Trump's Pardon of Blackwater Iraq Contractors Violates International Law, UN Says." *CNBC*. www.cnbc.com/2020/12/30/trumps-pardon-of-blackwater-iraq-contractors-violates-international-law-un-says.html
[81] Rona, Gabor. Dec. 24, 2020. "Can a Pardon Be a War Crime?: When Pardons Themselves Violate the Laws of War." *Just Security*. www.justsecurity.org/64288/can-a-pardon-be-a-war-crime-when-pardons-themselves-violate-the-laws-of-war/
[82] Ford, Stuart. 2020. "Has President Trump Committed a War Crime by Pardoning War Criminals?" *American University International Law Review* 35(4): 757–820.

time behind bars. Another issue is whether the command responsibility principle extends to leadership successions. This is relevant because several of the crimes took place before Trump entered office the first time in 2017. Judges have differed on this question at the International Criminal Tribunal for Rwanda, the Special Court for Sierra Leone, and the International Criminal Tribunal for the Former Yugoslavia. A final issue is whether the severity of the underlying offenses constituted "war crimes." Eddie Gallagher, in particular, was acquitted of murder and exclusively found guilty of posing with a dead victim.

Pragmatically, also at stake is whether an international court would adjudge some or any of Trump's clemencies to fall under its jurisdiction. Law professor Maj. Gen. Charles J. Dunlap (Ret.), for example, has argued that several of Trump's clemencies applied to cases that would not have met the ICC's standards for prosecuting war crimes. This is because, according to the ICC's governing Rome Statute, its war crimes jurisdiction only takes effect when acts occur "as part of a plan or policy" or "a large-scale commission of such crimes."[83] At the very least, it can be said that global prosecution of Trump's alleged crimes is unlikely to the point of implausible. One analysis, for instance, found no prior executive being tried for war crimes as a result of pardoning combatants.[84]

Discerning the legality of Trump's war crime clemencies is important. The intense scrutiny elicited by the cases in international law circles underscores their complexity. Yet resolving the issue is not essential for the purposes here. Regardless of whether Trump has technically violated the Geneva Conventions, Trump's main impact stems from his unabashed criticism of the validity of the law of war. His brazen defiance of military justice, evident in his public statements and actions, sets him apart from other Western leaders. Unlike previous U.S. presidents, Trump has not just pressed the boundaries of IHL. He has questioned the necessity of having the law of war at all. This aspect of his time as commander-in-chief, more than anything else, makes Trump distinctive.

[83] Dunlap, Charles J. 2019. "Reasonable People Can Differ on Trump's Military Justice Actions." *Small Wars Journal*.
[84] Ford, Stuart. 2020. "Has President Trump Committed a War Crime by Pardoning War Criminals?" *American University International Law Review* 35(4): 757–820.

1.4 A Challenge to the IHL Consensus

If there is one consensus to emerge from the literature on regime type and IHL, it is that Western democratic leaders tend to give public deference to the law of war, even if they do not always comply. This book challenges that consensus, but it is important to understand. It implies that if democratic leaders will breach IHL in private but not public, then expressed commitments are not just about internalizing normative principles. Rather, external constraints force public declarations. Although deference to IHL may be partially a function of norm diffusion, the consensus surrounding the strength of the Geneva Conventions has rarely presumed that democratic leaders would never be enticed to derogate from IHL. Instead, it has been based on more realist assumptions that underlie path dependency.

First, "structuralist" scholarship points to democratic leaders generally lacking the *means* to publicly challenge IHL. The logic is that, unlike in totalitarian regimes, they face a raft of veto players that threaten to block blatant violations of international law.[85] Structural accounts suggest that democratic forces both inside and outside of government tie the hands of leaders publicly.[86] Checks by bureaucrats and civil society actors – including media, NGOs, and other interest groups – may be strongest when democracies absorb international laws into their own body of national rules and customs.[87] Research

---

[85] Konig, Thomas, George Tsebelis, and Marc Debus, eds. 2010. *Reform Processes and Policy Change: Veto Players and Decision-Making in Modern Democracies.* New York: Springer. Tsebelis, George. 1999. "Veto Players and Law Production in Parliamentary Democracies: An Empirical Analysis." *American Political Science Review.* 93(3): 591–608. Tsebelis, George. 2002. *Veto Players: How Political Institutions Work.* Princeton: Princeton University Press.

[86] Finnemore, Martha and Kathryn Sikkink. 1998. "International Norms Dynamics and Political Change." *International Organization* 52(4): 887–917. Goldstein, Judith and Robert O. Keohane, eds. 1993. *Ideas and Foreign Policy: Beliefs, Institutions, and Political Change.* Ithaca: Cornell University Press. Ginsburg, Tom. 2006. "Locking in Democracy: Constitutions, Commitment, and International Law." *New York University Journal of International Law and Politics* 38: 707–759. Simmons, Beth A. 1998. "Compliance with International Agreements." *Annual Review of Political Science* 1: 75–93. Tacsan, Joaquín. 1992. *The Dynamics of International Law in Conflict Resolution.* Dordrecht: Martinus Nijhoff.

[87] Clark, Ann Marie. 2001. *Diplomacy of Conscience: Amnesty International and Changing Human Rights Norms.* Princeton: Princeton University Press.

shows that as domestic laws and constitutions become "enmeshed" with international law, leaders grow bound to a complex latticework of barriers that militate against obvious IHL misconduct.[88]

Second, the "domestic audience cost" theory indicates that democratic leaders have limited *motive* to overtly challenge IHL. The reason is that public opinion serves as a hard check on office-seeking politicians in making military and foreign policy decisions.[89] Scholars argue that democratic citizenries pressure elected leaders to act within certain normative parameters. Because voters hold underlying values that align with principles embodied in international law – such as reverence for rules, human rights, and minority protections – politicians expect to face electoral penalties for violating these tenets.[90]

DeMars, William E. 2005. *NGOs and Transnational Networks: Wild Cards in World Politics*. London: Pluto Press. Fisher, Roger. 1981. *Improving Compliance with International Law*. Charlottesville: University of Virginia Press. Garrett, Geoffrey and Barry R. Weingast. 1993. "Ideas, Interests, and Institutions: Constructing the EC's Internal Market." In Goldstein, Judith and Robert O. Keohane, eds. *Ideas and Foreign Policy: Beliefs, Institutions, and Political Change*. Ithaca: Cornell University Press. Ginsburg, Tom, Svitlana Chernykh, and Zachary Elkins. 2008. "Commitment and Diffusion: How and Why National Constitutions Incorporate International Law." *University of Illinois Law Review* 201(1): 201–237. Keck, Margaret E. and Kathryn Sikkink. 1998. *Activists Beyond Borders: Advocacy Networks in International Politics*. Ithaca: Cornell University Press.

[88] Keohane, Robert O. 1992. "Compliance with International Commitments: Politics within a Framework of Law." *Proceedings of the Annual Meeting (American Society of International Law)* 86: 176–180.

[89] Fearon, James D. 1994. "Domestic Political Audiences and the Escalation of International Disputes." *American Political Science Review* 88(3): 577–592. Kertzer, Joshua D. and Ryan Brutger. 2016. "Decomposing Audience Costs: Bringing the Audience Back into Audience Cost Theory." *American Journal of Political Science* 60(1): 234–249. Tomz, Michael. 2007. "Domestic Audience Costs in International Relations: An Experimental Approach." *International Organization* 61(4): 821–840. Tomz, Michael, Jessica L.P. Weeks, and Keren Yarhi-Milo. 2020. "Public Opinion and Decisions about Military Force in Democracies." *International Organization* 74(1): 119–143.

[90] Chilton, Adam. 2014. "The Influence of International Human Rights Agreements on Public Opinion: An Experimental Study." *Chicago Journal of International Law* 15: 110–137. Dai, Xinyuan. 2005. "Why Comply? The Domestic Constituency Mechanism." *International Organization* 59(2): 363–398. Morse, Julie C. and Tyler Pratt. 2022. "Strategies of Contestation: International Law, Domestic Audiences, and Image Management." *Journal of Politics* 84(4): 2080–2093. Simmons, Beth A. 2009. *Mobilizing for Human Rights*. Cambridge: Cambridge University Press. Zartner, Dana. 2014. *Courts, Codes, and Custom: Legal Tradition and State Policy toward International*

Studies show that the ratification of international laws can serve as an ethical and political impetus encouraging citizens to demand observance of global legal obligations.[91]

Third, "socialization" theory suggests that democratic leaders should be prevented from publicly challenging IHL because of the limited *opportunity* to affect the culture of professionalized militaries. Across the West, militaries have developed extensive socialization processes designed to instill in members key principles of battlefield ethics. A central goal is to forge new military identities steeped in restraint and respect for the law of war.[92] Scholars assert that as official training initiatives have proliferated, norms against openly challenging IHL have become ingrained into the organizational ethos of militaries.[93] Consequently, defying these dominant military cultures should be difficult because of deeply instilled mindsets defining the chains of command.

Taken collectively, the consensus is not that Western democratic leaders will never be tempted to break IHL. Instead, it is that Western leaders lack the "means, motive, and opportunity" to defy IHL openly. This book's thesis, however, is that these constraints may be more perceived than actual. Under certain conditions, democratic leaders may have more reason and ability to publicly reject IHL than is often

---

Human Rights and Environmental Law. Oxford: Oxford University Press. Zartner, Dana. 2020. "Internalization of International Law." *International Studies Association and Oxford University Press*.

[91] Kreps, Sarah E. and Geoffrey P.R. Wallace. 2016. "International Law, Military Effectiveness, and Public Support for Drone Strikes." *Journal of Peace Research* 53(6): 830–844. Wallace, Geoffrey. 2013. "International Law and Public Attitudes Toward Torture: An Experimental Study." *International Organization* 67(1): 105–140.

[92] International Committee of the Red Cross. 2018. *The Roots of Restraint in War*. Geneva: ICRC. www.icrc.org/en/publication/4352-roots-restraint-war / McQuinn, Brian, Fiona Terry, Oliver Kaplan, and Francisco Gutiérrez-Sanin. 2021. "Introduction: Promoting Restraint in War." *International Interactions* 47: 795–824.

[93] Checkel, Jeffrey T. 2017. "Socialization and Violence: Introduction and Framework." *Journal of Peace Research* 54(5): 592–605. Franke, Volker C. 2000. "Duty, Honor, Country: The Social Identity of West Point Cadets." *Armed Forces and Society* 26(2): 175–202. Jenks, Chris. 2020. "The Efficacy of the U.S. Army's Law of War Training Program." Lieber Institute West Point. Stubbins Bates, Elizabeth. 2014. "Towards Effective Military Training in International Humanitarian Law." *International Review of the Red Cross* 96(895–896): 795–816.

supposed. To make this argument, this book examines the case of Trump, whose direct tests of IHL have not just been the result of incidental words and deeds but part of a coherent, deliberate strategy. Later, the case selection of Trump is explained, followed by a preview of what has given Trump the means, motive, and opportunity to openly challenge IHL.

1.5 Case Selection: Trump

This book focuses on Trump not only because his defiance of the law of war has been so explicit but also because his infractions have occurred in such an unlikely context. As commander-in-chief of the world's most powerful military, Trump has not only pressed the boundaries of proper conduct in combat. He has openly questioned the relevance of having boundaries. Moreover, Trump has not done so in a pariah or rogue state, but in an advanced, Western democracy. For decades, American leaders have at least given public deference to the Geneva Conventions, both formally via official government policy and informally via expressed commitments. The U.S. military itself, as enshrined in its Law of War Manual, has also long championed principles consistent with rules-based fighting.[94]

One could argue that Trump's overt challenges to IHL are just a natural extension of his tumultuous leadership. To say that Trump's raison d'être is torching "the system," governing with lawlessness, and never apologizing is not to make a new point.[95] Neither is to observe Trump's well-known disdain for the "rules-based international order,"[96] which saw his first administration withdraw from

---

[94] Office of the General Counsel. 2015. *Department of Defense Law of War Manual*. Department of Defense. https://media.defense.gov/2023/Jul/31/2003271432/-1/-1/0/DOD-LAW-OF-WAR-MANUAL-JUNE-2015-UPDATED-JULY%202023.PDF

[95] Campbell, John L. 2022. *Institutions Under Siege: Donald Trump's Attack on the Deep State*. Cambridge: Cambridge University Press. Greenberg, Karen J. 2021. *Subtle Tools: The Dismantling of Democracy from the War on Terror to Donald Trump*. Princeton: Princeton University Press. Hart, Roderick P. 2020. *Trump and Us: What He Says and Why People Listen*. Cambridge: Cambridge University Press.

[96] Nye, Jr. Joseph S. 2019. "The Rise and Fall of American Hegemony from Wilson to Trump." *International Affairs* 95(1): 63–80.

1.5 Case Selection: Trump

the UN Human Rights Council,[97] terminate treaties like the Iran Nuclear Deal,[98] and threaten to abandon the North Atlantic Treaty Organization (NATO).[99] Yet compared to his predecessors, Trump's direct challenges to IHL are unique. His assaults on the validity law of war, aimed not just at attacking it, but at doing so overtly, are different from prior U.S. presidents. This is true despite several caveats.

First, to be clear, pointing out Trump's uniqueness is not to suggest that his predecessors in the White House had always led the maintenance and execution of IHL. The opposite might even be true. Historically, for example, the U.S. did not ratify the main Geneva Conventions of 1949 until 1955, following the armistice of the Korean War.[100] It has still never ratified the 1977 Additional Protocol I, which places the protection of civilians at the center of its provisions.[101] Furthermore, America has refused to be party to several major humanitarian global efforts, such as the Ottawa Convention to promote land mine bans[102] and various high-profile initiatives to restrict cluster munitions.[103] Detractors have routinely criticized U.S. leaders for trying to interpret IHL in ways that align with their own geopolitical ambitions.

Additionally, the point is not that American leaders before Trump had never run afoul of IHL. Modern U.S. presidents have regularly bent IHL strictures, and, in practice, a case can be made that several did so more severely than Trump. Political scientist John Tirman, for

---

[97] 2018. "US Quits 'Biased' UN Human Rights Council." *BBC*. www.bbc.co.uk/news/44537372
[98] Beauchamp, May 8, 2018. "Trump's Withdrawal from the Iran Nuclear Deal, Explained." *Vox*. www.vox.com/world/2018/5/8/17328520/iran-nuclear-deal-trump-withdraw
[99] Barnes, Julian E. and Helene Cooper. Jan. 14, 2019. "Trump Discussed Pulling U.S. From NATO, Aides Say amid New Concerns over Russia." *New York Times*. www.nytimes.com/2019/01/14/us/politics/nato-president-trump.html
[100] https://treaties.un.org/pages/showDetails.aspx?objid=0800000280158b1a
[101] Wahal, Anya. Jan. 7, 2022. "On International Treaties, the United States Refuses to Play Ball." Council on Foreign Relations. www.cfr.org/blog/international-treaties-united-states-refuses-play-ball
[102] Apr. 5, 2012. "Why Hasn't the U.S. Signed an International Ban on Land Mines?" *Los Angeles Times*. www.latimes.com/archives/blogs/worldnow/story/2012-04-05/why-hasnt-the-u-s-signed-an-international-ban-on-land-mines
[103] Crook, John R. 2008. "United States Opposes Ban on Cluster Munitions, Supports Alternative CCW Negotiations." *American Journal of International Law* 102(4): 889–892.

instance, in summing up its record on IHL, has observed that America has traditionally upheld "a two-tiered system of a policy" that "avows to uphold the Geneva Conventions" but with an "unacknowledged practice" of violating them.[104] From missile strikes bloodying civilians to CIA torture cells, recent U.S. presidents have routinely pressed the bounds of legality. Scores of texts with titles such as *Civilizing Torture: An American Tradition* and *American Immunity: War Crimes and the Limits of International Law* speak to the ubiquity of these controversies.[105]

Finally, it is not the case that American leaders prior to Trump had always zealously pursued justice for war crimes. For instance, foreign policy expert James Palmer has acknowledged that "while the violence of Trump's rhetoric is new, effective impunity for U.S. soldiers in foreign lands is not."[106] Perhaps the closest parallel to Trump's clemencies comes from the 1968 "My Lai Massacre" in Vietnam, in which Army Lt. William Calley, Jr., after being convicted in the murder of twenty-two civilians, had his sentence commuted to house arrest by President Richard Nixon.[107] The fraught relations between American leaders and military justice have also been reflected in consistently skeptical postures toward the ICC, with presidents from George W. Bush to Joe Biden finding themselves at odds with the court's operations.[108]

---

[104] Tirman, John. 2011. *The Death of Others: The Fate of Civilians in America's Wars.* Oxford: Oxford University Press.

[105] Brundage, W. Fitzhugh. 2018. *Civilizing Torture: An American Tradition.* Cambridge, MA: Belknap Press. Hagopian, Patrick. 2013. *American Immunity: War Crimes and the Limits of International Law.* Amherst: University of Massachusetts Press.

[106] Palmer, James. May 21, 2019. "America Loves Excusing Its War Criminals." *Foreign Policy.* https://foreignpolicy.com/2019/05/21/america-loves-excusing-its-war-criminals-trump-pardons/

[107] Jones, Howard. 2017. *My Lai: Vietnam, 1968, and the Descent into Darkness.* Oxford: Oxford University Press. Lane, Charles. May 20, 2019. "Trump's War-crime Pardons Could Be His Most Nixonian Moment Yet." *Washington Post.* www.washingtonpost.com/opinions/trumps-war-crime-pardons-could-be-his-most-nixonian-moment-yet/2019/05/20/c212d954-7b19-11e9-8bb7-0fc796cf2ec0_story.html

[108] Goldsmith, Jack. 2003. The Self-Defeating Criminal Court. *University of Chicago Law Review* 70(1): 89–104. "The U.S. Does Not Recognize the Jurisdiction of the International Criminal Court." Taylor, Adam. Mar. 16, 2023. "The United States and ICC Have an Awkward History." *Washington Post.* www.washingtonpost.com/world/2023/03/16/icc-us-cooperation-international-criminal-court-history/

1.5 Case Selection: Trump

Trump's overt challenges to IHL, however, are distinct. Other American presidents have sworn a commitment to IHL. This includes both Democrats and Republicans, in wartime and peacetime. U.S. leaders have not just claimed to operate within the limits of the law of war. They have professed to revere IHL and frequently to exceed the rules and regulations imposed by the Geneva Conventions. While critics often charge that such statements brim with double standards,[109] U.S. presidents have outwardly kept intact the aim of conforming to the law of war. What distinguishes Trump is not just that he has pressed the boundaries of IHL. It is that he has failed to pay homage to even its most basic pillars. Furthermore, he frames his behavior not as a necessary evil, but as worthy of praise.

With some notable exceptions,[110] this distinctiveness is not always recognized. Many observers treat Trump as following in the footsteps of other U.S. presidents who have plausibly violated IHL. The reasoning is that just as prior commanders-in-chief have sidestepped the Geneva Conventions, Trump has done the same, but no worse. The most obvious foil is George W. Bush, who more than any contemporary president was accused of riding roughshod over IHL. Following 9/11, opponents regularly attacked Bush's "war on terror" for violating the Geneva Conventions.[111] Some have made the case that Bush's transgressions on issues such as detentions, torture, the stripping of habeas corpus, and violating Iraq's sovereignty far outweigh Trump's infractions in their severity.

Yet while Trump and Bush have both challenged IHL, the crucial distinction is that Trump has done so overtly. Bush did not. While Bush was accused of breaching the Geneva Conventions, it was rarely for ignoring IHL altogether. Most experts observe that Bush routinely engaged in

---

[109] O'Toole, Fintan. May 26, 2022. "Our Hypocrisy on War Crimes." *New York Review*. www.nybooks.com/articles/2022/05/26/our-hypocrisy-on-war-crimes-fintan-otoole/

[110] Ford, Stuart. 2021. "Don Quixote or Darth Vader? President Trump's Views on Views on International Humanitarian Law." *Washington University Global Studies Law Review* 20(1): 45–98.

[111] Brody, Reed. 2011. *Getting Away with Torture the Bush Administration and Mistreatment of Detainees*. New York: Human Rights Watch. Haas, Michael. 2009. *George W. Bush: War Criminal? The Bush Administration's Liability for 269 War Crimes*. Westport, CT: Greenwood. Mayer, Jane. 2008. *The Dark Side: The Inside Story of How the War on Terror Turned into a War on American Ideals*. New York: Anchor Books.

legal and intellectual contortions to prove, even if futilely, that his policies were lawful. For example, one account described Bush's "torture memos," which justified his "enhanced interrogation" program, as "81 pages of twisted legal reasoning."[112] Another said that the document read like "the advice of a mob lawyer to a mafia don on how to skirt the law and stay out of prison."[113] A liberal columnist conceded that Bush "made torture a matter of hair-splitting, legalistic debate."[114]

Experts across the political spectrum have made similar points. Bush's former U.S. Assistant Attorney General Jack Goldsmith, for example, has written that, in dealing with national security, Bush was "excessively legalistic."[115] Legal expert Curtis Bradley has contended that "in some respects ... the [Bush] Administration was too focused on the law."[116] Law professor Rosa Brooks penned an op-ed expressly claiming that "Bush at least tried to cloak his administration's use of torture in legal sophistry, a backhanded testament to the strength of the norms his aides sought to circumvent.... In contrast to Bush, Trump makes no secret of his disdain for the laws of war."[117] In these ways, Bush's preoccupation with the law serves to reinforce Trump's uniqueness, rather than suggest an equivalence.

To put Trump in context, Table 1.1 highlights select quotes from U.S. presidents dating back to World War II. Unlike Trump, who has denigrated the Geneva Conventions as "the problem,"[118] other

---

[112] Editorial. Apr. 4, 2008. "There Were Orders to Follow." *New York Times*. www.nytimes.com/2008/04/04/opinion/04fri1.html

[113] Lewis, Anthony. July 15, 2004. "Making Torture Legal." *New York Review of Books*. www.nybooks.com/articles/2004/07/15/making-torture-legal/?pagination=false.

[114] Robinson, Eugene. July 30, 2008. "A Torture Paper Trail." *Real Clear Politics*. www.realclearpolitics.com/articles/2008/07/bushs_torture_logic_will_soon.html

[115] Goldsmith, Jack. 2007. *The Terror Presidency: Law and Judgment inside the Bush Administration*. New York. W.W. Norton

[116] Bradley, Curtis A. 2009. "The Bush Administration and International Law: Too Much Lawyering and Too Little Diplomacy." *Duke Journal of Constitutional Law and Public Policy* 4: 57–75.

[117] Brooks, Rosa. Jan. 8, 2020. "If Trump Orders War Crimes, the Military Will Face an Impossible Choice." *Washington Post*. www.washingtonpost.com/outlook/2020/01/08/if-trump-orders-war-crimes-military-will-face-an-impossible-choice/

[118] Schreckinger, Ben. Mar. 30, 2016. "Trump Calls Geneva Conventions 'The Problem.'" *POLITICO*. www.politico.com/blogs/2016-gop-primary-live-updates-and-results/2016/03/donald-trump-geneva-conventions-221394

1.5 Case Selection: Trump

Table 1.1 *Presidential quotes regarding the law of war*[119]

President	Quote	Years in office
Donald Trump	Called the Geneva Conventions "the problem"	2017–2021
Barack Obama	Declared that "the United States of America must remain a standard bearer in the conduct of war."	2009–2017
George W. Bush	Maintained that he "adher[ed] to the spirit of the Geneva Convention."	2001–2009

[119] Schreckinger, Ben. Mar. 30, 2016. "Trump Calls Geneva Conventions 'The Problem.'" *POLITICO*. www.politico.com/blogs/2016-gop-primary-live-updates-and-results/2016/03/donald-trump-geneva-conventions-221394/ Obama, Barack. Dec. 9, 2009. "Remarks on Accepting the Nobel Peace Prize in Oslo." www.presidency.ucsb.edu/documents/remarks-accepting-the-nobel-peace-prize-oslo, Jan. 28, 2002. "Text: Bush with Afghan Chairman Hamid Karzai." *Washington Post*. www.washingtonpost.com/wp-srv/nation/specials/attacked/transcripts/bushtext_012802.html/Clinton, William J. Aug. 21, 1996. "Statement on Signing the War Crimes Act of 1996." www.presidency.ucsb.edu/documents/statement-signing-the-war-crimes-act-1996/Bush, George. Dec. 2, 1989. "Letter to the Speaker of the House of Representatives and the President Pro Tempore of the Senate on United States Military Assistance to the Philippines." www.presidency.ucsb.edu/documents/letter-the-speaker-the-house-representatives-and-the-president-pro-tempore-the-senate/Reagan, Ronald. Jan 29, 1987. "Message to the Senate Transmitting a Protocol to the 1949 Geneva Conventions." www.presidency.ucsb.edu/documents/message-the-senate-transmitting-protocol-the-1949-geneva-conventions, Carter, Jimmy. Nov. 28, 2016. "America Must Recognize Palestine." www.cartercenter.org/news/editorials_speeches/jimmy-carter-nyt-112816.html/Ford, Gerald R. Jan. 22, 1975. "Statement on the Geneva Protocol of 1925 and the Biological Weapons Convention." www.presidency.ucsb.edu/documents/statement-the-geneva-protocol-1925-and-the-biological-weapons-convention/Nixon, Richard. Mar. 19, 1971. "Proclamation 4038 – National Week of Concern for Americans Who are Prisoners of War or Missing in Action." www.presidency.ucsb.edu/documents/proclamation-4038-national-week-concern-for-americans-who-are-prisoners-war-or-missing/Johnson, Lyndon B. July 20, 1966. "The President's News Conference." www.presidency.ucsb.edu/documents/the-presidents-news-conference-1169/Kennedy, John F. Feb. 1, 1963. "Proclamation 3516—Red Cross Month, 1963." www.presidency.ucsb.edu/documents/proclamation-3516-red-cross-month-1963. Eisenhower, Dwight. Dec. 11, 1959. "Remarks upon Receiving an Honorary Degree of Doctor of Laws at Delhi University." www.presidency.ucsb.edu/documents/remarks-upon-receiving-honorary-degree-doctor-laws-delhi-university/Truman, Harry S. Feb. 5, 1947. "Message to the Congress Transmitting First Annual Report on U.S. Participation in the United Nations." www.presidency.ucsb.edu/documents/message-the-congress-transmitting-first-annual-report-us-participation-the-united-nations

Table 1.1 (*cont.*)

President	Quote	Years in office
Bill Clinton	Expressed hope of achieving "further improvements in promoting respect for the laws of war."	1993–2001
George H.W. Bush	Insisted that he should act "in accordance with recognized principles of international law and pursuant to [his] constitutional authority ... as Commander in Chief."	1989–1993
Ronald Reagan	Lauded "[t]he United States ... [for] be[ing] in the forefront of efforts to codify and improve the international rules of humanitarian law in armed conflict."	1981–1989
Jimmy Carter	Advocated "that the Geneva Conventions and other human rights protections apply to all parties at all times."	1977–1981
Gerald Ford	Praised "the United States ... [for] long support[ing] the principles and objectives of the Geneva Protocol."	1974–1977
Richard Nixon	Said that "all civilized peoples are subject to the basic humanitarian standards long established in international law and custom."	1969–1974
Lyndon Johnson	Stated that he wanted "the Geneva Conventions of 1949 ... [to] be given fuller and more complete application."	1963–1969
John F. Kennedy	Praised the American Red Cross for "acting under the provisions of the Geneva Conventions," thereby "furnish[ing] volunteer aid to the sick and wounded of armies in time of war and ... protect[ing] prisoners of war."	1961–1963

1.5 Case Selection: Trump

Table 1.1 (cont.)

President	Quote	Years in office
Dwight Eisenhower	Proclaimed that although for "centuries nations have sent their youth, armed for war, to oppose their neighbors ... [t]he time has come for mankind to make the rule of law in international affairs as normal as it is now in domestic affairs."	1953–1961
Harry S. Truman	Praised the concept that "aggressive war is a crime against humanity for which individuals as well as states must be punished" and stated "[w]e cannot have lasting peace unless a genuine rule of world law is established and enforced."	1945–1953

past executives have all defended IHL. This again includes George W. Bush, who maintained that he always "adher[ed] to the spirit of the Geneva Convention"[120] and relentlessly couched his defenses in the language of IHL.[121] It also includes Richard Nixon, the other modern U.S. president most accused of trafficking in lawlessness, who affirmed that "all civilized peoples are subject to the basic humanitarian standards long established in international law and custom."[122] Other recent commanders-in-chief have made similarly aspirational statements.

Notably, Trump's overt challenges to IHL have come during a time of relative tranquility for the U.S. military abroad. Although American troops have remained engaged in conflict zones such as Afghanistan, Iraq, Libya, and Syria, the Trump era has in no way been marked by the heightened tensions faced by many of his predecessors. There has

---

[120] Jan. 28, 2002. "Text: Bush with Afghan Chairman Hamid Karzai." *Washington Post.* www.washingtonpost.com/wp-srv/nation/specials/attacked/transcripts/bushtext_012802.html
[121] Bush, George W. 2010. *Decision Points.* New York: Crown.
[122] Nixon, Richard. Mar 19, 1971. "Proclamation 4038 – National Week of Concern for Americans Who are Prisoners of War or Missing in Action." www.presidency.ucsb.edu/documents/proclamation-4038-national-week-concern-for-americans-who-are-prisoners-war-or-missing

been, for example, no equivalent "discourse of fear"[123] that suffused American politics like in the post-9/11 moment. Nor has there been any comparable anxiety like in the 1970s when much of the U.S. public demanded a swift end to the Vietnam War. Nowhere has there been a sense of impending insecurity as during the aftermath of Japan's strike on Pearl Harbor. And yet, Trump chose this period to attack IHL, despite an apparent lack of military urgency.

Compounding this is Trump's selection of former Fox News host Pete Hegseth as Secretary of Defense, who endured a bruising confirmation hearing before the Senate Armed Services Committee, due to, among other reasons, his vehement criticism of the need for the law of war. Hegseth has dismissed international law as a "folly" and derided the "crazy maze of rules of engagement" that bind combatants. He has called for "unleash[ing]" "our boys" to become the "most ruthless," "most uncompromising," and "most overwhelmingly lethal" force in the world. Hegseth has said that the U.S. should abandon the Geneva Conventions and instead "fight by its own rules."[124] He has further lambasted IHL as "written by dudes in cloakrooms in Europe [who] thought they could fight polite wars."[125]

All of this evidence points to the clear outlier nature of Trump, who has both declined to pay outward deference to IHL and, through unprecedented acts such as granting war crime clemencies, attacked the military justice system. Trump is not the first U.S. leader to undermine the law of war. But he is the first to flout the Geneva Conventions so blatantly, and without remorse. Before Trump, American presidents had been willing to brush aside adherence and exploit gray areas. Yet none had neglected to publicly affirm a belief in the validity of the law of armed conflict. What has given Trump the *means, motive,* and *opportunity* to overtly challenge the law of war? The remainder of this chapter previews the answers to these puzzles that guide the rest of the book.

---

[123] Altheide, David L. 2014. "'Constructing Psychological Terror Post 9/11." In Sinclair, Samuel Justin and Daniel Antonius, eds. *The Political Psychology of Terrorism Fears.* New York: Oxford University Press.

[124] De Luce, Dan and Courtney Kube. "Some Military Officers Worry That Pete Hegseth Could Turn a Blind Eye to U.S. War Crimes." *NBC News.* www.nbcnews.com/politics/national-security/military-officers-worry-pete-hegseth-turn-blind-eye-us-war-crimes-rcna183732

[125] Nov. 13, 2024. "The Man Picked as Defence Secretary Wants to Purge the Pentagon." *Economist.* www.economist.com/united-states/2024/11/13/the-man-picked-as-defence-secretary-wants-to-purge-the-pentagon

1.6 Preview of the Argument

The first puzzle this book will examine is how Trump has possessed the *means* to explicitly challenge IHL, and particularly, how he has cut through the multiple sources of influence, both within the federal government and civil society, that jealously guard its principles. As with most Western democracies, rules regulating U.S. military behavior have developed over generations and are the product of diverse actors. The law governing military conduct, the Uniform Code of Military Justice (UCMJ), is established by Congress, and while the commander-in-chief holds ultimate authority over the Department of Defense (DoD), an array of forces both inside and outside the military shape its operations. For these reasons, Trump's powers, both formal and political, to attack IHL would appear to be highly limited.

This book's answer, as explained in Chapter 2, is that Trump has not enacted his agenda alone. Instead, as a "political entrepreneur," he has done so by collectively mobilizing accomplices on America's political right. To explain how, the concept of the "impunity coalition" is developed, which consists of Trump himself, conservative media (especially Fox News), and Republican lawmakers on Capitol Hill. Drawing on original and secondary sources, case studies are presented of Trump's November 2019 and December 2020 war crime interventions to detail how Trump and his allies inspired and defended the impunity agenda. Additional illustrative examples, such as Trump's support for torture, depict how these acts are part of a broader strategy to push back against IHL.

The second puzzle this volume will address is Trump's *motive* to publicly challenge IHL. It is not obvious that a sizable constituency would support the impunity agenda, and especially not conservative voters who Trump has most aimed to court. Trump's strategy in every election has been to double down on mobilizing Republican turnout rather than trying to bridge partisan divides. But in domestic policy, conservatives are typically viewed as staunch law-and-order advocates. Indeed, Trump has spent considerable time expressly casting himself as the president of law and order and as an antidote to social unrest. To the extent that Trump has sought to galvanize the right-wing base, openly challenging IHL could be seen as inconsistent with what his constituents prioritize.

This book's answer, as laid out in Chapter 3, is that the values that make conservatives prioritize law and order in domestic criminal justice can take on different meanings in war. Drawing on studies of moral reasoning, it claims that, domestically, conservatives tend to support the law because they view victims of crime as the in-group, police as the ultimate authority, and blackletter law as embodying purity. In war, by contrast, conservatives tend to think of U.S. servicemembers as the in-group, the commander-in-chief as the ultimate authority, and American ideals as embodying purity. To show the resonance of this agenda and the impact of elite messaging, results are presented from a series of national experiments in 2020 that link support for rejecting IHL to the moral values held by conservatives.

The last puzzle this book will analyze is why Trump has perceived the *opportunity* to upend longstanding commitments to IHL within the U.S. military. For Trump, ensuring military support has been critical to prevent the impunity agenda from backfiring among his core Republican constituency. Because conservative voters hold the military in high esteem, outspoken rejection of the agenda might imperil its political success. Like most Western militaries, however, the individual branches of the U.S. military, in conjunction with the DoD, operate under an edifice of self-governing norms and regulations. Because of the military's extensive training in the law of war, one might have expected the military's fidelity to IHL to appear impervious to strain.

This book's answer, discussed in Chapter 4, traces to the U.S. military's well-known conservative composition. Specifically, it argues that Trump perceived that he could keep the military's support while openly challenging IHL because of three factors. The first was his strong electoral showings among active-duty servicemembers and veterans. The second was his expectation that he could use *Fox News* to spread impunity messaging. Last was Trump's belief that GOP Congress members, particularly veterans, could grant his agenda credibility with the military. In addition to reviewing data on the conservative makeup of America's military, a case study is presented of January 6, documenting how the rise of far-right extremism has made its ranks predisposed to Trump's messaging on violence.

Turning next to the future of the impunity agenda, Chapter 5 highlights why overt challenges to the law of war are likely to be self-executing now that its political advantages are clear. Especially

1.6 Preview of the Argument

with Trump back in the White House, it describes how built-in features of America's conservative landscape, especially competition in the right-wing media space and polarization in Congress, encourage direct challenges to IHL. It also traces how powerful lobbying organizations and court-martialed U.S. servicemembers continue to leverage their notoriety and political muscle to advance the impunity agenda. The chapter shows that the dense social and professional networks that bind the "war crime lobby" help to create a combustible mix that could sustain the impunity agenda.

Last, Chapter 6 recaps the book's main contributions. It discusses practical takeaways for IHL policymakers and practitioners and explains why future efforts to counteract public challenges to the law of war will run into political barriers. Drawing on evidence from the recent Israel-Hamas and Russia-Ukraine wars, it shows how parallels to the impunity agenda are increasingly evident outside the West. The book ends by posing questions for future research and returning to the theme that, despite the progress that Western democracies have made to promote the Geneva Conventions, these gains cannot be taken for granted. It concludes that preventing militaries from violating widely agreed-upon principles for deploying force requires grasping multifaceted political conditions that induce their decay.

2 | Means

How has Trump had the *means* to overtly challenge international humanitarian law (IHL)? Trump has drawn intense backlash for his attacks on the law of war. When he handed down his war crime clemencies in November 2019, for example, critics unleashed a fury of resistance.¹ On Capitol Hill, Democrat Sen. Seth Moulton of Massachusetts called the acts "appalling," insisting that they would "encourage … folks to start burning villages and pillaging like Genghis Khan."² Inside the Pentagon, a small number of military brass rebuked Trump³ or privately steered him toward different judgments.⁴ Combined with resistance from civil society actors, it is puzzling how Trump has overcome the steep political, legal, and institutional obstacles that militate against his agenda.

This chapter's answer is that Trump has overtly challenged IHL by partnering with influential allies on America's political right – conservative media (particularly Fox News) and Republican allies on Capitol Hill – that together comprise an "impunity coalition." Drawing on the

---

¹ Semones, Evan. Nov. 16, 2019. "Pete Buttigieg Hits Trump on Soldiers' Pardons." *POLITICO*. www.politico.com/news/2019/11/16/pete-buttigieg-hits-trump-soldier-pardons-071266
² Mitchell, Ellen. Dec. 11, 2019. "Pentagon Leaders: Trump Clemencies Won't Affect Military Order and Discipline." *The Hill*. https://thehill.com/policy/defense/474119-pentagon-leaders-trump-clemencies-wont-affect-military-order-and-discipline/
³ Spencer, Richard. Nov. 27, 2019. "Richard Spencer: I Was Fired as Navy Secretary. Here's What I've Learned Because of It." *Washington Post*. www.washingtonpost.com/opinions/richard-spencer-i-was-fired-as-navy-secretary-heres-what-ive-learned-because-of-it/2019/11/27/9c2e58bc-1092-11ea-bf62-eadd5d11f559_story.html
⁴ Myers, Meghann. Nov. 6, 2019. "Esper: 'Robust' Conversation with Trump about Proposed Pardons for SEAL, Two Soldiers." *Military Times*. www.militarytimes.com/news/your-military/2019/11/06/esper-will-ask-trump-to-reconsider-pardons-for-service-members-charged-with-convicted-of-war-crimes-report-says/

literature on collective action in government,[5] it claims that Trump has served as a "political entrepreneur"[6] enabling multiple diffuse actors to join forces. The impunity coalition's power has manifested in high-profile efforts to defeat and delegitimize rules and institutions that constrain U.S. military conduct. Fox News has formulated and projected talking points to advance Trump's rejection of IHL, while Republican legislators have encouraged and animated this agenda.

Trump's entrepreneurship solved a collective action problem. Before Trump, Fox News and Republicans in Congress each stood to gain from openly challenging IHL. Yet both were limited in what they could achieve alone. Fox News could endorse challenges to the law of war to its conservative audience. But it had no formal ability to affect U.S. military policy. GOP lawmakers had some purview over laws regulating the U.S. military. However, they lacked the power to take sweeping actions like pardoning servicemembers. Trump was also constrained. Without an influential media outlet to spin his agenda or high-ranking members of his party to legitimize it, Trump may have been reluctant to expend scarce capital on efforts to undermine the law of war.

As explained later, Trump has not just united Fox News and GOP lawmakers around the goal of calling into question IHL's validity. The

---

[5] Carpenter, Daniel P. 2001. *Forging Bureaucratic Autonomy: Reputations, Networks, and Policy Innovation in Executive Agencies, 1862–1928*. Princeton: Princeton University Press. Doig, Jameson W. and Erwin C. Hargrove. 1987. "'Leadership' and Political Analysis." In Doig, Jameson W. and Erwin C. Hargrove, eds. *Leadership and Innovation: A Biographical Perspective on Entrepreneurs in Government*. Baltimore: Johns Hopkins University Press. Kosack, Stephen. 2013. "The Logic of Pro-Poor Policymaking: Political Entrepreneurship and Mass Education." *British Journal of Political Science* 44(2): 409–444. Martin, Adam and Diana Thomas. 2013. "Two-tiered Political Entrepreneurship and the Congressional Committee System." *Public Choice* 154(1/2): 21–37. Schneider, Mark and Paul Teske. 1992. "Toward a Theory of the Political Entrepreneur: Evidence from Local Government" *American Political Science Review*. 86(3): 737–747. Sheingate, Adam D. 2003. "Political Entrepreneurship, Institutional Change, and American Political Development." *Studies in American Political Development* 17(2): 185–203.

[6] Moe, Terry M. 1988. *The Organization of Interests: Incentives and the Internal Dynamics of Political Interest Groups*. Chicago: University of Chicago Press. North, Douglass Cecil. 1990. *Institutions, Institutional Change, and Economic Performance: The Political Economy of Institutions and Decisions*. New York: Cambridge University Press. Riker, William H. 1986. *The Art of Political Manipulation*. New Haven: Yale University Press.

coalition has created a synergy of action, or a series of multi-iterated "feedback loops" on America's political right. Trump, Fox News, and Republican allies amplify each other's cues and maneuvers, generating greater political influence than any one actor could produce alone. The movement has fended off backlash from state and military bureaucracies and solidified public support by carrying out roles via implicit "divisions of labor." Fox News is a developer, not just a broadcaster, of information overtly straining the law of war. GOP lawmakers both lobby Trump to directly challenge IHL and defend his behavior.

The success of the impunity coalition casts doubt on the "structuralist" assumption that institutional barriers and veto points in advanced, Western democracies render undermining the law of war largely infeasible.[7] By assembling a coalition, Trump has effectively challenged IHL. The argument parallels extensive scholarship on democratic regression, which highlights the role of enablers in empowering leaders to achieve state capture.[8] Outside of government, leaders often use media, such as "state TV" or biased news, to court and manipulate publics, a role that Fox News has played for Trump.[9] Inside of

---

[7] Finnemore, Martha and Kathryn Sikkink. 1998. "International Norms Dynamics and Political Change." *International Organization* 52(4): 887–917. Goldstein, Judith and Robert O. Keohane, eds. 1993. *Ideas and Foreign Policy: Beliefs, Institutions, and Political Change*. Ithaca: Cornell University Press. Ginsburg, Tom. 2006. "Locking in Democracy: Constitutions, Commitment, and International Law." *New York University Journal of International Law & Politics* 38(4): 707. Simmons, Beth A. 1998. "Compliance with International Agreements." *Annual Review of Political Science* 1: 75–93. Tacsan, Joaquín. 1992. *The Dynamics of International Law in Conflict Resolution*. Dordrecht: Martinus Nijhoff.

[8] Diamond, Larry. 2021. "Democratic Regression in Comparative Perspective: Scope, Methods, and Causes." *Democratization* 28(1): 22–42. Haggard, Stephan and Robert Kaufman. 2021. *Backsliding: Democratic Regress in the Contemporary World*. Cambridge: Cambridge University Press. Haemin Jee, Hans Lueders, and Rachel Myrick. 2022. "Towards a Unified Approach to Research on Democratic Backsliding." *Democratization* 29(4): 754–767. Norris, Pippa. 2017. "Is Western Democracy Backsliding? Diagnosing the Risks." *HKS Working Paper No.* RWP17-012. www.hks.harvard.edu/publications/western-democracy-backsliding-diagnosing-risks/. Przeworski, Adam. 2019. *Crises of Democracy*. Cambridge: Cambridge University Press. Waldner, David and Ellen Lust. 2018. "Unwelcome Change: Coming to Terms with Democratic Backsliding." *Annual Review of Political Science* 21: 93–113.

[9] Gehlbach, Scott and Konstantin Sonin. 2014. "Government Control of the Media." *Journal of Public Economics* 118: 163–171. Guriev, Sergei, and Daniel Treisman. 2019. "Informational Autocrats." *Journal of Economic*

government, co-conspirators prop up leaders and insulate them from accountability,[10] similar to what congressional Republicans have done for Trump.

Section 2.1 of this chapter presents case studies of how Fox News and Trump allies in Congress both inspired and defended two rounds of high-profile clemencies during his first term. The first, occurring roughly six months after Trump had pardoned Michael Behenna in May 2019, pre-empted the court martial of Mathew Golsteyn, commuted the sentence of Clint Lorance, and restored the rank of Eddie Gallagher. The second set occurred roughly a year later, when Trump pardoned four Blackwater contractors, part of the "Raven 23" convoy, who had been jailed for murdering fourteen Iraqi civilians during the 2007 "Nisour Square Massacre." Section 2.2 documents how these clemencies are not isolated events but part of a broader challenge to international law.

2.1 War Crime Clemencies

Trump's political entrepreneurship first reached a high point in November 2019 when he granted clemency for Mathew Golsteyn, Clint Lorance, and Eddie Gallagher. Trump campaigned on the acts unapologetically, touting them as a bold defense of American

---

Perspectives 33(4): 100–127. Rozenas, Arturas and Denis Stukal. 2019. "How Autocrats Manipulate Economic News: Evidence from Russia's State-controlled Television." *Journal of Politics* 81(3): 982–996. Shadmehr, Mehdi and Dan Bernhardt. 2015. "State Censorship." *American Economic Journal: Microeconomics* 7(2): 280–307. Simon, Joel. 2006. "Muzzling the Media: How the New Autocrats Threaten Press Freedoms." *World Policy Journal* 23(2): 51–61. Treisman, Daniel and Sergei Guriev. 2023. *Spin Dictators The Changing Face of Tyranny in the 21st Century*. Princeton: Princeton University Press.

[10] Bermeo, Nancy. 2016. "On Democratic Backsliding." *Journal of Democracy* 27(1): 5–19. Levitsky, Steven and Daniel Ziblatt. 2019. *How Democracies Die*. New York: Penguin Random House. Gandhi, Jennifer. 2008. *Political Institutions under Dictatorship*. New York: Cambridge University Press. Haggard, Stephan and Robert Kaufman. 2021. "The Anatomy of Democratic Backsliding." *Journal of Democracy* 32(4): 27–41. Khaitan, Tarunabh. 2019. "Executive Aggrandizement in Established Democracies: A Crisis of Liberal Democratic Constitutionalism." *International Journal of Constitutional Law* 17(1): 342–365. Slater, Daniel. "Iron Cage in an Iron Fist: Authoritarian Institutions and the Personalization of Power in Malaysia." *Comparative Politics* 36(1): 81–101.

servicemembers. At an Oval Office press event on November 25, for example, Trump told reporters, "[W]e're going to protect our warfighters ... [T]here's never been a President that's going to stick up for [American servicemembers] ... and has, like I have."[11] Trump tweeted the next day, "I will always protect our great warfighters. I've got your backs!"[12] At a rally in Florida on November 26, Trump bragged, "I stuck up for three great warriors against the deep state. You know what I'm talking about.... People have to be able to fight."[13]

Just over a year later, in December 2020, Trump pardoned Blackwater contractors Nicholas Slatten, Paul Slough, Evan Liberty, and Dustin Heard.[14] The men, known colloquially as the "Biden Four" because then-Vice President Joe Biden had supported their prosecution, were implicated in a deadly 2007 incident in Baghdad with conflicting accounts over whether they had deliberately attacked unarmed citizens. Trump's interventions, which coincided with more than twenty pardons issued at the end of his term, again provoked a full-throated defense. The White House justified the pardons as "broadly supported by the public" and listed Fox News anchor Pete Hegseth and nine U.S. Congress members as endorsing them.[15] Both the lead-up to the interventions and their defense were the product of months of synchronization.

Fox News

Inspiration of Clemencies

Fox News first inspired the war crime clemencies by bringing the cases to Trump's attention. In 2018, a Fox News segment with

---

[11] Nov. 25, 2019. "Remarks Prior to a Meeting with Prime Minister Boyko Borisov of Bulgaria to the White House." American Presidency Project. www.presidency.ucsb.edu/documents/remarks-prior-meeting-with-prime-minister-boyko-borisov-bulgaria-the-white-house

[12] https://twitter.com/realDonaldTrump/status/1199290001143582721

[13] Nov. 26, 2019. "President Trump Rally in Sunrise, Florida." *C-SPAN*. www.c-span.org/video/?466539-1/president-trump-rally-sunrise-florida

[14] Wamsley, Laurel. Dec. 23, 2020. "Shock and Dismay after Trump Pardons Blackwater Guards Who Killed 14 Iraqi Civilians." *NPR*. www.npr.org/2020/12/23/949679837/shock-and-dismay-after-trump-pardons-blackwater-guards-who-killed-14-iraqi-civil

[15] Dec. 22, 2020. "Statement from the Press Secretary Regarding Executive Grants of Clemency." The White House. https://trumpwhitehouse.archives.gov/briefings-statements/statement-press-secretary-regarding-executive-grants-clemency-122220/

2.1 War Crime Clemencies

anchor and now Defense Secretary Pete Hegseth featured Mathew Golsteyn's wife pleading for clemency for her husband, who faced murder charges after admitting on Fox News to killing a suspected Taliban bombmaker. The clip set in motion a spiral of activity that eventually led Trump to intervene. One report, for example, explained that "Trump first signaled publicly that he might wade into war crimes cases … [in] December [2018], after Golsteyn's wife, Julie, appeared on Hegseth's program." Trump tweeted: "At the request of many, I will be reviewing the case of a 'U.S. Military hero,' Major Matt Golsteyn, who is charged with murder.… @PeteHegseth @FoxNews."[16]

Trump's tagging of Hegseth, the most outspoken Fox News personality advocating clemency, nodded to his centrality in the case. Known as "Trump's War Whisperer,"[17] one journalist reported that "Hegseth's behind-the-scenes work … underscores how heavily the president has relied on Fox News stars not just for support and messaging assistance but for actual counsel on policy."[18] Another writer said that observers should "give Fox News host Pete Hegseth credit if Trump pardons accused war heroes."[19] Referring to Hegseth, a *New York Times* article stated that "[a]mong the president's unofficial policy advisers and those who add to the echo chamber on Fox News talk shows, no one else channels Mr. Trump's … unexpected resort to force."[20]

As an anchor on Fox News's flagship morning show "Fox & Friends," Hegseth repeatedly lobbied for combatants implicated in war crime cases. In addition to on-air monologues, Hegseth hosted

---

[16] https://twitter.com/realDonaldTrump/status/1074319076766433280
[17] Bittle, Jake. Jan. 31, 2020. "Trump's War Whisperer." *The New Republic*. https://newrepublic.com/article/156377/trumps-war-whisperer-pete-hegseth-fox-news-friends
[18] Suebsaeng, Asawin, Sam Brodey, and Andrew Kirell. May 21, 2019. "Fox News Host Pete Hegseth Privately Lobbied Trump to Pardon Accused War Criminals." *Daily Beast*. www.thedailybeast.com/fox-and-friends-host-pete-hegseth-privately-lobbied-trump-to-pardon-accused-war-criminals
[19] Murdock, Sebastian. May 21, 2019. "Give Fox News Host Pete Hegseth Credit If Trump Pardons Accused War Criminals." *HuffPost*. www.huffingtonpost.co.uk/entry/pete-hegseth-fox-news-trump-pardons_n_5ce409d0e4b075a35a2dd9b3?ri18n=true
[20] Steinhauer, Jennifer. Jan. 6, 2020. "Fox Host's 'America First' Shift Makes an Exception for Trump's Iran Strike." *New York Times*. www.nytimes.com/2020/01/06/us/politics/pete-hegseth-trump-fox-news.html

the family members of servicemembers on his program[21] and wrote prominently on the topic. His recurring theme was that overzealous prosecutors had crippled America's ability to fight.[22] For instance, in a 2019 FoxNews.com op-ed, Hegseth wrote: "We send men to fight on our behalf, and too often second guess the manner in which they fight. Count me out on the Monday morning quarterbacking – I'm with the American warfighter, all the way."[23] On Fox News, Hegseth said of court-martialed troops, "They're not war criminals – they're warriors…. – it's all garbage, but they'll attack … [Trump] no matter what."[24]

As its "viewer in chief,"[25] Trump often live-tweeted to "Fox and Friends" and acted on Hegseth's recommendations.[26] Hegseth's comments triggered near-immediate responses on the war crime cases. For instance, one day after Hegseth published his Fox News op-ed and three days after he tweeted "#FreeEddie #FreeMatt #FreeClint,"[27] Trump made a White House appearance, aired on Fox Business, where he expressed his openness to Hegseth's pleas. "Some of these soldiers … have fought hard and long," Trump declared. "We teach 'em how to

---

[21] Lamothe, Dan and Josh Dawsey. Nov. 21, 2019. "'Insurgents' Lobbied Trump for War Crimes Pardons with Little Pentagon Involvement, Officials Say." *Washington Post*. www.washingtonpost.com/national-security/insurgents-lobbied-trump-for-war-crimes-pardons-with-little-pentagon-involvement-officials-say/2019/11/21/b6a0c62e-0c75-11ea-bd9d-c628fd48b3a0_story.html

[22] Wood, Graeme. Nov. 17, 2019. "War Crimes Are Not Difficult to Discern." *Atlantic*. www.theatlantic.com/ideas/archive/2019/11/trumps-latest-pardons-reveal-his-military-doctrine/602137/

[23] Hegseth, Pete. May 23, 2019. "Pete Hegseth: I'm With the Warfighters – Count Me out of Second-guessing Our Heroes." *Fox News*. www.foxnews.com/opinion/pete-hegseth-im-with-the-american-warfighters

[24] Rupar, Aaron. May 24, 2019. "Trump's Interest in Pardoning Troops Accused of War Crimes, Explained." *Vox*. www.vox.com/policy-and-politics/2019/5/24/18637360/trump-war-crimes-pardons-gallagher-golsteyn-fox-news-hegseth

[25] Aug. 28, 2019. "Fox News Advertisers Get a Direct Line to the Viewer in Chief." *Los Angeles Times*. www.latimes.com/business/story/2019-08-28/fox-news-advertisers-president-trump

[26] Marantz, Andrew. Jan. 8, 2018. "How "Fox & Friends" Rewrites Trump's Reality." *New Yorker*. www.newyorker.com/magazine/2018/01/15/how-fox-and-friends-rewrites-trumps-reality

[27] Rupar, Aaron. May 24, 2019. "Trump's Interest in Pardoning Troops Accused of War Crimes, Explained." *Vox*. www.vox.com/policy-and-politics/2019/5/24/18637360/trump-war-crimes-pardons-gallagher-golsteyn-fox-news-hegseth

2.1 War Crime Clemencies

be great fighters, and then when they fight, sometimes get treated really very unfairly."[28] One analysis said that the response amounted to Trump "taking cues from Fox News," adding that Hegseth appeared to be "doubl[ing] as an informal adviser to the president."[29]

Although Hegseth was Fox News's main voice championing war crime interventions, his "Fox & Friends" colleagues also joined the advocacy. Within the twelve-month span leading up to Trump's November 2019 clemencies, at least six of Hegseth's co-hosts – Jededia Bilah, Ed Henry, Sean Kilmeade, Peter Doocey, Ainsley Earhardt, and Jillian Mele – made supportive comments on behalf of the servicemembers or featured their stories sympathetically. Other Fox News anchors – including Jeanine Pirro, Martha McCallum, Shannon Bream, and Sandra Smith – also highlighted the cases and largely framed them as unjust prosecutions. Fox News platformed Eddie Gallagher's and Clint Lorance's lawyers and featured interviews with GOP lawmakers who led the campaign for leniency.[30]

Several analyses observed Fox News's sway in persuading Trump to grant the war crime clemencies. One report, for example, stated that "[i]f Trump were to issue the pardons, they would come after lobbying efforts from Republican members of Congress and persistent coverage in conservative media, where the cases are cast as the result of overzealous prosecutors and a military tainted by political correctness."[31]

---

[28] https://twitter.com/atrupar/status/1131966491962859521?ref_src=twsrc%5E tfw%7Ctwcamp%5Etweetembed%7Ctwterm%5E1131966491962859521% 7Ctwgr%5Efaa301f1819ed454a36e366021a623be73e6b632%7Ctwcon%5 Es1_&ref_url=https%3A%2F%2Fwww.vox.com%2Fpolicy-and-politics%2 F2019%2F5%2F24%2F18637360%2Ftrump-war-crimes-pardons-gallagher-golsteyn-fox-news-hegseth

[29] Rupar, Aaron. May 24, 2019. "Trump's Interest in Pardoning Troops Accused of War Crimes, Explained." *Vox.* www.vox.com/policy-and-politics/2019/5/24/18637360/trump-war-crimes-pardons-gallagher-golsteyn-fox-news-hegseth

[30] Hagle, Courtney and Grace Bennett. May 5, 2019 (updated Nov. 15, 2019). "A Fox Host Lobbied Trump to Pardon Accused and Convicted War Criminals. Here's How Fox Talked about the Cases over the Last Six Months." *Media Matters for America.* www.mediamatters.org/donald-trump/fox-host-lobbied-trump-pardon-accused-and-convicted-war-criminals-heres-how-fox-talked

[31] Darcy, Oliver. May 21, 2019. "Fox News Host Pete Hegseth Has Privately Encouraged Trump to Pardon Servicemen Accused of War Crimes." *CNN.* https://edition.cnn.com/2019/05/21/media/fox-news-pete-hegseth-trump-pardon-war-crimes/index.html

Referring to Gallagher's clemency, a retired senior Navy officer complained about a "'cable Cabinet' at Fox News that seems to be able to almost unilaterally convince the president to act on issues they care about."[32] Another analysis called "the war crimes lobby ... a metastasizing network of amateurish, enraged gawkers, gorging themselves on Fox News emissions."[33]

Lobbying at Fox News, however, was not just confined to TV appearances. Hegseth reportedly conversed one-on-one with Trump to persuade him to act. According to one analysis, "Trump called Hegseth numerous times to discuss the ... [clemencies] and told others about the conversation."[34] Multiple officials within the White House even became concerned that Hegseth was privately supplying Trump misleading or incorrect details about the cases, making the servicemembers appear more deserving. One official, for example, recounted that Defense Secretary Mark Esper and Chairman of the Joint Chiefs Gen. Mark Milley were placed in a position where "[t]hey were trying to convince the president these guys were actually criminals, not heroes."[35]

When Trump confirmed that he was officially reviewing Mathew Golsteyn's case on October 12, 2019, he did so via tweet, tagging "@PeteHegseth" and declaring, "We train our boys to be killing machines, then prosecute them when they kill!"[36] The tweet prompted

---

[32] Fritze, John and Tom Vanden Brook. Nov. 25, 2019. "Trump's Advocacy for Navy SEAL Eddie Gallagher Is Latest Intervention for Conservative Cause Celebre." *USA Today*. https://eu.usatoday.com/story/news/politics/2019/11/25/donald-trump-advocacy-eddie-gallagher-latest-conservative-cause/4297107002/

[33] Weinstein, Adam. May 20, 2019. "Who Actually Wants War Criminals Pardoned?" *The New Republic*. https://newrepublic.com/article/153948/actually-wants-war-criminals-pardoned?utm_content=bufferf1620&utm_medium=social&utm_source=facebook.com&utm_campaign=buffer

[34] Lamothe, Dan and Josh Dawsey. Nov. 21, 2019. "'Insurgents' Lobbied Trump for War Crimes Pardons with Little Pentagon Involvement, Officials Say." *Washington Post*. www.washingtonpost.com/national-security/insurgents-lobbied-trump-for-war-crimes-pardons-with-little-pentagon-involvement-officials-say/2019/11/21/b6a0c62e-0c75-11ea-bd9d-c628fd48b3a0_story.html

[35] Lamothe, Dan and Josh Dawsey. Nov. 21, 2019. "'Insurgents' Lobbied Trump for War Crimes Pardons with Little Pentagon Involvement, Officials Say." *Washington Post*. www.washingtonpost.com/national-security/insurgents-lobbied-trump-for-war-crimes-pardons-with-little-pentagon-involvement-officials-say/2019/11/21/b6a0c62e-0c75-11ea-bd9d-c628fd48b3a0_story.html

[36] https://twitter.com/realDonaldTrump/status/1183016899589955584

speculation, which turned out to be false, that Trump might intervene on Veterans Day, November 11, 2019. Trump was again counseled about the potential for fallout within parts of the military bureaucracy. Defense Secretary Mark Esper, for instance, reputedly engaged in a "robust" talk with the president in which he pleaded with Trump to resist Hegseth's recommendations. "I offered – as I do in all matters – the facts, the options, my advice, the recommendations and we'll see how things play out," Esper recalled.[37]

In addition to Trump's 2019 interventions, Fox News also laid the groundwork for Trump's pardoning of Blackwater contractors in December 2020. Similar to the prior clemencies, the process began with a "Fox & Friends" segment featuring family members. In April 2015, Jessica Slatten, sister of Blackwater agent Nicholas Slatten, and Kristin Slough, wife of agent Paul Slough, criticized the prosecutions on air. Slough described the case as being "blown entirely out of proportion" and accused the FBI of getting involved only after the Iraqi government had cleansed the crime scene, coached witnesses, and run advertisements to encourage civilians to come forward as victims. "I know you've talked to some Congressmen, some Senators," responded Fox News anchor Steve Doocy. "Let's see if something changes."[38]

Fox News's Sean Hannity also gave the Blackwater agents an early platform. According to the "Free Raven 23" website, Hannity .com published an op-ed in 2015 by Nicholas Slatten's sister, who complained that her brother and his colleagues would not be "wearing dress blues adorned with medals earned for honorable military service" but instead "jumpsuits and shackles."[39] In 2017, Nicholas Slatten penned a letter to Hannity, shared publicly, that called on him to broadcast details of the Blackwater cases. "I listen to your program every day through the week on my radio," he wrote, "[Y]ou will be outraged by this miscarriage of justice. I beg you, sir, please

---

[37] Myers, Meghann. Nov. 6, 2019. "Esper: 'Robust' Conversation with Trump about Proposed Pardons for SEAL, Two Soldiers." *Military Times*. www.militarytimes.com/news/your-military/2019/11/06/esper-will-ask-trump-to-reconsider-pardons-for-service-members-charged-with-convicted-of-war-crimes-report-says/

[38] Apr. 21, 2015. "Family Members of Sentenced Blackwater Guards Speak Out." *Fox News*. https://video.foxnews.com/v/4186281817001#sp=show-clips

[39] www.supportraven23.com/media

help us."⁴⁰ Hannity confirmed, "These guys were all over me constantly if I didn't do a segment the next number of months [on military justice] to get back on it. To their credit."⁴¹

Led again by Pete Hegseth, Fox News's Blackwater coverage gained momentum just before the clemencies of Golsteyn, Lorance, and Gallagher. On August 11, 2019, Hegseth interviewed the producers of the podcast "Presumption of Guilt," created on behalf of the Blackwater agents. In the "Fox & Friends" sit-down, Hegseth called the prosecutions "as bad as it gets" and blamed Joe Biden for making the contractors "vulnerable" to legal charges.⁴² On May 16, 2020, Hegseth also interviewed Rep. Louie Gohmert of Texas, where he insisted that the four men had been "thrown under the bus." After Gohmert praised Hegseth as "a great American" and attacked the Blackwater charges, Hegseth replied, "One hundred percent … they should have medals on their chest, not be behind metal bars."⁴³

As with Trump's 2019 clemencies, evidence points to Hegseth's lobbying as decisive in the Blackwater pardons. Journalist Peter Baker, for example, reported on the agents being "championed" by Hegseth, who he described as "a Fox News host and outspoken Trump supporter who has been influential with the president."⁴⁴ A *Los Angeles Times* story similarly recounted that "[t]he [Blackwater pardon] campaign got a boost from Pete Hegseth, a Fox News personality who had successfully pushed Trump to pardon servicemembers accused of war crimes."⁴⁵ Political scientist Norman

---

⁴⁰ Mar. 1, 2017. "Help Raven 23 Reach Sean Hannity." www.supportraven23.com/blog/2017/2/23/help-raven-23-reach-sean-hannity (last accessed Jan. 21, 2020)

⁴¹ Nov. 4, 2019. "Sean Hannity & Rep. Gohmert on the Breaking News about President Trump and Military Injustice." JFW Caucus. www.youtube.com/watch?v=aK81iNj0k3A

⁴² Aug. 11, 2019. "Podcast Tells the Story of How Four Veterans Ended up Serving Life Sentences for War Crimes." *Fox News*. https://video.foxnews.com/v/6071713887001?fbclid=IwAR2867eQMi1topNkvvhEJas6bfW5FkDbdK_NUwHdjmNfWMmE-OajdrlPFDk#sp=show-clips

⁴³ www.facebook.com/raven23support/posts/2768673599924984

⁴⁴ Baker, Peter. Dec. 24, 2020. "For a Defeated President, Pardons as an Expression of Grievance." *New York Times*. www.nytimes.com/2020/12/24/us/politics/trump-pardon-power.html

⁴⁵ Wilber, Del Quentin. Jan. 15, 2021. "This Blackwater Guard Pleaded Guilty. He Atoned. But Didn't Get a Pardon." *Los Angeles Times*. www.latimes.com/world-nation/story/2021-01-15/he-did-the-right-thing-but-his-blackwater-guard-didnt-get-a-pardon

Ornstein tweeted that "[i]t was Pete Hegseth who convinced Trump to pardon the Blackwater war criminals. May he burn in Hell."[46] The White House again expressly justified the pardons by saying that they were supported by Hegseth.[47]

As with Fox News, other conservative news outlets also denounced the Blackwater verdicts. For example, in 2016, right-wing radio network *TheBlaze* featured a segment on the agents, where the host complained that the prosecutions "can't be real" and accused the government of delivering "false justice."[48] On Townhall.com, writer Matt Vespa suggested that the prosecutions were the result of Joe Biden "crucify[ing] these contractors" in a politically motivated effort to "appease the Iraqi government."[49] Even right-leaning writer David French, known for his criticism of Trump, wrote a 2019 article in the *National Review* defending the Blackwater contractors. "It's time for the president to step in to correct a miscarriage of justice," he declared. "It's time to pardon the men of Raven 23."[50]

Defense of Clemencies

Fox News did not just inspire Trump's war crime clemencies. It also offered a robust defense of them. Following Trump's decisions to pardon Mathew Golsteyn and Clint Lorance and to grant clemency for Eddie Gallagher, Pete Hegseth tweeted, "God Bless our president and Commander-in-Chief @realDonaldTrump. A Hero for our warfighters,"[51] alongside a link to a Fox News story

---

[46] https://twitter.com/NormOrnstein/status/1342889377987514369

[47] Dec. 22, 2020. "Statement from the Press Secretary Regarding Executive Grants of Clemency." The White House. https://trumpwhitehouse.archives.gov/briefings-statements/statement-press-secretary-regarding-executive-grants-clemency-122220/

[48] Feb. 13, 2016. "Raven 23: False Justice." *TheBlaze*. https://soundcloud.com/the-jeff-fisher-show/raven-23-false-justice-21316?utm_source=www.supportraven23.com&utm_campaign=wtshare&utm_medium=widget&utm_content=https%253A%252F%252Fsoundcloud.com%252Fthe-jeff-fisher-show%252Fraven-23-false-justice-21316

[49] Vespa, May 14, 2020. "The Biden Four: Did the Former Vice President Screw Over Four Americans to Get Cozier Iraq?" *Townhall*. https://townhall.com/tipsheet/mattvespa/2020/05/14/the-biden-four-did-the-vice-president-seek-to-screw-over-four-americans-to-get-cozier-with-the-iraqis-n2568756?fbclid=IwAR1ldMshNj7KAMmcnoKE5rmOOSkh6hizWiDl1fBECVahDrXAFuWGZYjcYqA

[50] French, David. May 28, 2019. "Pardon the Men of Raven 23." *National Review*. www.nationalreview.com/2019/05/pardon-the-men-of-raven-23/

[51] https://twitter.com/PeteHegseth/status/1195493031715184645

headlined, "Trump grants clemency to 2 Army officers accused of war crimes, restores rank to Navy SEAL Eddie Gallagher." Trump responded by expressing gratitude to Hegseth and elaborating on his decision-making. "Thank you Pete," he said in a tweet collecting more than 30,000 "likes." "Our great warfighters must be allowed to fight. I would not have done this for Sgt. Bergdahl or Chelsea Manning!"[52]

After receiving his clemency, Eddie Gallagher thanked Hegseth explicitly, writing, "It was humbling to see all the veterans and veterans' companies come to my aid and support me.... Pete Hegseth ... you are true patriots."[53] Gallagher, Golsteyn, and Lorance all appeared on "Fox & Friends" after their release. Golsteyn told Hegseth that he was "stunned and awed by the president's generosity" and praised Trump for being "incredibly sanguine [and] warm." "I think it sends a clear signal that the president of the United States is paying attention," he remarked.[54] Lorance said that if he wanted Trump to know anything, it would be, "I love you, sir.... [I]f you're working in the White House or ... in the United States government, and you don't agree with something the president does, then go home."[55]

Fox News aired two exclusive interviews with Gallagher, both conducted by Hegseth, within the first week and a half of Trump's interventions. In the first, Gallagher declared that "it was pretty surreal ... to get a phone call from the White House and have them tell you that the president is on the line.... I had a feeling that it was coming because the president has shown the nation that he's been a man of his word."[56] In the second interview, aired after Navy leadership had attempted to remove his SEAL trident, Gallagher lashed out. "This is all about ego and retaliation," he pronounced. "I'm overjoyed that ... [Trump] stepped in again as being the leader that

---

[52] https://twitter.com/realdonaldtrump/status/1196061212833923072
[53] https://twitter.com/PeteHegseth/status/1198780634904383492/photo/1
[54] Musto, Julia. Nov. 16, 2019. "Former Green Beret Maj. Mat Golsteyn Praises Trump's 'Courage' for Pardon, Says He Woke Up 'Incredibly Stunned.'" *Fox News*. www.foxnews.com/media/major-mat-golsteyn-president-trump-pardon-fox-and-friends-weekend
[55] Nov. 18, 2019. "Exclusive: Clint Lorance Gives First Interview since Pardon by Trump." *Fox News*. www.youtube.com/watch?v=ne3AX9tasKY&t=448s
[56] Nov. 17, 2019. "Eddie Gallagher Speaks Out after Trump Orders His Naval Rank Restored." *Fox News*. www.youtube.com/watch?v=5UGPRMZC5KY

2.1 War Crime Clemencies

he is.... It's the higher echelon, the upper brass, who are the ones who are trying to put their thumb on me."[57]

For months after the interventions, Fox News continued to spotlight the cases. For example, in a March 2020 segment featuring Hegseth, Sean Hannity lauded his colleague's role in the clemencies, saying, "I like to kid Pete about his tattoos. But he served our country.... And what you did for Eddie Gallagher was amazing."[58] Fox News also platformed several other advocates of the interventions. For instance, on FoxNews.com, Clint Lorance's lawyer, Don Brown, blasted "inexcusable prosecutorial overreach" and praised Lorance, Golsteyn, and Gallagher as "brave patriots."[59] On FoxNews.com, Gen. Anthony Tata railed against the "suffocating pressure of a resource-rich bureaucracy" that he said had unduly borne down on Gallagher.[60]

Fox News's defense of the clemencies was so influential that Trump even appeared to borrow language directly from its coverage. On May 23, 2019, Hegseth on FoxNews.com complained about prosecutions of U.S. servicemembers "by lawyers who *never left their air-conditioned offices*."[61] From there, the phrase redounded. On June 24, former George W. Bush lawyer John Yoo, speaking on Fox News about the Gallagher trial, claimed that a military jury should not say "back now in our *air-conditioned courtroom*, we can impose our standard."[62] On September 18, Fox News's Sean Hannity echoed

---

[57] Nov. 24, 2019. "Eddie Gallagher on His Case: 'This Is about Ego and Retaliation.'" *Fox News*. www.youtube.com/watch?v=6dkz9MdRTZo
[58] Mar. 9, 2020. *Fox News*. www.foxnews.com/transcript/rep-devin-nunes-we-need-fisa-to-protect-america-but-not-at-the-expense-of-our-liberty
[59] Brown, Don. Nov. 26, 2019. "Don Brown: Military Men Who Got Trump Clemency – Lorance, Golsteyn & Gallagher – Are Heroes, NOT War Criminals." *Fox News*. www.foxnews.com/opinion/don-brown-military-men-who-got-trump-clemency-lorance-golsteyn-and-gallagher-are-not-war-criminals
[60] Tata, Anthony. Nov. 29, 2019. "Gen. Anthony Tata: Trump Was Right, Fired Navy Secretary Was Wrong on Eddie Gallagher Case." *Fox News*. www.foxnews.com/opinion/gen-anthony-tata-trump-was-right-to-fire-navy-secretary-and-intervene-on-behalf-of-seal-eddie-gallagher
[61] Hegseth, Pete. May 23, 2019. "Pete Hegseth: I'm With the Warfighters – Count Me out of Second-guessing Our Heroes." *Fox News*. www.foxnews.com/opinion/pete-hegseth-im-with-the-american-warfighters
[62] Yoo, John. June 24, 2019. "Discussing the Eddie Gallagher Case: Yoo on Fox News' 'The Daily Briefing with Dana Perino.'" AEI. www.aei.org/press/discussing-the-eddie-gallagher-case-yoo-on-fox-news-the-daily-briefing-with-dana-perino/

similar language on his radio program: "It's amazing how people can second-guess guys that are in combat ... from the comfort of their offices and their *air-conditioned military courtrooms*" [emphasis added in all the above quotes].[63]

Trump himself finally invoked the "air-conditioned" phrase at a MAGA rally in Florida on November 26, proclaiming "I will always stick up for our great fighters. *People can sit in air-conditioned offices* and complain, but it doesn't matter to me."[64] Two days later, on November 28, Sean Hannity, in an interview with Clint Lorance, declared, "How about those guys in *air-conditioned offices* that want to sit back and judge your three-second decision?"[65] During his confirmation hearings, Hegseth again railed against "people here in *air-conditioned offices* that like to point fingers at the guys in dark and dangerous places" [emphasis added in all the above quotes].[66] Collectively, the multiple, repeated references to judging U.S. servicemembers from "air-conditioned" rooms epitomized the symbiotic messaging between Trump, Fox News, and his supporters.

Alongside Fox News, other media voices on the far right also defended Trump's interventions. Talk radio host Rush Limbaugh, for example, praised Trump for "sid[ing] with the military hero, the down-in-the-dirt grunt who does the great, miraculous work, Eddie Gallagher, a Navy SEAL."[67] On RedState.com, a commentator wrote that "[i]t is insane to hold ... [U.S. troops] to some bullsh** peacetime 'use of deadly force' standard."[68] Townhall.com's John

---

[63] Hannity, Sean. Sept. 18, 2019. "Justice for Warriors." *Sean Hannity Show.* www.iheart.com/podcast/51-the-sean-hannity-show-24392822/episode/justice-for-warriors-49394778/

[64] Nov. 26, 2019. "President Trump Rally in Sunrise, Florida." *C-SPAN.* www.c-span.org/video/?466539-1/president-trump-rally-sunrise-florida

[65] Nov. 28, 2019. "Lt. Clint Lorance on Being Pardoned by Trump." *Fox News.* https://video.foxnews.com/v/6109800956001#sp=show-clips

[66] Jacobson, Louis and Sara Swann. Jan. 15, 2025. "Fact-check: What Did Pete Hegseth Say in Defence Confirmation Hearing?" *Al Jazeera.* www.aljazeera.com/news/2025/1/15/fact-check-what-did-pete-hegseth-say-in-defence-confirmation-hearing

[67] Nov. 25, 2019. "Trump Schiffcans Navy Secretary in SEAL Case." *Rush Limbaugh Show.* www.rushlimbaugh.com/daily/2019/11/25/trump-schiffcans-navy-secretary-in-seal-case/

[68] Streiff. Nov. 15, 2019. "Trump Issues Pardons in Three Highly Controversial War Crimes Court Martial Cases." *RedState.* www.redstate.com/streiff/2019/11/15/trump-issues-pardons-three-highly-controversial-war-crimes-court-martial-cases/

2.1 War Crime Clemencies

and Andy Schafly called criticism of Trump's pardons "a disgrace," and suggested that if there were any benefit of the pushback, it was that "disrespect for Trump's pardons smokes the Never-Trumpers out." On Gateway Pundit, writer Cristina Laila praised Trump for his actions "after overzealous Obama hacks hunted ... [Eddie Gallagher] down."

When initial reports emerged that Navy leadership planned to strip Gallagher of his SEAL trident, Fox News again rushed to his defense. On November 21, 2019, one of Gallagher's attorneys appeared on Fox News to impugn the commander of the Navy SEALs as a "coward."[69] Within hours, Trump turned to Twitter: "The Navy will NOT be taking away Warfighter and Navy Seal Eddie Gallagher's Trident Pin.... Get back to business!"[70] On November 24, Trump fired Navy Secretary Richard Spencer for plotting to override his order,[71] prompting Hegseth to slam Spencer as "an institutionalist" who "wanted to ... just bow to whatever the system was doing." He elaborated: "They ignored the president's clear guidance. 'You're not taking the Trident. Get back to business.' ... [Trump]'s the commander-in-chief. He won the election. You didn't."[72]

Others on Fox News echoed similar sentiments. For example, national security analyst Rebecca Grant penned an op-ed on FoxNews.com insisting that "[t]he Spencer case is sad proof there is indeed a 'deep state' anti-Trump resistance popping up within the Pentagon."[73] Fox Nation also hosted Eddie Gallagher's brother, who called the commander in charge of the matter a "clown" and stated that "the Navy got their asses handed to them."[74] One writer

---

[69] Crowley, James. Nov. 21, 2019. "Fox News Guest Calls Commander of the Navy Seals a 'COWARD.'" *Newsweek*. www.newsweek.com/fox-guest-calls-navy-seal-commander-coward-eddie-gallagher-1473249
[70] https://twitter.com/realdonaldtrump/status/1197507542726909952?lang=bn
[71] https://twitter.com/realDonaldTrump/status/1198746376420679680
[72] Nov. 25, 2019. "Hegseth to Pentagon Officials: The Obama Era Is Over. Understand that or See the Door." *Fox News*. https://video.foxnews.com/v/6108684683001#sp=show-clips
[73] Grant, Rebecca. Nov. 27, 2019. "Rebecca Grant: Fired Navy Secretary's Actions Prove a 'Deep State' Anti-Trump 'Resistance' Exists at Pentagon." *Fox News*. www.foxnews.com/opinion/rebecca-grant-fired-navy-secretarys-actions-prove-a-deep-state-anti-trump-resistance-exists-at-pentagon
[74] London, Matt. Mar. 2, 2020. "Critics Ignore Military Justice Failures in '60 Minutes' Profile of Navy SEAL Eddie Gallagher." *Fox News*. www.foxnews.com/media/eddie-gallagher-former-seal-60-minutes

opined that "Spencer's firing ha[d] its roots in the case of Edward Gallagher, a Navy SEAL who became a Fox News hero."[75] Analyst Sam Vinograd remarked, "[I]t's one thing for Fox analysts to offer their opinions, let's say on Gallagher's case. It is another thing for the president of the United States to make decisions based upon those analysts' opinions."[76]

After Trump issued the Blackwater pardons, Hegseth again promptly defended the moves. On "Fox & Friends," he declared, "God bless the president for having the courage which a lot of other presidents wouldn't do to pardon those men."[77] He insisted that the evidence that led to the convictions was "mischaracterized" and "mishandled" and complained that the agents had faced prosecution in a civilian court. According to Hegseth, Trump deserved "huge credit" and "kudos" for sending a clear signal to U.S. servicemembers: "We're going to have your back when you make tough calls on the battlefield, much like some of the pardons he gave for other members of the military before."[78] Hegseth also retweeted a message by "@freeraven23": "THEY ARE FREE!!! Thank you president @realDonaldTrump ! We love you and support you!"[79]

GOP Allies on Capitol Hill

Inspiration of Clemencies

Alongside Fox News, Republican lawmakers were crucial in inspiring Trump's war crime clemencies. On Capitol Hill, the Congressional Justice for Warriors Caucus (CJWC) was the primary

---

[75] Waldman, Paul. Nov. 25, 2019. "How Richard Spencer's Firing Illustrates Some of Trump's Most Corrupt Impulses." *Washington Post*. www.washingtonpost.com/opinions/2019/11/25/how-richard-spencers-firing-illustrates-some-trumps-most-corrupt-impulses/

[76] Palmer, Ewan. Nov. 28, 2019. "Donald Trump Running Military to Serve the Interests of Fox News Rather than the Country: CNN National Security Experts." *Newsweek*. www.newsweek.com/trump-fox-eddie-gallagher-richard-spencer-1474591

[77] Baragona, Justin. Dec. 23, 2020. "Fox's Pete Hegseth Applauds Trump for Pardoning War Criminals: 'God Bless the President.'" *Daily Beast*. www.thedailybeast.com/foxs-pete-hegseth-applauds-trump-for-pardoning-war-criminals-god-bless-the-president

[78] Dec. 23, 2020. "Pete Hegseth Praises Blackwater Guards Who Massacred 14 Civilians." *Raw Story*. www.youtube.com/watch?v=LP6l_LLoLwA&t=2s

[79] https://twitter.com/FreeRaven23/status/1341733087978381323

force advancing the agenda before the White House. Although individual Republicans in Congress had been lobbying for war crime clemencies even before Trump took office,[80] the caucus's formation institutionalized their effort. Founded in 2019 by Reps. Louie Gohmert of Texas and Duncan Hunter of California, the CJWC provided backing to court-martialed troops who it claimed had been "unfairly treated by the military justice system."[81] Encouraged by GOP Congress members, especially those with military backgrounds, Trump was motivated to intervene and gained credibility through the CJWC's support.

The CJWC first earned major traction in March 2019 when it wrote a letter to Navy leadership alleging the mistreatment of Eddie Gallagher while he was awaiting trial.[82] The letter earned the CJWC a national audience and showcased how it worked collaboratively with Fox News to gain Trump's attention. Fox News prominently covered the allegations, with the Gallagher family telling the network that it was "grateful [to] Members of Congress … [for] calling attention to … the abhorrent treatment of one of its most decorated warfighters."[83] After Rep. Ralph Norman of South Carolina appeared on "Fox & Friends" to discuss the case,[84] Trump tweeted that he would order Gallagher's removal from restrictive confinement, tagging both "@foxandfriends" and "@RepRalphNorman."[85]

Much of the early impetus for congressional lobbying came at the behest of Gallagher himself. On Instagram, for example, Gallagher

---

[80] Tan, Michelle. Jan. 14, 2015. "Congressmen to Army: Review LT's Murder Conviction." *Army Times*. www.armytimes.com/news/your-army/2015/01/14/congressmen-to-army-review-lt-s-murder-conviction/
[81] https://twitter.com/JFWCaucus
[82] Norman, Greg. Mar. 21, 2019. "Texas Rep. Dan Crenshaw Fighting for Fellow Navy SEAL Being Held on War Crimes Charges." *Fox News*. www.foxnews.com/us/eddie-gallagher-case-house-republicans-call-on-navy-leadership-to-review-treatment-of-seal-being-held-on-war-crimes-charges
[83] Norman, Greg. Mar. 21, 2019. "Texas Rep. Dan Crenshaw Fighting for Fellow Navy SEAL Being Held on War Crimes Charges." *Fox News*. www.foxnews.com/us/eddie-gallagher-case-house-republicans-call-on-navy-leadership-to-review-treatment-of-seal-being-held-on-war-crimes-charges
[84] Rupar, Aaron. May, 24, 2019. "Trump's Interest in Pardoning Troops Accused of War Crimes, Explained." *Vox*. www.vox.com/policy-and-politics/2019/5/24/18637360/trump-war-crimes-pardons-gallagher-golsteyn-fox-news-hegseth
[85] https://twitter.com/realdonaldtrump/status/1111965027483951105?lang=bg

wrote to his followers: "Our family is seeking Congressional Support for a presidential Pardon for Eddie.... Please call your Congressional Representative and ask them to sign onto our Letter to the POTUS to #FREEEDDIE from this Travesty of Justice." The post tagged "@justice_for_warriors_caucus" and several of the most active CJWC members, including co-chairs Reps. Louie Gohmert and Duncan Hunter.[86] Gallagher's lawyer, however, maintained that his client "didn't need to ask for a pardon, because that happened organically, because members of Congress are paying attention to what happened in this case."[87]

In subsequent months, several GOP lawmakers pushed Trump to take action in war crime cases. The most vocal was CJWC co-chair Duncan Hunter, who repeatedly lobbied for Gallagher specifically. In an op-ed for *USA Today* published in May 2019, Hunter decried prosecutorial misconduct by the Navy and insisted that "[a] pardon by Trump is fully warranted."[88] Hunter had previously said that, while he wanted Trump to help Gallagher, it was important for his court martial to proceed so that the public could witness "how disgusting the military justice system is when it's run by lawyers and bureaucrats [who] go after the war-fighter."[89] Gallagher's brother, Sean, praised Hunter as "one of those allies" whose "support for Eddie was immediate and unwavering."[90]

More than calling for Trump to intervene, Hunter appeared to minimize the significance of war crimes and to condone them as an

---

[86] www.instagram.com/p/B4SjG6yA3-i/?utm_source=ig_embed&hl=en

[87] Szoldra, Paul and Jared Keller. Nov. 1, 2019. "Navy SEAL Eddie Gallagher's Family Is Asking Trump for a Presidential Pardon." *Military.com*. www.military.com/daily-news/2019/11/01/navy-seal-eddie-gallaghers-family-asking-trump-presidential-pardon.html

[88] Hunter, Duncan. May 24, 2019. "Commander in Chief Donald Trump's Pardon Is Warranted." *USA Today*. https://eu.usatoday.com/story/opinion/2019/05/24/pardon-president-donald-trump-fully-warranted-navy-seal-editorials-debates/1213635001/

[89] Budryk, Zack. May 27, 2019. "GOP Rep Defends Accused War Criminal, Saying He Also Photographed Bodies." *The Hill*. https://thehill.com/homenews/house/445666-gop-rep-defends-accused-war-criminal-by-saying-he-also-photographed-bodies

[90] Gallagher, Sean. Oct. 24, 2019. "Congressman's Support of SEAL Immediate and Unwavering." *San Diego Union-Tribune*. www.sandiegouniontribune.com/opinion/story/2019-10-24/what-duncan-hunters-support-of-eddie-gallagher-reveals-about-his-character

2.1 War Crime Clemencies 53

inevitable byproduct of war. He argued for Trump to grant clemency for Gallagher because his acts were not rare in battle, saying that he "frankly [didn't] care" about his guilt or innocence.[91] Hunter had formerly sparked controversy for admitting that, as an artillery officer, his unit "killed probably hundreds of civilians" in Iraq, including "[p]robably ... women and children."[92] Referring to the charge of Gallagher posing with the corpse of a teenager, Hunter bragged that he had also taken illicit pictures "just like that when I was overseas" and said that "[a] lot of my peers ... have done the exact same thing."[93]

As momentum grew for clemencies in 2019, the CJWC sent a string of letters to Trump pleading for him to intervene, including one for Clint Lorance dated August 9[94] and one for Eddie Gallagher dated November 4.[95] The letters pilloried their verdicts and warned of the damage to troop morale if Trump neglected to intervene. After Pete Hegseth reported on Fox News that Trump intended to act soon, CJWC leaders again wrote to the White House on November 5 praising the president for defending "our nation's warriors." The text read that the "CJWC ... would like to commend you [President Trump] for your decision as reported by Fox News' Pete Hegseth to take action in the cases of 1Lt. Clint Lorance, Chief Petty Officer Eddie Gallagher, and Maj. Matt Golsteyn."[96]

On November 8, Reps. Duncan Hunter and Louie Gohmert followed up these letters with an op-ed at FoxNews.com entitled, "War Crimes Charges against 3 Military Combat Veterans Should be

---

[91] Fearnow, Benjamin. June 3, 2019. "'Keep Your Mouth Shut.' Retired General Shuts Down Republican Duncan Hunter's Defense of Alleged War Criminal." *Newsweek*. www.newsweek.com/duncan-hunter-general-war-crime-cnn

[92] Kelly, Caroline. June 2, 2019. "Rep. Duncan Hunter: Iraq Unit 'Killed Probably Hundreds of Civilians.'" *CNN*. https://edition.cnn.com/2019/06/01/politics/duncan-hunter-barstool-interview-killed-hundreds/index.html

[93] Budryk, Zack. May 27, 2019. "GOP Rep Defends Accused War Criminal, Saying He Also Photographed Bodies." *The Hill*. https://thehill.com/homenews/house/445666-gop-rep-defends-accused-war-criminal-by-saying-he-also-photographed-bodies

[94] https://gohmert.house.gov/uploadedfiles/scanned_letter_signed_for_lorance_with_hice.pdf (last accessed Mar. 14, 2021)

[95] https://gohmert.house.gov/uploadedfiles/pardon_eddie_gallagher.pdf (last accessed Mar. 14, 2021)

[96] https://gohmert.house.gov/uploadedfiles/11.5.19_letter_to_president_trump_from_louie_gohmert_and_duncan_hunter.pdf (last accessed May 14, 2021)

Thrown out by Trump."⁹⁷ In the piece, the legislators referred to Golsteyn, Lorance, and Gallagher as "brave men" and insisted that "[e]very commonsense, patriotic American would undoubtedly celebrate the dismissal of all the charges." Apart from lobbying for clemencies, Hunter and Gohmert touted the CJWC's role in "ensur[ing] miscarriages of justice like those suffered by these men never happen again." The op-ed was featured on Fox News's website with a video of Pete Hegseth stating that he was "able to confirm ... from the president of the United States himself ... that action is imminent."

When news emerged of pushback from inside the Pentagon, the CJWC took to social media to decry "Pentagon bureaucrats" bent on "'head[ing] off' president Trump from taking action."⁹⁸ On Facebook, the CJWC encouraged supporters to "[p]lease call the White House ... and Tweet our president @realDonaldTrump and encourage him to act on behalf of our nation's heroes."⁹⁹ Their pressure was rewarded when, days later, Pete Hegseth tweeted Trump's decision: "Army 1LT Clint Lorance is FULLY PARDONED and will be out of prison TONIGHT. Army Green Beret Matt Golsteyn is FULLY PARDONED and is free from Army harassment. Navy SEAL Eddie Gallagher gets his rank & record back. All thanks to @realDonaldTrump. #AmericaFirst #WarriorsFirst."¹⁰⁰

As with the 2019 clemencies, Republican Congress members also played an integral role in pushing for Trump's Blackwater pardons. On May 12, 2020, the CJWC issued a press release urging Trump to act.¹⁰¹ The statement, calling the contractors "brave men" who

---

⁹⁷ Hunter, Duncan and Louie Gohmert. Nov. 8, 2019. "Reps. Hunter and Gohmert: War Crimes Charges against 3 Military Combat Veterans Should Be Thrown Out by Trump." *Fox News*. www.foxnews.com/opinion/reps-hunter-and-gohmert-trump-should-throw-out-war-crimes-charges-against-3-brave-military-combat-veterans

⁹⁸ www.facebook.com/CongressionalJusticeForWarriorsCaucus/?ref=nf &hc_ref=ARSU9xcJhn28UKuDYzt0KhapYQn7nMjPE9vgZDW72A3PY-cNBGFQGkQTqzTSI9OhXv4&__tn__=%3C-R

⁹⁹ www.facebook.com/CongressionalJusticeForWarriorsCaucus/?ref=nf &hc_ref=ARSU9xcJhn28UKuDYzt0KhapYQn7nMjPE9vgZDW72A3PY-cNBGFQGkQTqzTSI9OhXv4&__tn__=%3C-R

¹⁰⁰ https://twitter.com/PeteHegseth/status/1195498456326004736

¹⁰¹ Press Release. May 12, 2020. "The Congressional Justice for Warriors Caucus Calls Upon President Trump to Pardon the Biden Four." https://gohmert.house.gov/news/documentsingle.aspx?DocumentID=399780 (last accessed Sept. 14, 2021)

"suffered grave injustices," ended with quotes from Reps. Louie Gohmert and Paul Gosar accusing Democrats and prosecutors of stymieing justice. According to Gohmert, the Blackwater agents were victims of "constitutional violations, prosecutorial misconduct, and media malpractice," as well as a malicious effort "[to] scapegoat[e] these men for political and diplomatic expediency." In the words of Gosar, "It was Hillary Clinton and Joe Biden who pushed for further prosecution," an act he described as "truly unconscionable."

Individual leaders of the CJWC also spoke out on the Blackwater cases. As early as June 2019, for example, Rep. Duncan Hunter called for unconditional pardons on FoxNews.com. Claiming that the contractors were being used as "political pawns" by Democrats, he wrote that "[o]ur warfighters deserve better" and "[i]t's time to have their backs."[102] On the same day that the CJWC formally advocated pardons, Rep. Louie Gohmert appeared on the "Raven 23: Presumption of Guilt" podcast,[103] the podcast that Pete Hegseth had earlier featured on Fox News.[104] Gohmert acknowledged that the CJWC did not originally intend to lobby for the Blackwater agents because they worked for a private firm. However, he said that this changed after realizing the men had prior military service and that "these were warriors."

Defense of Clemencies

GOP Congress members also rushed to defend Trump's war crime clemencies. When Trump intervened on November 15, 2019, the CJWC declared in a letter that it was "ecstatic and eternally grateful." It added that the clemencies were a "shining example of why [Trump] ... was elected in 2016" and called him a "bold and fearless leader who refuses to bow to establishment pressure when helping

---

[102] Hunter, Duncan. June 21, 2019. "Rep. Duncan Hunter: President Trump, 'The Biden Four' Deserve Your Attention." *Fox News*. www.foxnews.com/opinion/rep-duncan-hunter-trump-iraq-biden-four-blackwater-veterans-prison

[103] Keating, Gina. May 12, 2020. "Raven 23: Presumption of Guilt Special Episode: Interview with US Rep. Louie Gohmert." www.youtube.com/watch?v=oDGrQAU13b0

[104] Aug. 11, 2019. "Podcast Tells the Story of How Four Veterans Ended up Serving Life Sentences for War Crimes." *Fox News*. https://video.foxnews.com/v/6071713887001?fbclid=IwAR2867eQMi1topNkvvhEJas6bfW5FkDbdK_NUwHdjmNfWMmE-OajdrlFFDk#sp=show-clips

America's valiant warriors."[105] The CJWC's Twitter handle was celebrated by sharing tweets from its members, Trump, and Pete Hegseth.[106] One retweet included a message from Hegseth declaring, "@BarackObama traded terrorists for traitors. @realDonaldTrump backs real warfighters. Obama's war rules handcuffed our warriors – and then he prosecuted them. Trump let them fight and win – and tonight, he sets them free."[107]

Several CJWC members boasted on social media about their personal roles in the clemencies. For example, Rep. Paul Gosar of Arizona tweeted out a handwritten letter from Clint Lorance reading: "I want to personally thank you for sending a letter to the President on my behalf. You have made a permanent impact on my life. Thank you for your leadership. May God bless you." Gosar tagged @realDonaldTrump and declared that he would "never stop fighting for our men and women in uniform."[108] Rep. Ralph Norman tweeted, "This is who we fight for: those who fought for us. Well done, @realdonaldtrump."[109] His message responded to Trump's son, Eric, declaring, "I hope no one who serves our country and volunteers to do the unthinkable is ever treated like this again! Great job @realDonaldTrump!"[110]

Other GOP lawmakers defended Trump's clemencies, especially on Fox News. For example, Rep. Guy Reschenthaler of Pennsylvania lauded Trump on Fox News for "letting war fighters be war fighters."[111] On "Fox News Sunday," Rep. Steve Scalise of Louisiana complained that, before Trump, U.S. servicemembers "felt that they ... needed a team of attorneys before they could return fire in the battlefield."[112] In another example of how Fox News's messaging was used by other IT members, Rep. Michael Waltz of Florida

---

[105] www.facebook.com/CongressionalJusticeForWarriorsCaucus/photos/a.52879 3434597055/575858916557173/?type=3&theater
[106] https://twitter.com/jfwcaucus?lang=en
[107] https://twitter.com/PeteHegseth/status/1195500711259320322
[108] https://twitter.com/RepGosar/status/1195695801575628800
[109] https://twitter.com/RepRalphNorman/status/1195494279256379393
[110] https://twitter.com/EricTrump/status/1195491841506004992
[111] "GOP Rep. Weights in on Clemency Granted to Two Army Officers." *Fox News*. www.youtube.com/watch?v=HwLLFLI1rBs
[112] Semones, Evan. Nov. 17, 2019. "Steve Scalise: Trump's Military Pardons Boost Troop Morale." *POLITICO*. www.politico.com/news/2019/11/17/steve-scalise-trump-military-pardon-071306

told Pete Hegseth on "Fox & Friends" that "[w]hat we can't do is … have people back in Washington, DC, a bunch of lawyers, Monday morning quarterbacking."[113] The "Monday morning quarterbacking" phrase echoed precise words from Hegseth's 2019 FoxNews.com opinion piece.[114]

Soon after the interventions, a number of CJWC members urged Trump to go further in granting clemencies. For example, Rep. Louie Gohmert said that pardoning more servicemembers would be evidence of the White House's commitment to Americans serving in uniform. "Today," Gohmert said in a press release, "I am humbly requesting that the president also act in the cases of two more American heroes: Sgt. Derrick Miller and 1Sgt. John Hatley. All these men mentioned are deserving of having the findings and sentences of their cases disapproved." Gohmert added that "[t]hese warriors have been sacrificed at the altar of politically correct Rules of Engagement for far too long. It is time we take decisive action and put an end to the wrongful prosecution of our military heroes."[115]

Several Republican Congress members also defended Trump's firing of Navy Secretary Richard Spencer over his attempt to strip Eddie Gallagher of his SEAL trident. Rep. Duncan Hunter, for example, declared that Spencer was "just asking to be relieved as soon as possible."[116] Sen. Jim Inhofe of Oklahoma said that his past disagreements with Spencer were "no secret" and that he "look[ed] forward to … considering a nomination for the next Secretary of the Navy as soon as possible."[117] When Democrat Sen. Tim Kaine of Virginia demanded an inquiry into Spencer's firing, one reporter

---

[113] Nov. 17, 2019. "Rep. Michael Waltz: President Trump Did the Right Thing by Pardoning Clint Lorance." Rep. Michael Waltz. www.youtube.com/watch?v=IXmKv1yo2Ng&t=112s

[114] Hegseth, Pete. May 23, 2019. 'Pete Hegseth: I'm With the Warfighters – Count Me out of Second-guessing Our Heroes." *Fox News*. www.foxnews.com/opinion/pete-hegseth-im-with-the-american-warfighters

[115] www.facebook.com/RepLouieGohmert/posts/10157590336776904?comment_id=10157590386666904

[116] Stone, Ken. Nov. 25, 2019. "Rep. Duncan Hunter: Military Should Consider Trump Tweets a Direct Order." *Times of San Diego*. https://timesofsandiego.com/politics/2019/11/25/rep-duncan-hunter-military-should-consider-trump-tweets-a-direct-order/

[117] Morgan, Wesley. Nov. 24, 2019. "Esper Forces out Navy Secretary over Disputed SEAL Case." *POLITICO*. www.politico.com/news/2019/11/24/esper-navy-secretary-resign-seal-case-073436

noted "Republicans ... lined up in support of the president on the matter" and predicted that it was "doubtful an investigation would gain traction in the chamber where Republicans hold the majority."[118]

When Trump announced the Blackwater pardons in December 2020, the CJWC also released an official statement to celebrate.[119] In it, members alternated between praising Trump and criticizing lawyers and the Obama administration for allowing the men to be jailed. Rep. Louie Gohmert, for example, lauded Trump for "the most wonderful Christmas gift in the form of pardons." Rep. Bill Flores of Texas declared, "I commend president Trump for his action tonight to pardon the Biden Four." Rep. Daniel Webster of Florida wrote, "Thank you, president Trump, for standing up for these four veterans and righting this wrong." After accusing the Obama White House of "railroad[ing] four of our Iraq warriors," Rep. Paul Gosar ended his message with three words: "Welcome home boys."

The CJWC and various Republican politicians again took to social media to champion the interventions. On its Facebook page, the CJWC posted a red, white, and blue photo of the four Blackwater contractors, pronouncing: "THEY ARE FREE!!! Thank you President Donald J. Trump!! We love you and support you!"[120] On Twitter, the CJWC recounted the "wonderful news of @realDonaldTrump's pardons for the #BidenFour."[121] In response to a UN report criticizing the interventions, Rep. Matt Gaetz tweeted, "The UN is an America-Last organization. @realDonaldTrump was right to issue the Blackwater Pardons."[122] Even a Republican Texas state senator, Drew Springer, expressed his support on Twitter, tagging "@PeteHegseth": "Thank you Pres. Trump for pardoning them! Whiskey & Cigars seem like freedom to me."[123]

---

[118] Sisk, Richard and Gina Harkins. Nov. 27, 2019. "Lawmakers Call for Pentagon Investigation into Navy Secretary's Firing." *Military.com*. www.military.com/daily-news/2019/11/27/lawmakers-call-pentagon-investigation-navy-secretarys-firing.html

[119] Dec. 23, 2020. "CJWC Members Celebrate President Trump's Pardons for the Biden Four." Press Release. https://gohmert.house.gov/news/documentsingle.aspx?DocumentID=399894 (last accessed Feb. 13, 2022)

[120] www.facebook.com/CongressionalJusticeForWarriorsCaucus/

[121] https://twitter.com/freeraven23/status/1341733087978381323?lang=en

[122] https://twitter.com/mattgaetz/status/1344405861989576704?lang=en

[123] https://twitter.com/DrewSpringer/status/1344798100666376199

2.2 Additional Examples of IT Synchronization

As described earlier, Trump's war crime interventions exemplify the impunity agenda most clearly, as they overtly challenged IHL and the U.S. military justice system. However, they are not isolated events. As part of a broader attack on international laws governing the military, Trump has also tested bedrock principles pertaining to noncombatant immunity, state sovereignty, restraints on the use of force, and prohibitions on torture. As with the war crime clemencies, Trump, alongside Fox News and Republican Congress members, has carried out discrete tasks via divisions of labor to inspire and defend the behavior. By relying on right-wing partners, Trump has been able to avoid succumbing to resistance in publicly dismissing international laws.

First, Trump on multiple occasions has called for the deliberate killing of civilians, which, if acted on, would breach the IHL principle of "distinction" forbidding the intentional targeting of noncombatants. In December 2015, for example, Trump declared on "Fox & Friends" that killing family members of terrorists can be an effective tactic, pronouncing "When you get these terrorists, you have to take out their families."[124] At a GOP primary debate later that month, Trump refused to back down, saying that terrorists "may not care much about their lives, but they do care, believe it or not, about their families' lives."[125] According to a 2018 report, while being briefed on a drone strike in Syria, Trump also "[q]uestioned why [the] CIA avoided killing [a] terrorist's family."[126]

Fox News has given Trump multiple platforms to defend his views. In 2015, for example, Sean Hannity told Trump, "I actually agree with you" after Trump advocated killing the wives of terrorists.[127] When

---

[124] Hains, Tim. Dec. 2, 2015. "Trump: Islamic State Is Our No. 1 Threat." *Real Clear Politics*. www.realclearpolitics.com/video/2015/12/02/trump_isis_is_our_1_threat_--_we_cant_be_fighting_everybody_at_the_same_time.html

[125] Alter, Charlotte. Dec. 16, 2015. "Transcript: Read the Full Text of the Dec. 15 Republican Debate in Las Vegas." *TIME*. https://time.com/4150816/republican-debate-las-vegas-transcript/

[126] Hartmann, Margaret. Apr. 6, 2018. "Trump Questioned Why CIA Avoided Killing Terrorist's Family: Report." *New York Magazine*. https://nymag.com/intelligencer/2018/04/trump-asked-why-cia-drone-avoided-terrorists-family-report.html

[127] Dec. 4, 2015 "Trump Doubles Down on Targeting Terrorists' Families: 'Take Them Out!'" *Fox News*. https://insider.foxnews.com/2015/12/04/donald-trump-doubles-down-targeting-terrorists-families-hannity

Fox News's Bill O'Reilly asked Trump to clarify that he would really "put out hits on women and children," Trump insisted, "I would do pretty severe stuff."[128] One journalist noted that he had never witnessed "a political event at which people cheered for the murder of women and children."[129] Similar threats gained some approval in Congress. In 2015, for instance, Sen. Ted Cruz of Texas called for the U.S. military to "carpet-bomb … [ISIS] into oblivion," a move that would likely violate both distinction and proportionality principles. "I don't know if sand can glow in the dark," Cruz remarked, "but we're going to find out!"[130]

Related to noncombatant immunity, Trump also in his first term called for reversing Obama-era policies that had strengthened U.S. military rules of engagement (ROE).[131] Although the merits of loosening ROE are contested, and many experts acknowledge that they were previously more restrictive than required by IHL, reforms coincided with spikes in civilian deaths.[132] Trump's efforts culminated in a high-profile address in 2017 when he declared that "[r]etribution will be fast and powerful as we lift restrictions and expand authorities in the field."[133] Secretary of Defense General James Mattis reportedly took multiple steps on this front, including eliminating proximity requirements for launching air attacks.[134] Trump also oversaw the canceling of plans to stop the U.S. military's use

---

[128] Beauchamp, Zack. Jan. 25, 2016. "Donald Trump Said He'd Kill Terrorists' Families at a Rally. His Crowd Went Wild." *Vox*. www.vox.com/2016/1/25/10828770/trump-terrorist-family-appeal

[129] Beauchamp, Zack. Jan. 25, 2016. "Donald Trump Said He'd Kill Terrorists' Families at a Rally. His Crowd Went Wild." *Vox*. www.vox.com/2016/1/25/10828770/trump-terrorist-family-appeal

[130] Glueck, Katie. Dec. 5, 2015. "Cruz Pledges Relentless Bombing to Destroy ISIL." *POLITICO*. www.politico.com/story/2015/12/cruz-isil-bombing-216454

[131] Cooper, Helene. Apr. 5, 2017. "Trump Gives Military New Freedom. But With That Comes Danger." *New York Times*. www.nytimes.com/2017/04/05/us/politics/rules-of-engagement-military-force-mattis.html

[132] Crawford, Neta C. 2020. *Afghanistan's Rising Civilian Death Toll Due to Airstrikes, 2017–2020*. Brown University and Boston University.

[133] Aug. 21, 2017. "Full Transcript and Video: Trump's Speech on Afghanistan." *New York Times*. www.nytimes.com/2017/08/21/world/asia/trump-speech-afghanistan.html

[134] Mehta, Aaron. Oct. 3, 2017. "Mattis Reveals New Rules of Engagement." *Military Times*. www.militarytimes.com/flashpoints/2017/10/03/mattis-reveals-new-rules-of-engagement/

2.2 Additional Examples of IT Synchronization 61

of "cluster munitions," known for killing civilians indiscriminately through sub-explodables.[135]

Fox News commentators defended Trump's ROE reforms. Pete Hegseth, for example, praised Trump, quoting him as saying "I will ... untie the hands of my commanders. I will not micromanage from the White House." He further lamented "30 something graduate students second-guessing commanders on the battlefield," which he said occurred under Obama.[136] Sean Hannity lauded Trump for "t[aking] off the rules of engagement of Obama and bomb[ing] the living hell out of [the caliphate in Syria]."[137] On Capitol Hill, Rep. Michael Waltz of Florida complained that, prior to Trump, ROE were "often ... flawed" and "were dramatically over-restrictive."[138] Rep. Mac Thornberry of Texas also protested that, before Trump, troops "missed targets because they had to go back and have an NSC [National Security Council meeting] that met for weeks."[139]

Regarding accountability for noncombatant casualties, Trump has regularly taken aim at the ICC, accusing it of targeting U.S. servicemembers. Most notably, on June 11, 2020, Trump signed an executive order that froze financial assets and applied travel bans on ICC prosecutors. In a statement, Trump assailed the ICC's "illegitimate assertions of jurisdiction" and accused it of "imped[ing] the critical national security" work of the U.S.[140] The penalties came shortly after then

---

[135] Rogin, Josh. Nov. 30, 2017. "The Trump Administration Cancels a Plan to Curtail the Use of Cluster Bombs." *Washington Post.* www.washingtonpost.com/news/josh-rogin/wp/2017/11/30/the-trump-administration-cancels-a-plan-to-curtail-the-use-of-cluster-bombs/

[136] Apr. 24, 2017. "New Rules of Engagement for America's Military." *AM 560 The Answer.* https://560theanswer.com/podcast/episode/4897/new-rules-of-engagement-for-americas-military

[137] Staff. Jan. 3, 2020. "Sean Hannity Calls for Trump to Discard Rules of Engagement with Iran and 'Bomb the Living Hell out of Them.'" *Media Matters.* www.mediamatters.org/sean-hannity/sean-hannity-calls-trump-discard-rules-engagement-iran-and-bomb-living-hell-out-them

[138] Nov. 18, 2019. "Rules of Engagement 'Restrictive' under Obama: Rep. Waltz." https://video.foxnews.com/v/6105511944001#sp=show-clips

[139] Kheel, Rebecca. Mar. 28, 2017. "GOP Lawmakers Defend Trump Military Rules of Engagement." *The Hill.* https://thehill.com/policy/defense/326212-gop-lawmakers-defend-trump-military-rules-of-engagement

[140] June 11, 2020. "Executive Order on Blocking Property of Certain Persons Associated with The International Criminal Court." The White House. https://trumpwhitehouse.archives.gov/presidential-actions/executive-order-blocking-property-certain-persons-associated-international-criminal-court/

Secretary of State Mike Pompeo warned in May 2020 that the U.S. would be willing to "exact consequences" on the ICC.[141] It also followed 2018 comments by Trump national security adviser John Bolton who insisted that the U.S. "will not cooperate with the ICC" and that, "for all intents and purposes, the ICC is already dead to us."[142]

Fox News provided a platform for criticizing the ICC. For example, in a "Fox and Friends" interview with Pete Hegseth in March 2020, Pompeo complained that "these international bodies can turn ... against you, and that's precisely what's happened [with the ICC]."[143] On Foxnews.com, contributor Christian Whiton accused the ICC of being part of a "globaloney" agenda that was "more interested in prosecuting Americans than thugs."[144] In Congress, Sens. Ted Cruz, Marco Rubio, and Tom Cotton issued a press release in March 2020 condemning the ICC's "unacceptable" investigations of U.S. servicemembers.[145] Earlier that year, Cruz denigrated the ICC as a "kangaroo court" and "fundamentally illegitimate," vowing that "[t]he ICC's campaign against our troops will fail because the United States will ensure that it fails."[146]

Trump has also disregarded international laws on state sovereignty. Most notably, he has threatened to use the U.S. military to

---

[141] May 16, 2020. "Pompeo Warns ICC Against Asserting Authority Over Israel." *VOA News*. www.voanews.com/a/middle-east_pompeo-warns-icc-against-asserting-authority-over-israel/6189396.html

[142] Sept. 11, 2018. "John Bolton Threatens ICC with Sanctions: 'We Will Not Cooperate'." *Al Jazeera*. www.aljazeera.com/news/2018/9/11/john-bolton-threatens-icc-with-sanctions-we-will-not-cooperate

[143] US Secretary of State. Mar. 6, 2020. "Secretary Michael R. Pompeo With Steve Doocy, Jedediah Bila, and Pete Hegseth of Fox and Friends." https://2017-2021.state.gov/secretary-michael-r-pompeo-with-steve-doocy-jedediah-bila-and-pete-hegseth-of-fox-and-friends/index.html

[144] Whiton, Christian. Sept. 25, 2018. "Trump at UN: Elites May Laugh but Americans Can See Through the Globaloney." *Fox News*. www.foxnews.com/opinion/trump-at-un-elites-may-laugh-but-americans-can-see-through-the-globaloney

[145] Press Release. Mar. 13, 2020. "Rubio, Cotton, Cruz Urge POTUS to Ensures Service Members and Allied Armed Forces are Protected from ICC Prosecution." www.rubio.senate.gov/public/index.cfm/2020/3/rubio-cotton-cruz-urge-potus-to-ensures-service-members-and-allied-armed-forces-are-protected-from-icc-prosecution (last accessed Oct. 21, 2022)

[146] Press Release. Mar. 5, 2020. "Sen. Cruz: 'The ICC's Campaign against Our Troops Will Fail Because the United States Will Ensure That It Fails'." www.cruz.senate.gov/newsroom/press-releases/sen-cruz-and-039the-icc-and-039s-campaign-against-our-troops-will-fail-because-the-united-states-will-ensure-that-it-fails-and-039

2.2 Additional Examples of IT Synchronization 63

confiscate Middle Eastern oil for profit, a pledge that would likely constitute the war crime of "pillage."[147] In October 2019, for example, in reference to Syria, Trump said, "We're keeping the oil ... I've always said that – keep the oil.... $45 million a month."[148] Trump's comments prompted retired Gen. Barry R. McCaffrey to ask, "WHAT ARE WE BECOMING ... PIRATES?"[149] In 2017, Trump also said that the U.S. military "should have taken the oil" from Iraq during its 2003 invasion.[150] When told that the act would breach international law, Trump called experts holding the position "fools."[151] As far back as 2011, Trump had endorsed the U.S. military seizing oil from Iraq. "You're not stealing anything," he pronounced. "We're reimbursing ourselves ... at a minimum."[152]

On Fox News, anchors again rationalized Trump's arguments. For example, Fox Business host Charles Payne remarked that "what the president is saying ... [is] it's kind of crazy that we've spent trillions of dollars, that we lost all these amazing valuable lives to protect a region ... where the biggest asset is oil and we never tap into it."[153] In 2015, Sean Hannity told Trump that he "like[d] the idea" of confiscating oil.[154] On Capitol Hill, Sen. Lindsey Graham

[147] Stewart, James G. Nov. 5, 2019. "Trump Keeps Talking about 'Keeping' Middle East Oil. That Would Be Illegal." *Washington Post.* www.washingtonpost.com/outlook/2019/11/05/trump-keeps-talking-about-keeping-middle-east-oil-that-would-be-illegal/
[148] Finnegan, Conor. Oct. 28, 2019. "'We're Keeping the Oil' in Syria, Trump Says, but It's Considered a War Crime." *ABC News.* https://abcnews.go.com/Politics/keeping-oil-syria-trump-considered-war-crime/story?id=66589757
[149] https://twitter.com/mccaffreyr3/status/1188669495386071046
[150] Saadoun, Sarah. Jan. 27, 2017. "Trump, Iraq Oil and International Law." Human Rights Watch. www.hrw.org/news/2017/01/27/trump-iraqi-oil-and-international-law#
[151] Saadoun, Sarah. Jan. 27, 2017. "Trump, Iraq Oil and International Law." Human Rights Watch. www.hrw.org/news/2017/01/27/trump-iraqi-oil-and-international-law#
[152] Borger, Julian. Sept. 21, 2016. "Trump's Plan to Seize Iraq's Oil: 'It's Not Stealing, We're Reimbursing Ourselves.'" *Guardian.* www.theguardian.com/us-news/2016/sep/21/donald-trump-iraq-war-oil-strategy-seizure-isis
[153] Staff. Oct. 28, 2019. "Fox Business Host Defends Trump Plan to Tap Syria for Oil: 'The Idea Is to ... Alleviate the Economic Issues that Come with Policing that Part of the World.'" *Media Matters.* www.mediamatters.org/charles-payne/fox-business-host-defends-trump-plan-tap-syria-oil
[154] Aug. 12, 2015. "FOX 'Hannity'- Transcript: Trump Interview." https://votesmart.org/public-statement/1110867/fox-hannity-transcript-trump-interview#.Xj9B3FJKiqB

of South Carolina also backed Trump's oil threats. In 2019, after Trump proposed "mak[ing] a deal with ExxonMobil or one of our great companies to go in there and do it properly," Graham called Trump's plan "good common sense foreign policy"[155] and recommended "us[ing] some of the revenues from future oil sales to pay for our military commitment in Syria."[156]

Related to national sovereignty, in January 2020, Trump sparked debate about the legality of foreign assassinations after he authorized a drone strike killing Iranian Maj. Gen. Qasem Soleimani, who had previously been implicated in the deaths of Americans.[157] The White House initially justified Soleimani's targeting on the grounds that he was planning an "imminent" attack on U.S. citizens,[158] but then refused to substantiate the claim. After rebukes from opponents, Trump responded by criticizing the "Radical Left, Do Nothing Democrats" for "defending the life of Qasem Soleimani."[159] He also dismissed the need for legally justifying the act, tweeting that "whether or not the future attack by terrorist Soleimani was 'imminent' or not ... doesn't really matter because of his horrible past!"[160] A White House report released after Soleimani's killing offered no specific evidence of an imminent attack.[161]

---

[155] Hirsch, Lauren. Oct. 27, 2019. "Trump Wants to Make a Deal with Exxon or Others to Tap Syrian Oil: 'We Should Be Able to Take Some.'" *CNBC*. www.cnbc.com/2019/10/27/trump-wants-to-make-a-deal-with-exxon-or-others-to-tap-syrian-oil.html

[156] Press Release. Oct. 23, 2019. "Graham Statement on Syria." www.lgraham.senate.gov/public/index.cfm/2019/10/graham-statement-on-syria

[157] Loveluck, Louisa, Adam Taylor, and Michael Brice-Saddler. Jan. 3, 2020. "Trump Says Iranian Military Leader Was Killed by Drone Strike 'To Stop a War,' Warns Iran Not to Retaliate." *Washington Post*. www.washingtonpost.com/world/iran-strike-live-updates/2020/01/03/3779f55c-2e33-11ea-bcb3-ac6482c4a92f_story.html

[158] Hosenball, Mark. Jan. 3, 2020. "Trump Says Soleimani Plotted 'Imminent' Attacks, but Critics Question Just How Soon." *Reuters*. https://uk.reuters.com/article/us-iraq-security-blast-intelligence/trump-says-soleimani-plotted-imminent-attacks-but-critics-question-just-how-soon-idUSKBN1Z228N

[159] https://twitter.com/realDonaldTrump/status/1215998705557475328

[160] https://twitter.com/realDonaldTrump/status/1216754098382524422

[161] "Notice on the Legal and Policy Frameworks Guiding the United States' Use of Military Force and Related National Security Operations." The White House. www.documentcloud.org/documents/6776446-Section-1264-NDAA-Notice.html

2.2 Additional Examples of IT Synchronization 65

Fox News vigorously defended Trump over the Soleimani strike. Sean Hannity, for example, declared that "there's a new sheriff in town tonight," calling Soleimani's killing "a huge success."[162] Pete Hegseth said that Soleimani's death could be "about as big as bin Laden ... about as big as Baghdadi."[163] He also implied credit for Trump's decision: "If I was part of the narrative ... [in Soleimani's killing] well, that's a wonderful part of my day job."[164] In Congress, lone GOP voices like Sens. Rand Paul of Kentucky and Mike Lee of Utah questioned the legality of Soleimani's killing.[165] However, most high-profile lawmakers – including Sens. Marco Rubio of Florida, Tom Cotton of Arkansas, and Ben Sasse of Nebraska[166] – dismissed concerns about its lawfulness. Sen. Lindsey Graham accused some skeptics of the Soleimani strike of "empowering the enemy."[167]

Following Soleimani's death, Trump threatened to use "disproportionate" force against any Iranian response, a move that would expressly violate IHL's "proportionality" principle.[168] He also announced that retaliation would risk a U.S counterstrike against Iranian cultural

---

[162] Garcia, Victor. Jan. 6, 2020. "Sean Hannity: Iran Regime Knows 'That There's a New Sheriff in Town Tonight.'" *Fox News*. www.foxnews.com/media/sean-hannity-pelosi-iran-resolution-makes-us-less-safe

[163] Gage, John. Jan. 2, 2020. "'About as Big as Bin Laden': Fox's Pete Hegseth Hails Death of Iranian Gen. Qassim Soleimani." *Washington Examiner*. www.washingtonexaminer.com/news/about-as-big-as-bin-laden-foxs-pete-hegseth-hails-death-of-iranian-general-qassem-soleimani

[164] Steinhauser, Jennifer. Jan. 6, 2020. "Fox Host's 'America First' Shift Makes an Exception for Trump's Iran Strike." *New York Times*. www.nytimes.com/2020/01/06/us/politics/pete-hegseth-trump-fox-news.html

[165] Shabad, Rebecca and Mitch Felan. Jan. 8, 2020. "'Insulting and Demeaning': Two GOP Lawmakers Rip Trump Administration after Iran Briefing." *NBC News*. www.nbcnews.com/politics/congress/insulting-demeaning-lawmakers-rip-trump-administration-after-iran-briefing-n1112596

[166] Basu, Zachary. Jan. 2, 2020. "Republicans Celebrate Death of Qasem Soleimani." *Axios*. www.axios.com/2020/01/03/qassem-soleimani-death-reactions-iran

[167] Jan. 9, 2020. "Rand Paul Fires Back at Lindsey Graham: That's a Low, Gutter Type Response." *CNN*. www.youtube.com/watch?v=yfr6CoSmEBw

[168] https://twitter.com/realDonaldTrump/status/1213919480574812160?ref_src=twsrc%5Etfw%7Ctwcamp%5Etweetembed%7Ctwterm%5E1213919480574812160%7Ctwgr%5Ed81efe2-f135fd1e9c1a450199d7e046930dc1aa%7Ctwcon%5Es1_&ref_url=https%3A%2F%2Fwww.vox.com%2F2020%2F1%2F6%2F21051550%2Ftrump-iran-tweets-soleimani-war-powers-act

sites, which would breach the Geneva Conventions.[169] "Let this serve as a WARNING," Trump tweeted, "that if Iran strikes any Americans, or American assets, we have … targeted 52 Iranian sites…, some … important to Iran & the Iranian culture, and those targets, and Iran itself, WILL BE HIT VERY FAST AND VERY HARD."[170] Although Trump eventually walked back his comments,[171] it was not before he defended his original tweet, saying, "They're allowed to torture and maim our people…. And we're not allowed to touch their cultural site? It doesn't work that way."[172]

Trump's threats again received support on Fox News. Pete Hegseth, for example, pronounced, "I don't care about Iranian cultural sites, and I'll tell you why…. [I]f Iran could … they would destroy every single one of our cultural sites and build a mosque on top of it."[173] Co-host Ainsley Earhardt suggested, without evidence, that Iran was using cultural sites to conceal weapons.[174] Although Senate Majority Leader Mitch McConnell criticized targeting cultural sites,[175] Trump's warning was still met with a defense on Capitol Hill. After several Democrat senators tried to pass a unanimous resolution labeling force against cultural sites a war crime,[176] Republican Sen. James

[169] Bronin, Sara C. Jan. 5, 2020. "Destroying Cultural Heritage Sites Is a War Crime." *Los Angeles Times*. www.latimes.com/opinion/story/2020-01-05/iran-donald-trump-cultural-sites-war-crime
[170] https://twitter.com/realDonaldTrump/status/1213593974679769093
[171] Vazquez, Maegan and Allie Malloy. Jan. 7, 2020. "Trump Appears to Backtrack on Threat to Target Iranian Cultural Sites." *CNN*. www.cnn.com/2020/01/07/politics/donald-trump-iranian-cultural-sites-backtrack/index.html
[172] Haberman, Maggie. Jan. 5, 2020. "Trump Threatens Iranian Cultural Sites, and Warns of Sanctions on Iraq." *New York Times*. www.nytimes.com/2020/01/05/us/politics/trump-iran-cultural-sites.html
[173] Caruso, Justin. Jan. 6, 2020. "Fox News' Pete Hegseth: 'I Don't Care about Iranian Cultural Sites,' They Would Destroy Ours and Build Mosques." *Daily Caller*. https://dailycaller.com/2020/01/06/fox-news-pete-hegseth-dont-care-about-iranian-cultural-sites/
[174] Baragona, Justin. Jan. 8, 2020. "Fox News' Pete Hegseth: We Need to 'Rewrite the Rules' of War in Dealing With Iran." *Daily Beast*. www.thedailybeast.com/fox-news-pete-hegseth-says-we-need-to-rewrite-the-rules-of-war-in-dealing-with-iran
[175] O'Connor, Lydia. Jan. 7, 2020. "Mitch McConnell Says Targeting Iran's Cultural Sites Would Be 'Inappropriate.' It's Also Illegal." *HuffPost*. www.huffingtonpost.co.uk/entry/mitch-mcconnell-iran-cultural-site-attacks-inappropriate_us_5e14de2fc5b66361cb5be392?ri18n=true
[176] Jan. 8, 2020. "Senators Introduce Anti-War Crimes Resolution That Denounces Trump Threats to Attack Iranian Cultural Sites." www.warren

2.2 Additional Examples of IT Synchronization

Inhofe of Oklahoma blocked the effort. Echoing a concern from Fox News, he explained, "[I]t's simply not true that attacking cultural sites is always a war crime because ... cultural sites have been used as staging grounds for hostilities."[177]

Trump has further endorsed illegal interrogation techniques, including torture. On multiple occasions, Trump has expressly advocated waterboarding, despite the practice widely being deemed illegal under IHL. For example, in November 2015, Trump declared at a rally, "Would I approve waterboarding? You bet your ass I'd approve it.... In a heartbeat." Later that month, Trump proclaimed, "[T]hey say to me, 'What do you think about waterboarding?' I said, 'I think it's fine. I like it. I like it.'" In February 2016, Trump affirmed, "Those animals that are cutting off heads, when they hear that we're talking about waterboarding, you know, waterboarding is essentially a minor form of doing what they do." That month, Trump reiterated, "I think we should go much, much, much further than waterboarding." In June 2016, Trump pronounced that he did not think waterboarding was "tough enough."[178]

On Fox News, Trump's position has been met with support. Sean Hannity, who once offered to be waterboarded for charity,[179] posed a hypothetical to defend Trump. "OK, two guys ... kidnap your child," he said. "You don't waterboard that guy?"[180] Pete Hegseth said that Trump "understand[s] the appetite of the American people"

.senate.gov/newsroom/press-releases/senators-introduce-anti-war-crimes-resolution-that-denounces-trump-threats-to-attack-iranian-cultural-sites

[177] Carney, Jordain. Jan. 7, 2020. "Senate Republican Blocks Unanimous Consent on Resolution Calling Targeting Cultural Sites a War Crime." *The Hill.* https://thehill.com/homenews/senate/477231-senate-republican-blocks-resolution-calling-targeting-cultural-sites-a-war

[178] All quotes from: Apr. 4, 2018. "What Trump Said about Waterboarding." *Washington Post.* www.youtube.com/watch?v=ipLRLTc0uEE

[179] Linkins, Jason. May 23. 2009. "Hannity Offers To Be Waterboarded for Charity (By Charles Grodin!)." *HuffPost.* www.huffpost.com/entry/hannity-offers-to-be-wate_n_190354?guccounter=1&guce_referrer=aHR0cHM6Ly93d3cuZ29vZ2xlLmNvbS8&guce_referrer_sig=AQAAAJLFdrANR5xtnNFnQsiPFdIRPN5GFONkDtPfcPOnMdldAXv6xMj7X7fRmgXD6p16VRY5aBZqmhg1jcAEc82vdmPN9EMUMg1wUJcWsHWM8sRp0sTXAmsp7X8y63virv_NHqKBsvG5JOW6lrOmh5vGinLAWGOthZQgb5bnrPA9Lgpu

[180] Herbert, Geoff. Jan. 27, 2017. "Trump, Hannity Defend Waterboarding: What If David Muir's Kids Were Kidnapped?" Syracuse.com. www.syracuse.com/politics/2017/01/trump_hannity_waterboarding_david_muir_kidnapped.html

and is "willing to do something like waterboarding if it's going to keep us safe."[181] Fox News's Jesse Waters also called waterboarding "effective."[182] Despite generating more controversy within the Republican Party, some Congress members, including Sen. Ted Cruz, signaled openness to waterboarding.[183] After Trump's 2016 election, Sen. Tom Cotton suggested that waterboarding should be an option, affirming that "Donald Trump's a pretty tough guy, and he's ready to make those tough calls."[184]

In addition to waterboarding, Trump has also called for "much worse" forms of torture and other unspecified interrogation techniques against terrorists.[185] In 2016, for instance, Trump explicitly said, "Torture works, okay folks."[186] In a move that many critics saw as an implicit endorsement of torture, Trump nominated Gina Haspel as director of the CIA in 2018.[187] Haspel's record of running a CIA "black site" stirred backlash, with former American Civil Liberties Union deputy legal director Jameel Jaffer calling her "quite literally a war criminal."[188] Trump also nominated Marshall Billingslea, who had ties to Bush-era torture policies, to serve as an

[181] Apr. 12, 2016. "Pete Hegseth: Brennan's Rejection Of Waterboarding Was A "Stab At Cruz And Trump." Robert De Niro. www.youtube.com/watch?v=igfSzNqox6U

[182] May 26, 2018. "Green Beret Livestreams Himself Getting Waterboarded." Fox News. https://video.foxnews.com/v/5790088593001#sp=show-clips

[183] Feb. 6, 2016. "Ted Cruz, Donald Trump Advocate Bringing Back Waterboarding." ABC News. www.youtube.com/watch?v=u486WX1qHeQ

[184] Manduley, Christina. Nov. 9, 2016. "Sen. Tom Cotton: Waterboarding Isn't Torture." CNN. www.cnn.com/2016/11/09/politics/tom-cotton-waterboarding-torture/index.html

[185] Johnson, Jenna. Feb. 17, 2017. "Trump Says 'Torture Works,' Backs Waterboarding and 'Much Worse'." Washington Post. www.washingtonpost.com/politics/trump-says-torture-works-backs-waterboarding-and-much-worse/2016/02/17/4c9277be-d59c-11e5-b195-2e29a4e13425_story.html

[186] Feb. 17, 2016. "Donald Trump: Torture Works." Fox News. www.youtube.com/watch?v=Kpj3pp10wD8

[187] Jansen, Bart. Mar. 13, 2018. "Gina Haspel, Nominated by Trump as First Woman to Lead CIA, Has Controversial Past." USA Today. www.usatoday.com/story/news/2018/03/13/gina-haspel-trump-nominee-first-woman-leader-cia/419547002/

[188] Miller, Greg and Shane Harris. Mar. 13, 2018. "Gina Haspel, Trump's Pick for CIA Director, Tied to Use of Brutal Interrogation Measures." Washington Post. www.washingtonpost.com/world/national-security/trump-nominates-gina-haspel-to-head-cia-an-agency-veteran-tied-to-use-of-brutal-interrogation-measures/2018/03/13/bd47c8ce-26c6-11e8-874b-d517e912f125_story.html

2.2 Additional Examples of IT Synchronization 69

undersecretary of state.[189] One expert predicted that Trump made "a return to torture more likely."[190] Another journalist explained that "[t]orture was a key part of Trump's national-security platform."[191]

Several Fox News voices have endorsed or declined to criticize Trump's advocacy of torture. For instance, analyst Tom McInerney said that "torture worked" on Sen. John McCain as a prisoner of war, mocking "[t]hat's why they call him 'Songbird John.'"[192] Pete Hegseth called torture a "loaded term," adding that "what terrorists would do to you or to me … would [be] chop our heads off."[193] Anchor Greg Gutfield said, "Sure, it's easy to say, but we're better than [torturing] … from a shiny newsroom. But … what is your alternative?"[194] On Capitol Hill, Sen. Marco Rubio, according to one journalist, often resorted to his "favorite dog whistle" in explaining his stance on torture: Terrorists "are getting a one-way ticket to Guantanamo Bay."[195] Ted Cruz said that he only would rule out torture when it induced "excruciating pain equivalent to losing … organs and systems."[196]

---

[189] Berschinski, Rob and Benjamin Haas. Sept. 17, 2019. "Trump Wants a Torture Proponent to Lead US Human Rights Policy. The Senate Should Say No." *POLITICO*. www.politico.com/magazine/story/2019/09/17/trump-billingslea-torture-human-rights-228112/

[190] Jacobson, Adam D. 2017. "Could the United States Reinstitute an Official Torture Policy?" *Journal of Strategic Security* 10(2): 97–113.

[191] Serwever, Adam. Jan. 26, 2017. "Can Trump Bring Back Torture?" *Atlantic*. www.theatlantic.com/politics/archive/2017/01/trump-torture/514463/

[192] Wemple, Erik. May 10, 2018. "Fox Business Guest Says Torture 'Worked' on John McCain." *Washington Post*. www.washingtonpost.com/blogs/erik-wemple/wp/2018/05/10/fox-business-guest-says-torture-worked-on-john-mccain/

[193] Staff. May 9, 2018. "Fox & Friends Hosts Architect of CIA's Torture Program to Go to Bat for Gina Haspel." *Media Matters*. www.mediamatters.org/fox-friends/fox-friends-hosts-architect-cias-torture-program-go-bat-gina-haspel

[194] Mar. 14, 2018. "President Trump's CIA Pick Faces Questions over Her Role in Enhanced Interrogation Program." *Fox News*. www.foxnews.com/transcript/president-trumps-cia-pick-faces-questions-over-her-role-in-enhanced-interrogation-program

[195] Mora, Alberto. Mar. 13, 2016. "Is America on the Brink of Returning to Torture?" *Los Angeles Times*. www.latimes.com/opinion/op-ed/la-oe-0313-mora-election-return-to-torture-20160313-story.html

[196] Welna, David. Feb. 13, 2016. "Fact-Check: Could The Next President Bring Back Waterboarding?" *NPR*. www.npr.org/2016/02/13/466544830/fact-check-could-the-next-president-bring-back-waterboarding

Ultimately, as this chapter illustrates, Trump's overt challenges to IHL have been enabled by his alliance with powerful right-leaning partners. With Trump acting as a political entrepreneur, the impunity coalition has overcome collective action problems and surmounted barriers posed by state, military, and civil society. The overt strategy is crucial, freeing Trump, Fox News, and GOP allies in Congress from tempering their rhetoric and actions. Rather than relying on veiled language, Trump can push his agenda openly, both to supporters and in the face of detractors. Yet even if the impunity agenda's messaging has been effective, there is still a question of why conservative members of the public are so open to pursuits that explicitly undermine IHL. Chapter 3 turns to that question.

3 | Motive

Why has Trump had a *motive* to publicly challenge international humanitarian law (IHL)? Ultimately, as one journalist notes, the strategy amounts to "serving up red meat to the base."[1] Following Trump's November 2019 war crime clemencies, for example, a national poll showed that nearly 80 percent of Republicans approved of his actions.[2] At first glance, however, this overwhelming conservative support might seem puzzling. For Republicans especially, who Trump most sought to court,[3] openly attacking IHL might seem to run counter to their inclinations. With domestic criminal justice, conservatives are typically thought of as strong defenders of "law and order."[4] This contradiction

---

[1] Fritze, John and Tom Vanden Brook. Nov. 25. 2019. "Trump's Advocacy for Navy SEAL Eddie Gallagher Is Latest Intervention for Conservative Cause Celebre." USA Today. https://eu.usatoday.com/story/news/politics/2019/11/25/donald-trump-advocacy-eddie-gallagher-latest-conservative-cause/4297107002/

[2] Sagan, Scott D. and Benjamin A. Valentino. Dec. 16, 2019. "Do Americans Approve of Trump's Pardons for Court-Martialed Military Officers?" *Washington Post.* www.washingtonpost.com/politics/2019/12/16/do-americans-approve-trumps-pardons-court-martialed-military-officers/

[3] Allen, Jonathan. Apr. 8. 2019. "Inside Trump's All-about-that-base 2020 Strategy." *NBC News.* www.nbcnews.com/politics/2020-election/inside-trumps-all-about-base-2020-strategy-n991896 / Cizilla, Chris. July 7, 2020. "Donald Trump's Base-First Strategy is Working – And Dooming Him." *CNN.* https://edition.cnn.com/2020/07/07/politics/donald-trump-gallup-poll-2020-election/index.html/Galvin, Daniel J. 2020. "Party Domination and Base Mobilization: Donald Trump and Republican Party Building in a Polarized Era." *The Forum* 18(2): 135–168.

[4] Hetherington, Marc J. and Jonathan D. Weiler. 2009. *Authoritarianism and Polarization in American Politics.* Cambridge: Cambridge University Press. McCay, David. 2022. *American Politics and Society,* 10th ed. Oxford: Wiley. Jacobs, David and Jason Carmichael. 2001. "The Politics of Punishment across Time and Space: A Pooled Time-Series Analysis of Imprisonment Rates." *Social Forces* 80(1): 61–89. Lynch, Timothy J. Aug. 31, 2020. "Republicans Have Used a 'Law and Order' Message to Win Elections Before. This Is Why Trump Could Do It Again." *The Conversation.* https://theconversation.com/republicans-have-used-a-law-and-order-message-to-win-elections-before-this-is-why-trump-could-do-it-again-145306

seems even more striking given that Trump has expressly branded himself as "The president of Law and Order."[5]

This chapter resolves why Trump's overt challenges to IHL appeal to otherwise law-and-order conservatives. It does so by drawing on insights from moral foundations theory (MFT),[6] a framework in political psychology that has been used extensively to study ethically fraught issues, including conflict.[7] MFT presumes that all individuals prioritize five core moral values: in-group loyalty, authority, purity, harm, and fairness. Despite their universality, however, the literature has established a pair of important findings. First, ideology shapes how individuals prioritize these values: Conservatives tend to place a premium on in-group loyalty, authority, and purity, whereas liberals emphasize harm and fairness.[8] Second, these values can manifest differently depending on the context.[9]

---

[5] Burns, Alexander and Maggie Haberman. Aug. 27, 2020. "Trump Heads Into General Election He Casts as a Crusade for Law and Order." *New York Times*. www.nytimes.com/2020/08/27/us/politics/republican-national-convention-recap.html/. Waxman, Olivia B. June 2, 2020. "Trump Declared Himself the 'President of Law and Order.' Here's What People Get Wrong about the Origins of That Idea." *TIME*. https://time.com/5846321/nixon-trump-law-and-order-history

[6] Graham, Jesse, Ravi Iyer, Brian A. Nozek, Jonathan Haidt, Spassena Koleva, and Peter H. Ditto. 2011. "Mapping the Moral Domain." *Journal of Personality and Social Psychology* 101 (2): 366–385. Jesse, Graham, Jonathan Haidt, Sena Koleva, Matt Motyl, Ravi Iyer, Sean P. Wojcik, and Peter H. Ditto. 2013. "Moral Foundations Theory: The Pragmatic Validity of Moral Pluralism." *Advances in Experimental Social Psychology* 47: 55–130.

[7] Bell, Andrew M., Thomas Gift, and Jonathan Monten. 2022. "The Moral Foundations of Restraint: Partisanship, Military Training, and Norms of Civilian protection." *Journal of Peace Research* 59(5): 694–709. Smetana, Michal and Marek Vranka. 2021. "How Moral Foundations Shape Public Approval of Nuclear, Chemical, and Conventional Strikes: New Evidence from Experimental Surveys." *International Interactions* 47(2): 374–390.

[8] Day, Martin V., Susan T. Fiske, Emily L. Downing, and Thomas E. Trail. 2014. "Shifting Liberal and Conservative Attitudes Using Moral Foundations Theory." *Personality and Social Psychology Bulletin* 40(12): 1559–1573. Graham, Jesse, Jonathan Haidt, and Brian A. Nosek. 2009. "Liberals and Conservatives Rely on Different Sets of Moral Foundations." *Journal of Personality and Social Psychology* 96(5): 1029–1046. Haidt, Jonathan and Jesse Graham. 2007. "When Morality Opposes Justice: Conservatives Have Moral Intuitions that Liberals May Not Recognize." *Social Justice Research* 20(1): 98–116.

[9] Bowe, Brian J. 2018. "Permitted to Build? Moral Foundations in Newspaper Framing of Mosque-Construction Controversies." *Journalism and Mass Communication Quarterly* 95(3): 782–810. Clifford, Scott and Jennifer Jerit.

This chapter argues that the core values associated with conservatism inform conservative attitudes toward the law, but their expression varies by context. In domestic criminal justice, conservatives tend to embrace the law because they point to victims of crime as the in-group, the police as the central authority, and blackletter law as representing moral purity. Conversely, in war, conservatives are more inclined to see U.S. servicemembers as the in-group, the commander-in-chief as the prime authority, and America's military as reflecting moral purity. By presenting war crime clemencies and other direct challenges to IHL as consistent with conservatism, Trump and his allies play on latent impulses of right-leaning voters to discount the law of war.

This argument echoes broader studies on the politicization of the military via "civilian activation."[10] Considerable scholarship documents that leaders often co-opt the military to advance political ambitions. This includes manufacturing "rally-'round-the-flag" effects, using the military as a campaign artifice, diverting attention away from scandals, or cementing their authority through instigating foreign conflicts.[11] In a similar way, attacking IHL has yielded

---

2013. "How Words Do the Work of Politics: Moral Foundations Theory and the Debate Over Stem Cell Research." *Journal of Politics* 75(3): 659–671. Fulgoni, Dean, Jordan Carpenter, Lyle Ungar, and Daniel Preotiuc-Pietro. 2016. "An Empirical Exploration of Moral Foundations Theory in Partisan News Sources." Proceedings of the Tenth International Conference on Language Resources and Evaluation. Mucciaroni, Gary. 2011. "Are Debates about 'Morality Policy' Really about Morality? Framing Opposition to Gay and Lesbian Rights." *Policy Studies Journal* 39(2): 187–216. Mobayed, Tamim and Jet G. Sanders. 2022. "Moral Foundational Framing and Its Impact on Attitudes and Behaviours." *Behavioral Sciences* 12(5): 118. Nisbet, Matthew C., Dominique Brossard, and Adrianne Kroepsch. 2003. "Framing Science: The Stem Cell Controversy." *Harvard International Journal of Press/Politics* 8(2): 36–70

[10] Golby, Jim. 2021. "Uncivil-Military Relations: Politicization of the Military in the Trump Era." *Strategic Studies Quarterly* 15(2): 149–174. Ostrom, Jr. Charles W. and Brian L. Job. 1986. "The President and the Political Use of Force." *American Political Science Review* 80(2): 541–566. Robinson, Michael A. 2023. *Dangerous Instrument: Political Polarization and US Civil-Military Relations.* Oxford: Oxford University Press.

[11] Baker, William D. and John R. Oneal. 2001. "Patriotism or Opinion Leadership?: The Nature and Origins of the 'Rally 'Round the Flag' Effect." *Journal of Conflict Resolution* 44(5): 661–687. Howell, William G. and Jon C. Pevehouse. 2005. "Presidents, Congress, and the Use of Force." *International Organization* 59(1): 209–232. Meernik, James. 2001. "Domestic Politics and

clear payoffs for the impunity coalition. Trump has earned political support from a more energized base. For GOP Congress members, the advantages have also been electoral, as they court the same conservative voters. Finally, Fox News has benefited by appealing to its right-leaning audience.

These claims challenge the "domestic audience cost" assumption that voters in Western democracies largely reject open challenges to IHL.[12] They align with emerging studies showing that citizens will "trade off" adhering to the law of war to accomplish other aims.[13] Although some research has found that Republicans, and conservatives generally, tend to be more accepting of IHL violations,[14] studies

---

the Political Use of Military Force by the United States." *Political Research Quarterly* 54(4): 889–904.

[12] Chilton, Adam. 2014. "The Influence of International Human Rights Agreements on Public Opinion: An Experimental Study." *Chicago Journal of International Law* 15(1): 110–137. Dai, Xinyuan. 2005. "Why Comply? The Domestic Constituency Mechanism." *International Organization* 59(2): 363–398. Morse, Julie C. and Tyler Pratt. 2022. "Strategies of Contestation: International Law, Domestic Audiences, and Image Management." *Journal of Politics* 84(4): 2080–2093. Simmons, Beth A. 2009. *Mobilizing for Human Rights*. Cambridge: Cambridge University Press. Zartner, Dana. 2014. *Courts, Codes, and Custom: Legal Tradition and State Policy toward International Human Rights and Environmental Law*. Oxford: Oxford University Press. Zartner, Dana. 2020. "Internalization of International Law." *International Studies Association and Oxford University Press*.

[13] Carpenter, Charli, Alexander H. Montgomery, and Alexandria Nylen. 2020. "Breaking Bad? How Survey Experiments Prime Americans for War Crimes." *Perspectives on Politics* 19(3): 912–924. Chilton, Adam S. 2015. "The Laws of War and Public Opinion: An Experimental Study." *Journal of Institutional and Theoretical Economics* 171(1): 181–201. Gelpi, Christopher, Peter D. Feaver, and Jason Reifler. 2009. *Paying the Human Costs of War: American Public Opinion and Casualties in Military Conflicts*. Princeton: Princeton University Press. Hatz, Sophia. 2021. "What Shapes Public Support for Torture, and Among Whom?" *Human Rights Quarterly* 43(4): 683–698. Liberman, Peter. 2006. "An Eye for an Eye: Public Support for War against Evildoers." *International Organization* 60(3): 687–722. Sagan, Scott D., Benjamin A. Valentino, Charli Carpenter, and Alexander H. Montgomery. 2020. "Does the Noncombatant Immunity Norm Have Stopping Power? A Debate." *International Security* 45(2): 170–186. Wallace, Geoffrey P.R. 2013. "International Law and Public Attitudes toward Torture: An Experimental Study." *International Organization* 67(1): 105–140.

[14] Wallace, Geoffrey P.R. 2013. "International Law and Public Attitudes toward Torture: An Experimental Study." *International Organization* 67(1): 105–140. Chilton, Adam S. 2015. "The Laws of War and Public Opinion: An Experimental Study." *Journal of Institutional and Theoretical Economics*

3.1 "Law and Order" and Moral Foundations

mostly neglect why ideological splits exist or whether opinions can be activated. The analysis here fills that void by linking attitudes toward IHL to the foundational moral values of voters and explaining how elite cues can affect opinions through framing. Even if many conservative voters support law and order in the abstract, they may still be persuaded to dismiss it.

Section 3.1 of this chapter details how foundational moral values tend to make conservatives more receptive to overt challenges to IHL. It describes how Trump and various right-wing allies have activated these values, which mirrors tactics Trump has used in other areas of campaigning and governance. Section 3.2 presents findings from an original, national survey of U.S. respondents fielded in 2020 during Trump's first term. Results from four separate experiments show that conservatives tend to disregard IHL more than other respondents, which correlates with emphasizing their foundational moral values. Additionally, treatments using real-life video clips of Trump demonstrate that impunity coalition messaging can magnify these effects.

3.1 "Law and Order" and Moral Foundations

In-group Loyalty

In domestic criminal justice, Trump frequently presents himself as defending what he depicts as the main "in-group" (law-abiding citizens) against threats from the main "out-group" (criminals, disproportionately minorities in urban areas). For example, he has repeatedly called for protecting American suburbs from social unrest,[15] which reflects broader efforts by Republicans to combat domestic crime with in-group/out-group appeals.[16] However, the same logic does not necessarily make conservatives more supportive of IHL. Domestically,

---

171(1): 181–201. Hatz, Sophia. 2021. "What Shapes Public Support for Torture, and Among Whom?" *Human Rights Quarterly* 43(4): 683–693.

[15] Burnett, Sara and Michael Rubinkam. July 25, 2020. "Trump Plays on Fears in Play for the Suburbs." *Associated Press*. https://apnews.com/article/election-2020-campaigns-race-and-ethnicity-ap-top-news-elections-e433ef01c190799f046482e178e85e48

[16] Janoff-Bulman, Ronnie. 2009. "To Provide or Protect: Motivational Bases of Political Liberalism and Conservatism." *Psychological Inquiry* 20(2–3): 120–128.

conservatives tend to see victims of crimes as the in-group and perpetrators as the out-group. In war, however, they may be more inclined to see U.S. servicemembers as the in-group and foreign adversaries as the out-group.

Trump's war crime interventions have been the clearest manifestation of turning support for U.S. servicemembers into a litmus test of in-group loyalty. By framing his clemencies as helping in-group American fighters, Trump has commonly pivoted the discussion toward the moral duty of voters to defend their countrymen in uniform. According to one journalist, for example, Trump's war crime clemencies represent "a rational extension of Trumpist nationalism, which ... sees violence against outsiders as a redemptive expression of national *loyalty* [emphasis added]."[17] Another writer summarizes Trump's military agenda as reflecting the binary: "You're either uncritically and unconditionally with *us* – the U.S. military – or with *them* – the terrorists."[18]

One tactic that Trump has used to forge in-group connections with conservative voters is how he refers to court-martialed combatants. Trump rarely employs standard, impersonal identifiers such as "U.S. servicemembers" or "America's troops." Instead, he invokes the first-person plural pronoun, "our," to reinforce their in-group status. For example, he declared, "We're going to take care of *our* warriors.... I will always stick up for *our* great fighters."[19] Other allies of Trump have routinely borrowed from such phrasing. For example, Pete Hegseth has said "we need to back *our warfighters*."[20] Rep. Duncan Hunter of California has condemned prosecutors who have "been damning to *our warriors* on the front lines"[21] [emphasis added in all the above quotes].

[17] Serwer, Adam. Nov. 27, 2019. "The War-Crimes President." *The Atlantic.* www.theatlantic.com/ideas/archive/2019/11/trump-war-crimes/602731/
[18] Welsh, Erin. Feb. 10, 2020. "The Military Masculinity Trump Wants for America." *Medium.* https://medium.com/@ramman_erin/the-military-masculinity-trump-wants-for-america-85fe85f2fd8c
[19] Nov. 26, 2019. "President Trump Rally in Sunrise, Florida." *C-SPAN.* www.c-span.org/video/?466539-1/president-trump-rally-sunrise-florida
[20] Hegseth, Pete. May 23, 2019. "Pete Hegseth: I'm With the Warfighters – Count Me Out of Second-guessing Our Heroes." *Fox News.* www.foxnews.com/opinion/pete-hegseth-im-with-the-american-warfighters
[21] Stone, Ken. Nov. 15, 2019. "Trump Restores Navy SEAL Eddie Gallagher to Former Rank, Pardons 2 Others." *Times of San Diego.* https://timesofsandiego

3.1 "Law and Order" and Moral Foundations

Explicit appeals to "our boys" and "our warriors" mirror language that Trump employs in other contexts to draw a moral circle around in-groups. Scholar Victor Davis Hanson, for example, has observed that Trump's use of "our" is how he earns the loyalty of rank-and-file conservatives. "The supposedly callous, spoiled, egotistical and privileged Trump early in his campaign began using the first-plural personal pronoun our for the heartland's supposed losers," Hanson stated. "Suddenly the nation heard of 'our miners,' 'our farmers,' 'our vets,' and 'our workers.'"[22] Similarly, in reference to Trump calling on January 6 supporters to "take our country back," a writer noted that "[t]he implication of the word 'our' is that America has fallen into the wrong hands: Democrats, minorities and urban elites."[23]

By intervening on behalf of U.S. servicemembers who physically resemble a traditional image of "GI Joe" – that of a "red blooded, clean-cut" American in uniform – Trump has also reinforced an in-group connection with conservative voters. The apparent implication is that Trump's base can more easily empathize with troops who they could imagine being their brothers, friends, or neighbors.[24] This imagery reflects the accusation that Trump has used court-martialed troops as "political props"[25] and "mascot[s] for ... reelection."[26] Although Trump did not expressly mention race when granting his war crime clemencies, his defense of all-white servicemembers is notable given allegations of efforts to activate "white victimhood" in other contexts.[27]

.com/military/2019/11/15/trump-restores-navy-seal-eddie-gallagher-to-former-rank-pardons-2-others/

[22] Hanson, Victor Davis. 2019. *The Case for Trump*. New York: Basic Books.
[23] Bencks, Jarret. Jan. 12, 2021. "Trump and the Language of Insurrection." *BrandeisNOW*. www.brandeis.edu/now/2021/january/trump-language-capitol-riot-mcintosh.html
[24] Philipps, Dave and Tim Arango. Jan. 10, 2020. "Who Signs Up to Fight? Makeup of U.S. Recruits Shows Glaring Disparity." *New York Times*. www.nytimes.com/2020/01/10/us/military-enlistment.html
[25] Brennan, David. Dec. 9, 2019. "Trump Accused of Using 'War Criminals' He Pardoned as 'Political Props' at Florida Fundraiser." *Newsweek*. www.newsweek.com/donald-trump-accused-using-war-criminals-pardoned-political-props-florida-fundraiser-1476136
[26] Almond, Steve. Dec. 3, 2019. "Trump Is Using an Accused War Criminal as a Mascot For His Campaign." *WBUR*. www.wbur.org/cognoscenti/2019/12/03/edward-gallagher-donald-trump-steve-almond
[27] Armaly, Miles T. and Adam M. Enders. 2022. "'Why Me?' The Role of Perceived Victimhood in American Politics." *Political Behavior* 44:

Multiple observers have commented on the looks of the servicemembers whom Trump helped. For example, Paul Rieckhoff of Iraq and Afghanistan Veterans of America has stated that "[Eddie] Gallagher ... [was] a perfect fit [for Trump].... He's handsome, he's heroic, he's got a beautiful wife. He's a Rambo version of the same story Trump has been telling over and over."[28] A writer described Clint Lorance as having "the kind of bearing garrison commanders love: Blond and blue-eyed, he looked ... 'like Captain America.'"[29] On social media, one Twitter user commented, "When I saw Gallagher and his wife I thought 'central casting.' That's what 45* says whenever he's talking about appointing people. Those two look like characters in a movie."[30] A Reddit poster remarked, "Let's face it, Trump stepped in because Gallagher looks straight out of Central Casting and has a hot blonde wife."[31]

The idea of Trump's clemencies involving "central casting" extended to him hosting a photo-op with Eddie Gallagher[32] and telling aides that he "want[ed] to take his war criminal buddies on the campaign trail."[33] Trump has acknowledged using the tactic in other contexts. For example, he invoked the "central casting" phrase in nominating Vice President Mike Pence and Secretary of Defense James Mattis.[34]

1583–1609. Bebout, Lee. Jan. 6, 2021. "Trump Tapped into White Victimhood – Leaving Fertile Ground for White Supremacists." *The Conversation.* https://theconversation.com/trump-tapped-into-white-victimhood-leaving-fertile-ground-for-white-supremacists-150587

[28] Spiegelman, Ian. Jan. 3, 2020. "Court-Martialed Navy SEAL Eddie Gallagher Is Being Embraced as a Right-Wing Influencer." *Los Angeles Mag.* www.lamag.com/citythinkblog/eddie-gallagher-navy-seal/

[29] Penn, Nathaniel. Sept. 27, 2020. "The Last Patrol." *California Sunday Magazine.* https://story.californiasunday.com/clint-lorance-court-martial-pardon-the-last-patrol#:~:text=Under%20the%20command%20of%20First,t%20touched%20in%20a%20decade.&text=Lorance%20had%2-0the%20kind%20of,%2C%20"like%20Captain%20America."

[30] https://twitter.com/marythetrainer/status/1199311176829743106

[31] @allenahansen. 2019. "Trump's Pardon of Gallagher Just Got Even More Appalling." *Reddit.* www.reddit.com/r/politics/comments/eheqfs/trumps_pardon_of_gallagher_just_got_even_more/

[32] Keating, Joshua. Dec. 23, 2019. "Trump Hosts Convicted War Criminal at Mar-a-Lago." *Slate.* https://slate.com/news-and-politics/2019/12/gallagher-navy-seal-war-crimes-trump-mar-a-lago.html

[33] Lutz, Eric. Nov. 26, 2019. "Trump Wants to Take His War Criminal Buddies On the Campaign Trail." *Vanity Fair.* www.vanityfair.com/news/2019/11/trump-wants-to-take-war-criminal-buddies-on-campaign-trail-eddie-gallagher

[34] Benen, Steve. Apr. 9, 2019. "Trump's Preoccupation with 'Central Casting' Extends to Homeland Security." *MSNBC.* www.msnbc.com/

3.1 "Law and Order" and Moral Foundations

One journalist reported on Trump's "mostly white casting," noting that "[p]otential hires' appearances have always weighed heavily on Trump's decisions and he has been open about touting the 'central casting' appeal."[35] A *CNN* article entitled, "'Central Casting': Trump Is Talking More Than Ever about Men's Looks," recounted that "Trump likes people he believes look the part."[36]

Apart from in-group loyalty, Trump has also used its complement, out-group aversion, to solidify backing for publicly challenging IHL. By presenting fighters and even civilians from adversarial countries as out-group enemies, Trump has consistently tried to legitimize flouting military rules by presenting such individuals as undeserving of legal protections. The rationale is that just like being a U.S. servicemember entitles one to special privileges, being a foreigner with sympathies counter to America demonstrates a moral inferiority, and a lack of humanity. Trump has not only justified a permissive attitude toward openly challenging the law of war. He has regularly glorified illicit behavior and treated American servicemembers who perpetrated crimes as heroes.

Trump has aggressively used dehumanizing language to underscore the out-group nature of U.S. enemies. For example, at a Republican debate in 2016, Trump advocated for waterboarding by railing against "*animals* over in the Middle East."[37] At a rally later that year, Trump said that the U.S. was "dealing with *animals*" when it allowed immigrants to enter the country from terrorist nations.[38] In 2017, Trump described ISIS combatants as "sneaky, dirty *rats*" in a Fox News interview.[39]

---

rachel-maddow-show/trumps-preoccupation-central-casting-extends-homeland-security-msna1217371

[35] Liptak, Kevin. June 19, 2020. "Blindspots and Turncoats: How Trump's Mostly White Casting Has Backfired." *CNN.* www.cnn.com/2020/06/18/politics/donald-trump-central-casting-bolton/index.html

[36] Dale, Daniel. Aug. 13, 2019. "'Central Casting': Trump Is Talking More than Ever about Men's Looks." *CNN.* www.cnn.com/2019/08/13/politics/central-casting-trump-is-talking-more-than-ever-about-mens-looks/index.html

[37] Mar. 5, 2016. "Donald Trump Vows to 'Strengthen' Laws to Allow Torture, Waterboarding." *CBS News.* www.cbsnews.com/news/donald-trump-vows-to-strengthen-laws-to-allow-torture-waterboarding-election-2016/

[38] Alibutud, J.R. Aug. 12, 2016. "Philippines Talks of Barring Donald Trump for Calling It a 'Terrorist Nation." *New York Times.* www.nytimes.com/2016/08/13/world/asia/philippines-trump-terrorist-nation.html

[39] Hensch, Mark. Jan. 26, 2017. "Trump Calls ISIS Fighters 'Sneaky, Dirty Rats.'" *The Hill.* https://thehill.com/homenews/administration/316326-trump-isis-sneaky-dirty-rats

The next year, Trump referred to the culprits of a terrorist attack in London as *"animals* [that] are crazy."⁴⁰ After the high-profile killing of ISIS head Abu Bakr al-Baghdadi in 2019, Trump remarked that al-Baghdadi "died like a *dog*" and labeled him "a gutless *animal* [emphasis added in all the above quotes]."⁴¹

Dehumanizing language parallels references that Trump has made domestically. For example, Trump has called MS-13 gang members residing in America "animals."⁴² He compared former Black White House staffer Omarosa Manigault-Newman to a "dog."⁴³ He also referred to Baltimore as a "disgusting, rat and rodent infested mess."⁴⁴ Legal expert Andrew Cohen observes that "Trump rush[es] to call human beings 'animals' ... because the tactic always works – or at least always works well enough with a steady segment of the American population."⁴⁵ One journalist notes that "'[a]nimals' is so ingrained in ... [Trump's] rhetoric about immigrant criminals and terrorists – a group defined in part by themselves being foreigners ... – that he applies it liberally and often."⁴⁶

Trump has also leveraged out-group aversion to rationalize open challenges to IHL through inciting ethnic prejudice. According to one

---

⁴⁰ https://twitter.com/realDonaldTrump/status/1029332350969237504
⁴¹ Oct. 27, 2019. "Remarks by President Trump on the Death of ISIS Leader Abu Bakr al-Baghdadi." The White House. https://trumpwhitehouse.archives.gov/briefings-statements/remarks-president-trump-death-isis-leader-abu-bakr-al-baghdadi/
⁴² Fabian, Jordan. May 23, 2018. "Trump on MS-13: 'These Are Not People, These Are Animals.'" *The Hill*. https://thehill.com/homenews/administration/389037-trump-on-ms-13-these-are-not-people-these-are-animals
⁴³ https://twitter.com/realDonaldTrump/status/1029329583672307712?ref_src=twsrc%5Etfw%7Ctwcamp%5Etweetembed%7Ctwterm%5E1029329583672307712%7Ctwgr%5Ee2fc7fcfec216740aa228c15aaf787c61ad1e8b0%7Ctwcon%5Es1_&ref_url=https%3A%2F%2Fwww.vox.com%2Fpolicy-and-politics%2F2018%2F8%2F14%2F17688350%2Fomarosa-donald-trump-black-women-twitter-harassment
⁴⁴ https://twitter.com/realDonaldTrump/status/1155073965880172544
⁴⁵ Cohen, Andrew. May 22, 2018. "Trump's "Animal" Act Is an Old Racist Trope that Always Works." Brennan Center for Justice. www.brennancenter.org/our-work/analysis-opinion/trumps-animal-act-old-racist-trope-always-works
⁴⁶ Bump, Philip. May 17, 2018. "Trump's Long History of Referring to Nonwhite Groups He Sees as Dangerous as 'Animals.'" *Washington Post*. www.washingtonpost.com/news/politics/wp/2018/05/17/trumps-long-history-of-referring-to-nonwhite-criminals-as-animals/

3.1 "Law and Order" and Moral Foundations 81

writer, for example, Trump's war crime clemencies had a subliminal racial and religious tinge: "Murders, Trump is effectively telling the troops he commands, are not really murders when the corpses are brown and Muslim."[47] Elsewhere, Trump once claimed that in New Jersey he saw "thousands and thousands" of Muslims rejoice over 9/11.[48] In 2016, Trump said, "I think Islam hates us."[49] In 2020, following his order to kill Iranian Maj. Gen. Qassim Soleimani, Trump retweeted a fake picture of House Speaker Nancy Pelosi and Senate Minority Leader Chuck Schumer wearing traditional Islamic headwear, alongside the phrase "The corrupted Dems."[50]

Such words again echo tactics that Trump has employed in a domestic setting. Most clearly, this manifests in repeated allegations of racebaiting and xenophobia. Trump's activation of out-group aversion has been exhibited in policy: for instance, in issuing a travel ban on Muslim-majority countries[51] and in a national emergency declaration to build a U.S.–Mexico border wall.[52] It also comes in the form of inflammatory, racially charged language. For example, Trump has denounced immigration from "sh*thole countries,"[53] stoked fears

---

[47] MacDonald, Neil. Nov. 19, 2019. "No Need to Worry about War Crimes, Trump Has Soldiers' Backs: Neil Macdonald." *CBC*. www.cbc.ca/news/opinion/opinion-neil-macdonald-war-crimes-1.5363254

[48] Kessler, Glenn. Nov. 22, 2015. "Trump's Outrageous Claim that 'Thousands' of New Jersey Muslims Celebrated the 9/11 Attacks." *Washington Post*. www.washingtonpost.com/news/fact-checker/wp/2015/11/22/donald-trumps-outrageous-claim-that-thousands-of-new-jersey-muslims-celebrated-the-911-attacks/

[49] Schleifer, Theodore. Mar. 10, 2016. "Donald Trump: 'I Think Islam Hates Us.'" *CNN*. https://edition.cnn.com/2016/03/09/politics/donald-trump-islam-hates-us/index.html

[50] Samuels, Brett. Jan. 13, 2020. "Trump Criticized for Retweeting Image of Pelosi, Schumer in Muslim Attire." *The Hill*. https://thehill.com/homenews/administration/478017-trump-criticized-for-retweeting-image-of-pelosi-schumer-in-muslim

[51] Dec. 6, 2017. "Trump's US Travel Ban: What's the Full Story?" *BBC*. www.bbc.co.uk/newsround/38794001

[52] Collins, Michael, John Fritze, and David Jackson. Feb. 15, 2019. "Donald Trump Declares National Emergency to Free up Billions of Dollars for Border Wall." *USA Today*. www.usatoday.com/story/news/politics/2019/02/15/government-shutdown-trump-declare-emergency-get-wall-funding/2859532002/

[53] Watkins, Eli and Abby Phillip. Jan. 12, 2018. "Trump Decries Immigrants from 'Shithole Countries' Coming to US." *CNN*. www.cnn.com/2018/01/11/politics/immigrants-shithole-countries-trump/index.html

about "caravans" from Central America,[54] referred to Mexicans as "rapists" and people "bringing drugs ... [and] crime,"[55] and claimed that there were "very fine people on both sides" in the 2017 white supremacist rally in Charlottesville, Virginia.[56]

Authority

Trump has gone out of his way to aggressively tout and uphold the police as essential authority figures. One journalist, for example, has even described Trump's "'law and order' election message" as expressly "tak[ing] on an authoritarian tinge."[57] Deference to authority is a core element underpinning Republican respect for law enforcement. However, this value can again take on a different meaning in foreign wars. Rather than defer to legal officials, such as military lawyers, to determine the permissibility of military conduct, conservatives may be more apt to submit to the commander-in-chief. By downplaying the importance of IHL and by meddling in the U.S. military justice system, Trump has used his executive authority to justify the impunity agenda.

Trump has claimed authority over the military's legal code by making explicit pronouncements about it. In 2016, for instance, Trump insisted that he could compel U.S. servicemembers to violate IHL, declaring, "Believe me.... If I say do it, they're going to do it."[58] According to one journalist, Trump's assertion reflected

[54] Alvarez, Priscilla. Nov. 1, 2018. "The Latest Target of Trump's Immigration Attacks." *Atlantic*. www.theatlantic.com/politics/archive/2018/11/trump-escalates-rhetoric-against-migrant-caravan/574675/

[55] Schwartz, Ian. June 16, 2015. "Trump: Mexico Not Sending Us Their Best; Criminals, Drug Dealers and Rapists are Crossing Border." *Real Clear Politics*. www.realclearpolitics.com/video/2015/06/16/trump_mexico_not_sending_us_their_best_criminals_drug_dealers_and_rapists_are_crossing_border.html

[56] Gray, Rosie. Aug. 15, 2017. "Trump Defends White-Nationalist Protesters: 'Some Very Fine People on Both Sides.'" *Atlantic*. www.theatlantic.com/politics/archive/2017/08/trump-defends-white-nationalist-protesters-some-very-fine-people-on-both-sides/537012/

[57] Collinson, Stephen. July 23, 2020. "Trump Accused of Deploying 'Secret Police' as Part of 'Authoritarian' Law Enforcement Surge." *CNN*. www.cnn.com/2020/07/23/world/meanwhile-in-america-july-23-intl/index.html

[58] Mar. 4, 2016. "Transcript of the Republican Presidential Debate in Detroit." *New York Times*. www.nytimes.com/2016/03/04/us/politics/transcript-of-the-republican-presidential-debate-in-detroit.html

3.1 "Law and Order" and Moral Foundations

an "*authoritarian* misconception."[59] Another writer remarked that "Trump ... present[s] himself as a strong man ... ungoverned by rules or wimpy institutional norms or tenets such as the Geneva Conventions.... [H]e envisions ... an *authoritarian* state in which ... war criminals are misunderstood victims."[60] One commentator called Trump's war crime clemencies an effort to "hype *authoritarian* support among his most rabid supporters" [emphasis added in all of the above quotes].[61]

Trump has suggested that his authority over the military is so total that it allows him to legally deploy force against American civilians. In the wake of Black Lives Matter protests in 2020, for example, Trump proposed invoking the Insurrectionist Act to quell social unrest.[62] According to accounts, Trump called on the military to "[c]rack [protestors'] ... skulls!," "beat the f–k out [of them]," and "[j]ust shoot them."[63] Press Secretary Kayleigh McEnany said that Trump had "sole authority to invoke the Insurrection Act."[64] In an article entitled "Trump's Moves Are Right out of the Authoritarian Playbook," counterterrorism expert Stephen Tankel wrote that "[w]hether the president might ask military and paramilitary troops to shoot U.S. civilians ... is now something that needs to be considered."

---

[59] Rubin, Jennifer. Nov. 20, 2017. "Memo to Trump: The Military Will Not Follow Illegal Orders." *Washington Post*. www.washingtonpost.com/blogs/right-turn/wp/2017/11/20/memo-to-trump-the-military-will-not-follow-illegal-orders/

[60] Almond, Steve. Dec. 3, 2019. "Trump is Using an Accused War Criminal as a Mascot for His Campaign." *WBUR*. www.wbur.org/cognoscenti/2019/12/03/edward-gallagher-donald-trump-steve-almond

[61] Rosenberg, Paul. Nov. 24, 2019. "Republicans, A History: How Did the Party of "Law and Order" Become the Party of Crooks and Crime?" *Salon*. www.salon.com/2019/11/24/republicans-a-history-how-did-the-party-of-law-and-order-become-the-party-of-crooks-and-crime/

[62] Montanaro, Domenico. June 1, 2020. "What Is The Insurrection Act That Trump Is Threatening To Invoke?" *NPR*. www.npr.org/2020/06/01/867467714/what-is-the-insurrection-act-that-trump-is-threatening-to-invoke

[63] Cohen, Zachary. June 24, 2021. "Top US General Rejected Trump Suggestions Military Should 'Crack Skulls' during Protests Last Year, New Book Claims." *CNN*. www.cnn.com/2021/06/24/politics/bender-book-trump-milley-protests/index.html

[64] Schwartz, Ian. June 3, 2020. "McEnany on Insurrection Act: If Needed, President Trump Will Use It." *Real Clear Politics*. www.realclearpolitics.com/video/2020/06/03/mcenany_on_insurrection_act_if_needed_president_trump_will_use_it.html

Trump's assertions of operating above IHL reflect similar pronouncements that he has made about having nearly unfettered authority domestically. For example, in 2019, Trump insisted that "Article 2 [of the Constitution] ... gives the president powers you wouldn't believe."[65] Later that year, Trump boasted that Article 2 granted him "the right to do whatever I want as president."[66] In 2020, Trump asserted that "[w]hen somebody is the president of the United States, the authority is total. And that's the way it's got to be. It's total."[67] Trump also stated that local officials "can't do anything without the approval of the president of the United States."[68] The *Washington Post* compiled a video entitled, "All the Times Trump Said the Constitution Let's [sic] Him Do Whatever He Wants."[69]

Trump has further projected his authority over the military through his demeanor toward subordinates. In referencing top military leaders, for instance, Trump frequently uses the possessive "my generals," implying a legal power over the armed forces that draws its legitimacy more from him personally than the Constitution. According to one analysis, "Trump irked some military leaders right from the start when he rhapsodized over 'my generals.'"[70] Former CIA Director

---

[65] Diamond, Jeremy and Devan Cole. May 30, 2019. "Trump Unleashes Fury on Mueller, Again Disputes US Intelligence Findings on Russia." *CNN*. https://edition.cnn.com/2019/05/30/politics/trump-russia-election-interference-help/index.html

[66] User Clip. July 23, 2019. "Trump Says the Constitution Says 'I Can Do Whatever I Want as President.'" *C-SPAN*. www.c-span.org/video/?c4809509/user-clip-trump-constitution-i-president

[67] Sykes, Charlie. Apr. 16, 2020. "Trump's 'Total Authority' Boast Should've Enraged Republicans. Instead They Shrugged." *NBC News*. www.nbcnews.com/think/opinion/trump-s-total-authority-boast-should-ve-enraged-republicans-instead-ncna1184806

[68] Flynn, Meagan and Allyson Chiu. Apr. 14, 2020. "Trump Says His 'Authority is Total.' Constitutional Experts Have 'No Idea' Where He Got That." *Washington Post*. www.washingtonpost.com/nation/2020/04/14/trump-power-constitution-coronavirus/

[69] July 24, 2019. "All The Times Trump Said the Constitution Let's Him Do Whatever He Wants." *Washington Post*. www.youtube.com/watch?v=sl_gO3uOds8

[70] Vanden Brook, Tom, Michael Collins, and Deirdre Shesgreen. Sept. 10, 2020. "Trump's Tensions with the Military Grow after Reports that He Disparaged Soldiers, Generals." *USA Today*. https://eu.usatoday.com/story/news/politics/2020/09/10/trumps-relations-military-further-strained-over-loser-remarks/5719981002/

3.1 "Law and Order" and Moral Foundations 85

Leon Panetta has inveighed against Trump's invoking of the possessive, saying, "[T]he military belongs to the country.... [I]t's not the president's military."[71] Gen. Mark Milley, who served as Chairman of the Joint Chiefs under Trump, reportedly called Trump "the classic authoritarian leader."[72]

Trump's claims of unrestrained legal authority are again not confined to the military. Trump has routinely suggested that officials in the federal government are accountable to him personally. For instance, after berating U.S. Attorney General Jeff Sessions at the "Trump Justice Department," Trump told associates that he "finally" had "my attorney general" in William Barr.[73] Trump has applied the word "my" to a range of other individuals, from former presidential assistant Peter Navarro to Republican Minority Whip Steve Scalise. A biographer suggested that Trump's use of "my" is an unconscious power move, noting, "[I]t's not really about putting them on equal footing … [I]t's completely in the possessive, and it's about ownership, and it's about control."[74]

Just as Trump points to his own authority as taking precedence over IHL, he has suggested that devolving decision-making to others could subvert the U.S. military's proper functioning. In doing so, Trump has warned against the opposite of authority, anarchy, where political foes undermine not only his lawful power but also the interests of American troops. This is exemplified by Trump's allegation that a military "deep state" has tried to sabotage U.S. servicemembers in war crime cases. Headlines from multiple media sources – such as "Trump Says He Stood Up to the 'Deep State' by Intervening in War

---

[71] Abadi, Mark. Oct. 25, 2017. "Trump Won't Stop Saying 'My Generals' – And the Military Community Isn't Happy." *Insider*. www.businessinsider.com/trump-my-generals-my-military-2017-10?r=US&IR=T
[72] https://twitter.com/TheLeadCNN/status/1415806729254850561?ref_src=twsrc%5Etfw
[73] Sheth, Sonam. May 24, 2019. "Trump Is Said to Be Telling Confidants He 'Finally' Has 'My Attorney General' with William Barr." *Insider*. www.businessinsider.com/trump-william-barr-finally-my-attorney-general-2019-5?r=US&IR=T
[74] Parker, Ashley. Sept. 16, 2019. "From 'My Generals' to 'My Kevin,' Trump's Preferred Possessive Can Be a Sign of Affection or Control." *Washington Post*. www.washingtonpost.com/politics/from-my-generals-to-my-kevin-trumps-preferred-possessive-can-be-a-sign-of-affection-or-control/2019/09/16/52480d22-d895-11e9-a688-303693fb4b0b_story.html

Crime Cases" (*The Hill*)⁷⁵ and "Trump Ramps Up Attacks on 'Deep State,' Focuses on Pentagon amid Eddie Gallagher Controversy" (*USA Today*)⁷⁶ – evince its centrality to Trump's messaging.

Trump first invoked the "deep state" in regard to the military after his November 2019 war crime clemencies. At a Florida rally, he boasted, "Just this week, I stuck up for three great warriors against the Deep State. You know what I'm talking about."⁷⁷ The comments came after Clint Lorance pronounced that "'a big majority' of the 'people with stars on their collar that work in the Pentagon' are 'part of what president Trump calls the deep state.'"⁷⁸ Other allies have made similar comments. For example, Rep. Duncan Hunter tweeted to Trump, "I will continue to stand with you in your fight on behalf of our combat warriors and against the Deep State Military."⁷⁹ FoxNews.com published an op-ed arguing that a "'deep state' anti-Trump 'resistance' exists at [the] Pentagon."⁸⁰

Trump's charge of a deep state within the U.S. military justice system echoes conspiracy theories about federal bureaucrats undercutting his authority.⁸¹ For example, in 2018, Trump railed against a "Criminal Deep State" that he said had fabricated "Phony

---

75 Samuels, Brett. Nov. 26, 2019. "Trump Says He Stood up to the 'Deep State' by Intervening in War Crime Cases." *The Hill*. https://thehill.com/homenews/campaign/472201-trump-says-he-stood-up-to-the-deep-state-by-intervening-in-war-crime-cases

76 Fritze, John. Nov. 26, 2019. "Trump Ramps Up Attacks on 'Deep State,' Focuses on Pentagon amid Eddie Gallagher Controversy." *USA Today*. https://eu.usatoday.com/story/news/politics/2019/11/27/trump-calls-pentagon-deep-state-amid-eddie-gallagher-controversy/4323327002/

77 Nov. 26, 2019. "President Trump Rally in Sunrise, Florida." *C-SPAN*. www.c-span.org/video/?466539-1/president-trump-rally-sunrise-florida

78 Fritze, John. Nov. 27, 2019. "Trump Ramps up Attacks on 'Deep State,' Focuses on Pentagon amid Eddie Gallagher Controversy." *USA Today*. https://eu.usatoday.com/story/news/politics/2019/11/27/trump-calls-pentagon-deep-state-amid-eddie-gallagher-controversy/4323327002/

79 Dyer, Andrew. Nov. 21, 2019. "In a Tweet, Trump Tells Navy Not to Boot Gallagher from SEALs." *San Diego Tribune*. www.sandiegouniontribune.com/news/military/story/2019-11-21/in-a-tweet-trump-tells-navy-not-to-boot-gallagher-from-the-seals

80 Grant, Rebecca. Nov. 27, 2019. "Rebecca Grant: Fired Navy Secretary's Actions Prove a 'Deep State' Anti-Trump 'Resistance' Exists at Pentagon." *Fox News*. www.foxnews.com/opinion/rebecca-grant-fired-navy-secretarys-actions-prove-a-deep-state-anti-trump-resistance-exists-at-pentagon

81 Osnos, Evan. May 14, 2018. "Trump vs. The Deep State." *New Yorker*. www.newyorker.com/magazine/2018/05/21/trump-vs-the-deep-state

3.1 "Law and Order" and Moral Foundations 87

Collusion with Russia, a made up Scam."[82] Trump also complained of a "whistleblower ... from the Deep State!" during his 2019 impeachment proceedings stemming from his July 25 phone call with Ukraine President Volodymyr Zelensky.[83] At a campaign rally, Trump declared that "[u]nelected, deep state operatives who defy the voters, to push their own secret agendas, are truly a threat to democracy."[84] Trump further blamed a "deep state" for holding off on approving a COVID-19 vaccine until after the 2020 election.[85]

In the same vein, Trump has regularly insisted that U.S. military lawyers undermine proper chains of authority. This is reflected in Trump's recurring theme that "overzealous" prosecutors distort military justice. After Eddie Gallagher was acquitted on murder charges, for example, Trump moved to take away medals from the lawyers who prosecuted the case. In what amounted to what one journalist called a "remarkable rebuke by a president of his own Navy leadership,"[86] Trump tweeted about the prosecutors being "ridiculously given a Navy Achievement Medal"[87] and demanded that the Navy "immediately withdraw and rescind the awards."[88] One analyst commented that he "c[ould not] remember a time when a president involved himself in an award decision at this low a level."[89]

---

[82] https://twitter.com/realDonaldTrump/status/999242039723163648

[83] Grier, Peter and Story Hinckley. Oct. 17, 2019. "'Deep State' Versus a President? It didn't Begin with Trump." *Christian Science Monitor*. www.csmonitor.com/USA/Politics/2019/1017/Deep-state-versus-a-president-It-didn-t-begin-with-Trump

[84] Myre, Greg and Rachel Treisman. Nov. 6, 2019. "The Man Who Popularized the 'Deep State' Doesn't Like the Way It's Used." *NPR*. www.npr.org/2019/11/06/776852841/the-man-who-popularized-the-deep-state-doesnt-like-the-way-its-used

[85] Hall, Richard. Aug. 23, 2020. "Trump Claims 'Deep State' is Delaying Coronavirus Vaccine until after US election." *Independent*. www.independent.co.uk/news/world/americas/us-politics/trump-deep-state-coronavirus-vaccine-tweet-a9683406.html

[86] Baker, Peter. July 31, 2019. "Trump Orders Navy to Strip Medals from Prosecutors in War Crimes Trial." *New York Times*. www.nytimes.com/2019/07/31/us/politics/trump-navy-seal-war-crimes.html

[87] https://twitter.com/realDonaldTrump/status/1156655361711071232

[88] https://twitter.com/realDonaldTrump/status/1156655478740506977

[89] Diamond, Jeremy and Barbara Starr. July 31, 2019. "Trump Moves to Rescind Medals Awarded to Eddie Gallagher Prosecutors." *CNN*. www.cnn.com/2019/07/31/politics/trump-rescinds-navy-prosecutors-medals/index.html

Trump's criticism of "overzealous" lawyers has been part of a broader attempt to frame the U.S. military justice system as anti-authority. For instance, one analysis described how advocates of Mathew Golsteyn, Clint Lorance, and Eddie Gallagher frequently cast the men as "victims of overzealous prosecutors."[90] Echoing one of Trump's favorite phrases on Fox News, Pete Hegseth called the Navy's prosecution of Gallagher a "witch hunt."[91] He also complained about "overzealous prosecutors who were not giving the benefit of the doubt to the trigger-pullers."[92] Upon learning of Trump's interventions on behalf of Blackwater contractors, Rep. Steve King of Iowa protested against "overzealous prosecutors," declaring that "[i]f ever there was a justifiable set of pardons, president Trump has delivered it."[93]

Trump and his inner circle have articulated nearly identical language when defending Trump's nonmilitary pardons and choices not to prosecute allies. For example, in describing the 2020 pardon of longtime Trump associate Roger Stone, the White House condemned "overzealous prosecutors pursing [sic] a case that never should have existed."[94] In a 2020 memo justifying the discarding of criminal proceedings against former national security advisor Michael Flynn, Attorney General William Barr assailed the Justice Department's "hyper-aggressive extensions of the criminal law."[95] Additionally,

---

[90] Editorial Board. Nov. 5, 2019. "Editorial: Trump's Military Intervention Erodes Honor, Discipline." *San Diego Union-Tribune*. www.sandiegouniontribune.com/opinion/editorials/story/2019-11-05/trump-military-members-war-crimes

[91] https://twitter.com/Hoosier84/status/1142058738813218816

[92] Philipps, Dave, Peter Baker, Maggie Haberman, and Helene Cooper. Nov. 30, 2019. "Trump's Intervention in SEALs Case Tests Pentagon's Tolerance." *New York Times*. www.nytimes.com/2019/11/30/us/politics/trump-seals-eddie-gallagher.html

[93] Press Release. Dec. 23, 2020. "CJWC Members Celebrate President Trump's Pardons for the Biden Four." https://gohmert.house.gov/news/documentsingle.aspx?DocumentID=399894

[94] July 10, 2020. "Statement from the Press Secretary Regarding Executive Grant of Clemency for Roger Stone, Jr." The White House. https://trumpwhitehouse.archives.gov/briefings-statements/statement-press-secretary-regarding-executive-grant-clemency-roger-stone-jr/

[95] Mallin, Alexander. Sept. 17, 2020. "AG Barr Takes Aim at DOJ Prosecutors, Compares Lockdowns to Slavery." *ABC News*. https://abcnews.go.com/US/attorney-general-william-barr-accuses-doj-prosecutors-headhunters/story?id=73064588

3.1 "Law and Order" and Moral Foundations 89

Trump lawyer Rudolph Giuliani complained about "completely overzealous prosecutors" treating former Trump campaign manager Paul Manafort "like this was [mobster] John Gotti."[96]

Purity

Trump, like many Republicans, regularly claims that he will protect America's criminal justice system from a radical progressive agenda that ignores the law. By contrasting his message with that of Democrats who, in his words, "don't give a damn about crime,"[97] Trump has depicted himself as championing moral purity in the law. Yet while blackletter law is typically seen by conservatives as embodying purity domestically, the term can again assume a different definition in foreign wars. Instead of prioritizing the law as written, conservatives may view U.S. military conduct, by dint of the fact that it is done by Americans, as intrinsically ethical. Trump has used this logic to insist that, even when it breaches IHL, the U.S. remains firmly on the side of righteousness.

Trump has given short shrift to the atrocities committed by Americans to whom he granted clemency. Instead, he has focused on how these servicemembers, standing for pure U.S. values, need to be protected. By framing court-martialed troops as occupying the moral high ground, Trump has made the case that they should possess broad leeway to defeat their enemies. Military historian Waitman Wade Beorn, for example, has explained that Trump has "preferred to overlook serious war crimes in favor of a warped notion of patriotism and heroism" because he "subscribes to a 'bad things happen in war' mentality."[98] According to historian Nicole Hemmer, "Hate the war,

---

[96] Manchester, Julia. Mar. 8, 2019. "Giuliani Says Manafort Received Fair Sentence, Cohen Should Be Prosecuted for Perjury." *The Hill*. https://thehill.com/hilltv/rising/433212-giuliani-says-justice-served-fairly-for-manafort-but-cohen-should-be-prosecuted

[97] Jan. 10, 2019. "Trump: Democrats Don't Give a Damn about Crime." *CNN*. https://edition.cnn.com/videos/politics/2019/01/10/donald-trump-texas-democrats-dont-care-about-crime-sot-nr-vpx.cnn

[98] Beorn, Waitman Wade. May 9, 2019. "I Led a Platoon in Iraq. Trump Is Wrong to Pardon War Criminals." *Washington Post*. www.washingtonpost.com/outlook/i-led-a-platoon-in-iraq-trump-is-wrong-to-pardon-war-criminals/2019/05/09/15b10430-71d5-11e9-9eb4-0828f5389013_story.html

love the war criminal. That seems to be the mantra guiding President Donald Trump's foreign policy."[99]

Trump has depicted IHL violations by U.S. troops as not only permissible but also ethical. Douglas Porch of the U.S. Naval Postgraduate School, for example, has stated that Trump "encourag[ed] Fox News to promote war crimes as patriotic acts."[100] One journalist remarked that "[i]n the Trumpist worldview, [Eddie] Gallagher is not a hero in spite of his alleged atrocities, but because of them."[101] Foreign policy scholar Peter Certo similarly accused Trump of "encourag[ing] war crimes" and "glorifying serial killer-type behavior most service members would find appalling."[102] In the words of another writer, "Trump is sending a bright and clear message to troops in the field: Go ahead, do what you have to do, forget the rules of war, there'll be no punishment."[103]

Trump has attempted to reinforce the moral purity of his war crime clemencies by extolling the U.S. servicemembers granted reprieves and portraying them as brave men for fighting. For example, he praised Eddie Gallagher as "one of our ultimate fighters."[104] He similarly touted Mathew Golsteyn as "highly decorated"[105] and a "U.S. [m]ilitary hero."[106] After his 2019 clemencies, Trump told

---

[99] Hemmer, Nicole. Dec. 1, 2019. "Turning the Disgraced into War Heroes." *Sydney Morning Herald*. www.smh.com.au/world/north-america/turning-the-disgraced-into-war-heroes-20191130-p53fm3.html

[100] Edsall, Thomas B. Dec. 4, 2019. "The Savage Injustice of Trump's Military Pardons." *New York Times*. www.nytimes.com/2019/12/04/opinion/trump-military-pardons.html

[101] Levitz, Eric. Dec. 27, 2019. "Why Trump Vilifies Whistle-blowers and Venerates War Criminals." *New York Magazine*. https://nymag.com/intelligencer/2019/12/trump-edward-gallagher-ukraine-war-criminals-whistleblowers.html

[102] Certo, Peter. May 24, 2019. "Donald Trump May Spend Memorial Day Pardoning War Criminals." *In These Times*. https://inthesetimes.com/article/pardoning-war-criminals-honor-memorial-day-veterans-civilians

[103] MacDonald, Neil. Nov. 19, 2019. "No Need to Worry about War Crimes, Trump Has Soldiers' Backs: Neil Macdonald." *CBC*. www.cbc.ca/news/opinion/opinion-neil-macdonald-war-crimes-1.5363254

[104] Starr, Barbara and Ryan Browne. Nov. 26, 2019. "Esper 'Flabbergasted' to Learn of Navy Secretary's Secret White House Outreach about Navy SEAL." *CNN*. https://edition.cnn.com/2019/11/25/politics/esper-spencer-aftermath/index.html

[105] https://twitter.com/realDonaldTrump/status/1183016899589955584?ref_src=twsrc%5Etfw

[106] https://twitter.com/realDonaldTrump/status/1074319076766433280?ref_src=twsrc%5Etfw

3.1 "Law and Order" and Moral Foundations

his supporters that they should be "proud" of what he did to stand up for "our great fighters" who "are doing a job for us like nobody else in the world can do."[107] In a different context, while handing out an American military award, Trump stated that "[t]here is no love more *pure* than the love and courage that burns in the hearts of American patriots [emphasis added]."[108]

Supporters of Trump's military leadership have praised Trump as epitomizing pure American ideals. For example, Pete Hegseth has called Trump "a true warfighter's president."[109] Mathew Golsteyn applauded Trump's "incredible ... courage."[110] Clint Lorance called Trump "[a]wesome!"[111] Eddie Gallagher feted Trump as "a true leader" and "exactly what the military and this nation needs."[112] Rep. Louis Gohmert exalted Trump's "superb judgment" in issuing the 2020 Blackwater pardons.[113] One critic described the lobby advocating Trump's acts as "a cadre of conservative groups, right-wing politicians and cable TV hosts ... [who] wrap themselves up in the flag and squawk about patriotism and try to convince people that war crimes are not, in fact, crimes."[114]

---

[107] Nov. 26, 2019. "President Trump Rally in Sunrise, Florida." *C-SPAN*. www.c-span.org/video/?466539-1/president-trump-rally-sunrise-florida

[108] May 24, 2018. "Remarks on Presenting the Medal of Honor to Master Chief Petty Officer Britt K. Slabinski." *American Presidency Project*. www.presidency.ucsb.edu/documents/remarks-presenting-the-medal-honor-master-chief-petty-officer-britt-k-slabinski

[109] Darcy, Oliver. May 21, 2019. "Fox News Host Pete Hegseth Has Privately Encouraged Trump to Pardon Servicemen Accused of War Crimes." *CNN*. https://edition.cnn.com/2019/05/21/media/fox-news-pete-hegseth-trump-pardon-war-crimes/index.html

[110] Musto, Julia. Nov. 16, 2019. "Former Green Beret Maj. Mat Golsteyn Praises Trump's 'Courage' for Pardon, Says He Woke Up 'Incredibly Stunned.'" *Fox News*. www.foxnews.com/media/major-mat-golsteyn-president-trump-pardon-fox-and-friends-weekend

[111] Nov. 18, 2019. "Exclusive: Clint Lorance Gives First Interview since Pardon by Trump." *Fox News*. www.youtube.com/watch?v=ne3AX9tasKY&t=448s

[112] Nov. 25, 2019. "Who is Edward Gallagher – the Navy Seal Acquitted by Trump." *Voice of America*. www.voanews.com/usa/who-edward-gallagher-navy-seal-acquitted-trump

[113] www.facebook.com/photo/?fbid=885748102234918&set=pcb.885751248901270

[114] Kirby, John. Nov. 29, 2019. "Trump's Support for Navy SEAL Eddie Gallagher Is Misguided." *CNN*. https://edition.cnn.com/2019/11/29/opinions/trump-support-eddie-gallagher-richard-spencer-oped-kirby/index.html

In trying to highlight the U.S. military's moral purity even when it violates IHL, Trump has stressed the moral impurity of its enemies by pointing to how America's opponents debase standards for fighting. He has expressly said, "You have to play the game the way they [America's enemies] are playing the game."[115] Trump has argued not only that America's adversaries are unworthy of legal rights in combat, but that their actions are so morally impure that they deserve maltreatment. As one reporter writes, Trump "seemingly mak[es] the case for using similarly brutal tactics as terror groups."[116] According to another observer, Trump's mentality is that "torture is justified by the barbarism of others. It's the opposite of 'when they go low, we go high.'"[117]

Trump has routinely underlined the moral impurity of U.S. enemies to justify dismissing IHL. For example, in 2015, he affirmed that the U.S. should "be strong" because "over there" adversaries "put people in cages and … drown them in the ocean."[118] In 2016, Trump said that the U.S. should torture because its enemies possess "weapons that are so destructive … that the world could end."[119] The same year, Trump implored the U.S. military "to fight so viciously … [a]nd violently because we're dealing with violent people."[120] He also said that America should "go tougher than waterboarding" in response to "animals over in the Middle East that chop off heads."[121] In 2017, Trump called for

---

[115] Mar. 5, 2016. "Donald Trump: We Need to Change Law to Allow Torture, Waterboarding." *CBS*. www.cbsnews.com/video/donald-trump-we-need-to-change-law-to-allow-torture-waterboarding/

[116] Vitali, Ali. June 29, 2016. "Donald Trump on Terror: You Have to 'Fight Fire With Fire.'" *NBC News*. www.nbcnews.com/politics/2016-election/donald-trump-terror-you-have-fight-fire-fire-n600771

[117] Livni, Ephrat. Feb. 3, 2017. "For Better or Worse, Trump is Comfortable Using the Word 'Torture.'" *Quartz*. https://qz.com/901401/for-better-or-worse-trump-is-comfortable-with-the-word-torture/

[118] Hains, Tim. Nov. 23, 2015. "Trump: ISIS Is Chopping Off Heads And We Worry About Waterboarding." *Real Clear Politics*. www.realclearpolitics.com/video/2015/11/23/trump_isis_is_chopping_off_heads_and_we_worry_about_waterboarding.html

[119] Feb. 17, 2016. "Donald Trump: Torture Works." *CNN*. www.youtube.com/watch?v=Kpj3pp10wD8

[120] Vitali, Ali. June 29, 2016. "Donald Trump on Terror: You Have to 'Fight Fire With Fire.'" *NBC News*. www.nbcnews.com/politics/2016-election/donald-trump-terror-you-have-fight-fire-fire-n600771

[121] Berenson, Tessa. Mar. 3, 2016. "Donald Trump Defends Torture at Republican Debate." *TIME*. https://time.com/4247397/donald-trump-waterboarding-torture/

3.1 *"Law and Order" and Moral Foundations*

"fight[ing] fire with fire" because terrorists "chop … off [heads] and … put 'em on camera and … send 'em all over the world."[122]

That the moral impurity of the other side justifies almost any tactic is a theme that Trump has also invoked in domestic political fights. In 2019, for instance, Trump tweeted: "THE DEMOCRATS ARE TRYING TO DESTROY THE REPUBLICAN PARTY…. STICK TOGETHER, PLAY THEIR GAME, AND FIGHT HARD REPUBLICANS. OUR COUNTRY IS AT STAKE!"[123] Trump also implored Republicans to "get tougher and fight" because "the Democrats fight dirty … they're vicious."[124] In 2020, Trump retweeted a video of New Mexico politician Couy Griffin stating that "the only good Democrat is a dead Democrat."[125] One commentator said that, in aiding war criminals, Trump "sees parallels … to himself. He wants his own history of fighting dirty to be likewise excused."[126]

Trump has even suggested that U.S. troops should not be above committing war crimes that exploit views about purity held by the other side. For example, in 2016, Trump approvingly recounted an apocryphal story of U.S. General John Pershing from the early 1900s in the Philippines. He told supporters that Pershing dipped bullets in pig's blood, viewed as spiritually impure by Muslims, before executing terrorists. Trump elaborated: "He took 50 bullets and he dipped them in pig's blood, … and he lined up the 50 people, and they shot 49 of those people and the 50th person, he said, 'You go back to your

---

[122] Jan. 26, 2017. "TRANSCRIPT: ABC News Anchor David Muir Interviews President Trump." *ABC News*. https://abcnews.go.com/Politics/transcript-abc-news-anchor-david-muir-interviews-president/story?id=45047602

[123] Pettypiece, Shannon. Sept. 26, 2019. "Trump Says Those Who Gave Info to the Whistleblower Are Like Spies, Reports Say." *NBC News*. www.nbcnews.com/politics/white-house/trump-says-our-country-stake-whistleblower-account-made-public-n1059011

[124] Schwartz, Ian. Oct. 21, 2019. "Trump: Democrats Are 'Vicious' And Stick Together, 'They Don't Have A Mitt Romney In Their Midst.'" *Real Clear Politics*. www.realclearpolitics.com/video/2019/10/21/trump_democrats_are_vicious_and_stick_together_they_dont_have_a_mitt_romney_in_their_midst.html

[125] Silverstein, Jason. May 28, 2020. "Trump Shares Video of Supporter Saying 'The Only Good Democrat is a Dead Democrat'." *CBS News*. www.cbsnews.com/news/president-trump-shares-video-of-supporter-saying-the-only-good-democrat-is-a-dead-democrat/

[126] Kristian, Bonnie. Nov. 27, 2019. "Why Trump Identifies with War Criminals." *The Week*. https://theweek.com/articles/881173/why-trump-identifies-war-criminals

people and you tell them what happened.'"[127] Trump later alluded to the story in a 2017 tweet, declaring, "Study what General Pershing of the United States did to terrorists when caught."[128]

Trump has made similar arguments about adversaries getting what they ostensibly deserve when defending his war crime interventions. As one journalist commented, "Trump's justification of [Eddie] Gallagher's conduct (and his defense of torture) comes down to this: They'd do it to us if the shoe was on the other foot!"[129] In a similar vein, when members of Gallagher's platoon alleged that he had stabbed an ISIS captive, Gallagher reportedly replied, "Stop worrying about it; they do a lot worse to us."[130] Pete Hegseth has likewise asked, "What if we treated the enemy the way they treated us?" His answer was: "Hey, Al Qaeda: if you surrender, we might spare your life. If you do not, we will rip your arms off and feed them to hogs."[131]

A number of Trump's allies have also smeared opponents inside the U.S. military justice system as lacking moral purity. For example, one of Eddie Gallagher's and Trump's attorneys, Timothy Parlatore, vilified the effort to take away his client's SEAL trident as "pure retaliation."[132]

---

[127] Embury-Dennis, Tom. Mar. 19, 2019. "Trump Tells Fake Story about US General Slaughtering 49 Muslims Using Bullets Dipped in Pig's Blood, in Resurfaced Video." *Independent*. www.independent.co.uk/news/world/americas/us-politics/trump-muslims-general-pershing-pigs-blood-video-a8829676.html

[128] https://twitter.com/realDonaldTrump/status/898254409511129088?ref_src=twsrc%5Etfw%7Ctwcamp%5Etweetembed%7Ctwterm%5E898254409511129088%7Ctwgr%5Ea9fcc0b98211edcf8d0f0357f74a32f5ea8ee66d%7Ctwcon%5Es1_&ref_url=https%3A%2F%2Fwww.theatlantic.com%2Finternational%2Farchive%2F2017%2F08%2Fpershing-trump-terrorism%2F537300%2F

[129] Cillizza, Chris. Nov. 26, 2019. "What Donald Trump Doesn't Get about Eddie Gallagher and Being 'Tough.'" *CNN*. https://edition.cnn.com/2019/11/26/politics/donald-trump-eddie-gallagher/index.html

[130] Philipps, Dave, Peter Baker, Maggie Haberman, and Helene Cooper. Nov. 30, 2019. "Trump's Intervention in SEALs Case Tests Pentagon's Tolerance." *New York Times*. www.nytimes.com/2019/11/30/us/politics/trump-seals-eddie-gallagher.html

[131] Wilson, Jason. Nov. 25, 2024. "Trump Pentagon Pick Attacks UN and NATO and Urges US to Ignore Geneva Conventions." *Guardian*. www.theguardian.com/us-news/2024/nov/25/pete-hegseth-book-attacks-nato-alliances

[132] Philipps, Dave. Nov. 22, 2019. "As Admiral Moved to Expel a Navy SEAL, He Kept an Eye on Trump." *New York Times*. www.nytimes.com/2019/11/20/us/edward-gallagher-trident-letter.html

3.1 "Law and Order" and Moral Foundations 95

He also labeled the search of Gallagher's home, where he accused the Navy of "dragg[ing] ... [Gallagher's] kids out of the house at gunpoint in their underwear," as "pure intimidation."[133] Another one of Gallagher's lawyers, Marc Mukasey, referred to Gallagher's prosecution as "pure and simple retaliation."[134] Gallagher's brother, Sean, on Fox Nation, described the attempt by naval leadership to take away Gallagher's SEAL rank as an exercise in "pure vindictiveness."[135]

Such rhetoric extended beyond formal accusations, with many deploying derogatory labels to undermine their adversaries as morally compromised. For example, Eddie Gallagher dubbed fellow Navy SEAL Craig Miller, who described him as "freaking evil," as "Crying Craig Miller." He maligned SEAL Joshua Vriens, who labeled Gallagher "toxic," as "The Joker."[136] He also ridiculed *New York Times* journalist Dave Philipps as a "Sky Crane" because he was a "big tool" for allegedly defaming him.[137] The tags had clear parallels to Trump's own use of phrases like "Crooked Hillary" Clinton and "Crazy Joe" Biden.[138] Gallagher's wife added that her husband's

---

[133] Martin, David. Mar. 1, 2020. "Eddie Gallagher, Navy SEAL Acquitted of Stabbing Wounded ISIS Prisoner to Death, Tells His Story." *CBS News*. www.cbsnews.com/news/eddie-gallagher-navy-seal-isis-prisoner-60-minutes-interview-2020-03-01/

[134] Smith, Jennifer and David Martosko. Nov. 21, 2019. "Trump OVERRULES Navy Decision to Strip SEAL Eddie Gallagher of His 'Trident Pin' and Kick Him Out of Special Forces Despite Being Cleared of War Crimes." *Daily Mail*. www.dailymail.co.uk/news/article-7711235/Trump-overrules-Navy-let-Eddie-Gallagher-remain-SEAL-pardon.html

[135] London, Matt. Nov. 20, 2019. "Brother of Navy SEAL Chief Blasts Top Admiral: 'Two-star Is Defying an Order from the President.'" *Fox News*. www.foxnews.com/media/eddie-gallagher-trident-navy-seal-trump

[136] Crane, Emily. Jan. 28, 2020. "Retired Navy SEAL Eddie Gallagher Names and Shames 'Coward' Platoon Members Who Testified against Him at War Crimes Trial and Warns the 'Real Truth' Is Still Coming." *Daily Mail*. www.dailymail.co.uk/news/article-7939945/Retired-Navy-SEAL-Eddie-Gallagher-lashes-coward-platoon.html

[137] Nov. 29, 2020. "Black Rifle Coffee Podcast: Ep 080 Eddie Gallagher and Donut Operator." Black Rifle Coffee Podcast. www.youtube.com/watch?v=MSGhjYwVzFs

[138] Bennett, John T. Aug. 2, 2018. "Top 10 Trump Nicknames and Why They Stick to His Foes." *Roll Call*. www.rollcall.com/2018/08/02/top-10-trump-nicknames-and-why-they-stick-to-his-foes/ / Gstalter, Morgan. Dec. 26, 2018. "Trump's Most Memorable Insults and Nicknames of 2018." *The Hill*. https://thehill.com/homenews/administration/421948-18-nicknames-trump-invented-in-2018

prosecution was the result of "COWARDS & WHINERS"[139] and labeled his ex-platoon mates "mean girls."[140]

3.2 Survey of Attitudes toward War Crimes

As demonstrated earlier, Trump, Fox News, and congressional Republicans have presented overt challenges to IHL as consistent with the moral foundations of conservative voters. Even if conservatives support law and order domestically, and even if they reject war crimes in the abstract, the impunity coalition has marshaled support by activating the MFT values of in-group loyalty, authority, and purity. This strategy has benefited Trump's coalition. Trump has courted the right-wing base, Republican Congress members have ridden his political coattails, and Fox News has attracted conservative audiences that boost ratings. Whether Trump and his allies actually believe that their agenda serves America's military is secondary to it advancing their political interests.

To examine the effects of this strategy, an original, national survey was fielded in the U.S. while Trump was still in office to measure public reactions to challenges to IHL.[141] The objectives were threefold: first, to test whether conservatives support challenges to the law of war more than other voters; second, whether this effect results from underlying MFT values; and third, whether these views can be activated by appeals from the impunity coalition. The survey (N = 1,259 after cleaning[142]), fielded online by the market research firm Bovitz before the 2020 election (October 29 to November 2, 2020), used nonprobabilistic sampling intended to be broadly

---

[139] www.instagram.com/p/B_VjUfrJCOW/?hl=en

[140] Smith, Jennifer and Megan Sheets. Jul. 2, 2019. "'If This Was A Movie No One Would Believe It': How Navy SEAL Eddie Gallagher's Wife Stood by His Side through 'Farce' Trial and Lambasted the 'Mean Girls' Who Testified Against Him." *Daily Mail.* www.dailymail.co.uk/news/article-7201397/Navy-SEAL-Eddie-Gallaghers-wife-stood-farce-trial.html

[141] This study has been approved by the Indiana University Institutional Review Board, protocol #2008603055, joint with Andrew M. Bell.

[142] Of the initial 1,751 respondents, 230 did not reach the ideology question and were removed. Of the remaining 1,521 respondents, 262 failed at least one of two attention check questions taken from the Moral Foundations Questionnaire. They failed the attention checks if: (1) they said that whether or not someone is good at math is at least "somewhat relevant" to whether something is right or wrong; or (2) they at least "slightly disagree" that it is better to do good than to do bad.

3.2 Survey of Attitudes toward War Crimes

similar to established, national surveys (see Appendix Table 3.A.1 for summary statistics). Subjects in the Bovitz panel were compensated at an equivalent to just under $3.00.

The survey first assesses the overall willingness of voters to punish crimes in domestic criminal justice versus a battlefield setting. Next, it turns to attitudes toward deploying U.S. military force. It examines both support for loosening military rules of engagement (ROE), where ambiguity exists in what methods conform to the law of war, and support for violating the Geneva Conventions, where noncompliance is clear-cut. Finally, the survey investigates whether impunity coalition cues can activate respondent attitudes toward IHL. Waterboarding is the focus because it represents a challenging issue on which to alter opinions, as many citizens likely have preexisting views on it. To the extent that impunity messaging can alter attitudes, one might expect views on other IHL controversies to be even more malleable.

Each experiment conditions the estimates on respondent ideology and MFT values. Ideology is proxied with a standard self-reported measure on the conservative-liberal scale.[143] Moral foundations are based on the standard "MFQ30" questionnaire, where respondents answered thirty substantive questions intended to elicit how much they prioritized in-group loyalty, authority, purity, harm, and fairness.[144] In total, six questions relate to each of the MFT values, with a maximum of five points each. For simplicity, totals were rescaled from 0 to 1. As depicted in Figure 3.1, the ideological breakdown of the five MFT values is as expected. Comparatively, conservatives prioritize in-group loyalty, authority, and purity; liberals prioritize harm and fairness.

---

[143] Conservatives defined as "Extremely conservative," "Conservative," or "Slightly conservative"; liberals as "Extremely liberal," "Liberal," or "Slightly liberal"; and moderates as "Moderate, middle of the road." Moderates were included in all analyses but their results are not displayed.

[144] Fifteen of the substantive questions asked respondents to what extent certain considerations were "relevant" when ' decid[ing] whether something is right or wrong," with answers ranging from 0 ("not at all relevant") to 5 ("extremely relevant"). Fifteen of the substantive questions asked respondents about their "agreement" with certain declarative statements invoking moral values, with responses ranging from 0 ("strongly disagree") to 5 ("strongly agree").

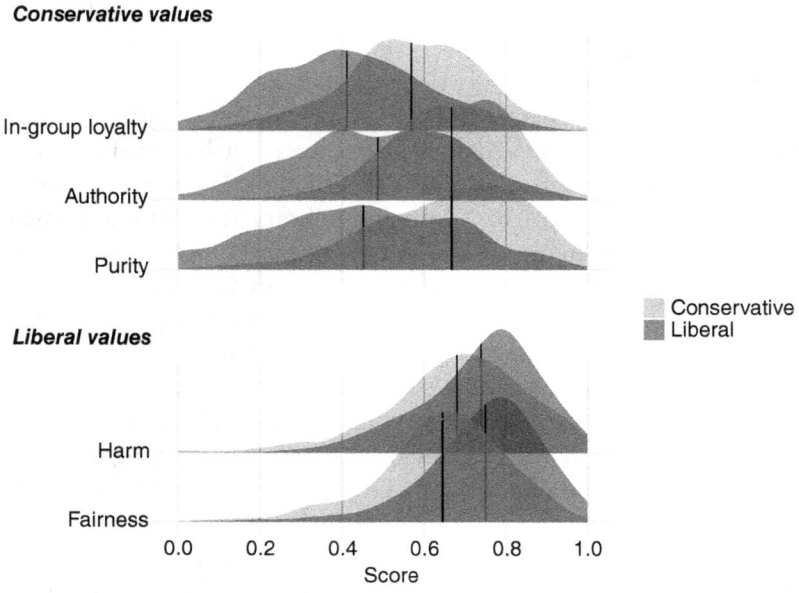

Figure 3.1 Distributions of MFT values, by ideology

Support for Exonerating Crimes

The first issue examined is how ideological and MFT divides affect support for punishing crimes domestically versus in combat. This speaks to the core claim regarding the motivations of the impunity agenda – that conservatives support law and order more in a criminal justice context than in foreign wars. To test this prediction, respondents were asked whether they supported punishing criminals to the full extent of the law, but the question randomly varied a key detail: whether the criminals were U.S. citizens who committed crimes in their communities or U.S. servicemembers who committed crimes on the battlefield. In response to a version of the following question, answers were coded on a 1–7 Likert scale, ranging from "Strongly agree" (1) to "Strongly disagree" (7) (i.e., higher numbers = more support for exoneration):

> *To what extent do you agree or disagree with the following statement: U.S. [citizens/servicemembers] who are found guilty of committing crimes [in their communities/on the battlefield] should be punished to the full extent of the law.*

3.2 Survey of Attitudes toward War Crimes

Table 3.1 *Support for exoneration from the law, by ideology*

	OLS (1)	OLS with covariates (2)	Ordered logit (3)
Constant	2.657***	2.697***	
	(0.094)	(0.176)	
ServicememberTreatment	−0.446***	−0.442***	−0.696***
	(0.130)	(0.130)	(0.160)
Conservative	−0.425**	−0.448**	−0.714***
	(0.141)	(0.143)	(0.174)
Conservative × ServicememberTreatment	1.384***	1.375***	1.911***
	(0.200)	(0.200)	(0.251)
N	1,256	1,254	1,256
Adjusted R^2	0.040	0.046	

*$p < .05$; **$p < .01$; ***$p < .001$. Two-tailed tests.
Model 2 includes covariates for age, gender, race, income, and education.
Larger values indicate greater support for exoneration.
Moderates were included in the analysis but not shown for legibility.

Table 3.1 reports the main findings by ideology, which confirm expectations.[145] Model 1 shows that conservatives are comparatively more inclined than liberals to exonerate U.S. servicemembers (significant at $p < .01$). Unlike liberals, their baseline levels of support for exonerating U.S. servicemembers are also higher than that for domestic criminals (significant at $p < .01$). As displayed in Figure 3.2a, the predicted level of disagreement for punishment on the 1–7 Likert scale is 3.17 for conservatives when criminals are depicted as U.S. servicemembers, compared to 2.23 when depicted as U.S. citizens. For liberals, these numbers were 2.21 and 2.66, respectively.[146] As predicted, Figure 3.2b also shows that placing greater emphasis on the conservative MFT values of in-group

---

[145] The linear model is: $Y = a0 + a1(ServicememberTreatment) + a2(Ideology) + a3(ServicememberTreatment \times Ideology) + E$, where Ideology is split into conservative, moderate, and liberal (liberal is the reference category, and results for moderates have not been displayed – this is the case for all applicable regressions).

[146] Robustness checks, which reestimate these regressions with both covariates (Model 2) and using ordered logit (Model 3), yield consistent results.

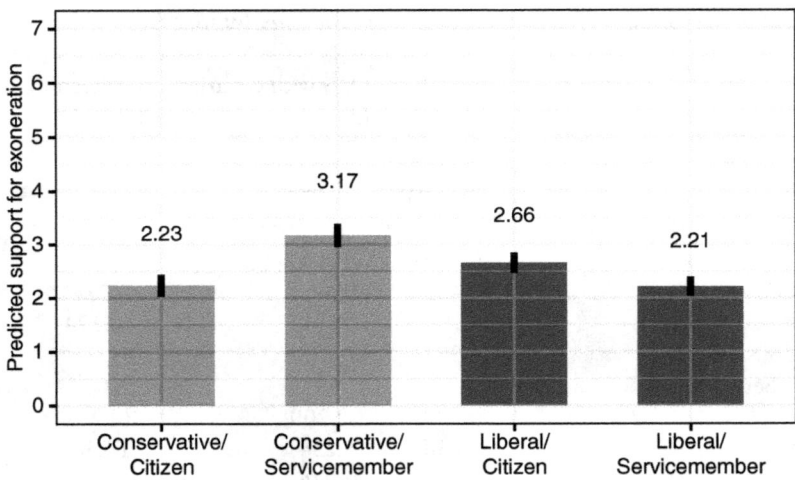

Figure 3.2a Support for exoneration from the law, by ideology

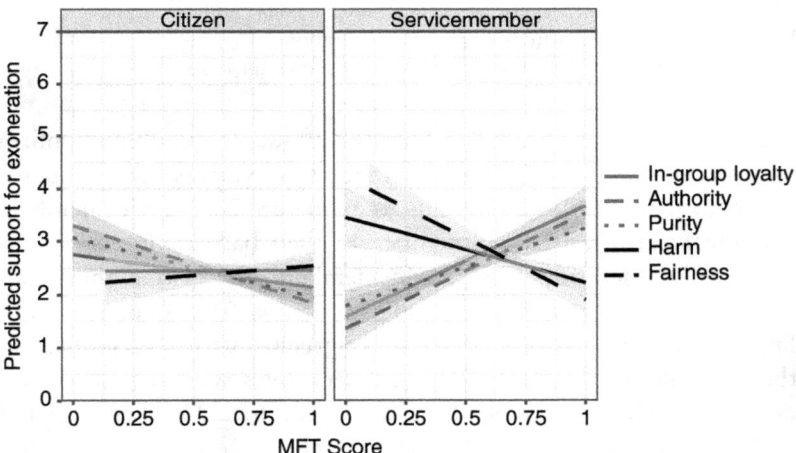

Figure 3.2b Support for exoneration from the law, by MFT values

loyalty, authority, and purity is correlated with both more support for exonerating U.S. servicemembers and less support for exonerating domestic criminals.[147] The opposite is true for respondents

---

[147] The linear model is: $Y = a0 + a1(ServicememberTreatment) + a2(In\text{-}group\ loyalty) + a3(In\text{-}group\ loyalty\ X\ ServicememberTreatment) + a4(Authority) + a5(Authority\ X\ ServicememberTreatment) + a6(Purity) + a7(Purity\ X$

3.2 Survey of Attitudes toward War Crimes

who prioritize the liberal values of harm and fairness (see Appendix Table 3.A.2 for full estimations).

Support for Challenges to IHL

The next set of experiments tests whether ideological and MFT divides exist in support for U.S. military actions that challenge IHL. Specifically, attitudes are examined toward: (1) military ROE; and (2) adherence to the Geneva Conventions. The topics were chosen not only because Trump has actively challenged IHL in these areas, but also because they offer variation in the degree to which the impunity agenda clearly breaches the law. Considerable debate exists about the appropriateness of particular ROE constraints. However, failure to comply with the Geneva Conventions is an unambiguous violation of IHL.

Constraints on U.S. Soldiers

Attitudes toward ROE were proxied by support for allowing troops to employ maximum firepower on the battlefield. Respondents were randomly assigned a version of the question below, which gauged assessments of the potential costs and benefits of loosening ROE. Answers were coded on a 7-point Likert scale from "Strongly disagree" (1) to "Strongly agree" (7) (i.e., higher numbers = less restraint):

> To what extent do you agree or disagree with the following statement: The United States should allow U.S. soldiers to use the maximum firepower necessary to target enemy forces [, even if it significantly increased civilian casualties/if doing so saved the lives of U.S. soldiers].

A *Control* group received only the baseline condition. Respondents assigned to *Treatment 1* (*CivilianCasualtiesTreatment*) not only read the same text but also received the caveat that allowing U.S. soldiers to use maximum firepower would significantly increase civilian casualties. Respondents assigned to *Treatment 2* (*SoldiersSavedTreatment*) also received the caveat that allowing U.S. soldiers to use maximum

$ServicememberTreatment) + a8(Harm) + a9(Harm \times ServicememberTreatment) + a10(Fairness) + a11(Fairness \times ServicememberTreatment) + E$

Table 3.2 *Support for using maximum firepower, by ideology*

	OLS (1)	OLS (2)	OLS with covariates (3)	Ordered logit (4)
Constant	3.828***	3.828***	2.756***	
	(0.155)	(0.152)	(0.220)	
Conservative	2.087***	2.087***	1.777***	2.222***
	(0.232)	(0.227)	(0.220)	(0.260)
CivilianCasualtiesTreatment		−1.033***	−1.135***	−1.188***
		(0.212)	(0.204)	(0.245)
SoldiersSavedTreatment		0.754***	0.709***	0.756**
		(0.212)	(0.203)	(0.239)
ComboTreatment		−0.737***	−0.731***	−0.758***
		(0.204)	(0.196)	(0.228)
Conservative × CivilianCasualtiesTreatment		−0.531	−0.373	−0.542
		(0.321)	(0.308)	(0.358)
Conservative × SoldiersSavedTreatment		−0.680*	−0.605*	−0.723*
		(0.319)	(0.307)	(0.353)
Conservative × ComboTreatment		−0.134	−0.106	−0.219
		(0.316)	(0.303)	(0.348)
N	316	1,256	1,254	1,256
Adjusted R^2	0.200	0.280	0.340	

*$p < .05$; **$p < .01$; ***$p < .001$. Two-tailed tests.
Model 3 includes covariates for age, gender, race, income, and education.
Larger values indicate greater support.
Moderates were included in the analysis but not shown for legibility.

firepower would save the lives of U.S. soldiers. Finally, *Treatment 3* (*ComboTreatment*) received both caveats.[148]

Table 3.2 reports the key results by ideology. The first analysis restricts the data to only respondents who received the *Control*. In line with expectations, Model 1 shows that conservatives agree more

[148] Treatment 3 used separate subtreatments to randomize the order of mentioning civilian casualties and saving the lives of U.S. soldiers, to ensure that receiving one before the other did not bias responses. These subtreatments were then collapsed into a main treatment.

3.2 Survey of Attitudes toward War Crimes

than liberals with using maximum firepower (significant at $p < .01$).[149] As depicted in Figure 3.3a, on the 1–7 Likert scale of agreement, the predicted value for conservatives is 5.91, compared to 3.83 for liberals. Model 2 estimates the fully interactive regression that disaggregates the individual treatments.[150] Consistent with predictions, conservatives in every scenario again agree more with using maximum firepower compared to liberals (for *CivilianCasualtiesTreatment*, significant at $p < .01$; for *SoldiersSavedTreatment* treatment, significant at $p < .01$; for *ComboTreatment*, significant at $p < .01$).[151] Predicted values are plotted in Figure 3.3b.

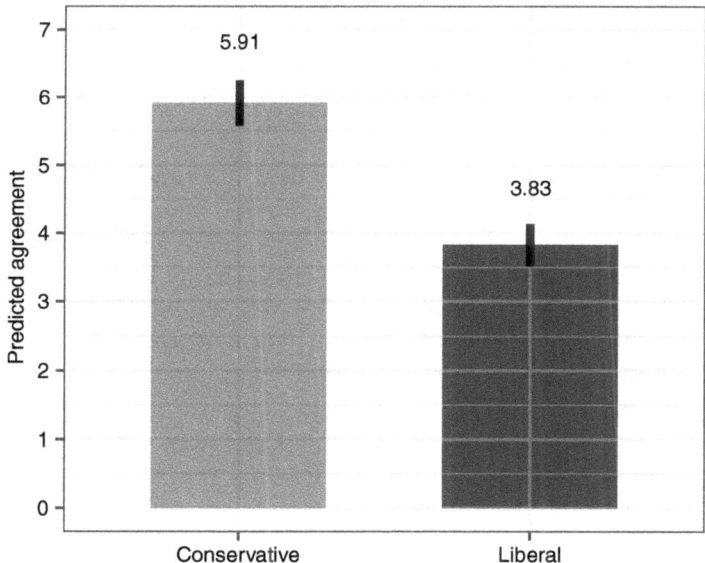

Figure 3.3a Support for using maximum firepower (control), by ideology

---

[149] The linear model is: $Y = a0 + a1(Conservative) + E$.
[150] The linear model is: $Y = a1(Ideology) + a2(CivilianCasualtiesTreatment) + a3(CivilianCasualtiesTreatment \times Ideology) + a4(SoldiersSavedTreatment) + a5(SoldiersSavedTreatment \times Ideology) + a6(ComboTreatment) + a7(ComboTreatment \times Ideology) - E$.
[151] As shown in Model 2, both conservatives and liberals agree less with using maximum firepower when told that it could increase civilian casualties (for conservatives, significant at $p < .01$; for liberals, significant at $p < .01$) and agree more when told that it could save the lives of U.S. soldiers (for conservatives, significant at $p < .01$; for liberals, significant at $p < .01$).

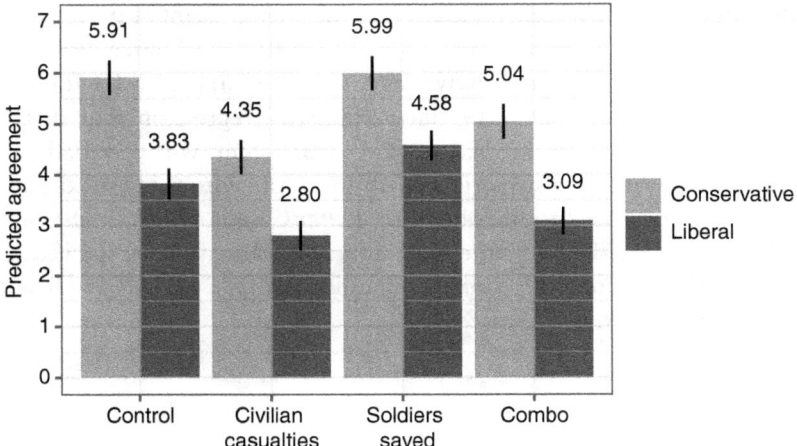

Figure 3.3b Support for using maximum firepower, by ideology

Figure 3.3c stratifies effects by MFT values.[152] As anticipated, the three conservative values (in-group loyalty, authority, and purity) are positively related to support for using maximum firepower in every condition. By comparison, the liberal values (harm and fairness) are both inversely related to this outcome (full results displayed in Appendix Table 3.A.3). Taken together, these results confirm that conservatives are more supportive of the U.S. challenging IHL in combat when legality is ambiguous. Associated MFT values of in-group loyalty, authority, and purity correspond with this preference.

Adherence to the Geneva Conventions

The next experiment turns to the clear-cut case of IHL violation by measuring support for rejecting U.S. abidance to the Geneva Conventions. All respondents were first given the following background information explaining that the Geneva Conventions constrain the use of force against civilians and that the U.S. had pledged to agree to its principles:

---

[152] The linear model is: $Y = a0 + a1(Treatment) + a2(In\text{-}group\ loyalty) + a3(In\text{-}group\ loyalty\ X\ ServicememberTreatment) + a4(Authority) + a5(Authority\ X\ Treatment) + a6(Purity) + a7(Purity\ X\ Treatment) + a8(Harm) + a9(Harm\ X\ Treatment) + a10(Fairness) + a11(Fairness\ X\ Treatment) + E$, where Treatment denotes which of the four treatments (including Control) the respondent was shown.

3.2 Survey of Attitudes toward War Crimes

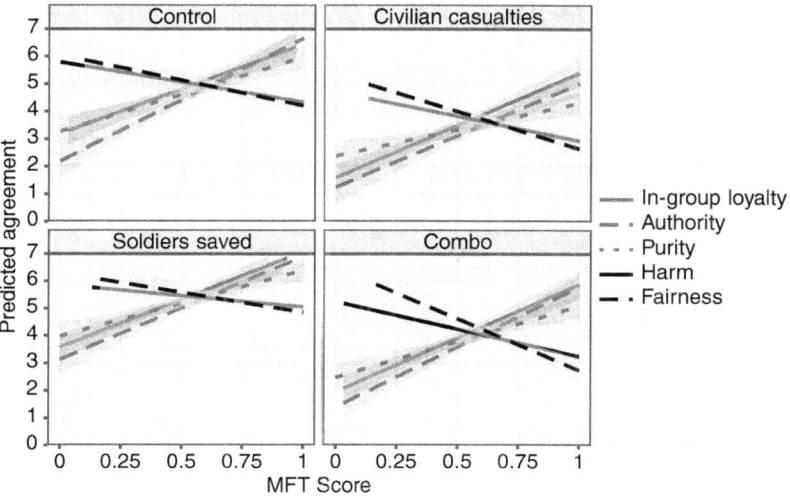

Figure 3.3c Support for using maximum firepower, by MFT values

> **Background information:** *The United States is a signatory to the Geneva Conventions, which constrain the use of force by soldiers in war in order to protect civilians and others not involved in fighting.*

Respondents were then randomly posed a version of the below question. Responses were coded on the Likert scale from "Strongly disagree" (1) to "Strongly agree" (7) (i.e., higher numbers = less restraint):

> *To what extent do you agree or disagree with the following statement: The United States should under certain conditions ignore the Geneva Conventions [, even if it significantly increased civilian casualties/if doing so helped the U.S. defeat its enemies more quickly].*

Respondents assigned to the *Control* only read the baseline text. In Treatment 1 (*CivilianCasualtiesTreatment*), respondents were informed that disregarding the Geneva Conventions would significantly increase civilian casualties. In Treatment 2 (*DefeatEnemiesTreatment*), respondents were told that disregarding the Geneva Conventions

Table 3.3 *Support for disregarding the Geneva Conventions, by ideology*

	OLS (1)	OLS (2)	OLS with covariates (3)	Ordered logit (4)
Constant	2.612***	2.612***	3.002***	
	(0.159)	(0.159)	(0.242)	
Conservative	0.997***	0.997***	0.927***	1.189***
	(0.230)	(0.230)	(0.231)	(0.244)
CivilianCasualtiesTreatment		−0.300	−0.324	−0.338
		(0.209)	(0.208)	(0.229)
DefeatEnemiesTreatment		0.092	0.037	0.134
		(0.225)	(0.224)	(0.243)
ComboTreatment		−0.181	−0.175	−0.239
		(0.225)	(0.223)	(0.247)
Conservative × CivilianCasualtiesTreatment		0.315	0.363	0.317
		(0.320)	(0.319)	(0.336)
Conservative × DefeatEnemiesTreatment		0.241	0.343	0.178
		(0.334)	(0.334)	(0.350)
Conservative × ComboTreatment		0.522	0.537	0.534
		(0.338)	(0.337)	(0.357)
N	323	1,256	1,254	1,256
Adjusted R^2	0.054	0.092	0.105	

*$p < .05$; **$p < .01$; ***$p < .001$. Two-tailed tests.
Model 3 includes covariates for age, gender, race, income, and education.
Larger values indicate greater support.
Moderates were included in the analysis but not shown for legibility.

would help the U.S. defeat its enemies more quickly. In *Treatment 3* (*ComboTreatment*), respondents were exposed to both caveats.[153]

Table 3.3 summarizes the main findings by ideology. The analysis starts again by restricting the data only to the *Control* group. Model 1 shows that conservatives are more willing than liberals

---

[153] Similar to the previous experiment, in Treatment 3, separate subtreatments were used to randomize the order of referencing civilian casualties and helping the U.S. to defeat its enemies more quality. These treatments were then collapsed.

3.2 Survey of Attitudes toward War Crimes

to disregard the Geneva Conventions (significant at $p < .01$).[154] As depicted in Figure 3.4a, conservatives have a predicted value of 3.61 and liberals 2.61 on the 1–7 Likert scale of agreement. Next is an analysis of the fully interactive model with the constituent treatments.[155] In line with projections, Model 2 confirms that conservatives remain more willing than liberals to disregard the Geneva Conventions under each situation (for *CivilianCasualtiesTreatment*, significant at $p < .01$; for *DefeatEnemiesTreatment*, significant at $p < .01$; for *ComboTreatment*, significant at $p < .01$).[156] Predicted values are plotted in Figure 3.4b.

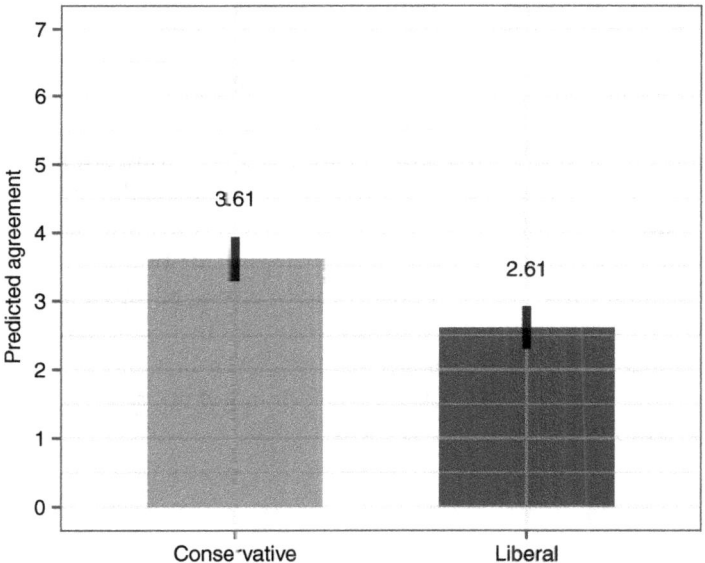

Figure 3.4a Support for disregarding the Geneva Conventions (control), by ideology

---

[154] The linear model is: $Y = a0 + a1(Ideology) + E$.
[155] The linear model is: $Y = a1(Ideology) + a2(CivilianCasualtiesTreatment) + a3(CivilianCasualtiesTreatment \times Ideology) + a4(DefeatEnemiesTreatment) + a5(DefeatEnemiesTreatment \times Ideology) + a6(ComboTreatment) + a7(ComboTreatment \times Ideology) + E$.
[156] There were no significant differences in the willingness of respondents to disregard the Geneva Conventions across the control and treatment groups for either conservatives or liberals.

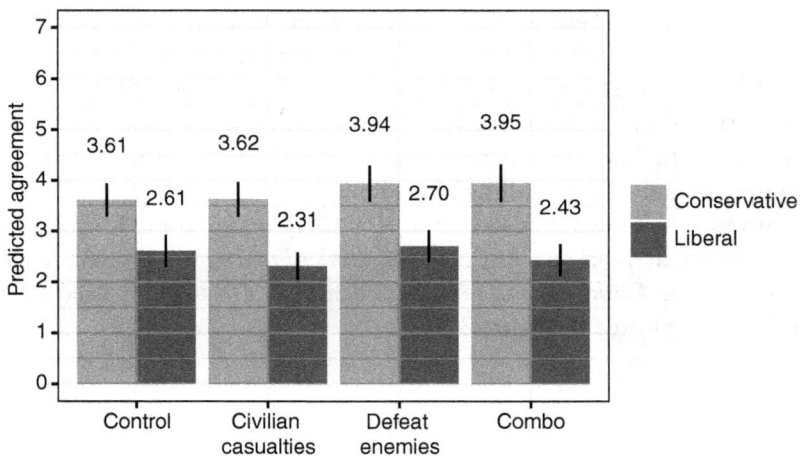

Figure 3.4b Support for disregarding the Geneva Conventions, by ideology

Figure 3.4c again disaggregates results by moral foundations.[157] As predicted, the three conservative values (in-group loyalty, authority, and purity) are positively linked to disregarding the Geneva Conventions, whereas the association is negative for the two liberal values (harm and fairness) (complete results displayed in Appendix Table 3.A.4). Overall, these findings indicate that conservatives are more inclined to violate the law of war when illegality is clear. These attitudes align with associated MFT values of in-group loyalty, authority, and purity.

Impunity Coalition Activation

The final question analyzed is whether appeals by the impunity coalition can actually activate citizens to reject the importance of IHL. This tests the prediction that, even if right-leaning voters are more receptive to challenges to IHL, elites can trigger the salience of these beliefs. To simulate impunity messaging, respondents were presented with

---

[157] The linear model is: $Y = a0 + a1(Treatment) + a2(\text{In-group loyalty}) + a3(\text{In-group loyalty} \times ServicememberTreatment) + a4(Authority) + a5(Authority \times Treatment) + a6(Purity) + a7(Purity \times Treatment) + a8(Harm) + a9(Harm \times Treatment) + a10(Fairness) + a11(Fairness \times Treatment) + E$, where Treatment denotes which of the four treatments (including Control) the respondent was shown.

3.2 Survey of Attitudes toward War Crimes

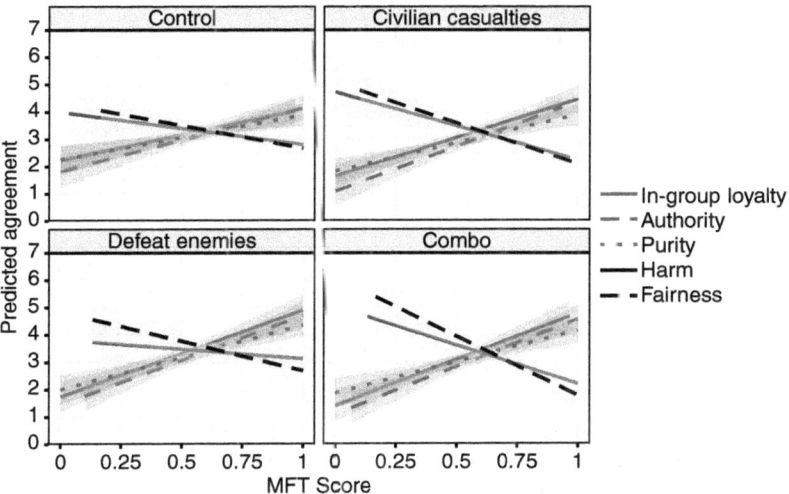

Figure 3.4c Support for disregarding the Geneva Conventions, by MFT values

a video of Trump endorsing waterboarding. The focus is on waterboarding because Trump supported its use, despite it being one of the most controversial techniques used by the U.S. government in recent decades.[158] Additionally, it should be a difficult case on which to move attitudes because citizens are likely to already have preexisting views on it. All respondents were first provided with the following definition of waterboarding:

> Background information: *"Waterboarding" refers to an interrogation technique usually regarded as a form of torture in which water is forced into a detainee's mouth and nose so as to induce the sensation of drowning.*

Those assigned to the *Control* group received no additional information. Respondents assigned to *Treatment 1 (TrumpOnlyTreatment)* watched a video of Trump advocating waterboarding. The video was taken from the March 3, 2016, GOP presidential debate in Detroit hosted by Fox News. Trump's words were:

---

[158] In the aftermath of 9/11, the CIA used waterboarding on a number of high-value terrorist targets. In 2009, however, President Barack Obama declared waterboarding to be illegal, prompting a bill that was later passed into law.

> **Trump:** *They then came to me, what do you think of waterboarding? I said, "It's fine, and if we want to go stronger, I'd go stronger too." Because frankly, that's the way I feel. Can you imagine, can you imagine these people, these animals, over in the Middle East that chop off heads, sitting around talking and seeing that we're having a hard problem with waterboarding? We should go for waterboarding, and we should go tougher than waterboarding.*

Respondents assigned to *Treatment 2* (*Trump+FoxNewsTreatment*) watched the same video. However, the clip was edited to include Fox News framing. A short snippet pulled from Fox News's debate coverage was played at the beginning of the video, which included sound, generic patriotic imagery (e.g., an animated White House, stars, and stripes), and the words "Fox News Debate." While Trump talked, the video was zoomed out to reveal a superimposed Fox News logo at the bottom left-hand corner of the screen, with chyron text: "FOX NEWS DEBATE." Two additional large Fox News signs flanked Trump on his back left and right. This branding, which was part of Fox News's original programming, did not include any substantive content by Fox News advocating waterboarding. It was intended only to simulate the partisan media environment in which voters consume information about the impunity agenda.

In contrast, respondents assigned to *Treatment 3* (*ObamaTreatment*) watched a video of Barack Obama expressing disapproval of waterboarding in 2011, with no media branding.[159] Obama's words were as follows:

> **Obama:** *Waterboarding is torture. It's contrary to America's traditions. It's contrary to our ideals. That's not who we are. That's not how we operate. We don't need it in order to prosecute the war on terrorism. And we did the right thing by ending that practice.*

The dependent variable was based on the question: "To what extent do you agree or disagree with the following statement: The United States should under certain conditions use interrogation methods involving waterboarding on captured terrorists." Respondents could

---

[159] The video was taken from CBS News footage, although all CBS logos were cut out of the video.

3.2 Survey of Attitudes toward War Crimes

Table 3.4 *Support for use of waterboarding, by ideology*

	OLS (1)	OLS (2)	OLS with covariates (3)	Ordered logit (4)
Constant	2.817***	2.817***	3.106***	
	(0.175)	(0.177)	(0.262)	
Conservative	1.489***	1.489***	1.530***	1.300***
	(0.271)	(0.274)	(0.276)	(0.250)
TrumpOnlyTreatment		−0.062	−0.032	−0.062
		(0.237)	(0.237)	(0.219)
Trump+FoxNewsTreatment		−0.150	−0.124	−0.178
		(0.251)	(0.251)	(0.235)
ObamaTreatment		−0.144	−0.114	−0.153
		(0.252)	(0.252)	(0.234)
Conservative × TrumpOnlyTreatment		0.836*	0.816*	0.851*
		(0.371)	(0.370)	(0.342)
Conservative × Trump+FoxNewsTreatment		1.322***	1.285***	1.258***
		(0.385)	(0.383)	(0.353)
Conservative × ObamaTreatment		0.088	0.037	0.179
		(0.385)	(0.385)	(0.357)
N	296	1,255	1,253	1,255
Adjusted R^2	0.090	0.183	0.190	

*$p < .05$; **$p < .01$; ***$p < .001$. Two-tailed tests.
Model 3 includes covariates for age, gender, race, income, and education.
Larger values indicate greater support.
Moderates were included in the analysis but not shown for legibility.

answer on a standard 7-point Likert scale, ranging from "Strongly disagree" (coded 1) to "Strongly agree" (coded 7).

Table 3.4 presents the main results by ideology. To begin, data are again restricted only to respondents who received the *Control*. Consistent with expectations, Model 1 shows that conservatives support waterboarding more than liberals (significant at $p < .01$).[160] As displayed in Figure 3.5a, the predicted level of agreement on the 1–7

---

[160] The linear model is: $Y = a0 + a1(Ideology) + E$.

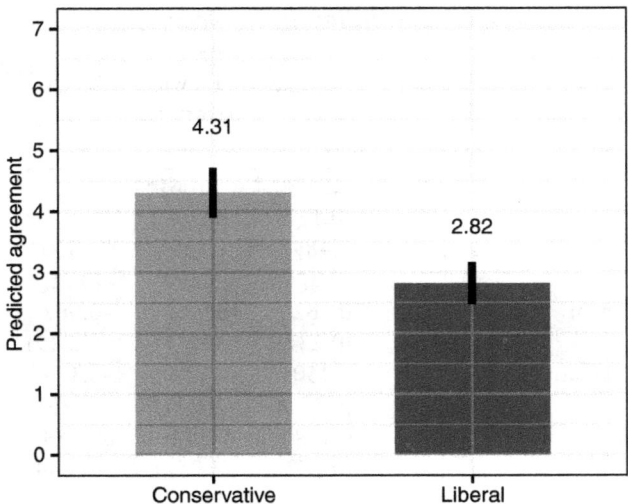

Figure 3.5a Support for use of waterboarding (control), by ideology

Likert scale is 4.31 for conservatives and 2.82 for liberals. Presented next is the fully interactive estimation.[161] Model 2 reports that, relative to the *Control*, receiving the *TrumpOnlyTreatment* raises support for waterboarding among conservatives (significant at $p < .01$), and the *Trump+FoxNewsTreatment* raises it directionally more.

The *ObamaTreatment* is correlated with reduced support for waterboarding among both conservatives and liberals, but again, the effects are not significant. Predicted values are illustrated in Figure 3.5b. Overall, results align with the expectation that conservatives express greater support for waterboarding as a baseline. Trump's advocacy further boosts favorability for this policy. Directionally, conservatives are more apt to support waterboarding when this message is filtered through Fox News.

Figure 3.5c disaggregates the findings by MFT values.[162] As anticipated, in each condition, support for waterboarding is positively

---

[161] The linear model is: $Y = a1(Ideology) + a2(TrumpOnlyTreatment) + a3(TrumpOnlyTreatment \times Ideology) + a4(Trump+FoxNewsTreatment) + a5(Trump+FoxNewsTreatment \times Ideology) + a6(ObamaTreatment) + a7(ObamaTreatment \times Ideology) + E$.

[162] The linear model is: $Y = a0 + a1(Treatment) + a2(In\text{-}group\ loyalty) + a3(In\text{-}group\ loyalty \times ServicememberTreatment) + a4(Authority) + a5(Authority$

3.2 Survey of Attitudes toward War Crimes

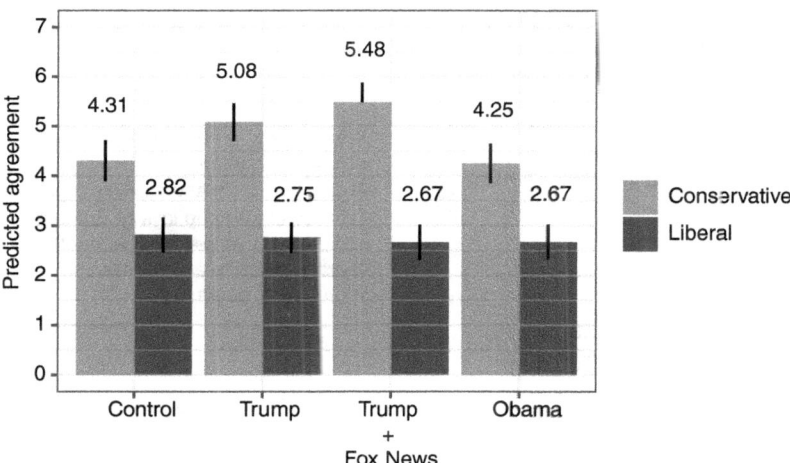

Figure 3.5b Support for use of waterboarding, by ideology

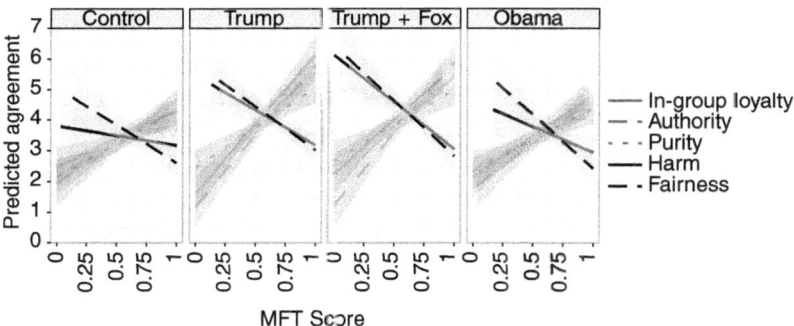

Figure 3.5c Support for use of waterboarding, by MFT values

linked to the conservative values of in-group loyalty, authority, and purity. By comparison, it is negatively linked to the liberal values of harm and fairness (full results presented in Appendix Table 3.A.5). To see more clearly the activation effects of the impunity coalition, Figure 3.5d shows the impact of receiving the *Trump+FoxNewsTreatment* on support for waterboarding relative

X Treatment) + a6(Purity) + a7(Purity X Treatment) + a8(Harm) + a9(Harm X Treatment) + a10(Fairness) + a11(Fairness X Treatment) + E, where Treatment denotes which of the four treatments (including Control) the respondent was shown.

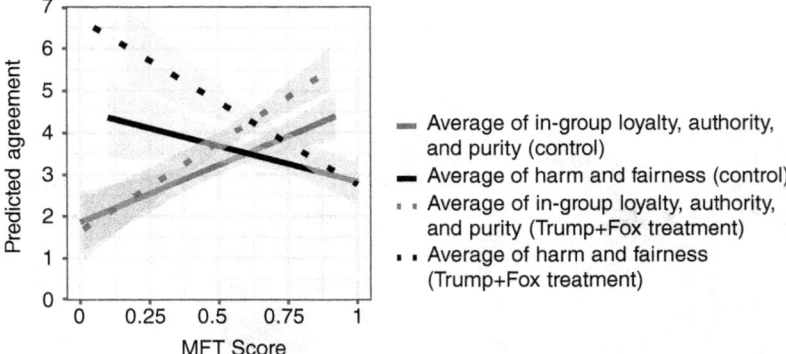

Figure 3.5d Support for use of waterboarding (Trump + Fox News treatment vs. control), combining MFT values

to the *Control*, by MFT values.[163] For readability, the three conservative and two liberal MFT values are averaged out, respectively. The graph illustrates that the more respondents prioritize conservative MFT values, the more their support for waterboarding is increased by seeing the *Trump+FoxNewsTreatment*. Conversely, the more that respondents prioritize liberal MFT values, the less this impact. The implication is that higher conservative support for waterboarding tracks MFT values of in-group loyalty, authority, and purity. Respondents who score higher on these associated values are more activated by impunity cues.

Follow-up, free-response questions also asked respondents to explain why they answered the waterboarding question how they did. Recurring themes implicated key conservative MFT values, which were coded and categorized in Table 3.5. Answers broadly included believing that waterboarding is acceptable because it protects fellow Americans (in-group loyalty), deferring to Trump's judgment about waterboarding (authority), and feeling that waterboarding is justified when it promotes a morally upright cause (purity). Although many of the strongest responses came from

---

[163] The linear model is: $Y = a0 + a1(ConservativeMFTValues) + a2(LiberalMFTValues) + a3(Trump+FoxNewsTreatment) + a4(ConservativeMFTValues \times Trump+FoxNewsTreatment) + a5(LiberalMFTValues \times Trump+FoxNewsTreatment) + E$.

Table 3.5 Free-response answers to waterboarding question, by MFT values and ideology

MFT value	Quote	Ideology
In-group Loyalty/ Out-group Aversion	"Do everything possible to protect the united states and it citizens."	Conservative
	"There should be no limit on what actions we take to protect the usa and its citizens."	Slightly conservative
	"Our security is far more important than the suffering of an enemy. If that's part of our Nation's path to survival, so be it."	Extremely conservative
	"I believe in America, they're killing our soldiers, and they're plotting against our America, we have to protect our people."	Conservative
	"Because they are not citizens of the USA and they are terrorists that do not follow the laws of God therefore torture is acceptable."	Conservative
	"[I] do not like the procedure as it is tortuous, but [I] will support it if it saves American lives."	Liberal
	"[T]he people we are dealing with act like animals and therefore we need to do the same…"	Moderate, middle of the road
	"I think it's justified at the enemy is evil I think we need to defend our rights and rights of our country."	Slightly Conservative
	"If America is in danger, then whatever is needed to be done!! Should be done. Regardless of the method!"	Extremely liberal
Authority / Anarchy	"… President Truump's point about them beheading POW is very true. In this case waterboarding is almost a compassionate alternative."	Conservative
	"Trump is so right fuck everyone in china iraq killing people its not fucking right make amercan graet again."	Slightly liberal

Table 3.5 (cont.)

MFT value	Quote	Ideology
	"I agree with trump. We have turned into a bunch of pansies. No ine is scared of us."	Moderate, middle of the road
	"I agree with president trump. We need to be tougher on these bad killer people."	Conservative
	"I do agree with what PResident Trump said – terrorists as far as I'm concerned don't deserve respect."	Moderate, middle of the road
	"The President"	Liberal
	"I totally agree with our president. Look what terrorists have done to our country. The caused 9/11."	Extremely conservative
	"I agree with President Trump for the most part … [O]ur country needs to be one step ahead and not afraid of upsetting sensitive people who disagree with these methods."	Moderate, middle of the road
	"… We should go harder like President Trump said. I stand by that."	Conservative
Purity/Impurity	"We need to clean house on terrizime no matter even if we take out children."	Slightly liberal
	"These people are cutting off heads and laughing about it. It's disgusting. Waterboarding is nothing compared to that."	Conservative
	"If waterboarding was the only option to save millions of lives and more to come, then yes, it's perfect.…"	Slightly liberal
	"Captured terrorists terrorized innocent others so we should waterboard and torture them when captured. Tit for tat!"	Liberal

	"War is never pretty. If our enemy is cutting off our soldiers heads then waterboarding is fair."	Conservative
	"… I believe that you should do onto others what that have done onto you. An eye for an eye if you will."	Moderate, middle of the road
	"They chop off our heads snd follow no rules. So we can break some to."	Conservative
	"Sometimes, the ugly necessary things need to be done to achieve justice."	Liberal
	"As a Veteran, I feel that if they can torture, maim and even kill our soldiers or even civiilian citizens, then by any means necessary…"	Moderate, middle of the road
Other / Miscellaneous	"… Personally, with a terrorist, think I'd start with a power drill first. Drill holes in the knee caps for starters."	Moderate, middle of the road
	"I would have chosen 'strongly agree' if you had available the option to consider harsher methods…"	Slightly conservative
	"War is war, 'rules of engagement' are bullshit and for LOSERS!…"	Extremely conservative
	"… [W]e need to force the enemy to talk [their] heads off, then kill them."	Extremely conservative
	"… [W]aterboarding could be considered one of the more benevolent methods when it comes down to it.…"	Conservative
	"All is fair in love and war."	Moderate, middle of the road
	"… If we show [other countries] that we are once again a force to be reckoned with, a lot of their antics would come to an end."	Extremely conservative
	"These folks hate America. They plot to kill Americans. They should be dealt with accordingly."	Conservative
	"… I really don't care what happens to someone that's been captured as a terrorist… [T]hey get what they deserve."	Moderate, middle of the road

self-identified conservatives, several moderate and liberal respondents also unequivocally favored the use of waterboarding as an interrogation technique.

In the miscellaneous category, some respondents displayed not just a willingness to discount IHL, but an eagerness to do so. For example, an ideologically moderate respondent stated, "Personally, with a terrorist, think I'd start with a power drill first. Drill holes in the knee caps for starters." Another respondent, who identified as slightly conservative, felt that the survey options did not go far enough in gauging support for waterboarding, declaring, "I would have chosen 'strongly agree' if you had available the option to consider harsher methods..." One extremely conservative respondent suggested that America should not have any rules at all in combat, pronouncing, "War is war, 'rules of engagement' are bullshit and for LOSERS!..."

Notably, across several of the categories, respondents either explicitly referenced Trump or paraphrased his words about "chop[ping] off heads" in justifying their answers. A conservative respondent, for instance, said that "President Trump's point about them beheading POW is very true" and declared that, by comparison, "waterboarding is almost a compassionate alternative." Another conservative respondent remarked that "people ... cutting off heads and laughing about it" is "disgusting" and that "[w]aterboarding is nothing compared to that." Even a slightly liberal respondent called Trump "so right," saying that it was time to "make amercan graet again" because "iraq killing people ... [is] not fucking right" [sic].

Overall, the evidence presented in this chapter suggests that Trump's motive for openly challenging IHL was to appeal to conservative voters. The foundational moral values that conservatives prioritize – in-group loyalty, authority, and purity – tend to make them less supportive of the law in wart contexts than in domestic criminal justice. Trump's messaging effectively activated and reinforced these values. The findings indicate that many conservatives are open to violating IHL in practice. However, even if Trump's core base abandoned attachments to law and order, conservative support could still have been jeopardized if the military itself pushed back against the impunity agenda. Chapter 4 explores Trump's efforts to secure the military's backing.

Appendix

Table 3.A.1 *Summary statistics for survey respondents*

Category	Mean	St. Dev.	Max	Min
Ideology				
Conservative	0.295	0.456	1	0
Liberal	0.401	0.490	1	0
Moderate, middle of the road	0.304	0.460	1	0
Age Brackets				
18–25	0.131	0.337	1	0
25–34	0.158	0.365	1	0
35–44	0.172	0.378	1	0
45–54	0.168	0.374	1	0
55–64	0.170	0.376	1	0
65 or older	0.201	0.401	1	0
Ethnicity				
White	0.784	0.412	1	0
Nonwhite	0.216	0.412	1	0
Gender				
Male	0.481	0.500	1	0
Female	0.519	0.500	1	0
Education				
Postsecondary education	0.780	0.414	1	0
No postsecondary education	0.220	0.414	1	0
Income				
Less than $25,000	0.223	0.416	1	0
$25,000 to $34,999	0.140	0.347	1	0
$35,000 to $49,999	0.138	0.345	1	0
$50,000 to $74,999	0.191	0.393	1	0
$75,000 to $99,999	0.119	0.324	1	0
$100,000 to $149,999	0.119	0.323	1	0
$150,000 or more	0.070	0.255	1	0

Table 3.A.2 *Support for exoneration from the law, by MFT values*

	OLS (1)	OLS with covariates (2)	Ordered logit (3)
Constant	2.765*** (0.316)	3.014*** (0.361)	
In-group loyalty	0.800 (0.446)	0.908* (0.450)	1.282* (0.591)
Authority	−1.488** (0.535)	−1.394** (0.537)	−2.420*** (0.687)
Purity	−0.708 (0.384)	−0.846* (0.387)	−0.958 (0.494)
Harm	0.258 (0.537)	−0.010 (0.543)	0.149 (0.700)
Fairness	0.531 (0.553)	0.602 (0.559)	0.922 (0.720)
ServicememberTreatment	0.425 (0.459)	0.420 (0.460)	0.325 (0.605)
ServicememberTreatment × In-group loyalty	0.328 (0.633)	0.309 (0.634)	0.083 (0.843)
ServicememberTreatment × Authority	2.776*** (0.736)	2.684*** (0.736)	4.327*** (0.968)
ServicememberTreatment × Purity	1.084 (0.553)	1.102* (0.553)	1.777* (0.731)
ServicememberTreatment × Harm	−0.900 (0.765)	−0.788 (0.765)	−1.115 (1.016)
ServicememberTreatment × Fairness	−2.821*** (0.784)	−2.855*** (0.784)	−4.120*** (1.036)
N	1,177	1,175	1,177
Adjusted R^2	0.097	0.102	

*$p < .05$; **$p < .01$; ***$p < .001$. Two-tailed tests.
Model 2 includes covariates for age, gender, race, income, and education.
Larger values indicate greater support for exoneration.

Table 3.A.3 *Support for using maximum firepower, by MFT values*

	OLS (1)	OLS with covariates (2)	Ordered logit (3)
Constant	4.185*** (0.505)	2.903*** (0.531)	
In-group loyalty	1.035 (0.631)	0.780 (0.616)	1.007 (0.813)
Authority	4.607*** (0.751)	4.195*** (0.734)	6.130*** (0.997)
Purity	0.149 (0.583)	0.412 (0.569)	-0.051 (0.723)
Harm	-2.280** (0.755)	-2.000** (0.740)	-2.486** (0.950)
Fairness	-1.483 (0.791)	-1.107 (0.771)	-1.662 (1.026)
CivilianCasualtiesTreatment	-0.509 (0.684)	0.085 (0.670)	-0.435 (0.831)
SoldierSavedTreatment	-0.008 (0.729)	0.103 (0.709)	0.420 (0.888)
ComboTreatment	0.061 (0.698)	0.447 (0.681)	0.346 (0.835)
CivilianCasualtiesTreatment × In-group loyalty	2.201* (0.943)	2.068* (0.918)	3.137** (1.185)
CivilianCasualtiesTreatment × Authority	-2.027 (1.112)	-2.353* (1.082)	-2.825* (1.420)
CivilianCasualtiesTreatment × Purity	-0.120 (0.826)	-0.053 (0.805)	0.343 (1.018)
CivilianCasualtiesTreatment × Harm	-0.883 (1.126)	-0.980 (1.101)	-1.585 (1.420)
CivilianCasualtiesTreatment × Fairness	-0.103 (1.170)	-0.520 (1.141)	-0.219 (1.476)
SoldierSavedTreatment × In-group loyalty	1.042 (0.953)	0.644 (0.933)	2.086 (1.198)
SoldierSavedTreatment × Authority	-2.203* (1.109)	-1.764 (1.081)	-3.311* (1.414)
SoldierSavedTreatment × Purity	-0.033 (0.867)	-0.177 (0.844)	-0.008 (1.077)
SoldierSavedTreatment × Harm	1.330 (1.128)	0.911 (1.100)	1.158 (1.414)
SoldierSavedTreatment × Fairness	0.510 (1.172)	0.819 (1.142)	0.414 (1.477)
ComboTreatment × In-group loyalty	1.065 (0.930)	0.743 (0.907)	1.625 (1.159)

Table 3.A.3 (cont.)

	OLS (1)	OLS with covariates (2)	Ordered logit (3)
ComboTreatment × Authority	−1.836 (1.079)	−1.707 (1.051)	−2.692 (1.375)
ComboTreatment × Purity	−0.016 (0.813)	−0.050 (0.791)	0.158 (0.986)
ComboTreatment × Harm	1.796 (1.157)	1.295 (1.127)	1.566 (1.419)
ComboTreatment × Fairness	−2.334* (1.168)	−2.194 (1.138)	−2.523 (1.438)
N	1,177	1,175	1,177
Adjusted R²	0.393	0.427	

*$p < .05$; **$p < .01$; ***$p < .001$. Two-tailed tests.
Model 2 includes covariates for age, gender, race, income, and education.
Larger values indicate greater support.

Table 3.A.4 *Support for disregarding the Geneva Conventions, by MFT values*

	OLS (1)	OLS with covariates (2)	Ordered logit (3)
Constant	3.674*** (0.495)	4.331*** (0.531)	
In-group loyalty	0.995 (0.737)	0.998 (0.734)	1.435 (0.817)
Authority	1.025 (0.870)	1.250 (0.866)	2.119* (1.048)
Purity	1.063 (0.689)	0.653 (0.694)	1.053 (0.799)
Harm	−1.548 (0.865)	−1.687 (0.864)	−2.285* (1.010)
Fairness	−1.581 (0.887)	−1.486 (0.887)	−2.190* (1.045)
CivilianCasualtiesTreatment	0.015 (0.724)	0.055 (0.720)	−0.109 (0.817)
DefeatEnemiesTreatment	−0.210 (0.727)	−0.289 (0.723)	−0.163 (0.818)
ComboTreatment	0.517 (0.746)	0.626 (0.741)	0.351 (0.842)
CivilianCasualtiesTreatment × In-group loyalty	0.627 (1.003)	0.447 (0.999)	0.567 (1.128)
CivilianCasualtiesTreatment × Authority	1.372 (1.198)	1.456 (1.192)	1.814 (1.443)
CivilianCasualtiesTreatment × Purity	−0.694 (0.914)	−0.475 (0.913)	−0.695 (1.059)
CivilianCasualtiesTreatment × Harm	−1.288 (1.206)	−1.296 (1.199)	−1.799 (1.400)
CivilianCasualtiesTreatment × Fairness	0.094 (1.222)	−0.056 (1.216)	0.487 (1.425)
DefeatEnemiesTreatment × In-group loyalty	1.034 (1.037)	1.062 (1.031)	0.782 (1.207)
DefeatEnemiesTreatment × Authority	0.038 (1.223)	−0.049 (1.220)	−0.427 (1.453)
DefeatEnemiesTreatment × Purity	0.453 (0.931)	0.733 (0.929)	0.958 (1.072)
DefeatEnemiesTreatment × Harm	0.329 (1.217)	0.423 (1.210)	0.114 (1.393)
DefeatEnemiesTreatment × Fairness	−0.860 (1.243)	−1.003 (1.235)	−0.507 (1.443)

Table 3.A.4 (cont.)

	OLS (1)	OLS with covariates (2)	Ordered logit (3)
ComboTreatment × In-group loyalty	0.902 (1.080)	0.965 (1.074)	1.047 (1.224)
ComboTreatment × Authority	1.276 (1.200)	1.091 (1.193)	2.130 (1.470)
ComboTreatment × Purity	−0.378 (0.943)	−0.143 (0.939)	−0.621 (1.093)
ComboTreatment × Harm	0.063 (1.320)	0.188 (1.312)	0.153 (1.524)
ComboTreatment × Fairness	−2.212 (1.370)	−2.525 (1.361)	−2.734 (1.583)
N	1,177	1,175	1,177
Adjusted R^2	0.205	0.218	

*$p < .05$; **$p < .01$; ***$p < .001$. Two-tailed tests.
Model 2 includes covariates for age, gender, race, income, and education.
Larger values indicate greater support.

Table 3.A.5 Support for use of waterboarding, by MFT values

	OLS (1)	OLS with covariates (2)	Ordered logit (3)
Constant	3.573*** (0.614)	3.782*** (0.652)	0.340 (0.837)
In-group loyalty	0.104 (0.827)	0.069 (0.824)	1.697 (0.993)
Authority	1.413 (1.021)	1.747 (1.019)	1.252 (0.670)
Purity	1.474* (0.726)	1.551* (0.724)	0.524 (1.045)
Harm	0.605 (1.049)	0.736 (1.048)	3.224** (1.066)
Fairness	−3.310** (1.092)	3.190** (1.088)	0.482 (0.816)
TrumpOnlyTreatment	0.278 (0.858)	0.374 (0.854)	1.149 (0.831)
Trump+FoxNewsTreatment	0.927 (0.875)	0.954 (0.871)	0.852 (0.836)
ObamaTreatment	0.755 (0.880)	0.688 (0.876)	2.271 (1.182)
TrumpOnlyTreatment × In-group loyalty	2.634* (1.179)	2.643* (1.171)	1.787 (1.368)
TrumpOnlyTreatment × Authority	1.661 (1.382)	1.386 (1.376)	−1.190 (0.982)
TrumpOnlyTreatment × Purity	−1.315 (1.006)	−1.249 (1.001)	−3.990** (1.436)
TrumpOnlyTreatment × Harm	−3.672* (1.428)	−3.622* (1.418)	1.899 (1.442)
TrumpOnlyTreatment × Fairness	1.857 (1.454)	1.877 (1.444)	0.680 (1.216)
Trump+FoxNewsTreatment × In-group loyalty	1.048 (1.215)	1.095 (1.209)	3.478* (1.413)
Trump+FoxNewsTreatment × Authority	3.541* (1.424)	3.500* (1.414)	−1.252 (1.000)
Trump+FoxNewsTreatment × Purity	−1.623 (1.058)	−1.680 (1.052)	−4.522** (1.468)
Trump+FoxNewsTreatment × Harm	−4.364** (1.478)	−4.354** (1.468)	1.330 (1.508)
Trump+FoxNewsTreatment × Fairness	1.572 (1.554)	1.594 (1.543)	0.787 (1.208)
ObamaTreatment × In-group loyalty	1.214 (1.196)	1.126 (1.191)	

Table 3.A.5 (cont.)

	OLS (1)	OLS with covariates (2)	Ordered logit (3)
ObamaTreatment × Authority	0.962 (1.438)	0.847 (1.430)	0.871 (1.445)
ObamaTreatment × Purity	−0.776 (1.074)	−0.761 (1.069)	−0.563 (1.059)
ObamaTreatment × Harm	−1.595 (1.500)	−1.383 (1.490)	−1.841 (1.515)
ObamaTreatment × Fairness	−0.277 (1.538)	−0.213 (1.528)	0.023 (1.488)
N	1,176	1,174	1,176
Adjusted R^2	0.217	0.228	

*$p < .05$; **$p < .01$; ***$p < .001$. Two-tailed tests.
Model 2 includes covariates for age, gender, race, income, and education.
Larger values indicate greater support.

4 Opportunity

Why has Trump perceived an opportunity to openly test the U.S. military's commitment to international humanitarian law (IHL)? Shortly before Trump issued his November 2019 war crime clemencies, a poll was released showing that only about half of active-duty servicemembers and veterans opposed the acts.[1] Given the U.S. military's intensive focus on combat ethics, it might be puzzling that this percentage was not higher.[2] Strategically, however, ensuring that sizable parts of the military are receptive to the impunity agenda has been vital for Trump. Co-opting militaries for political gain almost always requires either the tacit or explicit consent of insiders.[3] For Trump, creating a

---

[1] Rodman, Lindsay L. May 24, 2019. "Post-9/11 Veterans Have Mixed Feelings About Trump's War Crimes Pardons." *Just Security*. www.justsecurity.org/64256/post-9-11-veterans-have-mixed-feelings-about-trumps-war-crimes-pardons/

[2] Crawford, Neta C. 2013. *Accountability for Killing: Moral Responsibility for Collateral Damage in America's Post-9/11 Wars*. Oxford: Oxford University Press. Cronin, Bruce. 2018. *Bugsplat: The Politics of Collateral Damage in Western Armed Conflicts*. New York: Oxford University Press. Dill, Janina. 2014. *Legitimate Targets? Social Construction, International Law and US Bombing*. Cambridge: Cambridge University Press. Kahl, Colin H. 2007. "In the Crossfire or the Crosshairs? Norms, Civilian Casualties, and U.S. Conduct in Iraq." *International Security* 32(1): 7–46. Tirman, John. 2011. *The Deaths of Others: The Fate of Civilians in America's Wars*. Oxford: Oxford University Press.

[3] Brooks, Risa A. 2009. "Militaries and Political Activity in Democracies." In Nielsen, Suzanne C. and Don M. Snider, eds. *American Civil-Military Relations: The Soldier and the State in a New Era*. Baltimore: Johns Hopkins University Press: 213–238. Brooks, Risa. 2021. "Through the Looking Glass: Trump-Era Civil-Military Relations in Comparative Perspective." *Strategic Studies Quarterly* 15(2): 69–98. Finer, Samuel. 2002. *The Man on Horseback: The Role of the Military in Politics*. New Brunswick, NJ: Transaction Publishers. Geddes, Barbara, Joseph Wright, and Erica Frantz. 2018. *How Dictatorships Work: Power, Personalization, and Collapse*. New York: Cambridge University Press. O'Donnell, Guillermo, Philippe

"civil-military coalition"[4] that would not retaliate has maintained his credibility with the GOP base.

This chapter addresses the puzzle of why Trump has calculated that he could publicly challenge IHL with limited dissent from the U.S. military. Its answer traces to the military's well-known conservative composition. For years, America's military has not only exhibited a strong right-leaning bent. A nontrivial portion of its community has displayed more extremist, right-wing tendencies. When Trump first arrived in office in 2017, this made U.S. servicemembers and veterans appear susceptible to impunity messaging. Even if most combatants subscribe in principle to the importance of IHL, Trump discerned that these commitments could be compromised. This was especially true with Fox News and Republican Congress members supporting his agenda.

This argument challenges the "socialization" narrative that respect for IHL has thoroughly permeated Western militaries.[5] It aligns with new research showing that, although professionalized militaries have developed extensive programs to instill pro-IHL attitudes,[6] variation still exists in how combatants prioritize norms of restraint. Central is how the prevalence of military "subcultures" can contradict, and sometimes overwhelm, official doctrine

---

C. Schmitter, and Laurence Whitehead, eds. 1986. *Transitions from Authoritarian Rule: Comparative Perspectives*. Baltimore: Johns Hopkins University Press. Matanock, Aila M. and Paul Staniland. 2018. "How and Why Armed Groups Participate in Elections." *Perspectives on Politics* 16(3): 710–727. Svolik, Milan W. 2012. *The Politics of Authoritarian Rule*. New York: Cambridge University Press.

[4] Golby, Jim. 2021. "Uncivil-Military Relations: Politicization of the Military in the Trump Era." *Strategic Studies Quarterly* 15(2): 149–174.

[5] Checkel, Jeffrey T. 2017. "Socialization and Violence: Introduction and Framework." *Journal of Peace Research* 54(5): 592–605. Franke, Volker C. 2000. "Duty, Honor, Country: The Social Identity of West Point Cadets." *Armed Forces and Society* 26(2): 175–202. Jenks, Chris. 2020. "The Efficacy of the U.S. Army's Law of War Training Program." Lieber Institute West Point. Stubbins Bates, Elizabeth. 2014. "Towards Effective Military Training in International Humanitarian Law." *International Review of the Red Cross* 96(895–896): 795–816.

[6] International Committee of the Red Cross. 2018. *The Roots of Restraint in War*. Geneva: ICRC. www.icrc.org/en/publication/4352-roots-restraint-war/ McQuinn, Brian, Fiona Terry, Oliver Kaplan, and Francisco Gutiérrez-Sanin. 2021. "Introduction: Promoting Restraint in War." *International Interactions* 47: 795–824.

emphasizing IHL.[7] In the U.S. military, the surfacing of right-wing, "MAGA" factions has yielded subcultures that in some cases elevate allegiance to Trump over other principles. Combined with the military's broader conservative bent, Trump has activated these values to suppress political backlash.

Section 4.1 of this chapter analyzes the role of ideological subcultures in overriding formal doctrines relating to IHL. Section 4.2 turns to why Trump has perceived that Fox News and GOP Congress members could help him to appeal to conservatives and pockets of right-wing extremism in America's military. Section 4.3 documents the rise of far-right subcultures in the military, both before and after Trump's two electoral wins in 2016 and 2024. Finally, Section 4.4 presents a short case study of disproportionate military involvement in the January 6 Capitol riot. Although not a foreign battlefield, the case illustrates how Trump and his allies could lead combatants to discount norms of restraint, even to the point of attacking civilians on American soil.

4.1 Norm Socialization and Ideological Subcultures

Burgeoning literature shows that even professionalized militaries like the U.S. do not guarantee identical attitudes toward IHL.[8] Given their size and complexity, they tend to foster heterogeneous cultures. Research in military sociology, backed by findings in security studies, points to the existence of military "subcultures" that can operate in tandem

---

[7] Bell, Andrew. 2021. "Combatant Socialization and Norms of Restraint: Examining Officer Training at the US Military Academy and Army ROTC." *Journal of Peace Research* 59(2): 180–196. Bell, Andrew M., Thomas Gift, and Jonathan Monten. 2022. "The Moral Foundations of Restraint: Partisanship, Military Training, and Norms of Civilian Protection." *Journal of Peace Research* 59(5): 694–709. Stephens, Dale. 2019. "Roots of Restraint in War: The Capacities and Limits of Law and the Critical Role of Social Agency in Ameliorating Violence in Armed Conflict." *Journal of International Humanitarian Legal Studies* 10(1): 58–75.

[8] Bell, Andrew. 2021. "Combatant Socialization and Norms of Restraint: Examining Officer Training at the US Military Academy and Army ROTC." *Journal of Peace Research* 59(2): 180–196. Bell, Andrew M., Thomas Gift, and Jonathan Monten. 2022. "The Moral Foundations of Restraint: Partisanship, Military Training, and Norms of Civilian protection." *Journal of Peace Research* 59(5): 694–709. Stephens, Dale. 2019. "Roots of Restraint in War: The Capacities and Limits of Law and the Critical Role of Social Agency in Ameliorating Violence in Armed Conflict." *Journal of International Humanitarian Legal Studies* 10(1): 58–75.

with, and often in opposition to, official military doctrine.⁹ In the U.S., research has shown that Republican-leaning combatants are especially likely to devalue IHL.¹⁰ These partisan divides can stem from ideological predispositions, self-selection among recruits, or prevailing norms. Regardless of their origin, when taken to the extreme, they can contribute to right-wing subcultures that show indifference or contempt for IHL.

The potential for partisan "capture" of right-wing subcultures in the U.S. military has created an opportunity for Trump to openly dismiss the law of war while minimizing political fallout. Similar to how they activate other conservative voters, Trump, Fox News, and GOP Congress members have worked within a "division of labor" to court right-leaning servicemembers and veterans. At the top is Trump, willing to push unlike any prior U.S. president in explicitly challenging IHL. Underneath him, Fox News has formulated and vocalized messages suggesting that deference to IHL is more voluntary than imperative. Last, Republican Congress members, especially veterans, have stressed the optionality of strict adherence to IHL.

4.2 The Impunity Coalition's Influence over the Military

Trump

Trump's perception that he could persuade U.S. servicemembers to abandon IHL has likely come first and foremost from a belief in his own popularity with the military. In 2016, for example, Trump declared that he had been "endorsed ... at least conceptually, by the military."¹¹ As

---

[9] Ruffa, Chiara. 2018. *Military Cultures in Peace and Stability Operations: Afghanistan and Lebanon*. Philadelphia: University of Pennsylvania Press. Siebold, Guy L. 2007. "The Essence of Military Group Cohesion." *Armed Forces and Society* 33(2): 286–295. Soeters, Joseph. 2018. "Organizational Cultures in the Military." In Caforio, Giuseppe and Marina Nuciari, eds. *Handbook of the Sociology of the Military*. Cham: Springer International Publishing: 251–272. Soeters, Joseph L., Donna J. Winslow, and Alise Weibull. 2006. "Military Culture." In Caforio, Giuseppe, ed. *Handbook of the Sociology of the Military*. New York: Springer: 237–254.

[10] Bell, Andrew M., Thomas Gift, and Jonathan Monten. 2022. "The Moral Foundations of Restraint: Partisanship, Military Training, and Norms of Civilian Protection." *Journal of Peace Research* 59(5): 694–709.

[11] Engel, Pamela. Oct. 25, 2016. "Trump Says He's 'Been Endorsed Largely, At Least Conceptually, By the Military.'" *Insider*. www.businessinsider.com/trump-endorsed-by-military-2016-10

4.2 The Impunity Coalition's Influence over Military

president, Trump claimed that the "soldiers are in love with me."[12] Exit polling from 2016 showed that active-duty servicemembers and veterans voted for Trump over Hillary Clinton at a rate of nearly two to one.[13] Although this support declined over his first term, Trump still won the majority of military votes over Joe Biden in 2020.[14] A 2019 Pew poll found that more than 90 percent of Republican-leaning veterans approved of Trump as commander-in-chief.[15] In 2024, Trump won 65 percent of the military vote over Kamala Harris.[16]

In addition to rank-and-file support, Trump has received endorsements from several high-profile veterans groups. In 2016, for instance, nearly ninety retired military leaders, including four four-star generals, published an open letter praising Trump's candidacy.[17] In 2020, 235 retired senior military officers, including eight four-star generals and admirals and a Medal of Honor recipient, also published an open letter endorsing Trump.[18] In 2021, 124 retired admirals and generals, who dubbed themselves "Flag Officers 4 America," signed a letter endorsing Trump's baseless stolen election claims.[19] Even if

---

[12] Naughtie, Andrew. Sept. 8, 2020. "Trump Claims 'Soldiers Are in Love with Me' after Reports He Called Dead Troops 'Suckers.'" *Independent*. www.independent.co.uk/news/world/americas/us-politics/donald-trump-soldiers-love-me-military-scandal-atlantic-b413754.html

[13] "Election 2016: Exit Polls." *New York Times*. www.nytimes.com/interactive/2016/11/08/us/politics/election-exit-polls.html

[14] "National Exit Polls: How Different Groups Voted." *New York Times*. www.nytimes.com/interactive/2020/11/03/us/elections/exit-polls-president.html

[15] Pew. July 10, 2019. "Trump Draws Stronger Support from Veterans than from the Public on Leadership of U.S. Military." Pew Research Center. www.pewresearch.org/social-trends/2019/07/10/trump-draws-stronger-support-from-veterans-than-from-the-public-on-leadership-of-u-s-military/

[16] Guskin, Emily, Chris Alcantara, and Janice Kai Chen. Dec. 2, 2024. "Exit Polls from the 2024 Presidential Election." *Washington Post*. www.washingtonpost.com/elections/interactive/2024/exit-polls-2024-election/

[17] Haberman, Maggie. Sept. 6, 2016. "Donald Trump Is Endorsed by Nearly 90 Military Figures." *New York Times*. www.nytimes.com/2016/09/07/us/politics/donald-trump-earns-backing-of-nearly-90-military-figures.html

[18] Sisk, Richard. Sept. 15, 2020. "Dozens of Retired Generals, Admirals Sign Letter Backing Trump for Reelection." *Military.com*. www.military.com/daily-news/2020/09/15/dozens-of-retired-generals-admirals-sign-letter-backing-trump-reelection.html

[19] 2021. "Open Letter from Retired Generals and Admirals." https://img1.wsimg.com/blobby/go/fb7c7bd8-097d-4e2f-8f12-3442d151b57d/downloads/2021%20Open%20Letter%20from%20Retired%20Generals%20and%20Adm.pdf?ver=1620740665549

not representative, such support has enabled Trump to suggest that the impunity agenda is not outside the bounds of what many top military leaders want.

Trump has curried favor with what he called "my military"[20] by presenting its members as a core extension of his base. For example, shortly after his 2016 victory, Trump gave a speech at an Air Force base in Florida where he declared. "We had a wonderful election, didn't we? I saw those numbers, and you liked me and I liked you. That's the way it worked."[21] In 2018, after autographing MAGA hats for U.S. servicemembers during his first visit to Iraq as president, Trump was described by one retired major general as enjoying "a rock star kind of a status" among troops.[22] As an example of how he used his pro-military image to win voters, Trump's campaign in 2020 promised supporters who joined "the Trump Army" a camouflage "Keep America Great" hat.[23]

Trump's courting of the military, often in apparent violation of civil-military norms, has advanced both his appeal and the impunity agenda. For example, one journalist noted that "Trump's comments suggested that he saw service members as another constituency: Like factory workers, farmers and coal miners, they seemed to be cast as an interest group to be wooed."[24] Another analyst referred to Trump's "pander[ing] to excessively violent military personnel."[25] Ret. Air Force Major General Steven J. Lepper said that Trump "spent much of his time lavishing praise on the military, hailing himself as its savior, or pandering to it." By "treating the military … as his friend,"

[20] Abadi, Mark. Oct. 25, 2017. "Trump Won't Stop Saying 'My Generals' – and the Military Community Isn't Happy." *Business Insider*. www.businessinsider.com/trump-my-generals-my-military-2017-10
[21] https://twitter.com/cspan/status/828681692466515968?lang=en
[22] Cohen, Zachary. Dec. 18, 2018. "MAGA hat, Campaign Rhetoric Cast Cloud over Trump Iraq Visit." *CNN*. www.cnn.com/2018/12/27/politics/trump-political-war-zone-visit-iraq/index.html
[23] Grady, Constance. Oct. 1, 2020. "The Bizarrely Aggressive Rhetoric of Trump's Fundraising Emails, Explained." *Vox*. www.vox.com/culture/21440412/trump-emails-campaign-fundraising-rhetoric-explained
[24] Gordon, Micahel R. Feb. 17, 2017. "Trump's Mix of Politics and Military Is Faulted." *New York Times*. www.nytimes.com/2017/02/07/us/politics/trump-macdill-air-base.html
[25] Stevenson, Jonathan. June 4, 2020. "Trump Was Wrong to Deploy Troops. Will the Military Push Back?" *IISS*. www.iiss.org/sv/online-analysis/online-analysis/2020/06/trump-military-troops/

4.2 The Impunity Coalition's Influence over Military

he continued, it seemed to "explain why he pardoned three accused American war criminals."[26]

Trump's confidence in U.S. military support has likely been bolstered by the fact that he had elsewhere broken military norms with few consequences. For example, in 2015, Trump criticized Sen. John McCain, held as a prisoner in Vietnam, by declaring, "I like people who weren't captured."[27] In 2016, he pronounced, "I know more about ISIS than the Generals do."[28] That same year, Trump also lashed out at the parents of a Gold Star Muslim soldier who had died in Iraq.[29] In 2020, Trump reputedly referred to dead U.S. servicemembers as "suckers" and "losers" (although his staff denied this allegation).[30] An article in *Foreign Policy* claimed that "Trump has mocked the military his whole life."[31] Despite such behavior, Trump maintained high favorability among military voters.

Trump's ability to escape major backlash from the military with such statements has conceivably emboldened him to think that he could do the same in dismissing IHL. For example, in referencing some of Trump's most polemical comments, military expert Mark Perry wrote that "[t]he military noted … insults and repaid Trump in kind by overwhelmingly voting for him in the 2016 election."[32]

---

[26] Lepper, Steven J. June 5, 2020. "Retired General: 'I Must Speak Out' on Trump and the Military." *The Hill*. https://thehill.com/opinion/whitehouse/501300-retired-general-i-must-speak-out-on-trump-and-the-military/

[27] Schrecklnger, Ben. July 18, 2015. "Trump Attacks McCain: 'I Like People Who Weren't Captured.'" *POLITICO*. www.politico.com/story/2015/07/trump-attacks-mccain-i-like-people-who-werent-captured-120317

[28] Britzky, Haley. Jan. 5, 2019. "Everything Trump Says He Knows 'More About Than Anybody.'" *Axios*. www.axios.com/2019/01/05/everything-trump-says-he-knows-more-about-than-anybody

[29] Haberman, Maggie and Richard A. Oppel, Jr. July 30, 2015. "Donald Trump Criticizes Muslim Family of Slain U.S. Soldier, Drawing Ire." *New York Times*. www.nytimes.com/2016/07/31/us/politics/donald-trump-khizr-khan-wife-ghazala.html

[30] Goldberg, Jeffrey. Sept. 3, 2020. "Trump: Americans Who Died in War Are 'Losers' and 'Suckers.'" *Atlantic*. www.theatlantic.com/politics/archive/2020/09/trump-americans-who-died-at-war-are-losers-and-suckers/615997/

[31] Hirsch, Michael. Sept. 8, 2020. "Trump Has Mocked the U.S. Military His Whole Life." *Foreign Policy*. https://foreignpolicy.com/2020/09/08/trump-mocked-us-military-troops-losers-whole-life/

[32] Perry, Mark. June 8, 2020. "Why the U.S. Military Still Loves Donald Trump." *National Interest*. https://nationalinterest.org/feature/why-us-military-still-loves-donald-trump-161786

Trump's apparent trust in his military support closely mirrored the confidence that he displayed in his notoriously loyal civilian base, such as his remark that he "could stand in the middle of Fifth Avenue and shoot somebody ... and ... [not] lose any voters."[33] It also reflected Trump's "Teflon" reputation for scandals not sticking to him like they did with other politicians.[34]

Trump's overt attacks on IHL are not the only case where he has expected the U.S. military to follow orders on demand, regardless of whether they broke standard protocol. For example, in 2017, Trump reportedly asked for a "Red Square/North Korea-style parade" for his inauguration, replete with tanks, missile launchers, and jets flying over the U.S. Capitol and New York City.[35] In 2018, Trump also proposed hosting a "North Korea-style" parade to celebrate Veterans Day.[36] In describing his relationship to military subordinates, one expert said that Trump tried to "assert ownership over the armed forces."[37] Another writer noted that "Trump ... s[aw] the military as his personal plaything, little toy soldiers to move around on the map of America."[38]

Fox News

Fox News's reputation for courting a military audience also likely signaled to Trump that he could leverage the network to openly challenge

---

[33] Flores, Reena. Jan. 23, 2016. "Donald Trump: I Could 'Shoot Somebody and I Wouldn't Lose Any Voters.'" *CBS News*. www.cbsnews.com/news/donald-trump-i-could-shoot-somebody-and-i-wouldnt-lose-any-voters/

[34] Wren, Adam, Natalie Allison, Meridith McGraw, and Lisa Kashinsky. May 28, 2023. "Many GOP Insiders Fear that Teflon Don Is Back." *POLITICO*. www.politico.com/news/2023/05/28/trump-desantis-republican-2024-presidential-nominee-00099092

[35] Sanchez, Chris. Jan. 19, 2017. "The Military Reportedly Turned Down a Suggestion from Trump's Team for Tanks and Missile Launchers at the Inaugural Parade." *Insider*. www.businessinsider.com/trump-inauguration-parade-tanks-missile-launchers-2017-1

[36] Arkin. Feb. 7, 2018. "Trump's Desired Military Parade: Analysts Blast Plan as 'North Korea-Style' Event." *NBC News*. www.nbcnews.com/news/us-news/trump-s-desired-military-parade-analysts-blast-plan-north-korea-n845626

[37] Britzky, Haley. Nov. 20, 2018. "All the Times Trump Has Snubbed the Military." *Axios*. www.axios.com/2018/11/20/donald-trump-rhetoric-military-soldiers-armed-forces

[38] Ward, Alex. June 3, 2020. "The President Is a Danger to the US Military." *Vox*. www.vox.com/2020/6/3/21279391/george-floyd-protests-military-donald-trump-mattis

4.2 The Impunity Coalition's Influence over Military 135

the law of war. For Trump, Fox News has not only provided a mouthpiece through which to reach the military community. U.S. servicemembers and veterans almost uniformly regard it as pro-military. Even before Trump's presidency, Fox News had been the main media station shown on the Armed Forces Network, which broadcasts to military bases. It had a clear record of promoting pro-American, nationalist values. One journalist, for example, referred to Fox News as "patriotic" and "pugilistic" due to its stars-and-stripes programming.[39] Another called Fox News one of "the military's biggest cheerleaders."[40]

Timing-wise, Trump's initial ascent to the White House in 2016 occurred after Fox News's 2014 hiring of Pete Hegseth,[41] and just before the departure of moderates like military analyst Ralph Peters, who accused Fox News of being a "propaganda machine for a destructive and ethically ruinous [Trump] administration."[42] It also occurred as Fox News began to feature more outspoken military veterans. This included former Navy SEAL Rob O'Neill, known for killing Osama bin Laden, who declared on Fox News that "a commander in chief ... can do anything he wants."[43] It also included former U.S. Army Ranger Mat Best, who on Fox Nation blasted "political elitists sitting in some progressive ivory tower ... [who] if they heard a gunshot from afar, they'd be triggered."[44]

These and similar far-right voices on Fox News have provided Trump with reliable partners in broadcasting the impunity agenda.

---

[39] Folkenflik, David. Apr. 2, 2003. "Fox News Defends Its 'Patriotic' Coverage." *Baltimore Sun*. www.baltimoresun.com/news/bs-xpm-2003-04-02-0304020026-story.html

[40] Ponce De Leon, Charles L. May 23, 2015. "'Perilously Close to Propaganda': How Fox News Shilled for Iraq War, and Jon Stewart Returned Sanity." *Salon*. www.salon.com/2015/05/23/perilously_close_to_propaganda_how_fox_news_shilled_for_iraq_war_and_jon_stewart_returned_sanity/

[41] Stelter, Brian. Nov. 13, 2024. "How Pete Hegseth Went from Fox News Host to Trump's Defense Secretary Pick." *CNN*. www.cnn.com/2024/11/13/media/pete-hegseth-fox-news-trump-defense-secretary/index.html

[42] Wells, Emily. Mar. 21, 2018. "Fox Commentator Leaves Network, Calling it 'Propaganda Machine.'" *TD*. www.truthdig.com/articles/fox-commentator-leaves-network-calling-it-propaganda-machine/

[43] Nov. 26, 2019. "Rob O'Neill on President Trump's Decision to Intervene in Navy SEAL Eddie Gallagher's Case." *Fox News*. https://video.foxnews.com/v/6109272473001

[44] Nov. 12, 2019. "Mat Best Calls Out 'Political Elitists' Handling the Military Justice System." *Fox Nation*. www.youtube.com/watch?v=A7HJrFgwLo

For example, one analyst noted that "[f]or those who watch Fox News, the notion that the laws of war are inherently unfair and unnecessarily hinder our service members overseas will, most likely, seem acceptable."[45] Another analysis referred to Fox News anchors as "All the SEAL's Men," saying that their incessantly positive coverage of Eddie Gallagher made him "untouchable" to conservatives.[46] One account described the network's staunchly pro-Trump stance as sending a clear signal: "If you violate the laws of war, the commander-in-chief may well bail you out – especially if your case wins the sympathy of Fox News."[47]

Fox News's ubiquity on military bases has offered an indispensable medium for Trump to promote the impunity agenda. According to political scientist Tom Nichols, for example, Fox News remains the "default channel" in public military spaces.[48] Journalism professor Helen Benedict has likewise described "Fox News ... [as] the most popular TV channel on military bases."[49] Anecdotally, one source reported that "Fox News is always blaring in common spaces during duty hours" and that "[f]ar from always being a service member's choice ... everyone is subjected to it like it or not."[50] A recent schedule for the Armed Forces Network displayed Fox News running for eight out of twenty-four hours on a weekday, including programs like "The Five," "Jesse Watters Primetime," and "Hannity."[51]

[45] Rodman, Lindsay L. May 24, 2019. "Post-9/11 Veterans Have Mixed Feelings About Trump's War Crimes Pardons." *Just Security*. www.justsecurity.org/64256/post-9-11-veterans-have-mixed-feelings-about-trumps-war-crimes-pardons/

[46] Dyer, Andrew. Nov. 29, 2019. "All the SEAL's Men. The Fox News Campaign That Made Eddie Gallagher Untouchable." *San Diego Tribune*. www.sandiegouniontribune.com/news/military/story/2019-11-29/all-the-seals-men-the-fox-news-campaign-that-made-eddie-gallagher-untouchable

[47] Ford, Matt. May 8, 2019. "The Fox & Friends Pardon for War Crimes." *The New Republic*. https://newrepublic.com/article/153849/fox-and-friends-pardon-war-crimes

[48] Nichols, Tom. July 11, 2022. "Should the Military Censor Fox?" *Atlantic*. https://newsletters.theatlantic.com/peacefield/62cc57fc30d04800225a9f49/fox-news-censorship-us-military/

[49] Benedict, Helen. 2009. *The Lonely Soldier the Private War of Women Serving in Iraq*. Boston: Beacon Press.

[50] Lofgren, Mike and Jen Senko. Feb. 10, 2022. "It's Time the Pentagon Pulled the Plug on Fox News." *Common Dreams*. www.commondreams.org/views/2022/02/10/its-time-pentagon-pulled-plug-fox-news

[51] https://v3.myafn.dodmedia.osd.mil/

4.2 The Impunity Coalition's Influence over Military

Fox News's reach on military installations became so significant during Trump's first term that it inspired attempts to remove its content. For instance, in 2019, the Army & Air Force Exchange Service called for replacing TV news altogether on military bases because of its divisiveness.[52] After Trump left office in 2021, the progressive organization VoteVets launched a campaign to bar Fox News from military bases, accusing it of waging "information warfare that divides the troops, hurts unit cohesion, ... and threatens our national security."[53] Democrat Rep. Eric Swalwell of California suggested that Fox News should be banned on military bases.[54] The Lincoln Project, a group of anti-Trump Republicans, also circulated a petition with the hashtag "#BanFoxonBase."[55]

Although efforts to remove Fox News from military bases have largely been pegged to misleading 2020 election coverage,[56] criticism goes beyond these concerns. Several commentators have complained that Fox News undercuts proper conduct on the battlefield. According to one Navy officer, for example, "The values of Fox News are not aligned with those of the United States military, and undermine good order and discipline among the ranks."[57] Other experts have argued that because "[o]ur military leaders have a duty to maintain good

---

[52] Mervosh, Sarah. Apr. 13, 2019. "Retailer on Military Bases Says TV News Is Too 'Divisive.' Its Suggestion? Tune to Sports." *New York Times*. www.nytimes.com/2019/04/13/us/military-exchange-tv-news-sports.html

[53] Mastrangelo, Dominick. Mar. 7, 2023. "Veterans Group: Ban Fox News on Military Bases." *The Hill*. https://thehill.com/homenews/media/3887680-veterans-group-ban-fox-news-on-military-bases/#:~:text=A%20progressive%20veterans%20group%20has,coverage%20of%20the%202020%20election.

[54] https://twitter.com/RNCResearch/status/1634608324518748161?ref_src=twsrc%5Etfw%7Ctwcamp%5Etweetembed%7Ctwterm%5E1634608324518748161%7Ctwgr%5Ebc0ddb3bfd31274a66d9ee7869560117c13ff594%7Ctwcon%5Es1_&ref_url=https%3A%2F%2Fwww.dailywire.com%2Fnews%2Feric-swalwell-doesnt-want-to-dictate-what-channels-the-military-can-watch-unless-they-like-fox-news

[55] https://action.lincolnproject.us/_banfoxonbase

[56] Lapan, David. Oct. 4, 2022. "Why the US Military Should Ban Cable News Programs across its Bases." *Task and Purpose*. https://taskandpurpose.com/opinion/cable-news-on-military-bases/

[57] Spocchia, Gino. Mar. 11, 2021. "Calls for Fox News to be Turned Off on Military Bases after Tucker Carlson Attack on Women Soldiers." *Independent*. www.independent.co.uk/news/world/americas/us-politics/tucker-carlson-women-soldiers-fox-news-b1815996.html

order and discipline in the ranks … [a]llowing Fox News to blast into every barracks, orderly room, and enlisted club makes no more sense than allowing Radio Moscow to propagandize new recruits during the cold war."[58]

Fox News's pro-military slant has also enabled Trump to push the impunity agenda in civilian settings. For example, interviews with the wives of U.S. servicemembers pleading for clemencies have presented the impunity agenda as representing the plights of everyday military families.[59] Such efforts likely gain even more traction when aired alongside other military-themed programming. For instance, the network's franchise series "Proud American" expressly recognizes heroism in the armed forces.[60] Fox News's offer of a free year of paid subscription to "Fox Nation" for all active-duty U.S. combatants and retirees is another part of its military outreach.[61] Fox News maintains an entire webpage on "Military Families," which includes more than seventy stories from 2020 alone.[62]

GOP Allies on Capitol Hill

Trump's perception that GOP Congress members could shield the impunity agenda from military criticism has likely been bolstered by the fact that many of his allies on Capitol Hill are former veterans. For Trump, who never served in uniform (he received a medical deferment),[63]

---

[58] Lofgren, Mike and Jen Senko. Feb. 10, 2022. "It's Time the Pentagon Pulled the Plug on Fox News." *Common Dreams*. www.commondreams.org/views/2022/02/10/its-time-pentagon-pulled-plug-fox-news

[59] Aug. 24, 2019. "Wife of Major Mathew Golsteyn Gives Us an Update on the Case and His Pending Murder Charges." *Fox News*. www.foxnews.com/video/6076584965001

[60] O'Brien, Corney. May 26, 2021. "FOX News Media Donating $40,000 to Veteran and Military-focused Nonprofits for Proud American Series." *Fox News*. www.foxnews.com/media/fox-news-media-40000-military-focused-nonprofits-proud-american

[61] https://try.nation.foxnews.com/military/?cmpid=org=NAT::ag=inhouse::mc=CPC::src=google::cmp=brand&utm_source=CPC&utm_medium=google&utm_campaign=military&gclid=CjwKCAjwxr2iBhBJEiwAdXECw46gbaiOzlUgR3r5K7WK8Bwq8h46ErFBRF28n-RCgZCAM9zhtTzoJRoCFU0QAvD_BwE&gclsrc=aw.ds

[62] www.foxnews.com/category/us/military/military-families

[63] Rutenberg, Amy J. Jan. 2, 2019. "What Trump's Draft Deferments Reveal." *Atlantic*. www.theatlantic.com/ideas/archive/2019/01/trumps-military-draft-deferment-isnt-unusual/579265/

4.2 The Impunity Coalition's Influence over Military

such support has not only added to the impunity agenda's perceived credibility. Lawmakers have also been able to speak firsthand to the priorities of rank-and-file U.S. servicemembers. This includes playing to concerns that Pentagon bureaucrats make American troops vulnerable to prosecution. Shortly after Trump's inauguration, for example, Congressional Justice for Warriors Caucus (CJWC) co-founder Rep. Duncan Hunter wrote an opinion piece citing that less than a third of U.S. servicemembers felt that their leaders acted in their best interests.[64]

Republican Congress members who had pushed for war crime clemencies even before Trump first took office in 2017 gave a preview of what the impunity agenda would become. As early as 2015, for example, Reps. Duncan Hunter and Ryan Zinke of Montana, a former Navy SEAL, wrote a letter to the Obama administration demanding a review of Clint Lorance's verdict. The request, coinciding with a petition garnering more than 100,000 signatures, urged the White House "to tell the military … that when we send our young sons and daughters into harm's way, we do not turn against them." The effort made headlines in the *Army Times*,[65] *Washington Post*,[66] and *New York Times*,[67] giving Trump proof of the political traction that challenges to the military justice system could gain.

When Trump first entered office, the most strident voices challenging the U.S. military justice system on Capitol Hill were both ex-combatants and MAGA allies. This included CJWC co-chair Duncan Hunter, who served as an officer in the U.S. Marines with deployments to Iraq and Afghanistan. It also included CJWC co-chair Rep. Louie Gohmert, who worked as a defense lawyer in the U.S. Army JAG corps at Fort Benning in Georgia. Alongside the CJWC leaders were

---

[64] Hunter, Duncan. Apr. 14, 2017. "Average Soldiers Don't Trust Their Generals and They Have a Point." *Daily Beast*. www.thedailybeast.com/average-soldiers-dont-trust-their-generals-and-they-have-a-point

[65] Tan, Michelle. Jan. 14, 2015. "Congressmen to Army: Review LT's Murder Conviction." *Army Times*. www.armytimes.com/news/your-army/2015/01/14/congressmen-to-army-review-lt-s-murder-conviction/

[66] Shapiro, T. Ree. Jan. 31, 2015. "Lawyers Seek to Exonerate Ex-Army Officer Who Ordered Soldiers to Shoot Afghan Men." *Washington Post*. www.washingtonpost.com/world/national-security/lawyers-seek-to-exonerate-ex-army-officer-who-ordered-soliders-to-shoot-afghan-men/2015/01/31/396c25ec-a085-11e4-b146-577832eafcb4_story.html

[67] Philipps, Dave. Feb. 24, 2015. "Cause Célèbre, Scorned by Troops." *New York Times*. www.nytimes.com/2015/02/25/us/jailed-ex-army-officer-has-support-but-not-from-his-platoon.html

some of Trump's most firebrand, "ultra-MAGA" defenders generally. Among them were Rep. Dan Crenshaw of Texas, a former Navy SEAL who lost his right eye from an improvised explosive device (IED) in Afghanistan, and Rep. Brian Mast of Florida, who had both of his legs amputated after stepping on an IED in Afghanistan.[68]

CJWC members have regularly spotlighted their own military backgrounds to defend the impunity agenda. For instance, in a 2019 video posted to Sean Hannity's website, Louie Gohmert pointed to his time as "a former judge advocate general corps member" who "handled ... no telling how many court martials" to explain what inspired him to found the CJWC.[69] In an exchange with Pete Hegseth on Fox News, Rep. Michael Waltz of Florida said that he understood the clemency defense that "[w]ar is messy" and filled with "snap decisions of shoot or no shoot" because he himself "had to make those own decisions ... in combat." Affirming his service, Hegseth replied, "Congressman, very well said from someone who understands it and has been there himself."[70]

Duncan Hunter, in particular, routinely appealed to his own combat service to excuse illegal behavior on the battlefield. For example, in downplaying criminal charges against Eddie Gallagher, he declared, "A lot of us have done the exact same thing ... Eddie did one bad thing that I'm guilty of, too."[71] According to a reporter, Hunter insisted "that defending fellow veterans [wa]s at the very core of why he got into politics."[72] Speaking on the Zero Blog 30 podcast, Hunter

[68] Norman, Greg. Mar. 21, 2019. "Texas Rep. Dan Crenshaw Fighting for Fellow Navy SEAL Being Held on War Crimes Charges." *Fox News*. www.foxnews.com/us/eddie-gallagher-case-house-republicans-call-on-navy-leadership-to-review-treatment-of-seal-being-held-on-war-crimes-charges

[69] Staff. Oct. 18, 2019. "JUSTICE FOR WARRIORS: The Congressional Justice for Warriors Caucus Calls for the Release of a Wrongly Convicted Soldier." Hannity. https://hannity.com/media-room/justice-for-warriors-the-congressional-justice-for-warriors-caucus-calls-for-the-release-of-a-wrongly-convicted-soldier/

[70] Nov. 17, 2019. "Rep. Michael Waltz: President Trump Did the Right Thing by Pardoning Clint Lorance." Rep. Michael Waltz. www.youtube.com/watch?v=IXmKv1yo2Ng&t=112s

[71] Sisk, Richard. May 30, 2019. "Marine Vet Lawmaker Responds to Battlefield Photo Controversy." *Military.com*. www.military.com/daily-news/2019/05/30/marine-vet-lawmaker-responds-battlefield-photo-controversy.html

[72] Reston, Maeve. June 6, 2019. "Duncan Hunter's Defense of Accused Navy SEAL Brings New Scrutiny." *CNN*. www.cnn.com/2019/06/06/politics/duncan-hunter-political-future/index.html

4.2 The Impunity Coalition's Influence over Military 141

expressly said that his primary motivation in running for Congress was to represent the "millions of people ... who had served in Iraq and Afghanistan."[73] Eddie Gallagher's brother, Sean, praised Hunter's "advocacy, based in large part on a shared experience in combat."[74]

Republican Congress members have also leaned into their service in other ways to help both themselves and the impunity agenda. For example, Duncan Hunter used military imagery so aggressively in his campaigning that Marine leadership ordered him to stop using its official "Eagle, Globe, and Anchor" symbol in his electioneering.[75] CJWC members without military experience displayed their commitment by allying with court-martialed troops. For instance, in 2023, Rep. Matt Gaetz of Florida hired convicted war criminal Derrick Miller as a legislative aide. The move prompted headlines like "Matt Gaetz's Legislative Aide Is a Convicted War Criminal Who Murdered an Afghan Civilian and Dumped His Body in a Latrine" (*Insider*).[76] Gaetz's office insisted that Miller "served our country with honor."[77]

Equally critical has been an absence of pushback from other high-profile veteran Congress members in the GOP. This was especially true regarding Trump's war crime clemencies, which occurred after

---

[73] May 28, 2019. "ZBT #170: Interview w/ Rep. Duncan Hunter on Eddie Gallagher's Trial." *Zero Blog Thirty*. www.stitcher.com/show/zero-blog-thirty/episode/zbt-170-interview-w-rep-duncan-hunter-on-eddie-gallaghers-trial-61325806

[74] Dyer, Andrew. Dec. 8, 2019. "As Duncan Hunter Announces Plans to Resign, Supporters Recall a Tireless Supporter of Military, Veterans." *San Diego Tribune*. www.sandiegouniontribune.com/news/politics/story/2019-12-08/as-duncan-hunter-announces-plans-to-resign-supporters-recall-a-tireless-supporter-of-military-veterans

[75] Philipps, Dave. July 19, 2019. "Marine Corps Orders Duncan Hunter to Stop Using Emblem on Political Mailers." *New York Times*. www.nytimes.com/2019/07/19/us/duncan-hunter-marines-emblem.html

[76] Sheth, Sonam and John Haltiwanger. Mar. 30, 2023. "Matt Gaetz's Legislative Aide Is a Convicted War Criminal Who Murdered an Afghan Civilian and Dumped His Body in a Latrine." *Insider*. https://news.yahoo.com/matt-gaetzs-legislative-aide-convicted-185933521.html?guccounter=1&guce_referrer=aHR0cHM6Ly93d3cuZ29vZ2xlL mNvbS8&guce_referrer_sig=AQAAANOrmQpfpZPxhNCAZkQDMo cr01y9viEOItLv0CoQFqTNBHk-6t4YpBh7IuXoTq6ghAMK7L21Wo P8w5azRTbQpIRhCelkDvhixvB_gccNuv0ploCdGoIPlgb2JxEW_mxjt-VGuBh4G5QKgfs6gPzpgdsghfxOV8271X_i4C4MOgl4

[77] Blest, Paul. Mar. 30, 2023. "Matt Gaetz Hired a Real-Life War Criminal to Work In His Congressional Office" *Vice*. www.vice.com/en/article/epvdxw/matt-gaetz-derrick-miller-war-criminal?utm_source=vicenewstwitter

the 2018 death of Sen. John McCain, one of IHL's most lucid defenders.[78] Other Republican legislators, including South Carolina Sen. Lindsey Graham, an Air Force veteran, have seemingly undergone a volte-face on the issue. Following revelations of torture at Abu Ghraib in 2003, for example, Graham proclaimed, "Your goal has to be as an American to ... respect the concepts of the Geneva Convention."[79] By contrast, Graham expressed "some sympathy" for Trump's war crime clemencies because "the president believes that the rules of engagement were not clear, that we put our folks in a bad spot."[80]

4.3 Rise of Far-Right Extremism in the Military

Trump's rises to power in 2017 and again in 2025 both reflect and reinforce a subculture of political extremism within the U.S. military that has been key to carrying out the impunity agenda. Pro-Trump, right-wing servicemembers and veterans have bolstered Trump's calculation that he could inspire a critical, conservative mass of the military to support, or at least not oppose, overt challenges to IHL. Although the Department of Defense (DoD) does not officially collect data on partisanship, survey after survey dating back decades shows that its members lean to the right.[81] Despite more political diversity existing among enlistees than the officer corps,[82] studies still point to the U.S. military as a conservative organization.

---

[78] Senate. Sept. 28, 2006. Congressional Record. https://fas.org/irp/congress/2006_cr/s092806.html

[79] Senator Lindsey Graham, PBS Frontline "The Torture Question." Oct. 18, 2005. www.thirteen.org/programs/frontline/frontline-torture-question/

[80] Bolton, Alexander and Rebecca Kheel. Dec. 3, 2019. "Republicans Raise Concerns over Trump Pardoning Service Members." *The Hill*. https://thehill.com/policy/defense/472910-republicans-raise-concerns-over-trump-pardoning-service-members/

[81] Holsti, Ole. 2001–2002. "Politicization of the United States Military: Crisis or Tempest in a Teapot?" *International Journal* 57(1): 1–18. Liebert, Hugh and James Golby. 2017. "Midlife Crisis? The All-Volunteer Force at 40." *Armed Forces and Society* 43(1): 115–138. Urben, Heidi A. 2021. *Party, Politics, and the Post-9/11 Army*. New York: Cambria Press.

[82] Feaver, Peter D. and Richard H. Kohn, eds. 2001. *Soldiers and Civilians: The Civil-Military Gap and American National Security*. Cambridge, MA: MIT Press. Urben, Heidi A. 2014. "Wearing Politics on Their Sleeves? Levels of Political Activism of Active Duty Army Officers." *Armed Forces and Society* 40(3): 568–591.

4.3 Rise of Far-Right Extremism in the Military

Scholars have referred to this outcome as a partisan "gap" in civil-military relations.[83]

While conservatism does not equate to a far-right ideology, data show that perceptions of partisan divisions have become increasingly acute among the ranks.[84] During Trump's first term, for instance, more than three in four military members polled by the *Military Times* thought that the community was becoming more politically polarized.[85] A wave of independent reports – with titles like "The Violent Far-Right Terrorist Threat to the U.S. Military" (Council on Foreign Relations)[86] and "Right-Wing Extremism in the Military" (International Centre for Counter-Terrorism)[87] – cite a concomitant surge of far-right sympathies in the military after Trump's 2016 election. These movements have been characterized by adherence to fundamentalist, anti-government beliefs.

Indicative of this trend has been the gaining stature of right-wing paramilitary organizations like the Proud Boys and the Oath Keepers, whose ranks comprise disproportionate numbers of current and former military members. Based on estimates, upwards of a quarter of the membership of such groups is now made up of U.S. military veterans, with totals in the populations reaching the tens of thousands.[88] According to a federal prosecutor, the Proud Boys see themselves as "Donald Trump's army" who are willing to "line … up

---

[83] Golby, James T. 2011. "*The Democrat-Military Gap: A Re-Examination of Partisanship and the Profession.*" Chicago: Inter-University Seminar on Armed Forces and Society.

[84] Robinson, Michael A. 2023. *Dangerous Instrument: Political Polarization and US Civil-Military Relations.* Oxford: Oxford University Press.

[85] Shane, Leo III. 2018. "Troops See Rising Political Tension in the Ranks, Poll Shows." *Military Times.* www.militarytimes.com/news/pentagon-congress/2018/10/17/troops-see-rising-political-tension-in-the-ranks-poll-shows/

[86] Ware, Jacob. Jan. 31, 2023. "The Violent Far-Right Terrorist Threat to the U.S. Military." Council on Foreign Relations. www.cfr.org/blog/violent-far-right-terrorist-threat-us-military

[87] van Dongen, Teun, Yannick Veilleux-Lepage, Eviane Leidig, Hanna Rigault Arkhis. 2022. "Right-Wing Extremism in the Military A Typology of the Threat." International Centre for Counter Terrorism. www.icct.nl/sites/default/files/2022-12/Right-wing-extremism-in-the-military-1.pdf

[88] Steinhauer, Jennifer. Sept. 11, 2020. "Veterans Fortify the Ranks of Militias Aligned with Trump's Views." *New York Times.* www.nytimes.com/2020/09/11/us/politics/veterans-trump-protests-militias.html

behind Donald Trump and … commit violence on his behalf."[89] One analysis described the Oath Keepers as a radical-right militia "keen on supporting veterans while preying on their desire to defend the country once again."[90]

It is worth underscoring that extremism within the modern U.S. military is not a new problem.[91] Concerns about white supremacist infiltration, such as Ku Klux Klan membership, were prevalent during the Vietnam War.[92] In the 1980s, the DoD reported multiple instances of military participation in white supremacist groups.[93] In the 1990s, the Oklahoma City bombing, carried out by Timothy McVeigh and Terry Lynn Nichols, showcased the catastrophic damage wrought by two radicalized veterans.[94] After 9/11, the FBI counted "203 individuals with confirmed or claimed military service active in the extremist movement [from 2001 to 2008]."[95] In a 2006 publication, the Southern Poverty Law Center warned that "extremists are once again worming their way into a recruit-starved military."[96]

---

[89] Cheney, Kyle. Apr. 24, 2023. "'Donald Trump's Army': Prosecutors Close Seditious Conspiracy Case against Proud Boys Leaders." *POLITICO*. www.politico.com/news/2023/04/24/proud-boys-trial-closing-00093502

[90] Lawrence, Drew F. and Konstantin Toropin. Dec. 1, 2022. "Convicted Oath Keeper Leader Preyed on Veterans Looking for Meaning After Service." *Military.com*. www.military.com/daily-news/2022/12/01/convicted-oath-keeper-leader-preyed-veterans-looking-meaning-after-service.html

[91] Koehler, Daniel. 2019. "A Threat from Within? Exploring the Link between the Extreme Right and the Military." International Centre for Counter-Terrorism – The Hague.

[92] Gurhman, Hannah. Oct. 6, 2017. "As We Rethink the Vietnam War, We Have to Grapple with Its Racial Implications." *Washington Post*. www.washingtonpost.com/news/made-by-history/wp/2017/10/06/as-we-rethink-the-vietnam-war-we-have-to-grapple-with-its-racial-implications/

[93] Schmidt, William E. Apr. 15, 1986. "Soldiers Said to Attend Klan-Related Activities." *New York Times*. www.nytimes.com/1986/04/15/us/soldiers-said-to-attend-klan-related-activities.html

[94] Talley, Tim. Aug. 10, 1995. "Timothy McVeigh Known as Dedicated Soldier, Solitary Loner." *Associated Press*. https://apnews.com/article/69debb4c262e35ec720f1bb7b30e5522

[95] FBI. 2008. "White Supremacist Recruitment of Military Personnel since 9/11." https://documents.law.yale.edu/sites/default/files/White%20Supremacist%20Recruitment%20of%20Military%20Personnel%20Since%209-11-ocr.pdf

[96] Holthouse, David. Aug. 11, 2006. "Several High-Profile Racist Extremists Serve in the U.S. Military." Southern Poverty Law Center. www.splcenter.org/fighting-hate/intelligence-report/2006/several-high-profile-racist-extremists-serve-us-military

4.3 Rise of Far-Right Extremism in the Military

Still, Trump's record as commander-in-chief has appeared to empower extremism in the military.[97] In the final full year of Trump's first term in office, the FBI launched criminal probes into 143 current and ex-military members, nearly half of whom were connected to extremist behavior.[98] In 2020, the Pentagon recommended both banning servicemember participation in hate groups and revising the UCMJ to address the problem.[99] In 2021, Secretary of Defense Lloyd Austin issued a "stand down" order to counter military extremism.[100] The DoD also initiated a large-scale investigation into extremism.[101] The Center for Strategic and International Studies further found that, from 1994 to 2021, U.S. servicemembers were implicated "in a growing number of domestic terrorist plots and attacks."[102]

Available data, which tend to focus on legally defined criminal activity, likely capture only a fraction of U.S. military sympathies to radical, mostly far-right groups. More passive forms of extremism may not register in official counts, even if they raise the risks for illicit activity both on and off the battlefield. The extent of extremist

---

[97] Bembenek, Christina. Mar. 10, 2021. "Conspiracy Stand Down: How Extremist Theories Like Qanon Threaten the Military and What to Do About It." *War on the Rocks*. https://warontherocks.com/2021/03/conspiracy-stand-down-how-extremist-theories-like-qanon-threaten-the-military-and-what-to-do-about-it/

[98] Schmitt, Eric. Feb. 3, 2021. "Lloyd Austin Ramps up the Fight against Right-wing Extremism within the Military." *New York Times*. www.nytimes.com/2021/02/03/us/lloyd-austin-extremism-military.html

[99] Department of Defense Board on Diversity and Inclusion. 2020. "Recommendations to Improve Racial and Ethnic Diversity and Inclusion in the U.S. Military." https://media.defense.gov/2020/Dec/18/2002554852/-1/-1/0/DOD-DIVERSITY-AND-INCLUSION-FINAL-BOARD-REPORT.PDF

[100] Garamone, Jim. Feb. 3, 2021. "Austin Orders Military Stand Down to Address Challenge of Extremism in the Ranks." US Department of Defense. www.defense.gov/Explore/News/Article/Article/2492530/austin-orders-military-stand-down-to-address-challenge-of-extremism-in-the-ranks/

[101] Department of Defense Office of Inspector General. 2021. "Project Announcement: Evaluation of Department of Defense Efforts to Develop and Implement Policy and Procedures Addressing Ideological Extremism Within the U.S. Armed Forces (Project No. D2021-DEV0PB-0079.000)." www.dodig.mil/reports.html/Article/2472525/project-announcement-evaluation-of-department-of-defense-efforts-to-develop-and/

[102] Jones, Seth G., Catrina Doxsee, Grace Hwang, and Jared Thompson. "The Military, Police, and the Rise of Terrorism in the United States." Center for Strategic & International Studies. www.csis.org/analysis/military-police-and-rise-terrorism-united-states

proclivities is largely unknown due to the lack of a centralized, federal clearinghouse documenting the problem. Democrat Rep. Elissa Slotkin of Michigan, for instance, has acknowledged that data measuring military extremism is "really poor."[103] Mark Pitcavage of the Anti-Defamation League's Center on Extremism has lamented that "[t]he military has never set up the structure to track people who were kicked out for … extremism."[104]

Aggravating these patterns is that right-wing groups have prioritized recruiting military and ex-military members due to their transferable skills. Skills taught in basic training, such as tactical maneuvers, the use of weaponry, leadership, and management of high-stress situations, are prized by paramilitary groups. Political scientist Peter Feaver, for example, has observed that "[r]ight-wing groups targeted military veterans for having the skill sets that they were looking for," quipping "[t]hey weren't recruiting from among the Columbia Journalism School."[105] Former National Security Council member Jeff McCausland has similarly called the "unique training the military offers in weapons, communications and cyber" an "exploitable asset" for hard-right extremists.[106]

Concerns about the U.S. military's extremist problem have increasingly drawn attention. Democrat Rep. Jason Crow of Colorado, for instance, has referred to "the rise of extremism and white supremacy in the ranks" as a "crisis … fueled by President [Donald] Trump."[107] Thomas Kolditz, previously of the U.S. Military Academy, has remarked that among his "bigger concerns" is "a strong Trump following in

---

[103] Cammarata, Sarah. Mar. 24, 2021. "House Lawmakers Voice Concern over How to Address Extremism in the Military without Clear Data." *Stars and Stripes*. www.stripes.com/news/us/house-lawmakers-voice-concern-over-how-to-address-extremism-in-the-military-without-clear-data-1.667135

[104] Satter, Mark. May 13, 2021. "Capitol Insurrection Forces Military's Extremism Problem out of the Shadows." *Roll Call*. www.rollcall.com/2021/05/13/capitol-insurrection-forces-militarys-extremism-problem-out-of-the-shadows/

[105] Valentino-DeVries, Jennifer, Denise Lu, Eleanor Lutz, and Alex Leeds Matthews. Feb. 21, 2021. "A Small Group of Militants' Outsize Role in the Capitol Attack." *New York Times*. www.nytimes.com/interactive/2021/02/21/us/capitol-riot-attack-militants.html

[106] McCausland, Jeff. Mar. 4, 2021. "March 4 Capitol Attack Rumors Highlight Dangers of Far-right Extremism's Military Ties." *NBC Think*. www.nbcnews.com/think/opinion/march-4-capitol-attack-rumors-highlight-dangers-far-right-extremism-ncna1259546

[107] Bender, Bryan. Jan. 11, 2021. "The Military Has a Hate Group Problem. But It Doesn't Know How Bad It's Gotten." *POLITICO*. www.politico.com/news/2021/01/11/military-right-wing-extremism-457861

4.3 Rise of Far-Right Extremism in the Military

the military," noting that, when it comes to January 6 sympathizers, "[w]e're probably talking about thousands across the Department of Defense."[108] In reviewing major extremist incidents within the military since the 1970s, one group of national security experts has called for "future policies, strategies, and bureaucratic structures to counter extremism in the military."[109]

Efforts to crack down on military extremism, however, have been uneven. Intelligence specialist Kristofer Goldsmith, for instance, has criticized the DoD for treating extremists with "kid gloves."[110] Retired personnel, in particular, are often overlooked in lieu of a focus on current combatants.[111] To date, the Department of Veterans Affairs has not devised any permanent initiative aimed at opposing extremism. Among active-duty ranks, keeping extremism at bay is seen as difficult because so much activity occurs at the unit level. For example, the RAND Corporation's Heather Williams has observed that "[u]ltimately, the war to root out extremism is going to be fought in the trenches by individual military commanders and against specific bad apples."[112]

One reason for uneven political will to stop extremism likely stems from internal recruitment incentives. Because the U.S. military relies disproportionately on enlistees from Republican areas,[113]

---

[108] Colvin, Geoff. Jan. 8, 2021. "Retired Brigadier General Says Trump Loyalists in Military Need Rooting Out." *Fortune*. https://fortune.com/2021/01/08/trump-support-military-capitol-coup-attempt/

[109] Askew, Simone, Jack Lowe, Nette Monaus, and Kristin L. Cooper. Apr. 27, 2021. "We've Been Here Before: Learning from the Military's History with White Nationalism." *War on the Rocks*. https://warontherocks.com/2021/04/weve-been-here-before-learning-from-the-militarys-history-with-white-nationalism/

[110] Beynon, Steve and Konstantin Toropin. Nov. 5, 2021. "What Happened to Members of the Military Accused of Storming the Capitol on January 6?" *Military.com*. www.military.com/daily-news/2021/11/05/what-happened-members-of-military-accused-of-storming-capitol-january-6.html

[111] Sonne, Paul, Alex Horton, and Julie Tate. Apr. 20, 2021. "Post-riot Effort to Tackle Extremism in the Military Largely Overlooks Veterans." *Washington Post*. www.washingtonpost.com/national-security/veterans-extremism-capitol-attack/2021/04/19/3597018a-9651-11eb-8e42-3906c09073f9_story.html

[112] Williams, Heather. Feb. 1, 2021. "How to Root Out Extremism in the US Military." *Defense One*. www.defenseone.com/ideas/2021/02/how-root-out-extremism-us-military/171744/

[113] Philipps, Dave and Tim Arango. Jan. 10, 2020. "Who Signs Up to Fight? Makeup of U.S. Recruits Shows Glaring Disparity." *New York Times*. www.nytimes.com/2020/01/10/us/military-enlistment.html

efforts to eradicate extremism may also be seen as alienating a core part of its base. For instance, writer Matthew Kennard has argued that the military's under-recruitment problem dates back at least to the Iraq and Afghanistan wars, when it began lowering standards that allowed "neo-Nazis, gang members, and criminals" into the ranks.[114] According to a 2005 report by the DoD, the military informally maintained a "don't ask, don't tell" policy on extremism, stating, "If individuals can perform satisfactorily, without making their extremist opinions overt, they are likely to be able to compete their contracts."[115]

The military's recruiting challenges became even more pronounced after Trump left power the first time. In 2022, for example, the Army reported falling 15,000 recruits below its 60,000 recruitment target.[116] Due to fitness and other criteria, the fraction of Americans eligible to serve in the military based on age has fallen to below a quarter.[117] Analysis from the Council on Foreign Relations refers to U.S. military under-recruitment as a "crisis."[118] Experts David McCormick and James Cunningham describe the U.S. military's inability to reach targets as symptomatic of a "cultural rot" pervading the institution.[119] The need to replenish the ranks may partially

[114] Kennard, Matt. 2015. *Irregular Army: How the US Military Recruited Neo-Nazis, Gang Members and Criminals to Fight the War on Terror*. New York City: Verso Books. Lavin, Talia. May 17, 2021. "The U.S. Military Has a White Supremacy Problem." *The New Republic*. https://newrepublic.com/article/162400/us-military-white-supremacy-problem

[115] Fantz, Ashley. Mar. 31, 2021. "The Military Has Long Had an Extremism Problem. What Will It Do Now to Finally Solve It?" *CNN*. www.cnn.com/2021/03/31/us/us-military-extremism-invs/index.html

[116] Baldor, Lolita C. Oct. 2, 2022. "Army Misses Recruiting Goal by 15,000 Soldiers." *Army Times*. www.armytimes.com/news/your-army/2022/10/02/army-misses-recruiting-goal-by-15000-soldiers/

[117] Novelly, Thomas. Sept. 28, 2022. "Even More Young Americans Are Unfit to Serve, A New Study Finds. Here's Why." *Military.com*. www.military.com/daily-news/2022/09/28/new-pentagon-study-shows-77-of-young-americans-are-ineligible-military-service.html

[118] Kurilla, Michelle. June 16, 2023. "The President's Inbox Recap: The U.S. Military Recruiting Crisis." Council on Foreign Relations. www.cfr.org/blog/presidents-inbox-recap-us-military-recruiting-crisis

[119] McCormick, David and James Cunningham. Apr. 14, 2023. "The Military Recruitment Crisis Is a Symptom of Cultural Rot." *Wall Street Journal*. www.wsj.com/articles/the-military-recruitment-crisis-is-a-symptom-of-cultural-rot-american-exceptionalism-patriotism-health-c0f69bda

4.3 Rise of Far-Right Extremism in the Military

explain why the Pentagon has, despite pressure, yet to proscribe military membership in hate groups.[120]

Such challenges are only made more difficult by right-wing pushback. When in 2021 the Pentagon announced its inquiry into extremism after January 6, critics cast it as a targeted attack on Republicans. On Fox News, for example, Pete Hegseth warned against a "purge of the Defense Department led by a new and now powerful radical leftist."[121] Fox News's Laura Ingraham criticized an "ideological and un-American purge of the U.S. military."[122] On Fox News, Army veteran Rob Smith complained that the political left has "rush[ed] to define all of their political enemies right now as extremists," adding that "[s]tuff like this will destroy the military."[123] Republican Rep. Mike Rogers of Alabama insisted that extremism "is far from the largest military justice issue."[124]

A growing number of Republicans have cited specific instances of what they refer to as political retaliation. For instance, Pete Hegseth claims that he was prevented from working at Joe Biden's inauguration because of his Christian tattoo that read, "Deus Vult" ("God wills it," in Latin), which became popular with right-wing paramilitary groups involved in the U.S. Capitol storming.[125]

---

[120] Stafford, Kat and James Laporta. Dec. 29, 2021. "Military Still Grappling with Racism and Extremism, Investigation Finds." *PBS*. www.pbs.org/newshour/nation/military-still-grappling-with-racism-and-extremism-investigation-finds

[121] Fox News Staff. May 6, 2021. "Pete Hegseth: Meet Bishop Garrison, the Pentagon's 'Newly Minted MAGA Purge Man.'" *Fox News*. www.foxnews.com/media/pete-hegseth-meet-bishop-garrison-the-pentagons-newly-minted-maga-purge-man

[122] Creitz, Charles. Feb. 5, 2021. "Ingraham: Biden Defense Chief Starting 'Ideological and Un-American Purge of the US Military.'" *Fox News*. www.foxnews.com/media/laura-ingraham-biden-lloyd-austin-60-day-stand-down-extremism

[123] Stabile, Angelica. May 6, 2021. "Rob Smith Blasts Left for 'Woke' Influence on US Military: Will Destroy It 'from The Inside Out.'" *Fox News*. www.foxnews.com/media/rob-smith-blasts-left-for-woke-influence-on-us-military-will-destroy-it-from-the-inside-out

[124] Satter, Mark. May 20, 2021. "Divide over Scope of Military's Extremism Problem Impedes Culture, Policy Changes." *Roll Call*. www.rollcall.com/2021/05/20/divide-over-scope-of-militarys-extremism-problem-impedes-culture-policy-changes/

[125] Davis, Aaron C., Alex Horton, Dan Lamonthe, and Evan Hill. Nov. 16, 2024. "Pentagon Pick Left Guard after Being Reported as Possible 'Insider

Space Force lieutenant Lt. Col. Matthew Lohmeier, author of the book *Irresistible Revolution: Marxism's Goal of Conquest & the Unmaking of the American Military*, claims that he was demoted for criticizing the *New York Times*'s 1619 Project.[126] Many conservatives argue that such alleged maltreatment reflects hostility to Republicans that uses rooting out extremism as a pretense to justify politically motivated bias.

As part of this effort, right-wing personalities have been especially vocal in critiquing the U.S. military as overly "woke." In addition to arguing that "diversity, equity, and inclusion" (DEI) harms the military's lethality,[127] a common narrative is that left-wing activists hurt recruitment by punishing conservative-aligned servicemembers.[128] Following Trump's election in 2024, the White House released plans to create "Warrior Boards," with the intent of weeding out "woke generals" and "DEI hires."[129] Critics have cast the proposal as a loyalty vetting, in which senior military officials could be dismissed if they fail to express favored political positions. One Army lieutenant complained that "[i]t could be very hard to do our job if we have to constantly be making sure we're appeasing someone on a political or partisan level."[130]

It is important to caveat that the U.S. military is a sprawling organization, with approximately 1.3 million Americans currently serving

Threat' Due to Tattoo." *Washington Post*. www.washingtonpost.com/investigations/2024/11/16/pete-hegseth-tattoo-national-guard/

[126] Holmes, Kristen and Barbara Starr. May 17, 2021. "Space Force Commander Fired after Comments Made on Conservative Podcast." *CNN*. https://edition.cnn.com/2021/05/15/politics/space-force-lohmeier-fired-after-comments/index.html

[127] Fein, Jim. July 19, 2024. "DEI Is Distracting Our Military from Its Primary Task." Heritage Foundation. www.heritage.org/defense/commentary/dei-distracting-our-military-its-primary-task

[128] June 4, 2024. "Biden's 'Woke, Social Justice' Policies Causing Military Recruitment Crisis." *Fox News*. www.foxnews.com/video/6354289636112

[129] Salama, Vivian, Nancy A. Youssef, and Lara Seligman. Nov. 12, 2024. "Trump Draft Executive Order Would Create Board to Purge Generals." *Wall Street Journal*. www.wsj.com/politics/national-security/trump-draft-executive-order-would-create-board-to-purge-generals-7ebaa606

[130] Beynon, Steve. Nov. 13, 2024. "'It Could Be Very Hard to Do Our Job': Top Military Officers Brace for Trump's Potential Loyalty Review Boards." *Military.com*. www.military.com/daily-news/2024/11/13/it-could-be-very-hard-do-our-job-top-military-officers-brace-trumps-potential-loyalty-review-boards.html

in uniform and 18 million veterans. As such, its problem of right-wing radicalization, at least to some degree, reflects radicalization within America generally. As scholars Michael Robinson and Kori Schake have remarked, "To the extent that military service – active or prior – poses an extremist threat, we shouldn't expect only the military to solve this problem for us."[131] Still, extremist sympathies within the military appeared to grow during Trump's term in the White House, a trend that shows no signs of slowing in his second act. This helps to explain why Trump, as part of the impunity coalition, believed that he could exploit right-wing support.

4.4 Illustrative Case: Storming of the U.S. Capitol

None of Trump's efforts to tap into the military's right-wing extremism epitomizes his ability to undercut norms of restraint more than the storming of the U.S. Capitol on January 6, 2021. Despite not being a foreign battlefield, the insurrection, which killed five Americans,[132] was notable for the outsized number of military personnel who participated.[133] Rioters with military ties came to dominate a war-like zone. As Steven Sund, the former chief of the U.S. Capitol Police, testified, "[the insurrectionists] came prepared for war.... [w]hat we got was a military-style assault."[134] Journalist Carl Bernstein declared that January 6 proved that Trump was an "American war criminal," insisting that it should prompt Americans to see him as committing crimes "against our people."[135]

---

[131] Robinson, Michael and Kori Schake. Mar. 2, 2021. "The Military's Extremism Problem Is Our Problem." *New York Times*. www.nytimes.com/2021/03/02/opinion/veterans-capitol-attack.html

[132] Healy, Jack. Jan. 11, 2011. "These Are the 5 People Who Died in the Capitol Riot." *New York Times*. www.nytimes.com/2021/01/11/us/who-died-in-capitol-building-attack.html

[133] Pion-Berlin, David, Thomas Bruneau, and Richard B. Goetz, Jr. 2022. "The Trump Self-Coup Attempt: Comparisons and Civil–Military Relations." *Government & Opposition* 58(4): 1–18.

[134] Brown, Matthew. Feb. 23, 2021. "Steven Sund, Former Chief of the U.S. Capitol Police Testifies to Senate about Jan. 6 Riot." *USA Today*. https://eu.usatoday.com/story/news/politics/2021/02/23/live-politics-updates-capitol-riots-under-scrutiny-senate-hearing/4548115001/

[135] July 25, 2021. "Carl Bernstein: Donald Trump Is Our Own American War Criminal." *CNN*. www.youtube.com/watch?v=mYFcJit5Ol8

Pro-Trump, anti-state violence on the homeland is not identical to unauthorized aggression in war. However, it does reveal Trump's potential to shape, or activate, views toward the use of force among a military population. One January 6 rioter, Edward Richmond, had even been found guilty of manslaughter for killing a handcuffed civilian during a 2004 tour of duty in Operation Iraqi Freedom.[136] As with his overt challenge to IHL, Trump had the "means, motive, and opportunity" to incite violence on January 6. Trump gained the means with backing from Fox News and GOP lawmakers. He had the motive to court right-wing parts of the military community. Finally, Trump's delay in calling for the quelling of violence enabled military and other rioters to inflict far more damage than they would have otherwise.

Role of Current and Former Military Members

Although precise numbers vary, some estimates suggest that almost 20 percent of the Capitol rioters had military backgrounds,[137] a rate nearly triple their representation in the national population. Furthermore, nearly 40 percent of the military rioters had links to extremist organizations, a number roughly fourfold that of other January 6 participants.[138] Overall, more than eighty individuals with military ties were arrested across all four major branches of the armed forces. Five rioters were active-duty, with another enrolled in a U.S. Air Force boot camp.[139] Combat service spanned time in Vietnam, Afghanistan, and Iraq. At least one insurrectionist was a Purple Heart

---

[136] Graziosi, Graig. Jan. 22, 2024. "Defendant in Capitol Attack was Previously Convicted of Manslaughter in Iraq." *Independent*. www.independent.co.uk/news/world/americas/crime/capitol-riot-suspect-iraq-manslaughter-b2482885.html

[137] Dreisbach, Tom and Meg Anderson. Jan. 21, 2021. "Nearly 1 in 5 Defendants in Capitol Riot Cases Served in The Military." *NPR*. www.npr.org/2021/01/21/958915267/nearly-one-in-five-defendants-in-capitol-riot-cases-served-in-the-military?utm_term=nprnews&utm_medium=social&utm_campaign=npr&utm_source=twitter.com=twitter.com

[138] Milton, Daniel and Andrew Mines. 2021. "'This Is War': Examining Military Experience Among the Capitol Hill Siege Participants." Program on Extremism – The George Washington University and Combating Terrorism Center at West Point.

[139] Watson, Eleanor and Robert Legare. Dec. 15, 2021. "Over 80 of Those Charged in the January 6 Investigation Have Ties to the Military." *CBS News*. www.cbsnews.com/news/capitol-riot-january-6-military-ties/

4.4 Illustrative Case: Storming of the U.S. Capitol 153

recipient.[140] Collectively, rioters had careers totaling more than three centuries of military experience.[141]

Battlefield actions featured prominently among the insurrectionists on January 6. This included commonly taught maneuvers in the U.S. military, such as the so-called "Ranger File," which creates a human wall to infiltrate targets,[142] as well as "small unit tactics" like military-style hand signals and communications.[143] According to Ret. Admiral James Stavridis, "Many of the commands verbalized by the rioters to each other ('cover down,' 'flank them,' 'do a reconnaissance,' 'we are in') were drawn straight from Army and Marine Corps small tactical maneuver doctrine."[144] Even much of the gear used by the rioters – such as military boots, patches, ballistic goggles, zip ties, body armor, and helmets – appropriated or replicated standard-issue military products.

The deployment of military techniques significantly increased the efficacy of the rioters. Referring to their skills, for example, former FBI agent Michael German stated that "ISIS and al-Qaida would drool over having someone with the training and experience of a U.S. military officer."[145] Katrina Mulligan of the Center for American Progress similarly observed that "[p]art of what was so

---

[140] Sidner, Sara, Anna-Maja Rappard, and Marshall Cohen. Feb. 4, 2021. "Disproportionate Number of Current and Former Military Personnel Arrested in Capitol Attack, CNN Analysis Shows." *CNN*. https://edition.cnn.com/2021/01/31/us/capitol-riot-arrests-active-military-veterans-soh/index.html

[141] Cohen, Marshall. May 28, 2021. "1 in 10 Defendants from US Capitol Insurrection Have Military Ties." *CNN*. https://edition.cnn.com/2021/05/28/politics/capitol-insurrection-veterans/index.html

[142] Biesecker, Michael, Jake Bleiberg, and James LaPorta. Jan. 15, 2021. "Capitol Rioters Included Highly Trained Ex-military and Cops." *Associated Press*. https://apnews.com/article/ex-military-cops-us-capitol-riot-a1cb17201dfddc98291edead5badc257

[143] Herridge, Catherine. Jan. 15, 2021. "Capitol Rioters Communicated Using Military Hand Signals, Law Enforcement Official Says." *CBS News*. www.cbsnews.com/news/capitol-riots-military-hand-signal-communication/

[144] Stavridis, James. Feb. 5, 2021. "The U.S. Military Needs to Fight Extremism in Its Own Ranks. Here's How." *TIME*. https://time.com/5936355/u-s-military-extremists/

[145] Biesecker, Michael, Jake Bleiberg, and James LaPorta. Jan. 15, 2021. "Capitol Rioters Included Highly Trained Ex-military and Cops." *Associated Press*. https://apnews.com/article/ex-military-cops-us-capitol-riot-a1cb17201dfddc98291edead5badc257

horrifying about what happened that day [January 6] is you saw training in action."[146] During a criminal case, a judge opined that former Army Ranger Robert Morss was "willing to use his training or experience to organize with the rioters on January 6 ... thereby making their actions more effective, more forceful and more violent."[147] According to one of the rioters, January 6 was "everything we f------ trained for."[148]

Current and ex-military personnel were also instrumental in organizing January 6. Especially central were right-wing militias like the Proud Boys and Oath Keepers, comprised vastly of members with military ties.[149] For example, Oath Keepers founder and Army veteran Stewart Rhodes, who was sentenced to sixteen years in jail for "seditious conspiracy,"[150] was accused by prosecutors of behaving like "a general surveying his troops on a battlefield."[151] A federal indictment

[146] Budryk, Zack. Feb. 8, 2021. "Vets Defending Capitol Were Taunted by Vets Attacking It: Report." *The Hill*. https://thehill.com/policy/defense/537825-vets-defending-capitol-were-taunted-by-vets-attacking-it-report

[147] Rabinowitz, Hannah. July 21, 2021. "Ex-Army Ranger Weaponized Military Training to Aid Capitol Rioters, Judge Says." *CNN*. https://edition.cnn.com/2021/07/21/politics/robert-morss-army-ranger-capitol-riot/index.html

[148] Putterman, Samnatha. Sept. 23, 2021. "'Everything We Trained For': How the Far-right Oath Keepers Militia Planned for Violence on Jan. 6." *POLITIFACT*. www.politifact.com/article/2021/sep/23/everything-we-trained-how-far-right-oath-keepers-m/

[149] Beckett, Lois. Mar. 20, 2021. "Capitol Attack: More than 60 Proud Boys Used Encrypted Channel to Plan, Indictment Says." *Guardian*. www.theguardian.com/us-news/2021/mar/20/four-proud-boys-leaders-indicted-capitol-riot-donald-trump / Bing, Christopher. June 1, 2021. "Four More Oath Keepers Indicted in Jan. 6 Federal Conspiracy Case: Court Filing." *Reuters*. www.reuters.com/world/us/four-more-oath-keepers-indicted-jan-6-federal-conspiracy-case-court-filing-2021-05-31/ / Cheney, Kyle. Mar. 24, 2021. "New Evidence Suggests 'Alliance' between Oath Keepers, Proud Boys Ahead of Jan. 6." *POLITICO*. www.politico.com/news/2021/03/24/oath-keepers-proud-boys-alliance-capitol-riot-477741

[150] Richer, Alanna Durkin, Lindsay Whitehurts, and Michael Kunzelman. May 25, 2023. "Oath Keepers Founder Stewart Rhodes Sentenced to 18 Years for Seditious Conspiracy in Jan. 6 Attack." *Associated Press*. https://apnews.com/article/stewart-rhodes-oath-keepers-seditious-conspiracy-sentencing-b3ed4556a3dec577539c4181639f666c

[151] Durkin Richer, Alanna and Lindsay Whitehurst. Nov. 7, 2022. "Oath Keepers Leader Denies There Was a Plan for Group to Attack Capitol on Jan. 6." *PBS*. www.pbs.org/newshour/politics/oath-keepers-leader-says-there-was-no-plan-for-group-to-attack-the-capitol-on-jan-6

4.4 Illustrative Case: Storming of the U.S. Capitol

alleged that Rhodes "organised members into military-style units."[152] Active-duty Army officer Capt. Emily Rainey led a busload of Trump supporters to Washington on January 6.[153] Jessica Watkins, a transgender former Army Ranger, recruited insurrectionists for the invasion, who she said needed to be "fighting fit."[154]

Others with military backgrounds defended the storming. For example, Jacob Fracker, an Army National Guardsman who was pictured giving the "middle finger" inside the Capitol, posted on Facebook, "Lol to anyone who's possibly concerned about the picture of me going around ... Sorry I hate freedom? ... Not like I did anything illegal."[155] Thomas Robertson, an Army veteran, bragged on Facebook that "CNN and the Left are just mad because we actually attacked the government who is the problem.... The right IN ONE DAY took the f***** U.S. Capitol."[156] Jason Riddle, a military veteran, celebrated the violence by taking a "selfie" photo inside the Capitol while drinking a glass of stolen wine from the Office of the Senate Parliamentarian.[157]

Many military insurrectionists proudly admitted coming to Washington on January 6 with the explicit intent to wage war against the federal government. For example, Marine Cpl. Micah Coomer, who became the first rioter with military ties to be convicted of criminal activity, pronounced that he was "waiting for the boogaloo," a phrase

---

[152] Sept. 27, 2022. "January 6th Capitol Riot: Who Are the Oath Keepers and Why Are They on Trial?" *BBC*. www.bbc.com/news/world-us-canada-63013702

[153] Fitzsimons, Tim. Jan. 11, 2021. "Army Investigating Officer for Attending Pro-Trump Rally in D.C." *NBC News*. www.nbcnews.com/news/us-news/army-officer-quits-after-organizing-buses-dozens-attend-pro-trump-n1253712

[154] Nov. 16, 2022. "Storming Capitol Was 'Really Stupid,' Oath Keeper Testifies." *CBS*. www.cbsnews.com/texas/news/storming-capitol-was-really-stupid-oath-keeper-testifies/

[155] Rempfer, Kyle and Stephen Losey. Jan. 14, 2021. "Army Guardsman, First Known Service Member, Arrested after Capitol Riot." *Army Times*. www.armytimes.com/news/your-army/2021/01/14/army-guardsman-first-known-service-member-arrested-after-capitol-riot/

[156] Britzky, Haley. Jan. 14, 2021. "National Guard Infantryman Arrested after Taking Selfie Inside the Capitol during Riots." *Task & Purpose*. https://taskandpurpose.com/news/national-guard-army-arrested-capitol-riots/

[157] Voyles Pulver, Dinah, Doug Caruso, Rachel Axon, Katie Wedell, Erin Mansfield, Zshekinah Collier, and Tyreye Morris. Jan. 15., 2021. "Capitol Riot Arrests: See Who's Been Charged across the U.S." *USA Today*. www.usatoday.com/storytelling/capitol-riot-mob-arrests/

meaning "Civil War 2."[158] Ret. Air Force Lt. Colonel Larry Brock said that in preparing for January 6, he "bought ... body armor and a helmet for the civil war that is coming."[159] Retired Navy SEAL Kevin Newbold declared that he was "absolutely not above going to war," claiming he had "[d]one it before."[160] U.S. Army National Guard member Matthew Greene testified that he was "openly expecting a civil war."[161]

Means

Alongside Fox News and GOP Congress members, Trump again served as the political entrepreneur who mobilized military members to violence. After months of making false claims about election rigging, he called on supporters to join his "Save America March," scheduled to coincide with the certification of the 2020 election results. Moments before rioters broke the Capitol's security barrier, Trump pronounced: "We fight like hell, and if you don't fight like hell, you're not going to have a country anymore"; "Republicans are constantly fighting like a boxer with his hands tied behind his back.... [W]e're going to have to fight much harder"; and "[Y]ou'll never take back our country with weakness. You have to show strength."[162] Trump's attorney, Rudolph Giuliani, expressly advocated "trial by combat!"[163]

---

[158] Wentling, Nikki. May 18, 2023. "Marine Who Embraced Boogaloo Beliefs Pleads Guilty in Jan. 6 Case." *Marine Times*. www.marinecorpstimes.com/flashpoints/extremism-disinformation/2023/05/18/marine-who-embraced-boogaloo-beliefs-pleads-guilty-in-jan-6-case/

[159] Lawrence, Drew F. Nov. 16, 2022. "Retired Air Force Lt. Col. Who Wielded Zip Ties on Floor of Congress Found Guilty for Jan. 6 Breach." *Military.com*. www.military.com/daily-news/2022/11/16/retired-air-force-lt-col-who-wielded-zip-ties-floor-of-congress-found-guilty-jan-6-breach.html

[160] Dennis, Justin. Feb. 4, 2021. "'I'm Not Sorry for Being Angry' | Who is Adam Newbold and What Brought Him to the Capitol on Jan. 6?" *Mahoning Matters*. www.mahoningmatters.com/news/local/article262598952.html

[161] Whitehurst, Lindsay. Jan. 24, 2023. "Proud Boys Expecting 'Civil War' before Jan. 6, Witness Says." *Associated Press*. https://apnews.com/article/politics-united-states-government-district-of-columbia-proud-boys-donald-trump-a7e5b9f263868239c06c3826b49bf0c0

[162] Savage, Charlie. Jan. 10, 2021. "Incitement to Riot? What Trump Told Supporters Before Mob Stormed Capitol." *New York Times*. www.nytimes.com/2021/01/10/us/trump-speech-riot.html

[163] Derysh, Igor. "Rudy Giuliani Called for 'Trial by Combat' and Then Chaos Descended on Capitol Hill." *Salon*. www.salon.com/2021/01/06/rudy-giuliani-called-for-trial-by-combat-and-then-chaos-descended-on-capitol-hill/

4.4 Illustrative Case: Storming of the U.S. Capitol 157

Similar to his war crime clemencies, Trump would eventually give a blanket pardon to roughly 15,000 January 6 rioters on the first day of his second term, including defendants charged with committing violence against police.[164] Trump also commuted the sentences of fourteen members of the Proud Boys or the Oath Keepers. The decision capped off a barrage of first-day executive actions that Trump had pledged to carry out in his 2024 campaign. Before his election, for example, Trump promised to "treat those people from Jan. 6 fairly"[165] and insisted that the rioters were victims of a "persecution."[166] Several insurrectionists called on Trump to intervene personally in their cases. This included retired Navy SEAL Adam Newbold who expressed what he called a "cry for clemency."[167]

Both Fox News and Republican allies in Congress helped set the groundwork for January 6. At Fox News, a crucial voice was again Pete Hegseth, who before the riot declared, "The more you suppress it and tell these folks ... [that] it's just conspiracy theories, ... there was not widespread fraud, you're creating a bifurcation in the country."[168] One analysis found that "[a]mong those taking inspiration from Fox News figures ... [were] Ashli Babbitt, the U.S. Air Force veteran who ... was shot and killed while storming the Capitol."[169] Another rioter claimed in court that an acute case of "Foxitis" was to

---

[164] Matza, Max. Jan. 21, 2025. "Proud Boys and Oath Keepers among over 1,500 Capitol Riot Defendants Pardoned by Trump." *BBC*. www.bbc.co.uk/news/articles/c5y7l47xrpko

[165] Wallis, Daniel. Jan. 29, 2022. "Trump Says He Would Pardon Jan. 6 Rioters If He Runs and Wins." *Reuters*. www.reuters.com/world/us/trump-says-he-would-pardon-jan-6-rioters-if-he-runs-wins-2022-01-30/

[166] Palmer, Ewan. Feb. 2, 2022. "Donald Trump Doubles Down on Pardoning Jan. 6 Capitol Rioters, Says Many Not Guilty." *Newsweek*. www.newsweek.com/trump-pardon-jan6-capitol-lindsey-graham-newsmax-1675289

[167] Rector, Kevin and Chris Megerian. Jan. 17, 2021. "Alleged Capitol Rioters Argue Trump Invited Them In. They Want Pardons." *Los Angeles Times*. www.latimes.com/politics/story/2021-01-17/alleged-capitol-rioters-argue-they-were-invited-into-the-building-by-trump-seek-pardons

[168] Folkenflik, David and Tom Dreisbach. Jan. 13, 2021. "After Deadly Capitol Riot, Fox News Stays Silent On Stars' Incendiary Rhetoric." *NPR*. www.npr.org/2021/01/13/955694096/after-deadly-capitol-riot-fox-news-stays-silent-on-stars-incendiary-rhetoric

[169] Folkenflik, David and Tom Dreisbach. Jan. 13, 2021. "After Deadly Capitol Riot, Fox News Stays Silent On Stars' Incendiary Rhetoric." *NPR*. www.npr.org/2021/01/13/955694096/after-deadly-capitol-riot-fox-news-stays-silent-on-stars-incendiary-rhetoric

blame for his partaking in January 6.[170] A *Washington Post* headline read, "The Pro-Trump Media World Peddled the Lies that Fueled the Capitol Mob. Fox News Led the Way."[171]

As the Capitol storming unfolded, Fox News offered a selective framing of the events. For example, after reports of teargas being sprayed in the Capitol Rotunda, anchor Martha MacCallum called the breach a "huge victory for these protesters."[172] In response to an analyst on another news network observing, "We can't stand by idly and see people in uniform … have QAnon patches on," Fox News's Laura Ingraham disparaged the comment as "absolutely poisonous."[173] Later, Fox News then-anchor Tucker Carlson released a three-part series on January 6 entitled "Patriot Purge" where he implied that the insurrection was a "false flag" operation.[174] One writer observed that Fox News's audience was "subjected to a parade of rationalization and whataboutism" surrounding January 6.[175]

Many Republican lawmakers also helped to stoke the violence. For example, Rep. Mo Brooks of Alabama proclaimed, "Today is the day American patriots start taking down names and kicking ass…. Louder! Will you fight for America?"[176] Earlier, Rep. Madison

---

[170] Marcus, Josh. May 11, 2021. "Capitol Rioter Blames 'Foxitis' Addiction to Fox News for 6 January Riot." *Independent*. www.independent.co.uk/news/world/americas/us-politics/anthony-antonio-cnn-capitol-riot-b1845847.html

[171] Sullivan, Margaret. Jan. 7, 2021. "The Pro-Trump Media World Peddled the Lies that Fueled the Capitol Mob. Fox News Led the Way." *Washington Post*. www.washingtonpost.com/lifestyle/media/fox-news-blame-capitol-mob-media/2021/01/07/f15f668a-50ee-11eb-b96e-0e54447b23a1_story.html

[172] Baragona, Justin. Jan. 6, 2021. "Fox News: 'Peaceful' MAGA Mob Storming Capitol is 'Huge Victory.'" *Daily Beast*. www.thedailybeast.com/fox-news-peaceful-maga-mob-storming-capitol-is-huge-victory

[173] Gabbatt, Adam. Feb. 5, 2021. "Fox Lurches Further to the Right to Win Back 'Hard-Edge' Trump Supporters." *Guardian*. www.theguardian.com/media/2021/feb/05/fox-news-lunges-further-right-win-back-hard-edge-trump-supporters

[174] Folkenflik, David and Tom Dreisbach. Nov. 3, 2021. "'Off the Rails': New Tucker Carlson Project for Fox Embraces Conspiracy Theories." *NPR*. www.npr.org/2021/11/03/1051607945/tucker-carlson-fox-news-insurrection-conspiracy-new-show

[175] Allsop, Jon. Jan. 12, 2021. "Fox News and the Real Insurrection." *Columbia Journalism Review*. www.cjr.org/the_media_today/fox_news_trump_insurrection.php

[176] Edmondson, Catie and Luke Broadwater. Jan. 29, 2021. "Before Capitol Riot, Republican Lawmakers Fanned the Flames." *New York Times*. www.nytimes.com/2021/01/11/us/politics/republicans-capitol-riot.html

4.4 Illustrative Case: Storming of the U.S. Capitol

Cawthorn of North Carolina had instructed Republican voters to "lightly threaten" their Congress members, telling them to say, "if you don't start supporting election integrity, I'm coming after you ... everybody's coming after you."[177] Rep. Marjorie Greene Taylor of Georgia insisted she would "go on the attack" to ensure Trump's win and compared January 6 to a "1776 moment."[178] Rep. Paul Gosar of the CJWC declared, "Once we conquer the Hill ... Donald Trump is returned to being the president."[179]

After the riot, several GOP lawmakers refused to condemn the violence. Rep. Mo Brooks, for instance, stated, "I make no apology ... I encourage EVERY citizen to watch my entire rally speech and decide ... what kind of America they want: One based on freedom and liberty or ... Godless dictatorial power."[180] Rep. Matt Gaetz insisted, without evidence, that many of the Capitol rioters were disguised ANTIFA activists.[181] Rep. Paul Gosar pronounced that "in a better society, quislings like the strange sodomy-promoting General Milley would be hung" for being a "traitor" on January 6.[182] CJWC's Rep. Andrew Clyde of Georgia likened January 6 to a "normal tourist visit."[183] In a proposed resolution to honor Capitol

---

[177] Leonard, Ben. Jan. 12, 2021. "Cawthorn Expresses Concern about Election Fraud Claims after Earlier Stoking Them." *POLITICO*. www.politico.com/news/2021/01/12/cawthorn-election-fraud-concerns-458217

[178] Weissert, Will and Brian Slodysko. Jan. 28, 2021. "Rep. Marjorie Taylor Greene Routinely Expressed Support for Executing Democrats in Facebook Posts." *Chicago Tribune*. www.chicagotribune.com/nation-world/ct-nw-marjorie-taylor-greene-facebook-20210128-nlxroc2vkjdc5jl67pmskktlci-story.html

[179] Tolan, Casey, Curt Devine, Drew Griffin, and Scott Bronstein. Jan. 13, 2021. "GOP Lawmakers' Fiery Language under More Scrutiny after Deadly Capitol Riot." *CNN*. www.cnn.com/2021/01/12/politics/gop-lawmakers-fiery-language-under-scrutiny-invs/index.html

[180] Edmondson, Catie and Luke Broadwater. Jan. 29, 2021. "Before Capitol Riot, Republican Lawmakers Fanned the Flames." *New York Times*. www.nytimes.com/2021/01/11/us/politics/republicans-capitol-riot.html

[181] Teo, Armus, Jan. 7, 2021. "Rep. Matt Gaetz and Other GOP Politicians Baselessly Suggest Antifa Is to Blame for Pro-Trump Mob Rioting into Capitol." *Washington Post*. www.washingtonpost.com/nation/2021/01/07/antifa-capitol-gaetz-trump-riot/

[182] Sforza, Lauren. Sept. 25, 2023. "GOP's Gosar Suggests Milley Should be 'Hung' for Jan. 6 Response." *The Hill*. https://thehill.com/homenews/house/4221450-gosar-milley-hung/

[183] Schnell, Mychael. July 28, 2021. "GOP Rep. Clyde Defends 'Normal Tourist Visit' Comparison for Jan. 6." *The Hill*. https://thehill.com/homenews/

police for January 6, CJWC co-chair Rep. Louie Gohmert attempted to expunge references to the insurrection.[184]

Motive

As with his war crime clemencies, an irony of Trump's role in the Capitol storming is that it came even as he billed himself a "law-and-order" president. On January 6, for example, Trump tweeted, "WE are the Party of Law & Order."[185] Later, Trump affirmed, "I always have, and always will, be a champion for the unwavering rule of law ... [and] the heroes of law enforcement."[186] One journalist denounced Trump's words as "full of hypocrisy."[187] Rep. Liz Cheney of Wyoming said that Trump's behavior on January 6 "demonstrated he's at war with the rule of law."[188] Despite criticisms, Trump still garnered support among many members of the U.S. military community by again activating the MFT values of in-group loyalty, authority, and purity.

First, many military personnel who stormed the Capitol expressed their loyalty to Trump's "in-group" patriotism. In a large-scale textual analysis of insurrectionist statements, political scientist Eric Hodges found that "veterans' comments revealed that they believed they were acting patriotically."[189] For example, one former Navy SEAL said

house/565223-gop-rep-defends-description-of-normal-tourist-visit-on-jan-6/#:~:text=Andrew%20Clyde%20(Ga.),select%20committee%20probing%20the%20Jan.
[184] Zapler, Mike, Rachael Bade, Eli Okun, and Garrett Ross. Mar. 17, 2021. "POLITICO Playbook PM: Louie Gohmert tries to memory-hole Jan. 6." *POLITICO.* www.politico.com/newsletters/playbook-pm/2021/03/17/louie-gohmert-tries-to-memory-hole-jan-6-492145
[185] https://twitter.com/realDonaldTrump/status/1346912780700577792
[186] Easley, Jonathan. Feb. 13, 2021. "Trump on Acquittal: MAGA 'Has Only Just Begun.'" *The Hill.* https://thehill.com/homenews/senate/538766-trump-on-acquittal-maga-has-just-begun
[187] https://twitter.com/anacabrera/status/1360824769088794630
[188] Edgerton, Anna. Jan. 2, 2022. "Trump 'Went to War with Rule of Law' in Jan. 6 Riot, Cheney Says." *Bloomberg.* www.bloomberg.com/news/articles/2022-01-02/trump-went-to-war-with-rule-of-law-in-jan-6-riot-cheney-says
[189] Hodges, Eric B. 2021. "'Storming the Castle.' Examining the Motivations of the Veterans Who Participated in the Capitol Riots." *Journal of Veterans Studies* 7(3): 46–59.

approvingly of the siege: "our building, our house."[190] Such feelings were punctuated by the framing of opponents as out-group enemies. For instance, Gabriel Garcia, a retired Army captain, called police trying to prevent the storming "f**king traitors."[191] Retired Navy Lt. Cmdr. Thomas Edward Caldwell allegedly planned to ramp up the violence on January 6 by assembling a sniper team to "go hunting after dark … [for] cockroaches."[192]

A core aspect of in-group loyalty on January 6 was the extremist tie-in to white nationalism, which included the brandishing of Confederate flags and related paraphernalia.[193] Several analyses drew links between rioters with military backgrounds and advocacy for white supremacy. One reporter, for example, observed that "[t]he nation's military has a history of downplaying white nationalism…, but the siege of the Capitol has created a new urgency for dealing with them."[194] According to an expert, "Jan. 6 … exposed the crossover of military personnel to violent extremism and white supremacy."[195] Another writer alleged that "white supremacy … is now front and

---

[190] Biesecker, Michael, Jake Bleiberg, and James LaPorta. Jan. 15, 2021. "Capitol Rioters Included Highly Trained Ex-military and Cops." *Associated Press*. https://apnews.com/article/ex-military-cops-us-capitol-riot-a1cb17201d fddc98291edead5badc257

[191] Sidner, Sara. Anna-Maja Rappard, and Marshall Cohen. Feb. 4, 2021. "Disproportionate Number of Current and Former Military Personnel Arrested in Capitol Attack, CNN Analysis Shows." *CNN*. https://edition.cnn.com/2021/01/31/us/capitol-riot-arrests-active-military-veterans-soh/index.html

[192] Harkins, Gina. Feb. 15, 2021. "Veterans Used Their Military Training to Plot Violence in Capitol Riot, Feds Say." *Military.com*. www.military.com/daily-news/2021/02/15/veterans-used-their-military-training-plot-violence-capitol-riot-feds-say.html

[193] Brasher, Jordan. Jan. 14, 2021. "The Confederate Battle Flag, Which Rioters Flew inside the US Capitol, Has Long Been a Symbol of White Insurrection." *The Conversation*. https://theconversation.com/the-confederate-battle-flag-which-rioters-flew-inside-the-us-capitol-has-long-been-a-symbol-of-white-insurrection-153071

[194] Schmitt, Eric, Jennifer Steinhauer, and Helene Cooper. Jan. 18, 2021. "Pentagon Accelerates Efforts to Root Out Far-Right Extremism in the Ranks." *New York Times*. www.nytimes.com/2021/01/18/us/politics/military-capitol-riot-inauguration.html

[195] Lichtblau, Eric. Jan. 29, 2021. "The Military Said It Wants to Fight White Supremacy. What Is It Waiting for?" *Washington Post*. www.washingtonpost.com/outlook/military-white-supremacy-capitol-riot/2021/01/29/1693f124-61a1-11eb-afbe-9a11a127d146_story.html

center following signs that former military personnel played a role in the deadly attack on the U.S. Capitol."[196]

Evidence also indicates that respect for Trump's authority motivated military rioters. Not unlike troops on a battlefield, many appeared to believe that they were complying with the orders of their commander-in-chief. For example, former Navy officer Jeremey Butler observed, "If you're already suffering from some level of mental health issues and you have your ... commander-in-chief saying, 'Go to the Capitol and take back our democracy' with very strong martial language..., it's obvious to me why they interpreted it that way."[197] Legal scholar Leonard M. Niehoff noted that Trump's words offered "clear instruction" that he wanted rioters to "show strength" and "take the country back."[198] CNN anchor Anderson Cooper called Trump's words on January 6 "marching orders."[199]

Deference to Trump's authority became a common defense among those criminally charged over January 6. One report, for instance, recounted that "[a]s the cases against nearly 200 of the Capitol rioters begin to wind through federal court, many of the defendants blame the commander in chief."[200] A lawyer expressly said that his client, a retired Marine corporal, was "duped" and reacted "to the entreaties of the then commander in chief."[201] In an unprecedented

[196] Bender, Bryan. Jan. 11, 2021. "The Military Has a Hate Group Problem. But It Doesn't Know How Bad It's Gotten." *POLITICO*. www.politico.com/news/2021/01/11/military-right-wing-extremism-457861
[197] Grobe, Anna Mulrine. Feb. 2, 2021. "Military and Vets Stormed Capitol. Should They Get Special Treatment?" *Christian Science Monitor*. www.csmonitor.com/USA/Military/2021/0202/Military-and-vets-stormed-Capitol.-Should-they-get-special-treatment
[198] Helderman, Rosalind S., Spencer S. Hsu, and Rachel Weiner. Jan. 16, 2021. "'Trump Said to Do So': Accounts of Rioters Who Say the President Spurred Them to Rush the Capitol Could Be Pivotal Testimony." *Washington Post*. www.washingtonpost.com/politics/trump-rioters-testimony/2021/01/16/01b3d5c6-575b-11eb-a931-5b162d0d033d_story.html
[199] Jan. 15, 2021. "Anderson Cooper 360 Degrees." *CNN*. www.cnn.com/TRANSCRIPTS/2101/15/acd.01.html
[200] Axon, Rachel and Josh Salman. Feb. 10, 2021. "They Rioted at the Capitol for Trump. Now, Many of Those Arrested Say It's His Fault." *USA Today*. www.usatoday.com/in-depth/news/2021/02/10/trump-blamed-capitol-riot-some-who-were-arrested/4361411001/
[201] Cleveland, Will. Feb. 10, 2021. "Dominic Pezzola Held without Bail on Capitol Riot Charges, Says He Was Duped by Trump." *Democrat & Chronicle*. www.democratandchronicle.com/story/news/2021/02/10/

4.4 Illustrative Case: Storming of the U.S. Capitol

statement, the Joint Chiefs of Staff even circulated a memo to U.S. servicemembers reiterating that Joe Biden, not Trump, would be their next commander-in-chief.[202] A journalist remarked "[t]hat the chiefs ... found it necessary to remind their rank and file of their sworn oath to the country was extraordinary."[203]

Last, an impulse to fight for the ostensible purity of Trump's cause appeared to motivate military rioters. Rioters sought both to ensure what they falsely perceived as the correct 2020 election result and to purge defenders of Joe Biden's victory. Calls conjured up images of military heroes acting as the first line of defense against the "deep state." For example, Army veteran Joseph Biggs pronounced, "It's time for fucking War if they steal this shit."[204] Ethan Nordean, who served as a sailor recruit, declared, "We tried playing nice..., now you will deal with the monster you created. The spirit of 1776 has resurfaced."[205] One writer noted that later efforts to depict January 6 as a "false flag" were designed to "preserve ... the 'real American' *purity* of the participants" [emphasis added].[206]

At the center of the most extreme efforts to cleanse the federal government of supposedly impure actors were adherents of the far-right QAnon conspiracy. Human Rights First, for example, found that at least twenty-five military veterans loyal to QAnon were key to marshaling support for the insurrection.[207] Army intelligence officer Christina Bembenek noted that "QAnon supporters – including ... veterans, and current military members – ... led the mob on Jan. 6."[208] One report indicated that some of the "most elite,

dominic-pezzola-rochester-ny-charged-in-capitol-riot-said-he-was-duped-by-trump/4361809001/
[202] www.jcs.mil/Portals/36/Documents/JCS%20Message%20to%20the%20Joint%20Force%20JAN%2012%2021.pdf
[203] Schmitt, Eric. Jan. 12, 2021. "Military Chiefs Remind Troops of Their Oath After Fallout From Assault on Capitol." *New York Times*. www.nytimes.com/2021/01/12/us/politics/joint-chiefs-capitol-constitution.html
[204] www.justice.gov/usao-dc/case-multi-defendant/file/1377586/download
[205] www.justice.gov/usao-dc/case-multi-defendant/file/1377586/download
[206] Ganz, John. Jan. 6, 2022. "January 6 and the F Word." *The Forum*. www.aapf.org/theforum-january-6-fascism
[207] Human Rights First. 2022. "Digital Soldiers: QAnon Extremists Exploit U.S. Military, Threaten Democracy." https://humanrightsfirst.org/library/digital-soldiers/
[208] Bembenek, Chistina. Mar. 10, 2021. "Conspiracy Stand Down: How Extremist Theories Like QAnon Threaten the Military and What to

lethally trained members of the U.S.military" used secret Facebook groups to spread QAnon theories before the storming.[209] Notably, Jacob Anthony Chansley, the "QAnon shaman" pictured in countless January 6 photos wearing horns, covered in face paint, and draped in fur, was a Navy veteran.[210]

Opportunity

Insurrectionists were presented with an opportunity to do damage at the Capitol. After the storming began, Trump spent 387 minutes refusing to ask rioters to leave. Without his orders, it took the U.S. Army more than four hours to deploy the National Guard. While some have attributed the delay to unclear chains of command, others have speculated about ulterior causes. One possibility, as national security experts Ryan Goodman and Justin Hendrix have written, is that military leaders feared "injecting federal troops that could have been re-missioned by … [Trump] to advance his attempt to hold onto power."[211] Another, more critical interpretation of the military, as journalist Max Boot wrote, is that "Pentagon leaders … did not want to battle a mob that had been mobilized and incited by their commander in chief."[212]

The concern that Trump could have co-opted troops at the Capitol stemmed from conversations he reportedly had with high-level

Do About It." *War on the Rocks*. https://warontherocks.com/2021/03/conspiracy-stand-down-how-extremist-theories-like-qanon-threaten-the-military-and-what-to-do-about-it/

[209] Lee, Carol E. Apr. 16, 2021. "In Secret Facebook Groups, America's Best Warriors Share Racist Jabs, Lies about 2020, Even QAnon Theories." *NBC News*. www.nbcnews.com/news/military/secret-facebook-groups-america-s-best-warriors-share-racist-jabs-n1263985

[210] Ziezulewicz, Geoff. Jan. 11, 2021. "'QAnon Shaman' Charged with Storming the Capitol Is a Navy Veteran." *Navy Times*. www.navytimes.com/news/your-navy/2021/01/12/qanon-shaman-charged-with-storming-the-capitol-is-a-navy-veteran/

[211] Goodman, Ryan and Justin Hendrix. Dec. 21, 2021. "Crisis of Command: The Pentagon, The President, and January 6." *Just Security*. www.justsecurity.org/79623/crisis-of-command-the-pentagon-the-president-and-january-6/

[212] Boot, Max. Mar. 4, 2021. "How Trump's Politicized Pentagon Bungled the Response to the Capitol Invasion." *Washington Post*. www.washingtonpost.com/opinions/2021/03/04/how-trumps-politicized-pentagon-bungled-response-capitol-invasion/

4.4 Illustrative Case: Storming of the U.S. Capitol

advisers about declaring martial law to stop the peaceful transfer of power.[213] Some critics even went so far as to theorize that Trump's goal from the beginning was to create a putsch on January 6 as a pretext for staging a military coup. According to one report, Chairman of the Joint Chiefs Mark Milley allegedly "feared ... Trump's 'Reichstag moment,' in which, like Adolf Hitler in 1933, he would manufacture a crisis in order to swoop in and rescue the nation from it."[214] Enacting such a plan could have entailed Trump invoking the Insurrectionist Act to forcefully put down what he might have labeled a domestic rebellion.[215]

The accusation that Army leaders reacted slowly due to some supporting Trump's efforts to retake power gained traction amid Trump's efforts to root out detractors at the Pentagon after his election loss. In November 2020, Trump terminated Mark Esper as Secretary of Defense and replaced other top DoD personnel with partisan loyalists.[216] This reportedly prompted some remaining officials to plan a "Saturday Night Massacre in reverse," in which they would pledge to resign one by one to ensure that Trump could not execute a coup.[217] Charges of politicization were only amplified with reports that one of the individuals who failed to order the National Guard to the Capitol was the brother of former Trump national security adviser and election-denier Michael Flynn.[218]

---

[213] Goodwin, Jazmin. Dec. 21, 2020. "Trump's Talk of Martial Law Sends White House Staffers Rushing to the Press." *CNN*. www.cnn.com/2020/12/20/media/stelter-trump-martial-law/index.html

[214] Goodman, Ryan and Justin Hendrix. Dec. 21, 2021. "Crisis of Command: The Pentagon, The President, and January 6." *Just Security*. www.justsecurity.org/79623/crisis-of-command-the-pentagon-the-president-and-january-6/

[215] Alschuler, Albert W. Aug. 16, 2022. "Trump and the Insurrection Act: The Legal Framework." *Just Security*. www.justsecurity.org/82696/trump-and-the-insurrection-act-the-true-legal-framework/

[216] Bowman, Tom. Nov. 11, 2020. "Shake-Up At Pentagon Puts Trump Loyalists Into Senior Roles." *NPR*. www.npr.org/2020/11/11/933868828/shake-up-at-pentagon-puts-trump-loyalists-into-senior-roles

[217] Gangel, Jamie, Jeremy Herb, Marshall Cohen, Elizabeth Stuart, and Barbara Starr. July 14, 2021. "'They're Not Going to F**king Succeed': Top Generals Feared Trump Would Attempt a Coup after Election, According to New Book." *CNN*. www.cnn.com/2021/07/14/politics/donald-trump-election-coup-new-book-excerpt/index.html

[218] Liebermann, Oren and Barbara Starr. Jan. 21, 2021. "Army Now Acknowledges the Brother of Michael Flynn Was a Part of Army Response

What led to the military's delayed response on January 6 continues to prompt debate. Trump claimed, falsely, that he requested 10,000 National Guard troops be sent to the Capitol but was denied by House Speaker Nancy Pelosi.[219] Although the Pentagon's inspector general defended the military's reaction, others have been more critical. Most prominently, whistleblower Col. Earl Matthews, who served on Trump's National Security Council, published a thirty-six-page memo in which he accused the Army's rationalization of its actions on January 6 as "worthy of the best Stalinist or North Korea propagandist."[220] Matthews wrote that leaders in the D.C. Guard were ready to respond, but were held back, leaving them "stunned watching in the Armory."[221]

Ultimately, the U.S. Capitol was not a foreign battlefield, and the men and women who rioted on January 6 were not fighting an enemy state or terrorist group. Yet if even a small part of the U.S. military community could be persuaded to attack American civilians at the Capitol, it raises concerns about potential implications for foreign combat. For months, Trump, alongside Fox News and GOP Congress members, urged retaliation over baseless election rigging claims. January 6 reflected Trump empowering right-wing extremists to relinquish prior commitments to norms of restraint. Although exact parallels cannot be drawn to American servicemembers in war, the case suggests Trump's power to change the basic orientation toward the use of force among a military population.

More broadly, this chapter showed that the political advantages of Trump's overt challenges to IHL rested on the receptivity of the U.S. military community. By tapping into the military's conservative,

---

to Capitol Riot." *CNN*. www.cnn.com/2021/01/21/politics/michael-flynn-brother-capitol-hill-riot/index.html#:~:text=Charles%20Flynn%2C%20 the%20brother%20of,violence%20at%20the%20US%20Capitol.

[219] Mazetti, Mark and Maggie Haberman. July 21, 2022. "A Jan. 6 Mystery: Why Did It Take So Long to Deploy the National Guard?" *New York Times*. www.nytimes.com/2022/07/21/us/politics/national-guard-january-6-riot.html

[220] Swan, Betsy Woodruf and Meridith McGraw. Dec. 6, 2021. "'Absolute Liars': Ex-D.C. Guard Official Says Generals Lied to Congress about Jan. 6." *POLITICO*. www.politico.com/news/2021/12/06/jan-6-generals-lied-ex-dc-guard-official-523777

[221] Matthews, Ear G. Dec. 1, 2021. "The Harder Right: An Analysis of a Recent DoD Inspector General Investigation and Other Matters." *POLITICO*. www.politico.com/f/?id=0000017d-8aca-dee4-a5ff-eeda79e90000

4.4 Illustrative Case: Storming of the U.S. Capitol

especially right-wing, elements, Trump was able to preempt pushback and frame his agenda as pro-military. The rise of far-right radicalization among active-duty servicemembers and veterans provided an opportunity that Trump, along with Fox News and GOP lawmakers, exploited. These developments reflected mounting politicization within the ranks, increasing the perceived validity of open attacks on IHL. The result shielded Trump from potential backlash with his GOP base, which might otherwise have been wary of straying from official military principles.

5 Impunity Here to Stay

"For those who have and continue to slander my name, the truth is coming."[1] Those words, uttered by Eddie Gallagher in 2020 after his release from prison, served as a warning shot to critics. In his fight against what he labeled "domestic terrorists"[2] in the U.S. military justice system, Gallagher was defiant. His words were not empty rhetoric. Since receiving clemency from Trump in 2019, the former Navy SEAL has penned a book,[3] founded a nonprofit dedicated to overhauling military prosecutions,[4] and morphed into a right-wing celebrity and martyr.[5] Gallagher is not alone. His work is now mirrored by countless individuals and organizations that, both in Washington and nationally, lobby for the release of jailed U.S. servicemembers.

This chapter explains the persistence of the impunity agenda. It argues that Trump's resurgence in 2024 has already thrust the agenda back to the forefront and that it could even be self-executing after Trump eventually leaves office. Sections 5.1 and 5.2 show how the conservative media space and an emboldened right wing in Congress discourage advocates from backing away from publicly testing IHL. Section 5.3 traces the expanding coalition of the impunity movement, which now not only includes Fox News and Republican lawmakers but also lobbyist organizations and troops granted clemency by Trump. Section 5.4 describes how close-knit professional and social

---

[1] Allassan, Fadel. Jan. 28, 2020. "Eddie Gallagher Attacks Navy SEALs Who Testified against Him." *Axios*. www.axios.com/2020/01/28/navy-seal-eddie-gallagher-attack-video
[2] www.instagram.com/p/B3aozb7gh3l/
[3] Gallagher, Eddie and Andrea Gallagher (with Andy Symonds). 2021. *The Man in the Arena: From Fighting ISIS to Fighting for My Freedom*. Washington, DC: Ballast Books.
[4] https://pipehitterfoundation.org
[5] Levin, Bess. Jan. 2, 2020. Edward Gallagher, "Trump's Favorite War Criminal, Is a 'CONSERVATIVE INFLUENCER' Now." *Vanity Fair*. www.vanityfair.com/news/2020/01/edward-gallagher-navy-seal-influencer

networks amplify the power of the impunity coalition, even more now given Trump's re-ascendance to the White House and Pete Hegseth's selection as Defense Secretary.

5.1 Trends in Conservative Media

Fox News shows little sign of retreating from its aggressive advocacy for the impunity agenda. Even when Trump was out of office, the network's most outspoken advocacy for "Trumpism" continued to come from reliable backers, not least Pete Hegseth prior to his cabinet appointment. Fox News's reluctance to peel away from the impunity agenda in part reflects inertia. Since 2016, Fox News built up anchors and producers who positively covered Trump's military leadership and were influential in steering White House policy. As one analysis observed, "The end of a presidential campaign is often a time for news organizations to take stock and recalibrate their strategies. But [with Fox News] never before had a network been so closely affiliated with a commander-in-chief."[6]

Since his second election, no act has more clearly demonstrated Trump's commitment to Fox News and the impunity agenda than his appointment of Hegseth as Defense Secretary. The pick was not only symbolically important in elevating a Fox News host to lead the Pentagon, formalizing a previously informal relationship. Trump's doing so against considerable pressure, and accusations that Hegseth was unqualified, showed his personal commitment to Hegseth. Shortly after his appointment, allegations emerged accusing Hegseth of sexual misconduct, financial mismanagement, alcoholism, and later, spousal abuse, all of which Hegseth denied.[7] Hegseth also sparked controversy for his previously stated position that women should not fight in front-line combat.[8]

---

[6] Ellison, Sarah and Jeremy Barr. Feb. 2, 2021. "Sean Hannity Is the Face of the Post-Trump Identity Crisis at Fox News." *Washington Post*. www.washingtonpost.com/lifestyle/media/fox-ratings-sean-hannity-cnn-msnbc/2021/02/02/9a604eac-650d-11eb-8c64-9595888caa15_story.html

[7] Mayer, Jane. Dec. 1, 2024. "Pete Hegseth's Secret History." *New Yorker*. www.newyorker.com/news/news-desk/pete-hegseths-secret-history

[8] Baldor, Lolita C. Nov. 18, 2024. "Should Women be Allowed to Fight on the Front Lines? Trump's Defense Pick Reignites the Debate." *Associated Press*. https://apnews.com/article/military-women-defense-hegseth-combat-916d50a7b465ccfea1aeb13bb91064b3

Trump first floated the idea of making Hegseth the Secretary of Defense on "Fox & Friends," with one analysis reporting "pride among Fox hosts that one of their own" had been tapped.[9] Hegseth's appointment now reinforces a direct line of communication between the White House and Fox News. With Hegseth's appointment, Fox News loses an anchor but gains an ally with the direct ear of the commander-in-chief. During Trump's first term, Hegseth, both privately and on air, needed to lobby Trump and work against forces inside the Pentagon anathema to the impunity agenda. Now, Hegseth can take unilateral action against subordinates. Fox News also has an incentive to champion their former anchor and face of the network, which it has consistently done.[10]

In his new role, indications are that Hegseth will continue to prioritize the impunity agenda, alongside Fox News. After Trump lost in 2020, Hegseth continued to make the case on Fox News for standing behind jailed U.S. servicemembers. Notably, just months before his nomination, Hegseth released the book *The War on Warriors: Behind the Betrayal of the Men Who Keep Us Safe*, published in conjunction with Fox News Books.[11] A Fox Nation clip of Hegseth went viral from just before the book's release, where Hegseth decried that "wars keep going ... because we are not doing what we did in Japan [drop a nuclear bomb]." He claimed that, in World War II, the military "had barrel-chested men saying 'we are going to win this war,'" whereas today it has lawyers.[12]

In Trump's second term, Fox News is again poised to advance the impunity agenda through its interactions both with Trump and its conservative audience. One account recently called Trump the channel's "de facto programming executive."[13] Another said that Trump

---

[9] Barr, Jeremy. Dec. 12, 2024. "Fox News and the Blurred Lines of Pete Hegseth." Dec. 12, 2024. www.washingtonpost.com/style/media/2024/12/12/fox-news-pete-hegseth-hannity-trump/
[10] Dec. 5, 2024. "How Fox News Is Defending Pete Hegseth." *WBUR*. www.wbur.org/hereandnow/2024/12/05/hegseth-defense-scrutiny & Stelter, Brian. Dec. 4, 2024. "Fox News Stars Defend Imperiled Ex-colleague Pete Hegseth amid Misconduct Allegations." www.cnn.com/2024/12/04/media/fox-news-pete-hegseth-defend-misconduct-allegations/index.html
[11] Pete, Hegseth, 2024. *The War on Warriors: Behind the Betrayal of The Men Who Keep Us Free*. New York: Broadside and Fox News Books.
[12] https://x.com/DecodingFoxNews/status/1860793202904555872
[13] Jan. 11, 2024. "'A Pathetic Surrender': Why Fox News Just Can't Quit Donald Trump." *Vanity Fair*. www.vanityfair.com/news/

has "commented so frequently on the coverage of his favourite conservative networks," including Fox News, that he has become "a sort of politician-media columnist."[14] After stepping down from Fox News following his appointment as Defense Secretary, Hegseth went on Fox News's "Hannity" to plug his credentials. In the interview, he praised Trump for having a "backbone of steel" and pledged to "clean out all the social justice, politically-correct garbage on top" so that the military could get back to "lethality."[15]

There is also evidence that Pete Hegseth is controlling media access to reduce scrutiny of his leadership at Department of Defense (DoD). Soon after becoming Secretary of Defense, Hegseth instituted a new annual "media rotation program" at the Pentagon.[16] Venues that lost workspace in the building included the *Washington Post*, CNN, the *Hill*, NBC News, National Public Radio, and the *New York Times*. Outlets that gained space were Newsmax, One America News Network (OAN), *Breitbart*, the *New York Post*, *Free Press*, *Daily Caller*, and *HuffPost* – with all but the latter leaning conservative. Fox News kept its existing office space. The Pentagon Press Association, which acts on behalf of journalists who report on the U.S. military, denounced the decision as an "unprecedented move by DoD to single out highly professional media."[17]

In addition to Fox News, new rivalries in conservative media are likely to reinforce the impunity agenda. Competition from the right of Fox News could foster even more extreme echo chambers amplifying overt challenges to IHL. This includes cable outlets Newsmax and OAN. Although the professed goal of these networks is to

donald-trump-fox-news-2024-election?srsltid=AfmBOoqvcVJtjJm9ULm2dSkWs9BMyquO6i10UYdGPYxQAkcKQs2xd1QE

[14] Marcus, Josh. Nov. 11, 2021. "Jim Jordan Says He Would Talk with Trump 'Through Fox News' Despite Ex-president Claiming He Didn't Watch TV." *Independent*. www.independent.co.uk/news/world/americas/jim-jordan-donald-trump-fox-b1956164.html

[15] Dec. 10, 2024. "Hegseth Praises Trump for Standing by Him: 'Backbone of Steel'." *Fox News*. www.youtube.com/watch?v=A2A9i5qqnjs

[16] Stelter, Brian. Feb. 7, 2025. "Pentagon Boots CNN and the Washington Post from Workspace in Favor of Smaller Conservative Outlets." *CNN*. https://edition.cnn.com/2025/02/07/media/pentagon-press-rotation-defense-department/index.html

[17] Stewart, Phil and Idrees Ali. Feb. 1, 2025. "Trump's Pentagon Says It Will 'Rotate' Out Some Media from Offices." *Reuters*. www.reuters.com/world/us/trumps-pentagon-says-it-will-rotate-out-some-media-offices-2025-02-01/

ideologically counterbalance the likes of CNN and MSNBC on the left, it is also to "outfox Fox News."[18] One analysis, for instance, has described a "race unfolding among several conservative outlets who don't think Fox is pro-Trump enough."[19] Another has observed that "[Trump] followers now have multiple options to feed their fix for right-wing opinions – some of them far more extreme than … Fox News."[20]

Like Fox News, Newsmax and OAN have aggressively championed Trump's record as commander-in-chief. A key difference, however, is that these networks have tended to air even more extreme views and to tolerate less dissent. For example, a Newsmax interview with Eddie Gallagher's brother began with the host affirming, "I admit my bias. Your brother to me is an American hero, and frankly, I think … should be given a medal … Why is … [he] enduring this hell?"[21] In another Newsmax interview, a guest blasted military prosecutors for "target[ing]" and "harass[ing]" Gallagher, who he said had "annihilated the government … and exposed their corruption."[22] One Newsmax headline condemned the charges against Gallagher as a "Persecution."[23] Newsmax also hosted Gallagher to promote his book[24] and to champion Pete Hegseth.[25]

[18] Folkenflik, David. Nov. 30, 2020. "Newsmax Rises on Wave of Resentment Toward Media – Especially Fox News." *NPR*. www.npr.org/2020/11/30/939030504/newsmax-rises-on-wave-of-resentment-toward-media-especially-fox-news

[19] Fischer, Sara and Mike Allen. Nov. 17, 2020. "The Race to Out-Fox Fox News." *Axios*. www.axios.com/fox-news-conservative-cable-tv-newsmax-oann-352677fb-b6ae-4500-9dea-588788ab3a99.html

[20] Battaglio, Stephen and Meg Jones. Feb. 18, 2021. "Fox News Tries to Keep Trump Fans Satisfied, but at What Cost?" *Los Angeles Times*. www.latimes.com/entertainment-arts/business/story/2021-02-18/trump-fox-news-conservative-viewers-murdoch-newsmax

[21] Jan. 23, 2019. "The Real Story Behind the Charges against Eddie Gallagher." *Newsmax*. www.youtube.com/watch?v=PmxFMphdC4A

[22] https://twitter.com/newsmax/status/1199019342794543104

[23] Kerik, Bernard. Dec. 3, 2018. "The Persecution of US Navy Special Warfare Operator Eddie Gallagher." *Newsmax*. www.newsmax.com/bernardkerik/us-navy-eddie-gallagher/2018/12/03/id/892926/

[24] Fitzgerald, Sandy. July 3, 2021. "Eddie Gallagher to Newsmax: Book about War Charges 'Therapeutic.'" *Newsmax*. www.newsmax.com/newsmax-tv/gallagher-navy-seals-book/2021/07/03/id/1027356/

[25] Solange, Reyner. Nov. 13, 2024. "Eddie Gallagher to Newsmax: Hegseth 'Great Pick'." *Newsmax*. www.newsmax.com/newsmax-tv/eddie-gallagher-pete-hegseth-military/2024/11/13/id/1187975/

5.1 Trends in Conservative Media

Similar narratives have been featured by OAN voices, who echo Fox News rhetoric. For example, in berating the court-martial of U.S. troops, OAN's Neil McCabe railed against military lawyers wanting the "scalps of the war criminals," which he insisted was "creating a detrimental effect among our trigger pullers."[26] In one segment, Gallagher himself argued that his interactions with military prosecutors were a harbinger of "January 6th individuals ... being mistreated."[27] In another clip, an OAN anchor introduced Gallagher by declaring, "You were a SEAL ... You know exactly what it takes to get the job done."[28] One OAN interview advertised a $100 per ticket "cocktail benefit" in Florida hosted by Gallagher to help military personnel finance their criminal defenses.[29]

As with Fox News, OAN and Newsmax have fostered close interactions with Republican lawmakers. For instance, when Reps. Duncan Hunter and Louie Gohmert established the Congressional Justice for Warriors Caucus (CJWC) in 2019, OAN aired a special feature on the organization. The anchor predicted that "if the Justice for Warriors Caucus is successful, it may soon be a force for enduring freedom."[30] Newsmax has continued to host CJWC members, with highly favorable coverage. This included a 2022 interview with Rep. Ralph Norman of South Carolina to discuss proposed reforms to the Uniform Code of Military Justice (UCMJ). In it, one of the show's hosts, himself a retired Navy SEAL, referred to Eddie Gallagher as "basically the poster child for the military justice system's corruption and failures."[31]

---

[26] Carr, Julie. July 10, 2019. "War on Warriors: The Tennessee Star Report Talks to OANN's Neil McCabe about the Anti-Military Cadre Within the Pentagon." *Tennessee Star.* https://tennesseestar.com/2019/07/10/war-on-warriors-the-tennessee-star-report-talks-to-oanns-neil-mccabe-about-the-anti-military-cadre-within-the-pentagon/

[27] Newsroom. Apr. 13, 2023. "Navy SEAL Hero: My Ordeal Foretold J6 Prisoner, Vax Mandate Nightmares." *OAN.* www.oann.com/video/oan-contribution/navy-seal-hero-my-ordeal-foretold-j6-prisoner-vax-mandate-nightmares/

[28] Oct. 7, 2022. "One America News REAL AMERICA – Dan Ball with Navy Seal Chief Eddie_Gallagher." Pipe Hitter Foundation. www.youtube.com/watch?v=dptV8QUsi1A

[29] Newsroom. Apr. 12. "Eddie Gallagher Touts Ben Darby's Release at Fla. Event." *OAN.* www.oann.com/video/oan-contribution/eddie-gallagher-touts-ben-darbys-release-at-fla-event/

[30] June 28, 2019. "Hunter, Gohmert Team up to Launch 'Justice for Warriors Caucus'." *OAN.* www.youtube.com/watch?v=iHv_ohGZFFU

[31] www.facebook.com/CongressionalJusticeForWarriorsCaucus/

To the extent that right-wing cable outlets like Newsmax and OAN are still seen as too moderate, conservatives can also increasingly access a panoply of far- and "alt-right" websites, blogs, and other platforms that support explicit challenges to IHL. As one journalist has written, "true believers [of Trump] can get their information elsewhere."[32] Right-wing and "new media" websites have become incubators for hardline, pro-Trump content, from QAnon conspiracy theories to the "Big Lie." These mediums have also routinely defended efforts to test IHL. For instance, numerous platforms – such as *Red State*, *TheBlaze*, and *Gateway Pundit* – have endorsed positions that the U.S. military should take a less binding stance in upholding norms of restraint on the battlefield.

The byproduct of this competition is not only that more right-wing media sources exist to push the impunity movement. By threatening to capture Fox News's market share, Newsmax, OAN, and like-minded outlets also impose "market discipline" on Fox News that may disincentivize it from veering from the impunity agenda. Fox News executive Steve Tomsic, for instance, has acknowledged that the network "do[es]n't take lightly the potential for competition, whether it's the existing sort of classic MSNBC or CNN or the sort of emerging ones like Newsmax and OAN."[33] As one reporter has summarized, "Onscreen and off, in ways subtle and overt, Fox News has adapted to the post-Trump era by moving in a single direction: Trumpward."[34]

What is unlikely to change is that right-wing media outlets driving the impunity agenda will continue to have as their audience not just conservative voters but also Trump himself. For example, Republican Rep. Jim Jordan of Ohio said that, during Trump's first term, "every time we were on TV," including Fox News, "we weren't just talking to people in the television audience; we were

---

[32] DiResta, Renee. Nov. 23, 2020. "Right-Wing Social Media Finalizes Its Divorce from Reality." *Atlantic*. www.theatlantic.com/ideas/archive/2020/11/right-wing-social-media-finalizes-its-divorce-reality/617177/

[33] Easley, Jonathan. Dec. 15, 2020. "Fox News Confident in Face of New Rivals from Right in Newsmax, OAN." *The Hill*. https://thehill.com/homenews/media/530178-fox-news-confident-in-face-of-new-rivals-from-right-in-newsmax-oan

[34] Grynbaum, Michael M. May 28, 2021. "Fox News Intensifies Its Pro-Trump Politics as Dissenters Depart." *New York Times*. www.nytimes.com/2021/05/28/business/media/trump-fox-news.html

talking to POTUS."³⁵ This dynamic was underscored when Fox News anchors joked on air that Trump should turn off and on lights at the White House to prove that he was listening. Moments later, the lights appeared to flash on screen. Although Fox News conceded the video was edited, the anecdote reflects the reality of Trump leaning on Fox News as his primary information source.³⁶

5.2 Trends among GOP Allies on Capitol Hill

Even before Trump re-entered office, Republican Congress members had continued to advocate for U.S. troops implicated in war crime cases. Particularly through the CJWC, many have coordinated campaigns involving social media, TV spots, and events, such as a 2022 reception honoring Eddie Gallagher.³⁷ Indicative of the CJWC's resilience is its sustained activity despite both of its original chairmen leaving Congress. In 2020, Rep. Duncan Hunter resigned in the wake of corruption charges related to campaign finance violations.³⁸ In 2022, Louie Gohmert stepped down from his seat in an unsuccessful bid to become Texas attorney general.³⁹ CJWC executive director, Derrick Miller, himself a convicted war criminal,⁴⁰ has remained in his position since 2019.⁴¹

---

35 Crilly, Rob. Nov. 11, 2021. "'We could talk to Trump through Fox News or MSNBC': GOP Rep Jim Jordan says He Didn't Need to Schedule Phone Calls or Meetings with the President and Instead Communicated through News Network Interviews." *Daily Mail*. www.dailymail.co.uk/news/article-10192747/Jim-Jordan-says-didnt-need-calls-meetings-Trump-simply-used-TV-appearances-instead.html

36 Wemple, Erik. Aug. 1, 2022. "'Fox & Friends,' at Its Transparent Best." *Washington Post*. www.washingtonpost.com/opinions/2022/08/01/fox-friends-trump-kilmeade-sycophancy/

37 www.facebook.com/CongressionalJusticeForWarriorsCaucus/

38 Zanona, Melanie. Jan. 7, 2020. 'Rep. Duncan Hunter Resigns from Congress." POLITICO. www.politico.com/news/2020/01/07/rep-duncan-hunter-resigns-from-congress-095725

39 Akin, Stephanie. Mar. 2, 2022. " Gohmert Comes up Short in Bid for Texas Attorney General." *Roll Call*. https://rollcall.com/2022/03/02/gohmert-comes-up-short-in-bid-for-texas-attorney-general/#:~:text=Texas%20Rep.,in%20a%20four-person%20primary.

40 Nava, Victor. Mar. 29, 2023. "Matt Gaetz Staffer was Previously Convicted of a War Crime in Afghanistan." *New York Post*. https://nypost.com/2023/03/29/rep-matt-gaetz-staffer-was-previously-convicted-of-war-crimes/

41 www.linkedin.com/in/derrick-miller-04ba09212/

Alongside other initiatives, the CJWC has continued to petition for the release of U.S. troops held in pretrial confinement and imprisoned for convictions.[42] Republican Congress members have maintained a presence at parole hearings[43] and broadcasted their efforts through public relations channels.[44] CJWC members have also lobbied for concrete reforms before Congress. In 2023, for example, a draft bill of the National Defense Authorization Act included several "Gohmert amendments," named after Rep. Louie Gohmert. One proposed lowering the bar for the U.S. Supreme Court to hear a servicemember's criminal case irrespective of a verdict issued by the Court of Appeals for the Armed Forces. Another proposed requiring unanimous verdicts of guilt in U.S. military courts.[45]

Polarization in Congress, and particularly the rise of Trumpist, far-right legislators, is likely to keep the impunity agenda front and center. One way is simply by reducing the Republican Party to its most polemical manifestations on military issues.[46] With "MAGA" Republicans especially, this could lead to the continued mainstreaming of fringe views, including open attacks on IHL, that would be muted in a more centrist environment. As scholar Stephen Walt has observed, "Once foreign policy begins to oscillate between two increasingly divided factions, each of the groups has an incentive to pursue its most ambitious, controversial, or extreme projects."[47] So long as conservative voters respond positively to impunity appeals, Republican politicians are likely to embrace them.

---

[42] https://twitter.com/JFWCaucus/status/1527372127401574402
[43] Staff. "JUSTICE FOR WARRIORS: The Congressional Justice for Warriors Caucus Calls for the Release of a Wrongly Convicted Soldier." Hannity. https://hannity.com/media-room/justice-for-warriors-the-congressional-justice-for-warriors-caucus-calls-for-the-release-of-a-wrongly-convicted-soldier/
[44] https://twitter.com/RepBrianMast/status/1582785901129740288
[45] https://rules.house.gov/bill/117/hr-7900
[46] Friedrichs, Gordon M. and Jordan Tama. 2022. "Polarization and US Foreign Policy: Key Debates and New Findings." *International Politics* 59: 767–785. Smeltz, Dina, Ivo Daalder, Karl Friedhoff, Craig Kafura, and Brendan Helm. 2020. *Divided We Stand: Democrats and Republicans Diverge on US Foreign Policy*. Chicago: Chicago Council on Global Affairs. Trubowitz, Peter, and Nicole Mellow. 2011. "Foreign Policy, Bipartisanship and the Paradox of Post-September 11 America." *International Politics* 48: 164–187.
[47] Walt, Stephen M. Mar. 11, 2019. "America's Polarization Is a Foreign Policy Problem, Too." *Foreign Policy*. https://foreignpolicy.com/2019/03/11/americas-polarization-is-a-foreign-policy-problem-too/

Self-reinforcing feedback loops may also increase both elite and mass Republican support for the impunity agenda. When Trump or GOP lawmakers promote the impunity agenda, these positions, in turn, may perpetuate a cycle of electorates (and, again, politicians) moving further to the right. For example, many Republican voters have pivoted to support Russia in recent years as a result of Trump's pro-Kremlin rhetoric.[48] Similarly, at the height of the GOP primaries in 2015, which were marked by hawkish rhetoric on the Middle East, one analysis found that nearly a third of Republican voters would support bombing Agrabah, a nonexistent country.[49] Deference to party leaders may push conservative voters to endorse open challenges to IHL, causing GOP politicians to become even more extreme.

Partisan conflict in Congress could also promote the impunity agenda by giving Trump or an eventual predecessor more leeway to directly challenge IHL. With many lawmakers moving to the ideological poles, consensus on military policy has grown increasingly elusive on Capitol Hill. This has allowed recent U.S. presidents, including Trump, to exploit gaps in congressional oversight to expand their authority over the military.[50] Political scientists James M. Goldgeier and Elizabeth N. Saunders, for instance, have referred to the rise of "unconstrained ... executive power" by American presidents in international affairs.[51] This de facto expanded control over the armed forces could empower a commander-in-chief to unilaterally downplay the importance of the law of war.

At the same time, the pullback of some Congress members from military affairs could actually give anti-establishment Republicans like

---

[48] Prokop, Andrew. Dec. 14, 2016. "The Change in Republican Voters' Views of Putin Since Trump's Rise Is Remarkable." *Vox.* www.vox.com/2016/9/9/12865678/trump-putin-polls-republican

[49] Timm, Trevor. Dec. 18, 2015 "Republicans Are So Bullish on War that 30% Would Bomb a Fictional Country." *Guardian.* www.theguardian.com/commentisfree/2015/dec/18/republicans-are-so-bullish-on-war-that-30-percent-would-bomb-a-fictional-country

[50] Mann, Thomas E., and Norman J. Ornstein. 2012. *It's Even Worse than It Looks.* New York: Basic Books. Fowler, L. L. 2015. *Watchdogs on the Hill: The Decline of Congressional Oversight of US Foreign Relations.* Princeton: Princeton University Press.

[51] Goldgeier, James M., and Elizabeth N. Saunders. 2018. "The Unconstrained Presidency: Checks and Balances Eroded Long before Trump." *Foreign Affairs* 97: 144–156.

CJWC members more clout. Even if Congress as a whole continues to play a lesser role in the military, polarization may increase power for small groups of the most ambitious lawmakers.[52] Scholars Kevin Marsh and Jeffrey S. Lantis, for example, have written on how polarization in Washington has led to an expanded role for "revolutionary" foreign policy entrepreneurs (driven by strategic or philosophical aims) and "mercenary" foreign policy entrepreneurs (motivated to advance their political stature).[53] Given both the high levels of organization and commitment of the CJWC, this could augment its relative power in Congress.

Finally, entrenched polarization on Capitol Hill reduces the likelihood that presidents will be held to account for clear violations of the law of war. While Congress holds the power of executive oversight, recent events such as Trump's two impeachment trials have demonstrated that lawmakers now rarely sanction a leader of their own party.[54] Although presidents may occasionally face intra-party criticism, the lack of formal accountability mechanisms leaves ample room for commanders-in-chief to maneuver. The absence of any serious debate within Congress about holding Trump accountable for violating IHL highlights this dynamic. Consequently, Trump or a successor may perceive free rein to overtly flout IHL, without fear of repercussions.

5.3 Other Political Pressures

Beyond conservative media and GOP lawmakers, pressure from lobbyist organizations and court-martialed U.S. servicemembers themselves may also "re-up" the impunity agenda. Following Trump's 2019 and 2020 military clemencies, some activists pushed for even

---

[52] Homan, Patrick, and Jeffrey S. Lantis. 2020. *The Battle for US Foreign Policy: Congress, Parties, and Factions in the 21st Century*. Switzerland: Palgrave Macmillan.

[53] Marsh, Kevin and Jeffrey S. Lantis. 2018. "Are All Foreign Policy Innovators Created Equal? The New Generation of Congressional Foreign Policy Entrepreneurship." *Foreign Policy Analysis* 14(2): 212–234.

[54] Cassidy, John. Jan. 13, 2021. "The House Impeaches Trump Again, but Most Republicans Stick with Him." *New Yorker*. www.newyorker.com/news/our-columnists/the-house-impeaches-trump-again-but-most-republicans-stick-with-him

5.3 Other Political Pressures

more war crime interventions.[55] This included eight former U.S. servicemembers who petitioned Trump for pardons, including, most notoriously, Staff Sgt. Robert Bales, who pleaded guilty to murdering three men, four women, and nine children in Afghanistan.[56] Although unsuccessful, the efforts set the groundwork for attempts to retry cases, to downplay the severity of alleged crimes, and to provide combatants with well-financed legal defense teams. With Trump back in the Oval Office, these cases have not faded from public view.

Lobbyist Organizations

Several lobbyist organizations continue to advocate for war crime interventions. By far, the most well-known is United American Patriots (UAP), whose self-stated goal is to create "positive public awareness and support for our Nation's Warriors."[57] Since its inception in 2005, UAP has worked with dozens of U.S. servicemembers, flagging attention to what it deems illegitimate verdicts and sentences.[58] Headquartered near Washington, DC, the organization maintains annual revenues of more than $700,00 and operating expenses of more than $1.4 million.[59] In addition to its full-time staff, volunteers, and a board of directors, UAP claims a membership of "hundreds of thousands of highly patriotic, dedicated, and concerned American citizens" who fund or support its efforts.[60]

As of 2024, UAP reports a total of twenty-four "presently supported warriors" (seven Marine, two Navy, and fifteen Army personnel).[61] Much of the legal work done by UAP is contracted to a national cadre of attorneys, who it hires through its "Warrior Fund"[62] at firms like MilitaryDefender.com and Military Justice

---

[55] Sisk, Richard. Dec. 23, 2020. "There May Be More Military Pardons to Come from Trump, Advocates Say." *Military.com*. www.military.com/daily-news/2020/12/23/there-may-be-more-military-pardons-come-trump-advocates-say.html

[56] Sisk, Richard. Dec. 4, 2020. "Robert Bales Among 8 Former Troops, Contractors Petitioning Trump for Pardons." *Military.com*. www.military.com/daily-news/2020/12/04/robert-bales-among-8-former-troops-contractors-petitioning-trump-pardons.html

[57] www.uap.org/uap-mission [58] www.uap.org/uap-mission

[59] https://projects.propublica.org/nonprofits/organizations/412172043

[60] www.uap.org/who-we-are/ [61] www.uap.org/who-we-support/

[62] www.uap.org/warrior-fund/

Attorneys.⁶³ Among its highest-profile current clients are Army Staff Sgt. Robert Bales and paroled Army First Sgt. John Hatley, sentenced in 2019 for the killings of four Iraqi civilians. UAP also lists as past "success stories" numerous combatants who have received pardons from Trump (Michael Behenna, Mathew Golsteyn, and Clint Lorance), had their charges dismissed or sentences reduced, or received discharge upgrades for their service.⁶⁴

Although it manages legal cases, UAP is perhaps most influential as a public relations apparatus. It launches targeted political campaigns on behalf of court-martialed servicemembers and fights against what it labels "lynchings" by U.S. military courts.⁶⁵ As part of these efforts, supporters can donate to UAP, subscribe to UAP's newsletter "One Team, One Fight," and purchase UAP-themed gear, such as ball caps, hoodies, cell phone cases, and mugs.⁶⁶ In 2020, UAP sponsored a stock car in NASCAR's XFINITY series at Daytona, emblazoned with the photos of Mathew Golsteyn, Clint Lorance, and other court-martialed U.S. servicemembers.⁶⁷ UAP's Facebook,⁶⁸ Youtube,⁶⁹ and Instagram⁷⁰ pages post regular updates about cases to its followers.

UAP is one of several groups involved in the space. For example, it recently joined with the Combat Clemency Project (CCP) at the University of Chicago Law School,⁷¹ which, according to a *New York Times* description, offers legal services toward a "shared mission to pardon U.S. soldiers who killed civilians."⁷² Founded in 2015 as part of a legal clinic, the project has written clemency petitions and lists among its current and ex-clients seven combatants, including Clint Lorance. CCP says that all "have been excessively punished, and the Army bears some degree of responsibility for their crimes."⁷³ According to director Mark Heyrman, CCP exists in part because

---

⁶³ www.militaryjusticeattorneys.com/firm/attorneys/gerald-healy/
⁶⁴ www.uap.org/success-stories/   ⁶⁵ www.uap.org/post/veterans-legal-help/
⁶⁶ https://store.uap.org/   ⁶⁷ www.uap.org/nascar/
⁶⁸ www.facebook.com/UAPINC/
⁶⁹ www.youtube.com/channel/UCeYGzfELwMAAZwyz2sEYwSg
⁷⁰ www.instagram.com/uapatriots/?hl=en
⁷¹ For more information, see: www.law.uchicago.edu/clinics/mandel/mental/combat
⁷² Philipps, Dave. May 19, 2016. "Shared Mission to Pardon U.S. Soldiers Who Killed Civilians." *New York Times*. www.nytimes.com/2016/05/20/us/clemency-war-crimes.html
⁷³ www.law.uchicago.edu/clinics/mandel/mental/combat

5.3 Other Political Pressures

"[w]e owe more to our veterans than to just use them in our wars, traumatize them, and throw them away when they behave badly."[74]

The nonprofit Save Our Heroes (SOH) has also played a visible role in efforts to reform U.S. military prosecutions.[75] According to SOH, its members travel monthly to the nation's capital "to help educate Congressional leadership" on "inherent flaws within the military judicial system."[76] SOH's Facebook page has depicted Clint Lorance as "one of our wrongfully convicted Heroes."[77] Its blog contains posts like "Unlawful Command Influence Exposed at the Highest Levels of Military Legal Leadership."[78] SOH boasts a "client base" of more than 300 individuals, several legislative proposals introduced before Congress, and the instruction of lawmakers about the "national security threat posed by the military justice judicial system."[79] In 2018, SOH convened its first annual meeting in Texas.[80]

Other organizations have also aggressively lobbied for war crime clemencies. For example, the Navy SEALs Fund (NSF)-Brotherhood beyond Battle organization, which brands itself as a "Veterans-helping-Veterans" nonprofit,[81] shouldered much of the financial burden for Eddie Gallagher's court case. NSF started an online fundraiser to counter what it characterized as "absurd charges" against the "tried and true Warrior," asserting that Gallagher sacrificed in battle so that "you and your family can sleep peacefully in the warmth of your beds at home."[82] In total, NSF raised more than $750,000 for Gallagher's

---

[74] Gillespie, Becky Beaupre. Apr. 13, 2016. "The Hardest Stories to Tell." University of Chicago Law School. www.law.uchicago.edu/news/hardest-stories-tell-what-intense-new-clinic-project-teaching-seven-students-about-war-mercy
[75] www.saveourheroesproject.org/
[76] www.saveourheroesproject.org/news-events/congressional/
[77] www.facebook.com/SaveOurHeroesProject/posts/1174920312595029
[78] Conzachi, Michael. Oct. 27, 2017. "Unlawful Command Influence Exposed at the Highest Levels of Military Legal Leadership." Save Our Heroes. www.saveourheroesproject.org/unlawful-command-influence-exposed-highest-levels-military-legal-leadership/
[79] www.saveourheroesproject.org/accomplishments/
[80] www.saveourheroesproject.org/accomplishments/
[81] https://navysealsfund.org/
[82] https://navy-seals-fund.networkforgood.com/projects/60396-justice-for-eddie-gallagher-support-fund#:~:text=fight%20for%20Justice!-,The%20Navy%20SEALs%20Fund%20%E2%80%93%20Brotherhood%20Beyond%20Battlefield%C2%AE%20is%20Honored,system%20standing%20on%20its%20head.

case. Following Gallagher's not guilty verdict for murder, NSF declared on its website that "Truth has prevailed!" and posted a Fox News video of Gallagher and Pete Hegseth.[83]

Even corporate interests have joined the lobbying efforts. For example, Nine Line Apparel CEO Tyler Meritt raised at least $80,000 for Eddie Gallagher's legal case via a "Free Eddie" campaign.[84] He also created limited-edition Gallagher t-shirts and defended Gallagher on Fox News.[85] Merritt posted a tongue-in-cheek article on Nine Line's website entitled "Navy SEAL Kills 8lb 6oz Baby Jesus on Easter" that mocked the charges against Gallagher. In it, he offered a "disclaimer" that "[n]o babies (including the son of GOD) were murdered by any Navy Seal EVER" and disparaged a "BS story [about Gallagher] published by the garbage news agency known as the NY Times." He further posted online a mock-up of a *New York Times* article suggesting many of the charges against Gallagher were bogus.[86]

Beyond large organizations, a defining aspect of the impunity movement under Trump has been the growth of online, grassroots organizing. A notable example during Trump's first term was supportraven23.com, created on behalf of the Blackwater agents,[87] which also published a newsletter that eclipsed 50,000 recipients.[88] With newsletter titles like "Sign & Share Our Pardon Petition to Free Raven 23," the organization kept its followers updated on how to contribute. It championed the CJWC,[89] published regular calls for prayers,[90] requested that members share the cases with their

---

[83] https://navy-seals-fund.networkforgood.com/projects/60396-justice-for-eddie-gallagher-support-fund#:~:text=fight%20for%20Justice!-,The%20Navy%20SEALs%20Fund%20%E2%80%93%20Brotherhood%20Beyond%20Battlefield%C2%AE%20is%20Honored,system%20standing%20on%20its%20head.

[84] www.ninelineapparel.com/blogs/news/freeeddie-update

[85] https://video.foxnews.com/v/video-embed.html?video_id=6050562533001

[86] Merritt, Tyler. Apr. 29, 2019. "Navy SEAL Kills 8lb 6oz Baby Jesus on Easter." Nine Line. ninelinenews.com/nine-line-news/inthepress/navy-seal-kills-8lb-6oz-baby-jesus-on-easter/

[87] www.supportraven23.com/

[88] https://us11.campaign-archive.com/home/?u=7d183eb6e4095556b7c9195bc&id=c6c78ca2c7

[89] https://us11.campaign-archive.com/?u=7d183eb6e4095556b7c9195bc&id=64da202e44

[90] https://us11.campaign-archive.com/?u=7d183eb6e4095556b7c9195bc&id=2347ede96f

5.3 Other Political Pressures

churches,[91] and asked supporters to "please keep tweeting President Trump and emailing him and calling and snail mailing him to say that you support presidential pardons."[92]

On social media, legions of supporters have also been inspired to participate in discussion forums[93] and fundraisers[94] to raise awareness of troops accused or convicted of war crimes. Hashtags like "#FreeEddie [Gallagher]" and "#KeeptheFaith" became calling cards for court-martialed combatants. Independent websites and magazines additionally publish blogs[95] and articles[96] clamoring for and celebrating clemencies. To fill ongoing demand, internet companies continue to sell paraphernalia with taglines like "Edward Gallagher: Never Out of the Fight."[97] Smaller, more amateur advocates in this space, such as Justice4NavySeals, have also gained niche followings, which amplify content from organizations like Fox News, OAN, UAP, and the NSF.[98]

Today, advocates for war crime clemencies have increasingly begun convening face-to-face through large, public gatherings that attract like-minded attendees. A particularly high-profile example is SHOT Show, described by Fox News as "the greatest gun show on Earth."[99] The trade show has found natural partnerships with advocates of the impunity agenda. UAP, for instance, routinely arranges a booth at SHOT Show, where attendees can learn about its lobbying and buy UAP-themed "swag."[100] In 2020, the organization featured

---

[91] https://us11.campaign-archive.com/?u=7d183eb6e4095556b7c9195bc&id=66c6b5e6a4

[92] https://us11.campaign-archive.com/?u=7d183eb6e4095556b7c9195bc&id=1a28504ac5

[93] For example, www.reddit.com/r/ExDemFoyer/comments/ql4rtr/video_the_true_story_behind_the_eddie_gallagher/

[94] For example, www.customink.com/fundraising/fight4clint?side=front&type=2&zoom=false

[95] For example, https://feraljundi.com/

[96] For example, www.sofmag.com/who-are-the-biden-four/

[97] For example, www.amazon.com/Free-Eddie-Gallagher-Vintage-Gift/dp/B07QY3QFHC/ref=sr_1_2?crid=1NNNUJF4JYLVT&keywords=free+eddie+gallagher+t-shirt&qid=1699811387&sprefix=free+eddie+gallagher+t-shir%2Caps%2C97&sr=8-2

[98] https://twitter.com/Justice4SEALs

[99] Barrie, Allison. Jan. 23, 2018. "SHOT 2018: The Greatest Gun Show on Earth." Fox News. www.foxnews.com/tech/shot-2018-the-greatest-gun-show-on-earth

[100] www.facebook.com/UAPINC/posts/5168394979857841/?paipv=0&eav=AfbMQtD5NOSQ_OFkr--eIyhLpoJJY199eICqVdtO_qefJ4tmvMe3odeXQiNomip5XDU&_rdr

a "meet-and-greet" with Clint Lorance.[101] In 2022, *Shot Show TV* interviewed UAP CEO David "Bull" Gurfein.[102] The same year, Shot Show hosted Eddie Gallagher, who boasted in a video of his "f[inding] a way to beat the [military justice] system."[103]

Troops Granted Clemency

Individual troops granted clemency by Trump also continue to perpetuate the impunity agenda. The most visible has been Eddie Gallagher, who has made a new career presenting himself as a victim of a corrupt military justice system. Since receiving clemency, Gallagher has launched his own website, TheEddieGallagher.com, and founded the Pipe Hitter Foundation, a charity that lobbies for U.S. servicemembers who purportedly "find themselves in legal crosshairs simply for doing their jobs."[104] He has published an autobiography, *The Man in the Arena: From Fighting ISIS to Fighting for My Freedom*.[105] He has also made headlines for suing both Navy Secretary Kenneth Braithwaite[106] and *New York Times* writer Dave Philipps,[107] who has penned a book, *Alpha*, critical of Gallagher.[108]

Most notably, Gallagher has established himself as a right-wing "influencer." In *Vanity Fair*, for instance, one writer called Gallagher

[101] UAP. 2020 Update – Annual Report. www.uap.org/wp-content/uploads/2021/02/UAP-Year-in-Review-2020.pdf
[102] www.facebook.com/watch/?v=301054021989529
[103] Feb. 15, 2022. "Justice for all – A Chat with Eddie and Andrea Gallagher of the Pipe Hitter Foundation at SHOT Show." Back to the Lodge Podcast. www.youtube.com/watch?v=B6o1GRDrnBM
[104] Pipe Hitter Foundation. 2021. "Justice for All." https://pipehitterfoundation.org
[105] Gallagher, Eddie and Andrea Gallagher (with Andy Symonds). 2021. *The Man in the Arena: From Fighting ISIS to Fighting for My Freedom*. Washington, DC: Ballast Books.
[106] Dyer, Andrew. June 1, 2020. "Former SEAL Edward Gallagher Sues New Navy Secretary, New York Times Reporter." *San Diego Union-Tribune*. www.sandiegouniontribune.com/news/military/story/2020-06-01/former-seal-eddie-gallagher-sues-new-navy-secretary-and-new-york-times-reporter
[107] Bruno, Bianca. Sept. 27, 2021. "New York Times Reporter Dodges Some Defamation Claims by Navy SEAL." *Courthouse News Service*. www.courthousenews.com/nyt-reporter-dodges-some-defamation-claims-by-navy-seal/
[108] Philipps, David. 2021. *Alpha: Eddie Gallagher and the War for the Soul of the Navy SEALS*. New York: Crown.

5.3 Other Political Pressures

"an online micro-celebrity,'" detailing how he has used his image to sell products, including fitness supplements and t-shirts with phrases like "Waterboarding Instructor" and "KILL BAD DUDES."[109] In 2020, Nine Line Apparel officially launched Gallagher-themed merchandise, including clothing and drinkware, under its "Salty Frog" line.[110] One writer observed that "[t]his commodification of criminality and toxic patriotism chimes with Trump's attitudes toward his presidency.... It looks like Trump has found his own brand ambassadors."[111] A *New York Times* profile called Gallagher a "pitchman and conservative activist."[112]

To bolster his brand, Gallagher has created a personal logo, comprised of a skull and crossbones, alongside the phrase "Seek Battle: FAFO" (F*&K Around and Find Out – reportedly a favored slogan of the paramilitary group the Proud Boys). On his website, Gallagher advertises that supporters can "train with Eddie" in the use of high-powered weaponry and in "home defense and preparation."[113] Courses, which take place at a veteran-owned shooting range in Florida, include "Operator for a Day," "Advanced Pistol/Rifle Training," and private one-on-one training with Gallagher. Gallagher additionally sponsors the sale of ammunition, knives, and rifles.[114] For $15 per month, supporters can become "Tier 1" members of Gallagher's Patreon page, which finances his content creation.[115]

Gallagher's Instagram account, which has more than a quarter million followers as of 2024 and includes more than 6,000 posts, offers a sampling of his content.[116] Gallagher consistently posts updates on the Pipe Hitter Foundation, inspirational quotes, "shorts" of personal

---

[109] Levin, Bess. Jan. 2, 2020. Edward Gallagher, Trump's Favorite War Criminal, Is a "CONSERVATIVE INFLUENCER" Now." *Vanity Fair*. www.vanityfair.com/news/2020/01/edward-gallagher-navy-seal-influencer

[110] Baker, Sinead. Jan. 2, 2020. "Navy SEAL Edward Gallagher Has Launched a Lifestyle Brand after Trump Reversed a Military Court's Sentence." *Business Insider*. www.businessinsider.com/navy-seal-edward-gallagher-lifestyle-brand-after-war-crime-acquittal-2020-1?r=US&IR=T

[111] Beorn, Waitman Wade. Nov. 27, 2019. "The War-Crimes Presidency." *The New Republic*. https://newrepublic.com/article/155857/war-crimes-presidency

[112] Philipps, Dave. Dec. 31, 2019. "From the Brig to Mar-a-Lago, Former Navy SEAL Capitalizes on Newfound Fame." *New York Times*. www.nytimes.com/2019/12/31/us/navy-seals-edward-gallagher-trump.html

[113] https://theeddiegallagher.com/training/

[114] https://theeddiegallagher.com/   [115] www.patreon.com/EddieGallagher

[116] www.instagram.com/eddie_gallagher/?hl=en

interviews, advertisements for sponsored products like hot sauce and fitness machines, and other news about his daily life. Some features include a photo of Gallagher giving two "middle fingers" to the Naval Consolidated Brig building in San Diego; Gallagher posing with his latest designed "Free Eddie" t-shirt, on sale for followers; clips with titles like "Exposing the Legal System" and "Why the System is Broken"; and a photo that simply says "The Media Wants to Scare Us."

Gallagher is also a regular guest for online videos and podcasts.[117] Examples include a 2020 YouTube video where Gallagher mockingly reads "Mean Tweets" about him,[118] an interview that declares that "Eddie's story can be paralleled with the story of Joseph in the bible,"[119] and a podcast that urges fans to order his book alongside images of beer and barbecue.[120] Gallagher's own long-form videos, posted under the YouTube handle "theeddiegallagher," depict an ultra-masculine, all-American "bro." One video, for example, features Gallagher working out in an American-flag muscle shirt.[121] Another shows him at a shooting range and gym, ending with his lifting partner advertising "Battle Tested" post-workout supplement.[122]

Several prominent platforms have boosted Gallagher's online celebrity. The most notable was a 2019 video by popular YouTuber "Donut Operator."[123] The upload, which went viral with 3.9 million views, played a large role in introducing Gallagher's case to a mass audience. Elsewhere, Gallagher was described as "serv[ing] honorably" on the popular *Joe Rogan Podcast*.[124] In a two-part podcast,

---

[117] https://theeddiegallagher.com/news/
[118] Jan. 15, 2020. "Mean Tweets – Navy Seal Eddie Gallagher Responds." Nine Line Apparel. www.youtube.com/watch?v=eY57Jd5Ee-A
[119] https://teamneverquit.com/podcast/eddie-andrea-gallagher/
[120] Nov. 29, 2020. "Black Rifle Coffee Podcast: Ep 080 Eddie Gallagher and Donut Operator." Black Rifle Coffee Podcast. www.youtube.com/watch?v=MSGhjYwVzFs
[121] Mar. 9, 2023. "Full Mobility Training with Navy Seal Eddie Gallagher Part 1 #darustrong." Eddie Gallagher. www.youtube.com/watch?v=bRWRmrXyvGc
[122] Mar. 5, 2023. "Tactical Shooting & Lifting with Navy Seal Eddie Gallagher." Eddie Gallagher. www.youtube.com/watch?v=DZ2cTMzLpMQ
[123] Feb. 16, 2019. "The Story of Navy SEAL Chief Eddie Gallagher." Donut Operator. www.youtube.com/watch?v=qFe-n4Eu6Mw
[124] Oct. 20, 2022. "Joe Rogan: Mike and Andy TALK about Eddie Gallagher and the UNFAIR TREATMENT He Received." JRE Notes. www.youtube.com/watch?v=uz5qG3SWYnM

5.3 Other Political Pressures

Gallagher also appeared with Rob O'Neill, who reportedly killed Osama Bin Laden.[125] Comments on the video included: "Gallagher and O'Neil Save America ... F-YEA!!!!!!!!!!!!!!!!!!!!! LOVE YOU GUYS!!!!!!!!!!!!!!"; "[H]e's a fucking warrior I'm so glad Trump pardoned him"; and Jeopardy answer: "Who are two of the baddest Muther F***ers to ever walk this planet?"

Gallagher has also created or participated in several major production ventures. In 2020, for instance, he posted a three-minute, cinematic video that called the Navy SEALs who testified against him in court "cowards." The footage begins with Gallagher maintaining his innocence and insisting, "The fight to clear my name is not over."[126] In 2021, Apple featured Gallagher in its first-ever podcast-TV original series.[127] Entitled "The Line," the high-budget production, which included six podcast episodes and a four-part documentary, was criticized by one expert for being "too credulous of the SEAL's self-aggrandizing mythology."[128] An independent, pro-Gallagher documentary, entitled "Navy Seals in the Crosshairs: The Eddie Gallagher Story," is also reportedly in the works.[129]

As a testament to his reputation within right-wing circles, the conservative *Washington Examiner* published a special feature on Gallagher in 2019 speculating how he might use his notoriety to earn money or to advocate for political causes after he left the Navy.[130] In the article, one Navy SEAL urged Gallagher to write publicly about his experiences to provide a "warning for the future generations." Another SEAL said that he believed "there's a lot of defense businesses out there that Eddie could potentially get into" and that "he's

---

[125] Mar. 15, 2023. "Eddie Gallagher Part 1 – The Operator Ep: 31." Drinkin Bros Studio. www.youtube.com/watch?v=kkKXFVIQ3xA

[126] www.instagram.com/eddie_gallagher/?hl=en

[127] Spangler, Todd. Apr. 6, 2021. "Apple TV Plus Launches True-Crime Podcast 'The Line' Ahead of Docu-Series Premiere." *Variety*. https://variety.com/2021/digital/news/apple-tv-plus-the-line-podcast-docu-series-1234944780/

[128] https://twitter.com/Brian_Castner

[129] "Navy SEAL in the Crosshairs – The Eddie Gallagher Story (Official Trailer)." Time for a Hero. www.youtube.com/watch?v=8hfowJG3axE

[130] Read, Russ. July 5, 2019. "Upcoming Documentary Just One of Many Opportunities for Acquitted Navy SEAL Eddie Gallagher." *Washington Examiner*. www.washingtonexaminer.com/policy/defense-national-security/upcoming-documentary-just-one-of-many-opportunities-for-acquitted-navy-seal-eddie-gallagher

going to have enough patriots out there that will gainfully employ him." Discussing Gallagher's connection to Pete Hegseth, the article reported that "observers have speculated Gallagher could join ... [Fox News] as a military analyst."

In 2024, Fox News also featured a special report on Gallagher's Pipe Hitter Foundation, spotlighting his advocacy and fundraising efforts on behalf of court-martialed U.S. servicemembers.[131] The feature opened with the claim that "Eddie Gallagher knows how it feels to have a target on your back, both on and off the battlefield." It advertised Gallagher's "Operator for a Day" fundraiser where supporters could spend $3,000 to receive ammunition and gain access to "two-story live-fire shoot house on site" that simulates close-quarter combat. In an accompanying interview, Gallagher told Fox News that the U.S. military has "a nasty epidemic of overpunishing people." He further described the UCMJ as "an outdated and archaic system."

Besides Gallagher, other troops granted clemency by Trump have also remained in the spotlight. Clint Lorance, dubbed a conservative "*cause celebre*" by the New York Times,[132] released his own book in 2020 entitled *Stolen Honor: Falsely Accused, Imprisoned, and My Long Road to Freedom*.[133] The memoir was advertised as a "captivating account of how Clint Lorance ... became a scapegoat for a corrupt military hierarchy." A *Military.com* feature published that year detailed Lorance's distrust of a "bureaucratic deep state" and his plans to become an attorney so that he could revamp the UCMJ.[134] In a Q&A with UAP, Lorance also described his openness

---

[131] Pandolfo, Chris. Oct. 8 2024. "Retired Navy SEAL Who Spent Months behind Bars in War Crimes Probe Vows to Not Let It Happen to Others." *Fox News*. www.foxnews.com/us/retired-navy-seal-who-spent-months-behind-bars-war-crimes-probe-vows-not-let-happen-others

[132] Philipps, Dave. Feb. 24, 2015. "Cause Célèbre, Scorned by Troops." *New York Times*. www.nytimes.com/2015/02/25/us/jailed-ex-army-officer-has-support-but-not-from-his-platoon.html

[133] Lorance, Clint. 2020. *Stolen Honor: Falsely Accused, Imprisoned, and My Long Road to Freedom*. New York: Center Street.

[134] Sisk, Richard. Oct. 25, 2020. "He Was Convicted of War Crimes and Pardoned by Trump. Now He Wants to Reform Military Justice." *Military.com*. www.military.com/daily-news/2020/10/25/he-was-convicted-of-war-crimes-and-pardoned-trump-now-he-wants-reform-military-justice.html

5.3 Other Political Pressures

to what he labeled a "nuclear option": running for Congress so that he can "jump up and down on people's desks in Washington."[135]

Even before his pardon, Lorance starred from prison in the Starz documentary "Leavenworth," a six-part miniseries available on Amazon. A *New York Times* headline described the production as "Putting the Army on Trial."[136] Lorance was also the subject of his attorney's 2019 book, *Travesty of Justice: The Shocking Prosecution of Lt. Clint Lorance*.[137] Following Trump's Blackwater pardons, Lorance began a Change.org petition to "bring … more of our comrades home."[138] Since his release from jail, Lorance has continued to make public appearances. For example, in 2020, he was interviewed on the far-right *Conservative Business Journal Podcast,* which was billed as part of "The Biden Scam Series," alongside an interview with MyPillow CEO Mike Lindell.[139]

Lorance, who graduated from Appalachian School of Law in 2023[140] and has described himself as a "military justice reform advocate,"[141] has also taken part in several high-profile legal battles since his clemency. In 2021, as an appellant, he won a landmark victory in the Tenth Circuit U.S. Court of Appeals, which ruled that his receipt of a pardon did not constitute acknowledgment of guilt for war crimes.[142] The *Lorance v. Commandant* decision, which overturned a 2019 lower court judgment in Kansas, was the first time the U.S. court system had ruled on whether accepting a pardon intrinsically

---

[135] Oct. 1, 2020. "Q&A With Clint Lorance, Author of The New Book 'Stolen Honor.'" United American Patriots. www.uap.org/post/clint-lorance-author-q-a/
[136] Hale, Mike. Oct. 18, 2019. "Review: 'Leavenworth' Puts the Army on Trial." *New York Times.* www.nytimes.com/2019/10/18/arts/television/leavenworth-review.html
[137] Brown, Don. 2019. *Travesty of Justice: The Shocking Prosecution of Lt. Clint Lorance.* Denver: WildBlue Press.
[138] Lorance, Clint. Dec. 29, 2020. "New Mission for Team Freedom." www.change.org/p/president-donald-j-trump-mr-president-please-pardon-the-biden-four/u/28280845
[139] www.instagram.com/p/CIjqmwRgcPv/
[140] www.instagram.com/p/Cr4CYpFveax/?hl=en
[141] Hussain, Murtaza. Aug. 5, 2023. "War Criminal's Bid to Become Lawyer Faces Obstacle: His Own Troops." *Intercept.* https://theintercept.com/2023/08/05/war-criminal-clint-lorance-trump-pardon/
[142] https://law.justia.com/cases/federal/appellate-courts/ca10/20-3055/20-3055-2021-09-23.html

implies imputation or acceptance of guilt.[143] UAP heralded the case on social media, praising it for "now being cited as #precedent in other federal civilian appellate courts."[144]

In 2023, Lorance again made headlines when his application for the Oklahoma bar was questioned by two former soldiers with whom he served in Afghanistan. In a Twitter post receiving more than 3 million views, Todd Fitzgerald wrote that Lorance had "no moral fiber." He recounted that, after the shooting that led to his arrest, Lorance told a group of "crying women and children" to "[s]hut the fuck up or I'll kill you too."[145] In an op-ed for the *Army Times*, another platoon mate, Mike McGuiness, wrote a scathing indictment of Lorance's bar application, claiming that "at no point should he ever again hold a position of power or influence."[146] Lorance's application was also featured in the American Bar Association Journal, which asked whether he was "unfit for practice."[147]

Mathew Golsteyn has also waged a public relations campaign aimed at rehabilitating his image. In 2021, for example, Golsteyn made national headlines for "blast[ing]" a decision by the Army not to restore his special forces insignia and medals for valor after it ruled that his pardon was not a technical wiping clean of his war record.[148] He has reputedly weighed launching a formal appeal. Like Clint Lorance, UAP continues to list Golsteyn as a "presently supported warrior."[149] Golsteyn's wife, Julie, has also remained a vigorous

---

[143] Raymond, Nate. Sept. 23, 2021. "Ex-soldier's Acceptance of Trump Pardon Didn't Constitute Confession of Guilt, Court Rules." *Reuters*. www.reuters.com/legal/litigation/ex-soldiers-acceptance-trump-pardon-didnt-constitute-confession-guilt-court-2021-09-23/#:~:text=(Reuters)%20-%20A%20federal%20appeals,for%20murdering%20two%20Afghan%20civilians.

[144] https://twitter.com/UAPatriots/status/1541456612858011648

[145] https://twitter.com/fucking_fitzy/status/1672012731371618306?s=20

[146] McGuinness, Mike. July 7, 2023. "Clint Lorance Wants to Be a Lawyer. A Soldier He Led Says He's Unfit." *Army Times*. www.armytimes.com/opinion/2023/07/07/clint-lorance-wants-to-be-a-lawyer-a-soldier-he-led-says-hes-unfit/

[147] Weiss, Debra Cassens. July 11, 2023. "Pardoned Ex-soldier Plans to Take the Bar Exam; Is He Unfit for Practice?" *ABA Journal*. www.abajournal.com/news/article/pardoned-ex-soldier-plans-to-take-the-bar-exam-is-he-unfit

[148] Brook, Tom Vanden. Mar. 17, 2021. "Army Denies Medals, Special Forces Insignia to Soldier Trump Pardoned for Alleged Murder." *USA Today*. www.usatoday.com/story/news/politics/2021/03/17/army-denies-medals-soldier-trump-pardoned-alleged-afghan-murder/4730488001/

[149] www.uap.org/who-we-support/

5.3 Other Political Pressures

advocate for her husband. In 2022, she wrote a children's book about "bravery" based on her "life experiences." The book was promoted on "Fox and Friends," where Pete Hegseth called her a "powerful spokesman for [Mathew]."[150]

The four Blackwater contractors pardoned by Trump have also continued to express outrage over their alleged mistreatment. Before receiving a pardon, for example, Nicholas Slatten decried that he was a "POW in … [his] own country."[151] Shortly after his pardon, an *Associated Press* headline described Evan Liberty as "defiant."[152] Newspapers have documented gallant returns of the Blackwater agents to their hometowns.[153] Dustin Heard benefited from a "Go Fund Me" campaign.[154] The Blackwater Memorial Alumni Association additionally raised funds for all four agents.[155] Today, supporters can still purchase "Raven 23 support shirts" through

---

[150] Mackey, Maureen. July 17, 2022. "Wife of Former Green Beret Writes Children's Book about Bravery, Courage and Compassion." *Fox News*. www.foxnews.com/lifestyle/wife-green-beret-childrens-book-bravery-courage

[151] Collins, Michael. Sept. 24, 2017. "Tennessee Native and Former Blackwater Security Guard Nick Slatten: 'I Am a POW in My Own Country.'" *Tennessean*. https://eu.tennessean.com/story/news/politics/2017/09/24/former-blackwater-security-guard-nick-slatten-i-am-pow-my-own-country/692745001/

[152] Tucker, Eric. Jan. 2, 2021. "After Pardon, Blackwater Guard Defiant: 'I Acted Correctly.' *Associated Press*. https://apnews.com/article/donald-trump-shootings-baghdad-only-on-ap-iraq-7b3e202ac353db544180fb2a61d2902c

[153] Choate, Trish. Dec. 29, 2020. "Olney Welcomes Heard Home after Presidential Pardon." *Wichita Falls Times Record News*. www.timesrecordnews.com/story/news/2020/12/29/dustin-heard-welcomed-home-after-trump-pardon/4043832001//Greene, Melissa. Dec. 24, 2020. "WATCH: Pardoned Blackwater Guard Returns Home to Kids in Time for Christmas." *WJHL*. www.wjhl.com/news/regional/tennessee/watch-pardoned-blackwater-guard-returns-home-to-kids-in-time-for-christmas//Sullivan, Cole. Sept. 9, 2021. "Convicted of a Massacre, Pardoned Former Blackwater Contractor Thanks People Who Supported Him." *10 News*. www.wbir.com/article/news/national/military-news/convicted-of-a-massacre-pardoned-former-blackwater-contractor-thanks-people-who-supported-him/51-fa4b582e-a311-4cab-82cf-86d41a05e21c

[154] Coate, Trish. Dec. 29, 2020. "Olney Welcomes Heard Home after Presidential Pardon." *Times Record News*. https://eu.timesrecordnews.com/story/news/2020/12/29/dustin-heard-welcomed-home-after-trump-pardon/4043832001/

[155] https://blackwater-memorial-alumni-association.networkforgood.com/projects/120295-raven-23-freedom-fund

BlackwaterWorldWide.com.[156] The Support Raven23 organization still maintains a Twitter handle, where it follows Donald Trump Jr., the CJWC, UAP, and the rapper "Ice Cube."[157]

The Free Raven 23 Facebook page, which has 17,000 followers as of 2024 and has published numerous celebrations of the Blackwater pardons, offers a sampling of the often religious-like fervor that such initiatives have inspired.[158] Following Trump's pardons, for example, one user remarked: "Thank you, president TRUMP!!! This has me bawling my face off!!!" Another user stated: "Praise the Lord! I cried when I heard the news." On Free Raven 23's Twitter page, certain tweets were equally emotional.[159] One poster declared, "Amen. Would love for y'all to write a book. #TrumpWasRightAboutEverything."[160] Another wrote, "Praise God! I got to watch a video tonight of little Lily Slough be surprised by the best Christmas present in the world-her daddy walking in the front door."[161]

5.4 Impunity Synergies

In his second term, Trump is not just inheriting a loose impunity coalition with a temporary interest in advancing military justice reform. Instead, he is re-entering an active, well-established network of political actors dedicated to openly challenging the law of war – a network built around Trump, by Trump, and for Trump. Alongside Fox News and Republican Congress members, the organizations and individuals involved continue to amplify their influence through close, overlapping interactions with one another and the public. Both online and in-person, these activists promote Trump's impunity agenda, resulting in a vast array of content spotlighting the cases of court-martialed American servicemembers and, more broadly, questioning the need for IHL.[162]

---

[156] https://blackwaterworldwide.com/raven-23-support-shirt/
[157] https://twitter.com/FreeRaven23/following
[158] www.facebook.com/raven23support/
[159] https://twitter.com/freeraven23?lang=en
[160] https://twitter.com/YourBattleAxe/status/1617718512138715138
[161] https://twitter.com/SharonO08/status/1341743468478156810
[162] www.youtube.com/@uapinc5550/videos

5.4 Impunity Synergies

Compared to Trump's first term, however, the "Trump 2.0" impunity movement stands out in an important way – it appears to have even more capacity to mobilize. A key reason is the significant new role of its most prominent figure behind Trump, Pete Hegseth, who now leads the Defense Department. Indeed, Hegseth's Senate confirmation battle alone, a months-long saga that eventually saw him confirmed on a knife's edge, 51-50, with Vice President J.D. Vance casting the tie-breaking vote, typifies the impunity coalition's invigorated capacity. When it became unclear if Hegseth would earn the support of enough moderate Republican senators to become Secretary of Defense, Fox News and GOP allies in Congress launched an aggressive campaign behind him.

One report documented a "full-court press" at Fox News for Hegseth.[163] Hegseth's former co-anchors defended him on air,[164] even welcoming Hegseth's mother to talk about how her son had been redeemed.[165] Other reporting confirmed that Fox News stars were "personally contacting Senators to push for Hegseth" and to provide character references. Fox News host Will Cain called allegations against Hegseth "100 percent bul_s***."[166] Fox News headlines during Hegseth's hearing included: "Hegseth Was 'Incredibly Talented, Battle-Proven Leader,' Military Evaluations Show"[167] and "'Clear Vision': Conservatives Rally around Hegseth after 'Crushing' Fiery Confirmation Hearing."[168] North Dakota

---

[163] Baragona, Justin. Dec. 5, 2024. "Fox News Colleagues Jump on Bandwagon to Back Pete Hegseth as Trump Defense Secretary Pick." *Independent*. independent.co.uk/news/world/americas/us-politics/hegseth-fox-news-defense-secretary-trump-pick-b2659638.html

[164] Stelter, Brian. Dec. 4, 2024. "Fox News Stars Defend Imperiled Ex-colleague Pete Hegseth amid Misconduct Allegations." *CNN*. https://edition.cnn.com/2024/12/04/media/fox-news-pete-hegseth-defend-misconduct-allegations/index.html

[165] Dec. 4, 2024. "Pete Hegseth's Mother Sets Record Straight on Allegations against Son." *Fox News*. www.foxnews.com/video/6365525205112

[166] Bickerton, James. Dec 4, 2024. "Pete Hegseth's Fox News Colleagues Speak Out." *Newsweek*. www.newsweek.com/pete-hegseth-fox-news-colleagues-speak-out-1995427

[167] Wallace, Danielle. Jan. 13, 2025. "Hegseth Was 'Incredibly Talented, Battle-Proven Leader,' Military Evaluations Show." *Fox News*. www.foxnews.com/politics/hegseth-incredibly-talented-battle-proven-leader-military-evaluations-show

[168] Miller, Andrew Mark. Jan. 14, 2025. "'Clear Vision': Conservatives Rally around Hegseth after 'Crushing' Fiery Confirmation Hearing." *Fox News*.

Sen. Kevin Cramer said that "[t]hey [Fox News] love him," which he described as "very reassuring."[169]

Similar support came from Republicans on Capitol Hill. For example, thirty-two military veterans serving in the House of Representatives penned a letter backing Hegseth.[170] The letter specifically claimed that Hegseth's "media expertise" would be "crucial in executing a clear vision that cuts through bureaucratic inertia." Sen. Mike Rounds of North Dakota told Newsmax that Hegseth was "refreshing," especially because of his focus on "mak[ing] the department more lethal."[171] Sen. Rick Scott of Florida lauded Hegseth for being "clearly committed to making sure we have a lethal military that scares the crap out of our enemies."[172] When faced with the accusation that Hegseth had a drinking problem, Sen. Markwayne Mullin of Oklahoma offered the excuse that "[t]here's a lot of alcohol that flows through Washington."[173]

Other right-wing groups and individuals also defended Hegseth. The Heritage Foundation filmed a pro-Hegseth TV ad[174] and published an open letter backing Hegseth signed by dozens of "prominent veterans," including Eddie Gallagher.[175] A member of the Navy SEAL Foundation, which hosts an annual swim in New York City that Hegseth has participated in, organized a march of more than 100 Navy SEALs in favor of Hegseth during the first day of

www.foxnews.com/politics/clear-vision-conservatives-rally-around-hegseth-crushing-fiery-confirmation-hearing

[169] Vaillancourt, William. Dec. 11, 2024. "Fox Stars Are Personally Contacting Senators to Push for Pete Hegseth." *Daily Beast.* www.thedailybeast.com/fox-stars-are-personally-contacting-senators-to-push-for-pete-hegseth/

[170] https://x.com/RepPfluger/status/1867026100007698446/photo/1

[171] Thomas, Jim. Dec. 7, 2024. "Sen. Rounds to Newsmax: Hegseth's Approach Focuses on Lethality, Success." *Newsmax.* www.newsmax.com/newsmax-tv/rounds-hegseth-candidate/2024/12/07/id/1190732/

[172] Kight, Stef W. Dec. 2, 2024. "GOP Senators Defend Hegseth after Private Meeting." *Axios.* www.axios.com/2024/12/03/senators-pete-hegseth-defense-secretary-trump

[173] Hawkinson, Katie. Dec. 8, 2024. "GOP Senator Offers Curious Defense for Pete Hegseth Drinking Claims: 'There's A Lot of Alcohol that Flows through Washington.'" *Independent.* www.independent.co.uk/news/world/americas/us-politics/pete-hegseth-markwayne-mullin-alcohol-fox-news-b2660897.html

[174] https://x.com/Heritage/status/1865132829782479278

[175] N.D. "Letter in Support of Pete Hegseth's Military Record." Heritage Foundation.

5.4 Impunity Synergies

his confirmation hearings.[176] Turning Point USA CEO Charlie Kirk, a right-wing celebrity, took to X to call crossing Hegseth a "red line."[177] Alongside other conservative outlets, a commentator at the Daily Signal blasted the "corporate media" for being on a "search-and-destroy mission" against Hegseth.[178]

Hegseth himself turned to conservative allies to argue his case and used his celebrity to make public appeals. He appeared on the Megyn Kelly podcast where he accused Democrats of operating a "classic art of the smear" against him.[179] In the *Wall Street Journal*, Hegseth wrote an op-ed titled, "I've Faced Fire Before. I Won't Back Down." Hegseth also personally thanked Trump on X after he doubled down in calling Hegseth a "WINNER."[180] As he walked around Capitol Hill with an entourage (including his personal guard, a former Army Special Forces master sergeant who once beat up a civilian and hogtied him in a pool),[181] Hegseth ripped open his suit jacket in "Superman style" to reveal an American flag lining, declaring, "This is how we're feeling today, right here."[182]

A striking example of the impunity coalition's coordination came in response to suggestions that Republican Sen. Joni Ernst of Iowa was wavering in her support of Hegseth. A pro-Trump, dark-money group took out a TV ad in Iowa claiming that the "deep state" was trying to block Hegseth's nomination.[183] Reports also documented a pressure campaign in Washington against Ernst to confirm Hegseth. According to an anonymous Trump ally, Hegseth became a "cause ...

---

[176] Mack, Ericc. "Navy SEALs, Veterans to March for Hegseth Confirmation." *Newsmax*. www.newsmax.com/newsfront/defense-secretary-confirmation-pete-hegseth/2024/12/08/id/1190824/
[177] https://x.com/charliekirk11/status/1864697921125650819
[178] www.instagram.com/thedailysignal/reel/DDfXg34JbMW/
[179] Brest, Mike. "Pete Hegseth Says He's a Victim of the 'Art of the Smear' Designed to Tank Defense Secretary Nomination." *Washington Examiner*. www.washingtonexaminer.com/policy/defense/3249299/pete-hegseth-victim-tank-secretary-defense-nomination/
[180] https://x.com/PeteHegseth/status/1865025967376269819
[181] Philipps, Dave and Sharon LaFraniere. Dec. 16, 2024. "Hegseth's Guard Left the Army After the Beating of a Civilian During Training." *New York Times*. www.nytimes.com/2024/12/16/us/politics/hegseth-bodyguard-army.html
[182] https://x.com/bennyjohnson/status/1866877678772437220
[183] Dec. 8, 2024. "Mullin: 'There's Been Absolutely No Noes from Republican Senators' on Hegseth Yet." *CNN*. https://edition.cnn.com/2024/12/08/politics/video/sotu-markwayne-mullin-defends-hegseth-nomination

[n]ot even for the official Trump operation, but the movement who is going apeshit for him."[184] One well-known conservative commentator offered a stark threat: "Warning to Joni Ernst – Pete Hegseth will be just fine if you sabotage his deserved spot as SecDef ... You, however, will not be fine."[185]

On the eve of his confirmation hearing, the *New York Times* ran a feature titled "Trump Supporters Go All In for Pete Hegseth with Money and Coordination."[186] The article described a "phalanx of well-financed groups" backing Hegseth, including podcasters, political advocacy groups, and donors helping to make Hegseth's "political survival a cause célèbre." Former Trump adviser Steve Bannon reflected on how Trump's backers had grown "more sophisticated" since Trump's first term, commenting that "it's got more money ... a whole media and influencer ecosystem, and it started earlier, because a lot of it came out of the campaign."[187] Another account described how pro-Hegseth advocates intimidated possible witnesses and suppressed an FBI background check on Hegseth.[188]

All of this support unfolded within the broader MAGA network, where activist members of the public made clear to party officials the imperative of voting for Hegseth. For example, in response to charges that Hegseth had once drunkenly yelled "Kill all Muslims! Kill all Muslims!" (allegations that Hegseth denies), one writer commented

---

[184] McGraw, Meredith and Natalie Allison. Dec. 10, 2024. "Trump Allies Adopt New Strategy for Nominees: Make the Doubters Pay." *POLITICO*. www.politico.com/news/2024/12/10/trump-hegseth-controversial-nominee-playbook-00193349

[185] Peterson, Kristina, John McCormick, and Lindsay Wise. Dec. 10, 2024. "Pete Hegseth Gets Boost from Trump Allies' Pressure Campaign." *Wall Street Journal*. www.wsj.com/politics/policy/pete-hegseth-trump-pressure-republican-senators-50ee71c7

[186] Kelly, Kate and Kenneth P. Vogel. Jan. 13, 2025. "Trump Supporters Go All in for Pete Hegseth with Money and Coordination." *New York Times*. www.nytimes.com/2025/01/13/us/politics/pete-hegseth-defense-secretary-trump.html

[187] Kelly, Kate and Kenneth P. Vogel. Jan. 13, 2025. "Trump Supporters Go All in for Pete Hegseth with Money and Coordination." *New York Times*. www.nytimes.com/2025/01/13/us/politics/pete-hegseth-defense-secretary-trump.html

[188] Mayer, Jane. Jan. 13, 2025. "The Pressure Campaign to Get Pete Hegseth Confirmed as Defense Secretary." *New Yorker*. www.newyorker.com/news/the-lede/the-pressure-campaign-to-get-pete-hegseth-confirmed-as-defense-secretary

5.4 Impunity Synergies

on how "it doesn't dim his star in MAGA world. Instead, it signals that he's reliable. That's a bond that neither Trump nor most of the G.O.P. caucus will want to mess with."[189] The flurry of online support for Hegseth mirrored that of U.S. servicemembers jailed for war crimes. Supporters cast Hegseth as a folk hero, called for the primarying of Republicans who failed to back him, and expressed feelings of near-religious zeal for his confirmation.

After Hegseth was confirmed, the impunity coalition celebrated. On Hannity, Fox News's Joe Concha heralded Hegseth as the ultimate "soldier-secretary" and praised his Fox News colleagues for being the "only people" who "both on and off camera" said that "everything reported by from the likes of NBC, and CNN, the *New York Times*, and others in our dying legacy media was all BS."[190] Republican Sen. Markwayne Mullin of Oklahoma posted on X, "We did it, America. It was an honor to be in the fight with my friend, and your SecDef: @PeteHegseth."[191] Sen. Mike Lee of Utah declared, "Heck yeah! @PeteHegseth is the man for the job."[192] Hegseth thanked his supporters, exclaiming, "This is for the troops. For the warriors.... We will never back down."[193]

Beyond just Hegseth, the few degrees of separation between members of the "war crime lobby" are now facilitated by tight-knit personal and professional ties. "Revolving doors" produce a constant churn of activists across like-minded institutions. For example, among the members of the Pipe Hitter Foundation's board of directors is Tommy Marquez, formerly a caseworker for CJWC co-founder Duncan Hunter. Also on the board is Carl Higbie, a *Newsmax* contributor.[194] Derrick Miller, the current CJWC executive director, was previously represented in his war crime case

---

[189] Stephens, Brett. Jan. 22, 2025. "What It Means That Republicans Aren't Acting on the Pete Hegseth Allegations." *New York Times*. www.nytimes.com/2025/01/22/opinion/pete-hegseth-republicans-trump-loyalty.html
[190] https://x.com/JoeConchaTV/status/1882985910922612995
[191] https://x.com/SenMullin/status/1882989455650472062
[192] Mion, Landon. Jan. 25, 2025. "Republicans React to Pete Hegseth's Confirmation as Defense Secretary: 'He is the Change Agent'." *Fox News*. www.foxnews.com/politics/republicans-react-pete-hegseths-confirmation-defense-secretary-he-change-agent
[193] https://x.com/PeteHegseth/status/1883022600676188588
[194] https://pipehitterfoundation.org/who-we-are/

by UAP.[195] Conservative attorney Tim Parlatore, who has penned articles for *Newsmax* under the heading "In Defense of Justice,"[196] has represented Eddie Gallagher,[197] Pete Hegseth,[198] and Trump.[199]

With the second Trump administration, however, one organization still stands out as a key node connecting national security staff who have expressed views challenging the law of war: Fox News. In addition to supplying Pete Hegseth as Defense Secretary, Trump's national security adviser, Rep. Michael Waltz, previously a Fox News commentator, has been a vociferous critic of America's rules of engagement.[200] Sebastian Gorka, a former Fox News contributor and Trump's counterterrorism director, has described the West as being in a civilizational struggle against Islam, claimed that Palestine does not exist, and, according to one analysis, advocated views that "presag[ed] an approach [to the war in Gaza] that has led to tens of thousands of civilians killed in airstrikes and other attacks."[201]

In short, a cottage industry on the American right is now devoted to overturning IHL prosecutions. At its center are Trump, Fox News, and Republican lawmakers. The movement extends to numerous complementary actors. Notable is the movement's scale and reach, tapping into millions of right-wing supporters and would-be

---

[195] www.uap.org/success-stories/
[196] www.newsmax.com/insiders/timothyparlatore/bio-573/
[197] Wallace, Danielle. July 16, 2019. "Navy SEAL Edward Gallagher's Defense Lawyer Wants to Rejoin the Navy to Teach Prosecutors, Says He Fears for Law-abiding Warfighters." *Fox News*. www.foxnews.com/us/navy-seal-edward-gallaghers-defense-lawyer-timothy-parlatore-rejoin-navy-teach-prosecutors
[198] Dec. 6, 2024. "Pete Hegseth's Lawyer Responds to Allegations That Could Jeopardize Hegseth's Nomination." *CNN*. https://edition.cnn.com/2024/12/05/politics/video/pete-hegseth-tim-parlatore-lawyer-nomination-src-digvid
[199] Alemany, Jacqueline. May 17, 2023. "Attorney Tim Parlatore Says He Is Leaving Donald Trump's Legal Team." *Washington Post*. www.washingtonpost.com/national-security/2023/05/17/parlatore-trump-quits-classified-documents/
[200] Nov. 18, 2019. "Rep. Michael Waltz: Rules of Engagement Were Restrictive under Obama." Rep. Michael Waltz. www.youtube.com/watch?v=_cb9UNVGwJo
[201] Horton, Alex and John Hudson. Nov. 23, 2024. "Gorka and His Hard-right Views on Islam Head back to the White House." *Washington Post*. www.washingtonpost.com/politics/2024/11/23/sebastian-gorka-trump-islam/

5.4 Impunity Synergies

supporters. Its multiple layers of advocacy – from top-down lobbying in government and media, to bottom-up activities by grassroots organizers – synergistically advance the impunity agenda. For now, these efforts seem unlikely to dissipate. As UAP CEO David Gurfein has predicted, "I think what we're seeing now is the tip of the iceberg ... [in] supporting those warriors who have been improperly accused of war crimes and unjustly convicted."[202]

---

[202] Laporta, James. Nov. 26, 2019. "After Gallagher, Military Activists Lobby Trump to Intervene in These Other Cases." *Newsweek*. www.newsweek.com/trump-pardons-gallagher-military-activists-lobby-intervene-other-cases-1474007

6 | *Trumpism and the Future of Impunity*

It is hard to imagine any other U.S. president responding with such contempt for the law of war. In November 2019, Trump was preparing to offer clemency to Mathew Golsteyn, Clint Lorance, and Eddie Gallagher. Chairman of the Joint Chiefs Gen. Mark Milley recalled the chilling response he received when urging Trump to reconsider. After telling him, "Mr. President, we have military ethics and laws about what happens in battle. We can't do that kind of thing. It's a war crime," Trump reportedly demurred: "You guys ... are all just killers. What's the difference?"[1] The words were telling. Trump saw U.S. servicemembers as agents of death, as "killing machines." For him, the Geneva Conventions were mere formalities, not to be taken seriously, and not to be shown public deference.

Chapters 1–5 explained how Trump has shattered a consensus, solidified after the signing of the Geneva Conventions in 1949, that Western leaders would at least pay lip service to international humanitarian law (IHL). But as the impunity agenda escalates, what lessons can be drawn from Trump's experience, and his return to power? This final chapter closes with several forward-looking discussions. Section 6.1 highlights practical takeaways from the book for IHL policymakers and practitioners. Section 6.2 explores what, if anything, can be done to curb the impunity agenda at its source. Sections 6.3 and 6.4 examine the future of Trump's impunity agenda, both in America and globally, including in major conflicts involving Russia and Israel. Section 6.4 poses questions for further research.

6.1 Practical Takeaways

For policymakers and practitioners, several practical takeaways from the book stand out. Most notably, for stewards of the Geneva

---

[1] Golberg, Jeffrey. Sept. 21, 2023. "The Patriot." *Atlantic.* www.theatlantic.com/magazine/archive/2023/11/general-mark-milley-trump-coup/675375/.

6.1 Practical Takeaways

Conventions, the Trump case underscores the imperative of not taking for granted public deference to IHL as a "first duty" of signatory nations. Historically, most of the focus on the Geneva Conventions has been on ensuring point-by-point, legalistic compliance with technical provisions. However, Common Article 1 of the Geneva Conventions formally demands that party states first "undertake to respect and to ensure respect for the present Convention in all circumstances."[2] This requires two-sided reciprocity: nations must publicly uphold IHL to qualify for its safeguards by demonstrating broad deference to its principles and values.[3]

This first duty is even more demanding than it appears. In 2016, the International Committee of the Red Cross (ICRC) published a new "Commentaries" on the Geneva Conventions for the first time in over sixty years, clarifying that party states have both a "positive" and a "negative" duty to uphold IHL.[4] Under the conventional, negative duty, "High Contracting Parties may neither encourage, nor aid or assist in violations of the Conventions by Parties to a conflict." Under the positive duty, however, they must go beyond this requirement to "do everything reasonably in their power to prevent and bring such violations to an end." This positive duty can again be construed as a responsibility to proactively ensure that third parties and other nations visibly respect IHL.

These obligations matter because, for centuries, armed fighters have committed atrocities on the battlefield, often with the tacit or explicit support of political leaders. By viewing the recent past, an era defined by a professed commitment to the Geneva Conventions, as the exception, experts can more appropriately weigh the risk of open challenges to IHL in the West. The failure of even party states to outwardly defer to the Geneva Conventions may give fodder for skeptics to question the integrity of their protocols. The public may lose confidence in the institution, especially given an inability to prevent many atrocities. A "domino effect" may also result in leaders of party states refusing

---

[2] https://ihl-databases.icrc.org/en/ihl-treaties/gci-1949/article-1#:~:text=The%20High%20Contracting%20Parties%20undertake,present%20Convention%20in%20all%20circumstances.
[3] U.S. State Department. "Digest of United States Practice in International Law." www.state.gov/wp-content/uploads/2019/05/2017-Digest-Chapter-18.pdf
[4] https://ihl-databases.icrc.org/en/ihl-treaties/gci-1949/preamble/commentary/2016?activeTab=undefined

to pay public respect to IHL when others do the same. This, in turn, could aid in delegitimizing IHL.

The Trump case not only underlines the limits of U.S. hegemony in fostering public respect for the law of war abroad. It also raises a question of how much other nations will follow suit when America's leader expressly champions illicit acts in combat. Given its superpower status and military dominance, a key source of America's "soft power" has traditionally been setting normative precedents regarding outward respect for the Geneva Conventions.[5] By failing to live up to its own ethical standards, however, the U.S. will be unable to admonish other countries that fail to honor the Geneva Conventions. Unless other nations step into this role, it again heightens the risks that other leaders will also "revise deviancy downward," and ultimately, overtly reject IHL.

Shifting next to Western militaries, this book highlights the importance of taking concrete steps to preempt public challenges to the law of war. This includes efforts to inoculate troops against ideological subcultures where unofficial norms inspired by political actors can degrade the military's official ethos. Under Trump, respect for IHL was jeopardized not just via policies but also verbally to a rare degree. Trump showed how political messaging could contravene rules and norms that servicemembers learn in basic training. This may inform what types of counter-messaging can blunt its negative effects. Commanders, trainers, and legal officers within Western militaries could leverage lessons to improve curricula, operations manuals, and field exercises related to IHL.

As part of this training, Western militaries need to instill in troops, in apolitical terms, that upholding the law of war is not just an ethical imperative but a strategic one. Discounting the value of IHL or committing war crimes can jeopardize long-term tactical objectives, especially in contexts with high levels of interaction with local populations. As political scientist Janina Dill has observed, "Figuring out how to fight wars without the long-term alienation of the civilian population is the critical strategic task.... (whispered: it's also a legal requirement & moral imperative.)"[6] Ethical lapses in conflict put a

---

[5] Nye, Jr. Joseph S. 1990. *Bound to Lead: The Changing Nature of American Power*. New York: Basic Books.
[6] https://x.com/JaninaDill/status/1882743452150182169

6.1 Practical Takeaways

target on the backs of Western combatants, even in peacekeeping missions, and also make affected populaces more likely to align with rebel groups or terrorist organizations.

In the U.S. military, Trump's presidency also exposed worrying levels of right-wing extremism among current and ex-servicemembers who devalue IHL. Military leaders insist that they have a "no tolerance" policy for extremism, and that existing regulations already bar memberships in hate groups.[7] However, as evidenced by January 6, enforcement remains inadequate. Needed is more systematic screening of recruits and training of commanders about how to identify and deal with threats. The balance, however, comes in distinguishing between radical behavior and simply right-leaning opinions. The perception that militaries are targeting Republicans or Trump voters will not only provoke backlash and hurt recruitment efforts[8] but also weaken military readiness.

For judges, prosecutors, and other legal actors within Western militaries, the Trump case further calls attention to the limits of their authority. Ultimately, a commander-in-chief can overrule lower-ranking officials in prosecutions and sentences. This raises the stakes of getting as close to "right" as possible elements of jurisprudence that subordinates do control. Flaws in the court system increase the likelihood that future leaders, legitimately or not, grant military clemencies. This could make such interventions seem more routine, and thus justifiable. In the U.S., achieving just outcomes may require conceding that some proposals for military justice reform, such as the requirement for unanimous verdicts,[9] have merit or that judicial procedures could be made better or more transparent.

Next, for civilian governments in the West, the Trump case offers reason to rethink how existing democratic guardrails fail to guarantee public commitments to IHL. In the U.S., much of the attention on Trump's rule-breaking has centered on institutions such as Congress,

---

[7] Garamone, Jim. Jan. 14, 2021. "No Place in DOD for Extremism, White Supremacy, Officials Say." U.S. Department of Defense. www.defense.gov/News/News-Stories/Article/Article/2472928/no-place-in-dod-for-extremism-white-supremacy-officials-say/.

[8] Jan. 25, 2021. "Dems Pushing to Purge Military of Political Opponents." *Fox News*. www.foxnews.com/video/6226110921001

[9] Maurer, Dan. 2023. "Why Are Non-Unanimous (Court-Martial) Guilty Verdicts Still Alive After Ramos?" *American Criminal Law Review* 60(1): 127.

elections, or the free press.[10] Experts have observed the hazards of Trump's military leadership,[11] especially for civil-military relations,[12] but without a paradigm for how it fits into a larger political agenda. However, Trump relied on many of the same tactics and allies to disrupt both domestic checks on his power and the law of war. This calls attention to an emergent, but often overlooked, threat: how open attacks on IHL and those on national institutions can go hand in hand.

The failures of democratic guardrails to impede the impunity agenda heighten the responsibility of civic leaders, when possible, to strengthen cultural respect for the law of war. For elected officials, the institutionalization of efforts to minimize civilian harm and strengthen the military justice system should be paramount. While such initiatives may not always prevent leaders from flagrantly violating the law of war, they may reduce collateral damage. Task forces and "blue ribbon" commissions can get these initiatives underway. However, "bureaucratizing" reforms, through the creation of permanent, inter-agency administrative and staffing positions, may be more effective.[13] Advice and input from military experts can secure buy-in and forge bipartisan consensus.

In the U.S., notable developments have occurred on this front, even if it is unclear whether some can survive four more years of

---

[10] Howell, William G., and Terry M. Moe. 2020. *Presidents, Populism, and the Crisis of Democracy*. Chicago: University of Chicago Press. Jacobs, Lawrence R. 2002. *Democracy under Fire: Donald Trump and the Breaking of American History*. New York: Oxford University Press. Peters, Jeremy W. 2022. *How Republicans Lost Their Party and Got Everything They Ever Wanted*. New York: Penguin Random House.

[11] Dombrowski, Peter and Simon Reich. 2017. "Does Donald Trump Have a Grand Strategy?" *International Affairs* 93(5): 1013–1037. Lynch, Timothy. 2020. *In the Shadow of the Cold War American Foreign Policy from George Bush Sr. to Donald Trump*. Cambridge: Cambridge University Press.

[12] Binkley, John C. 2022. "Civil–Military Relations During the Trump Administration: Rejection of Military Professionalism and the Deterioration of Civil–Military Relations." *Armed Forces & Society* 50(1): 55–80. Feaver, Peter D. 2023. *Thanks for Your Service*. Oxford: Oxford University Press. Owens, Mackubin Thomas. 2021. "Maximum Toxicity: Civil-Military Relations in the Trump Era." *Strategic Studies Quarterly* 15(2): 99–119. Schake, Kori. 2020. "The Military and the Constitution Under Trump." *Survival* 62(4): 31–38.

[13] Hodges, Doyle. Feb. 10, 2021. "Bureaucratizing to Fight Extremism in the Military." *War on the Rocks*. https://warontherocks.com/2021/02/bureaucratizing-to-fight-extremism-in-the-military/

6.1 Practical Takeaways

Trump. One is the 2023 creation of the DoD's Civilian Protection Center of Excellence (CP CoE), which emerged from the Civilian Harm Mitigation and Response Action Plan approved by Defense Secretary Lloyd Austin in 2022. The Center's aim is to serve as "the hub and facilitator of Department-wide analysis, learning, and strategic approaches" that "institutionalize[s] good practices for civilian harm mitigation and response during operations."[14] As part of the initiative, the CP CoE supports operational command, crafts policy doctrine, and facilitates research. Following Trump's inauguration, however, the administration put in place potential plans to "disestablish" the office.[15]

Structural reform also took root during the Biden administration in how criminal charges are brought within the military. Traditionally, senior military commanders have held nearly total discretion over charging crimes in their units, with little oversight. The result had been acute disparities in charge rates that have fueled suspicions of selective prosecutions.[16] In 2022, Congress used the National Defense Authorization Act to transfer prosecutions for numerous crimes away from commanders and to military lawyers who report to civilian service secretaries.[17] In 2023, Joe Biden signed a largely bipartisan executive order amending the UCMJ to assign decision-making in serious offenses, including murder, to specialized, independent military prosecutors.[18]

Although not applying to U.S. combatants, Congress in 2022 also passed the Justice for Victims of War Crimes Act, which aims to promote

---

[14] U.S. Department of Defense. 2023. "Report on the Civilian Protection Center of Excellence." https://policy.defense.gov/Portals/11/Documents/CHMR/Report-on-the-Civilian-Protection-Center-of-Excellence-Final-Report.pdf

[15] Ismay, John. Jan. 23, 2025. "U.S. Army Plans to Eliminate Office for Reducing Civilian Harm in War." *New York Times*. www.nytimes.com/2025/01/23/us/pentagon-civilian-deaths.html

[16] VanLandngham, Rachel. Jan. 5, 2024. "The U.S. Military Moves Closer to Just Military Justice – But More Work Remains." *Just Security*. www.justsecurity.org/91004/the-u-s-military-moves-closer-to-just-military-justice-but-more-work-remains/

[17] www.congress.gov/bill/117th-congress/senate-bill/1605

[18] July 28, 2023. "FACT SHEET: President Biden to Sign Executive Order Implementing Bipartisan Military Justice Reforms." The White House. https://bidenwhitehouse.archives.gov/briefing-room/statements-releases/2023/07/28/fact-sheet-president-biden-to-sign-executive-order-implementing-bipartisan-military-justice-reforms/

accountability for global violations of IHL.[19] Under the prior War Crimes Act of 1996, U.S. authorities had been restricted from prosecuting alleged war criminals unless either the victim or offender was an American national. With the reform, the only requirement for bringing charges is that the suspect be arrested on U.S. soil. While the bill was introduced in response to Russia's atrocities in Ukraine, it extends to any foreign combatant accused of war crimes visiting or residing in the U.S. Advocates say that the law reflects America's commitment to ensuring that the country does not become a safe haven for war criminals.

Finally, for humanitarian organizations seeking to advance IHL and security sector reform, this book highlights that large-scale programming cannot be enacted divorced from political context. Despite outsized investments into initiatives to bolster IHL promotion,[20] much is unknown about how macro-level political variables interact with meso-level leadership to foster, or undermine, humanitarian goals. Practitioners typically concentrate on instilling combat ethics at the unit or subunit level. Yet the Trump experience reveals how leaders, alongside other state and nonstate actors, can openly subvert law of war principles. Programmatic efforts to uphold IHL may fail when influential figures, to whom combatants have a political affinity, dismiss its basic precepts.

These insights can encourage global human rights organizations, such as the ICRC or Geneva Call, to recognize vulnerabilities caused by state leadership that impinge on military ethics programs. An impediment, however, is the paucity of knowledge about how the effects of training initiatives are conditioned by politics. When organizations like the ICRC partner with armed groups to help instill norms of restraints, evaluations are critical to assess efficacy and identify "best practices." However, internal and external politics, budget constraints, and fears of exposing poor performance may disincentivize scrutiny. This underlines the importance of donors and contributing governments insisting on the establishment of long-term, independent monitoring of IHL programs.

---

[19] Kavi, Aishvarya. 2022. "Congress Votes to Expand U.S. Power to Prosecute International War Crimes." *New York Times*. www.nytimes.com/2022/12/22/us/politics/congress-war-crimes.html

[20] Blank, Laurie R. and Gregory P. Noone. *Law of War Training: Resources for Military and Civilian Leaders*. US Institute of Peace. https://law.emory.edu/_includes/documents/sections/clinics/law-of-war-training-manual-01.pdf/ Oberleitner, Gerd. 2015. *Human Rights in Armed Conflict: Law, Practice, Policy*. Cambridge: Cambridge University Press.

These challenges highlight the need for humanitarian organizations to apply appropriate social science methods to test pro-IHL initiatives. While surveys and randomized controlled trials are indispensable tools, researchers cannot always manipulate political dynamics that affect military cultures surrounding IHL. This makes it essential to integrate innovative empirical techniques, such as exploiting natural and quasi-natural experiments, to explore a wider set of questions and to improve causal identification.[21] In-depth qualitative case studies may also help to illuminate causal chains from how a leader's behavior shapes the attitudes of combatants toward IHL. Collaborating with academics, think tanks, and freelance scholars can enhance evaluation quality.

6.2 Can Anything Stop Impunity at the Source?

Besides addressing its downstream consequences, can the impunity agenda be stopped at its source? Later, several possible remedies are examined. These include "nonbinding" methods that lack enforcement power but could tilt public opinion away from impunity or make the calculus of overtly straining IHL less appealing. They also include "binding" methods that could legally constrain executives or hold them accountable for wrongdoing. The main challenge, however, lies in execution. In light of both Trump's return to power and international obstacles to change, the prospects for short- to medium-term reform appear bleak. U.S. presidents are highly likely to retain considerable discretion, both formal and informal, in whether to defer to the law of war.

Nonbinding Methods

Appeals from Military Voices
First, greater pressures from U.S. military voices might discourage presidents from overtly challenging IHL.[22] Even modest pleas could raise

---

[21] Sekhon, Jasjeet S. and Rocio Titiunik. 2012. "When Natural Experiments Are Neither Natural nor Experiments." *American Political Science Review* 106(1): 35–37. Jones, Benjamin F. and Benjamin A. Olken. 2005. "Do Leaders Matter? National Leadership and Growth since World War II." *The Quarterly Journal of Economics* 120(3): 335–864.

[22] David, Jovana. Jan. 15, 2021. "Should the Military Leadership Speak Up on Partisan Politics?" U.S. Army War College. https://warroom.armywarcollege.edu/articles/partisan-politics/

public awareness given the high regard with which Americans, and conservatives particularly, hold the military.[23] While Democrats and left-wing media routinely attacked Trump on military matters, accountability may carry more weight from inside the organization.[24] Some high-profile military leaders did criticize Trump's attacks on IHL. Former Chairman of the Joint Chiefs Martin Dempsey, for instance, called Trump's war crime clemencies an "[a]bdication of moral responsibility."[25] Ret. Gen. David Petraeus also declared that Trump's pardons "tell ... the world that Americans abroad can commit the most heinous of crimes with impunity."[26] Yet many were silent, while others endorsed Trump's acts.

One obvious hindrance to more military voices speaking out is the predominantly right-leaning bent of the officer corps. Political scientist Heidi Urben, for example, has summarized that, even more than enlistees, "[p]ast surveys have shown senior military officers to generally be conservative and identify with the Republican Party, a trend which has solidified with the advent and professionalism of the all-volunteer force."[27] Because of this right-leaning composition, a nontrivial fraction of high-ranking officers may either favor the impunity agenda or inhabit social circles where pressures exist to toe the party line. This may be especially true amid rising levels of polarization within the U.S. military, which reflect broader divides in American politics, compounded by Trump's return to commander-in-chief.[28]

[23] https://news.gallup.com/poll/1597/confidence-institutions.aspx
[24] Bovens, Mark, Robert E. Goodin, and Thomas Schillemans, eds. 2014. *The Oxford Handbook of Public Accountability*. Oxford: Oxford University Press. Keohane, Robert O. 2006. "Accountability in World Politics." *Scandinavian Political Studies* 29(2): 75–87.
[25] Gage, John. May 21, 2019. "Obama's Top General Slams Trump Military Pardons as 'Abdication of Moral Responsibility.'" *Washington Examiner*. www.washingtonexaminer.com/news/obamas-top-general-slams-trump-military-pardons-as-abdication-of-moral-responsibility
[26] Rubin, Trudy. Dec. 27, 2020. "Petraeus, Crocker: Trump's Pardons to War Criminals Undermine Rule of Law, Endanger U.S. Troops." *Philadelphia Inquirer*. www.inquirer.com/opinion/trump-pardons-ryan-crocker-david-petraeus-nisour-square-iraq-20201227.html
[27] Urben, Heidi A. 2010. Civil-Military Relations in a Time of War. Georgetown University. Ph.D. Dissertation. https://nation.time.com/wp-content/uploads/sites/8/2012/11/urben-diss-1-5.pdf
[28] Kirisci, Mustafa, Ibrahim Kocaman, and Cagil Albayrak. Mar. 3, 2023. "Why Polarization in the Military Is a Growing Concern for Democracies." *National Interest*. https://nationalinterest.org/feature/why-polarization-military-growing-concern-democracies-206267

6.2 Can Anything Stop Impunity at the Source?

Among Trump's detractors, other reservations may mute criticism of the impunity agenda. Most practically is the UCMJ's formal ban on active-duty officers expressing "contemptuous words against the President."[29] Although retired leaders are subject to fewer legal checks, years of acculturation can make them disinclined to speak out. Additionally, veterans may have principled concerns against using their uniforms as "political currency."[30] Trump critics may also be reluctant to admit that the military will fall victim to direct challenges to IHL. After Trump's war crime clemencies, for instance, Gen. Mark Milley insisted that the U.S. military "will not turn into a gang ... raping, burning and pillaging."[31] This reflects a belief that the military is immune to the worst effects of overt attacks on IHL.

Pushback from Moderate Republicans

Pushback from moderate Republican politicians might also raise awareness about the dangers of the impunity agenda. Centrist voices could balance out the party's advocacy for direct breaches of the law of war. A small minority of Republicans on Capitol Hill did raise concerns about war crime clemencies and urged Trump to reevaluate his stances during his first term. Most notably, Sen. Mitt Romney of Utah, a frequent Trump critic, called pardoning war criminals "a terrible idea" and "unthinkable."[32] Sen. Joni Ernst of Iowa, a veteran of the Iowa National Guard, more modestly conceded that there could be "some issues" with war crime clemencies.[33] Such defections, however,

---

[29] www.law.cornell.edu/uscode/text/10/888
[30] Dunlap, Charlie. Sept. 21, 2019. "Why an Apolitical Military Is So Important in an Era of an 'All-Volunteer' Force." *Lawfire*. https://sites.duke.edu/lawfire/2019/09/21/why-an-apolitical-military-is-so-important-in-an-era-of-an-all-voluntary-force/
[31] O'Brien, Connor. Dec. 11, 2019. "Top General: Military Won't Be a 'Raping, Burning and Pillaging' Gang after Trump's War Crimes Pardons." *POLITICO*. www.politico.com/news/2019/12/11/top-general-military-wont-be-a-raping-burning-and-pillaging-gang-after-trumps-war-crimes-pardons-082467
[32] Bobic, Igor. May 21, 2019. "'Terrible Idea': Senators Slam Trump Plan to Pardon Vets Accused of War Crimes." *HuffPost*. www.huffpost.com/entry/trump-pardon-war-crimes-mitt-romney_n_5ce4697ae4b0547bd12e82e8
[33] Bobic, Igor. May 21, 2019. "'Terrible Idea': Senators Slam Trump Plan to Pardon Vets Accused of War Crimes." *HuffPost*. www.huffpost.com/entry/trump-pardon-war-crimes-mitt-romney_n_5ce4697ae4b0547bd12e82e8

were notable exceptions. GOP criticism was mostly dwarfed by either support for Trump's interventions or silence.

One reason why more moderate Republicans are unlikely to speak out is simply their small and diminishing numbers.[34] Particularly in the U.S. House, electoral trends and institutional setups coinciding with polarization have sidelined many "establishment" figures. Scholars point to causes like gerrymandering (the drawing of districts to create "safe" seats),[35] the growth of out-of-state donor contributions (which encourages politicians to court moneyed interests that are ideologically extreme),[36] and the role of low-turnout primaries (which drive candidates to court fringe voters).[37] Given growing right-wing clout and Trump's re-ascendance to power, Republicans who fail to support the Trumpian line on IHL may fear retribution, such as losing committee memberships or being shut out of fundraisers.

Even if moderate Republicans did take stronger stands in favor of IHL, there is reason to doubt that large blocs of conservative voters would reject the impunity agenda. It could even be counterproductive. Many MAGA Republicans, for example, have worn criticism from moderates as "badges of honor" that boost their right-wing credibility.[38] To the degree that impunity sympathizers in Congress stand in opposition to moderates, they can depict themselves as "true conservatives" fighting against "RINOs" ("Republicans in name only"). This likelihood is especially high given Trump's reclaiming of

---

[34] Packer, George. Nov. 5, 2018. "The Demise of the Moderate Republican." *New Yorker*. www.newyorker.com/magazine/2018/11/12/the-demise-of-the-moderate-republican / Thomsen, Danielle M. 2017. *Opting out of Congress: Partisan Polarization and the Decline of Moderate Candidates*. Cambridge: Cambridge University Press.

[35] McGann, Anthony J., Charles Anthony Smith, Michael Latner, and Alex Keena. 2016. *Gerrymandering in America: The House of Representatives, the Supreme Court, and the Future of Popular Sovereignty*. Cambridge: Cambridge University Press.

[36] Skocpol, Theda and Alexander Hertel-Fernandez. 2016. "The Koch Network and Republican Party Extremism." *Perspectives on Politics* 14(3): 681–699.

[37] Jacobson, Gary C. 2004. *The Politics of Congressional Elections*, 6th ed. New York: Pearson.

[38] Antle III, W. James. Aug. 26, 2022. "'The Definition of Fascism': Biden Uses F-word to Describe Trump Republicans." *Washington Examiner*. www.washingtonexaminer.com/news/white-house/biden-uses-the-f-word-trump-republicans

6.2 Can Anything Stop Impunity at the Source? 211

the White House.[39] In some policy areas, more belligerent wings of the "MAGAverse" have arguably even radicalized beyond Trump,[40] including on U.S. military justice issues.

Critiques from Conservative Intellectual Circles

Conservative intellectual circles, encompassing right-of-center think tanks, research institutes, and policy organizations, could counter open challenges to IHL.[41] Operating with a degree of independence from partisan politics, a muscular defense of the law of war from well-known conservative entities could be influential. During the first Trump administration, for example, the Heritage Foundation played a pivotal role in shaping the White House's policy agenda.[42] With *Project 2025,* a right-wing policy manual outlining plans for Trump's second term, Heritage is again poised to guide Trump's second term.[43] Similarly, the American Enterprise Institute (AEI) provided the intellectual groundwork for George W. Bush's Iraq invasion[44] and major battlefield strategies like the 2007 troop "surge."[45]

---

[39] Edsall, Thomas B. Apr. 20, 2022. "With or Without Trump, the MAGA Movement Is the Future of the Republican Party." *New York Times.* www.nytimes.com/2022/04/20/opinion/trump-trumpism-republican-party.html/ Tharoor, Ishaan. Nov. 5, 2020. "Trumpism Is Here to Stay." *Washington Post.* www.washingtonpost.com/world/2020/11/05/trumpism-here-to-stay/

[40] Gift, Thomas. Jan. 5, 2022. "Has Trump Become Too Tame for the MAGAverse?" *The Hill.* https://thehill.com/opinion/white-house/588289-has-trump-become-too-tame-for-the-magaverse/

[41] Arin, Kubilay Yado. 2014. *Think Tanks: The Brain Trusts of US Foreign Policy.* Grafelfing, Germany: Springer. Stahl, Jason. 2016. *The Conservative Think Tank in American Political Culture Since 1945.* Chapel Hill: University of North Carolina Press. Wiarda, Howard J. 2008. "The New Powerhouses: Think Tanks and Foreign Policy." *The Journal of the National Committee on American Foreign Policy* 30(2): 96–117.

[42] Kopan, Tal. Dec. 7, 2016. "Meet Donald Trump's Think Tank." *CNN.* www.cnn.com/2016/12/06/politics/donald-trump-heritage-foundation-transition/index.html

[43] Quinn, Melissa and Jacob Rosen Nov. 8, 2024. "What Is Project 2025? What to Know about the Conservative Blueprint for a Second Trump Administration." *CBS News.* www.cbsnews.com/news/what-is-project-2025-trump-conservative-blueprint-heritage-foundation/

[44] Altheide, David L. and Jennifer N. Grimes. 2005. "War Programming: The Propaganda Project and the Iraq War." *Sociological Quarterly* 46: 617–643.

[45] Kagan, Kimberly. 2010. *The Surge: A Military History.* New York: Encounter Books.

Scholars at such institutions, however, have shown limited engagement with IHL controversies and might even be open to more military clemencies. As of early 2021, website searches revealed only three articles in total on Trump's war crime interventions penned by experts at Heritage, AEI, and the Hudson Institute. Although none clearly endorsed the interventions, neither did any unequivocally condemn them. For example, a group of Heritage scholars observed that "executive leniency ... is best done after serious consultation..., and only when leniency is deserved."[46] Gary Schmitt of AEI said that "pardons are a tool to be used decisively" albeit "rarely."[47] Hudson senior fellow Rebeccah L. Heinrichs argued that "[w]ith war-crime pardons, President Trump should proceed with an abundance of caution."[48]

AEI, in particular, has also housed two experts arguably most associated with recent White House challenges to IHL. John Yoo, a visiting scholar at AEI and a former Justice Department lawyer, authored George W. Bush's infamous "torture memos," which rationalized his enhanced interrogation program.[49] Moreover, John Bolton, previously a senior fellow at AEI before serving as Trump's national security adviser, consistently questioned the right of the International Criminal Court (ICC) to uphold various facets of IHL. This included calling the ICC an "illegitimate court" and claiming that the Trump White House would "let the ICC die."[50] If anything, these affiliations offer reason to doubt that such major conservative organizations will defend against direct threats to IHL.

[46] Spoehr, Thomas, Dakota Wood, John Venable, and James Jay Carfano. Dec. 6, 2019. "The Case of Navy SEAL Eddie Gallagher: Trusting the Military Justice System and Its Essential Role in National Security." Heritage Foundation. www.heritage.org/defense/commentary/the-case-navy-seal-eddie-gallagher-trusting-the-military-justice-system-and-its

[47] Schmitt, Gary J. Nov. 26, 2019. "Unpardonable Pardons." *The Bulwark.* www.aei.org/op-eds/unpardonable-pardons/

[48] Heinrichs, Rebeccah L. June 3, 2019. "Caution Needed as Trump Ponders Pardons." Hudson Institute. www.hudson.org/research/15075-caution-needed-as-trump-ponders-pardons /

[49] Borger, Julian. July 20, 2020. "Trump Consults Bush Torture Lawyer on How to Skirt Law and Rule by Decree." *Guardian.* www.theguardian.com/us-news/2020/jul/20/trump-john-yoo-lawyer-torture-waterboarding

[50] Bowcott, Owen, Oliver Holmes, and Erin Durkin. Sept. 10, 2018. "John Bolton Threatens War Crimes Court with Sanctions in Virulent Attack." *Guardian.* www.theguardian.com/us-news/2018/sep/10/john-bolton-castigate-icc-washington-speech

"Guerrilla Sabotage"

Another mechanism for curbing overt challenges to IHL is for critics to defy ostensibly unlawful orders by the commander-in-chief or to resist implementation. A large literature on "guerrilla sabotage" in government, for example, explains how public servants, often obliquely or through subterfuge, thwart "unprincipled" superiors.[51] In essence, this amounts to what Trump labeled the "deep state." A case in point was Navy Secretary Richard Spencer, who refused Trump's command to restore Eddie Gallagher's SEAL status.[52] Only after his termination did Spencer go public, writing a stinging op-ed in the *Washington Post* accusing Trump of having "very little understanding of what it means to … fight ethically or to be governed by a uniform set of rules and practices."[53]

Guerrilla sabotage, however, carries risks, particularly when it implicates the possibility of high-stakes battlefield incidents. Law professor Rosa Brooks, for instance, has written that "military leaders – and, for that matter, lower-ranking service members – have only one legally permissible response if confronted with a presidentially initiated unlawful order: 'No, sir.'"[54] At the same time, even orders that seem to conflict with IHL can often be ambiguous. Noncompliers may be labeled mutinous. As the National Constitution Center's Lyle Deniston has written, "[I]t is not the function of the military to make

---

[51] O'Leary, Rosemary. 2013. *The Ethics of Dissent: Managing Guerrilla Government,* 2nd ed. London: Sage. Schuster, Christian, Kim Sass Mikkelsen, Izabela Correa, and Jan-Hanrik Meyer-Sahling. 2022. "Exit, Voice, and Sabotage: Public Service Motivation and Guerrilla Bureaucracy in Times of Unprincipled Political Principals." *Journal of Public Administration Research and Theory* 32(2): 416–435.

[52] Starr, Barbara and Nicole Gaouette. Nov. 25, 2019. "Navy Secretary Forced out after Trump's War Crimes Intervention Causes Division and Chaos in Military." *CNN.* www.cnn.com/2019/11/24/politics/pentagon-mark-esper-richard-spencer/index.html

[53] Spencer, Richard. Nov. 27, 2019. "Richard Spencer: I Was Fired as Navy Secretary. Here's What I've Learned Because of It." *Washington Post.* www.washingtonpost.com/opinions/richard-spencer-i-was-fired-as-navy-secretary-heres-what-ive-learned-because-of-it/2019/11/27/9c2e58bc-1092-11ea-bf62-eadd5d11f559_story.html

[54] Brooks, Rosa. Jan. 8, 2020. "If Trump Orders War Crimes, the Military Will Face an Impossible Choice." *Washington Post.* www.washingtonpost.com/outlook/2020/01/08/if-trump-orders-war-crimes-military-will-face-an-impossible-choice/

a decision that the policy choices of civilian government leaders are outrageous, or even that they violate norms of international law."[55]

Besides its legal pitfalls, crossing military superiors can imperil careers. Servicemembers may face punishment, harassment, or even threats of dishonorable discharge. At higher levels, the Trump White House offered extreme warning shots on this count. For example, in 2020, Trump staffers leaked a "hit list" of alleged "deep state" members who they wanted to eliminate from government roles.[56] In a non-IHL context, Lt. Col. Alexander Vindman was subjected to what he called "bullying, intimidation and retaliation,"[57] as well as death threats,[58] after acting as a "whistleblower" in Trump's impeachment trial over Ukraine. In a second Trump term, an unwillingness of U.S. servicemembers to risk rejecting orders may explain why many are likely to submit even to a president who defiles IHL.

Cabinet Resistance

Cabinet members, by resigning and speaking out against the commander-in-chief, could try to sway public opinion against U.S. presidents for openly challenging IHL. Likely candidates would include the Secretaries of Defense, Homeland Security, or State. Such acts are not unprecedented, even if most resignations result from policy disagreements or are preemptive moves before firings. During Trump's first term, for example, Defense Secretary James Mattis resigned in protest in 2018 largely over disputes about Syria. Similarly, after January 6, a string of top officials, including multiple cabinet members, abruptly

---

[55] Denniston, Lyle. Mar. 1, 2016. "Constitution Check: Could the Military Disobey Orders Issued by a President Trump?" National Constitution Center. https://constitutioncenter.org/blog/constitution-check-could-the-military-disobey-orders-issued-by-a-president-

[56] Swan, Jonathan. Feb. 23, 2020. "Exclusive: Trump's 'Deep State' Hit List." *Axios*. www.axios.com/2020/02/23/trump-memos-deep-state-white-house

[57] Brook, Tom Vanden, Nicholas Wu, and Deirdre Shesgreen. July 8, 2020. "Alexander Vindman Retires from Army, Citing 'Bullying' from Trump for Impeachment Testimony." *USA Today*. www.usatoday.com/story/news/politics/2020/07/08/alexander-vindman-resigns-army-after-trump-impeachment-testimony/5397752002/

[58] Lubold, Gordon. July 8, 2020. "Impeachment Witness Vindman Retiring from Military, Lawyer Says." *Wall Street Journal*. www.wsj.com/articles/impeachment-witness-vindman-retiring-from-military-lawyer-says-11594224136

6.2 Can Anything Stop Impunity at the Source?

left the White House.[59] Such resistance helps to explain why Trump was so intent on nominating loyalists to his cabinet for a second term, including Pete Hegseth to lead the DoD.[60]

Practically, however, even cabinet secretaries who resist a president are unlikely to possess enough influence to impact a president's approvals. Pronouncements about resignations tend to quickly fade from the news cycle. Moreover, even protest resignations often result in cabinet officials soft-pedaling their criticism. In his resignation letter, for example, Mattis stated merely that Trump deserved a Defense Secretary whose views were more "aligned" with his own.[61] One account of Mattis's book said that his "disapproval [of Trump] is so veiled that it is practically shrouded."[62] It took Mattis roughly two years to label Trump a threat to the Constitution after resigning.[63] Meanwhile, Trump earned praise from GOP supporters for calling Mattis "the world's most overrated general."[64]

Another problem is that principled resignations could actually increase, not decrease, the chances of a president openly challenging IHL. When cabinet officials who serve as the "adults in the room" resign, they leave a void often filled by "yes men."[65] When Trump took office in 2017, for instance, some critics were reassured that his

---

[59] New York Times. Jan. 17, 2021. "The Trump Administration Officials Who Resigned Over Capitol Violence." *New York Times*. www.nytimes.com/article/trump-resignations.html

[60] Montanaro, Domenico. Nov. 16, 2024. "Trump Is Creating Team of Loyalists after Conflicts with Cabinet Members in 1st Term." *NPR*. www.npr.org/2024/11/16/g-s1-34532/trump-cabinet-loyalists

[61] Dec. 21, 2018. "James Mattis' Resignation Letter in Full." *BBC*. www.bbc.com/news/world-us-canada-46644841

[62] Jurecic, Quinta. Aug. 20, 2019. "Did the 'Adults in the Room' Make Any Difference with Trump?" *New York Times*. www.nytimes.com/2019/08/29/opinion/james-mattis-trump.html

[63] Rummler, Orion. Jun 3, 2020. "James Mattis Condemns Trump as a Threat to the Constitution." *Axios*. www.axios.com/2020/06/03/james-mattis-trump-protests

[64] Shane III, Leo. "Trump Blasts Mattis as 'The World's Most Overrated General.'" *Military Times*. www.militarytimes.com/news/pentagon-congress/2019/10/17/trump-blasts-mattis-as-the-worlds-most-overrated-general/

[65] McCarthy, Tom. Dec. 21, 2018. "With Jim Mattis Gone, Has the Last Proverbial Adult Left the White House?" *Guardian*. www.theguardian.com/us-news/2018/dec/20/jim-mattis-resign-trump-administration

cabinet was comprised of esteemed public servants who could check his more unfiltered impulses. However, Trump had more cabinet turnover in his first eighteen months in office than Reagan, Clinton, the two Bushes, and Obama had in their whole first terms.[66] As officials left, most were replaced by party loyalists or others lacking commensurate experience, leaving fewer top officials willing or able to rein in Trump on IHL.

"Self-Policing" by Other Western Leaders

By calling out behavior clearly inconsistent with IHL, other Western leaders can create normative incentives for U.S. presidents not to openly flout the law of war. This aligns with a substantial scholarship on "social deterrence" in IR – the extralegal, informal mechanisms that shame or shun leaders into complying with globally recognized standards. Political scientists Hyena Ho and Beth Simmons, for example, have pointed out that social deterrence "may be especially relevant precisely when norms are strong but the formal institutions of law – policing, courts, and formal confinement – are weak."[67] Social deterrence could morph into "prosecutorial deterrence" if Western leaders also call for their peers to face charges before the ICC.

Some Western leaders have accused non-Western autocrats of war crimes. President Joe Biden, for example, said that Russian President Vladimir Putin "clearly committed war crimes" in Ukraine and that ICC efforts to prosecute him were "justified."[68] Yet a willingness to hold other leaders accountable generally does not extend to the "inner sanctum" of Western allies. Such leaders have strong incentives not to upset bilateral relations, especially with powerful countries like the U.S., because of fears of blowback, such as countersanctions or diplomatic isolation. An even greater disincentive, however, may be the

---

[66] Joung, Madeleine. July 12, 2019. "Trump Has Now Had More Cabinet Turnover Than Reagan, Obama and the Two Bushes." *TIME*. https://time.com/5625699/trump-cabinet-acosta/

[67] Jo, Hyeran and Beth A. Simmons. 2016. "Can the International Criminal Court Deter Atrocity?" *International Organization* 70(3): 443–475.

[68] Carvajal, Nikki, Jeremy Diamond, and Kylie Atwood. "Biden: ICC's War Crimes Case against Putin is 'Justified'." *CNN*. www.cnn.com/2023/03/17/politics/biden-putin-war-crimes-ukraine/index.html

6.2 Can Anything Stop Impunity at the Source?

"karma effect." By publicly assigning liability, Western leaders put themselves at greater risk for legally dubious decisions that they take as heads of their own militaries.[69]

Furthermore, criticisms from other Western leaders could actually be politically empowering for U.S. presidents who overtly challenge IHL. As both a candidate and as president, for example, Trump has consistently tapped into populist, "anti-globalist" sentiments to rally his base.[70] This has included not just attacks on international organizations like the UN and NATO, but also *ad hominem*, "bully" attacks on individual Western leaders.[71] In the same way that pushback from moderate Republicans could galvanize support for a Trump-like leader, so too could pushback from Western allies who could be denigrated as cosmopolitan "elitists." Trumpist leaders might welcome criticism from their peers, which they could exploit as evidence of "shaking up" the international system.

UN Resolutions

Passing a UN resolution, requiring a simple majority of party states, could be another means to reproach a U.S. president like Trump for overtly defying IHL. Article 14 of the UN Charter stipulates that the General Assembly "may recommend measures for the peaceful adjustment of any situation … which it deems likely to impair the general welfare … among nations."[72] Such a measure would be nonbinding. Only Security Council measures carry the force of law, and as a permanent member, the U.S. would hold veto power over any resolution that reprimanded an American leader. However, a nonbinding resolution might widen the set of possible countries willing to rebuke a U.S.

---

[69] Sherman, Michael J. 2018. "Standards in Command Responsibility Prosecutions: How Strict, and Why?" *Northern Illinois University Law Review* 38(2): 298–347.
[70] Hattem, Julian. Apr. 26, 2016. "Trump Warns against 'False Song of Globalism'." *The Hill.* https://thehill.com/policy/national-security/277879-trump-warns-against-false-song-of-globalism/
[71] Kaufmann, Sylvie. July 25, 2018. "Trump Reveals Himself as the Bully of His Allies." *New York Times.* www.nytimes.com/2018/07/25/opinion/trump-bully-allies-nato.html
[72] United Nations Charter, Chapter IV: The General Assembly. United Nations. www.un.org/en/about-us/un-charter/chapter-4

president. American actions have been criticized, albeit rarely, in UN resolutions in the past, such as in its 1983 invasion of Grenada.[73]

Still, the possibility of a UN resolution against a U.S. leader like Trump is unlikely. Arriving at a simple majority for passage remains a high bar. The same reasons why Western leaders might not call out a U.S. president – fear of antagonizing the U.S. or being subject to the same type of resolution themselves – might dissuade other nations from signing. Even UN resolutions that observers might think would be uncontroversial have had trouble reaching majority support in the past. For example, after the October 7, 2023, terrorist attacks in Israel, a UN resolution could not garner a majority to name Hamas in its official condemnation.[74] A resolution that pointed a finger at a U.S. leader would prove exponentially more difficult, especially without evidence of flagrant crimes.

Moreover, even if a UN resolution were passed, it could again play into the domestic political hands of Trump or a Trump-like leader. During his first term, the Trump administration repeatedly attacked the UN to score political points. For instance, at a speech before the UN General Assembly, Trump declared that "the future does not belong to the globalists."[75] His UN ambassador, Nikki Haley, announced in 2018 that the U.S. would withdraw from the UN Human Rights Council, calling it a "self-serving organization."[76] For his second term, Trump has appointed GOP firebrand Elise Stefanie as UN ambassador, who has been critical of the UN's position on the Gaza war.[77] The chance to berate the UN as engaged in a "witch-hunt" against the U.S. would likely be welcomed by Trump.

---

[73] Oct. 29, 1983. "Text of the UN Resolution." *New York Times*. www.nytimes.com/1983/10/29/world/text-of-the-un-resolution.html

[74] Oct. 27, 2023. "General Assembly Adopts Resolution Calling for Immediate, Sustained Humanitarian Truce Leading to Cessation of Hostilities between Israel, Hamas." United Nations. https://press.un.org/en/2023/ga12548.doc.htm

[75] Borger, Julian. Sept. 24, 2019. "Donald Trump Denounces 'Globalism' in Nationalist Address to UN." *Guardian*. www.theguardian.com/us-news/2019/sep/24/donald-trump-un-address-denounces-globalism

[76] Dwyer, Colin. June 19, 2018. "U.S. Announces Its Withdrawal from U.N. Human Rights Council." *NPR*. www.npr.org/2018/06/19/621435225/u-s-announces-its-withdrawal-from-u-n-s-human-rights-council#:~:text=After%20more%20than%20a%20year,and%20Ambassador%20to%20the%20U.N.

[77] Halpert, Madeline. Nov. 11, 2024. "Who is Elise Stefanik, Trump's Pick for UN Ambassador?" *BBC*. www.bbc.co.uk/news/articles/c3vlndv0yxpo

Binding Methods

Limit to Executive Powers

In terms of "binding" methods for constraining leaders from overtly challenging IHL, one way to check presidential overreach is for Congress to formally limit executive powers. In the specific case of disallowing war crime clemencies, many experts agree that this would align with customary law under IHL, a legal framework inherent to the general functioning of militaries. For example, Lt. Col. Dan Maurer of the U.S. Military Academy has written about the potential of Congress to introduce a "war crime pardon exception,"[78] which would carve out criteria under which the president could not grant clemencies. Article 2 of the Constitution grants broad purview to the president to pardon federal crimes, but this authority could be constrained through either an amendment or reform of the UCMJ.

Either pathway, however, seems infeasible, even without a GOP-controlled Congress. Passing a constitutional amendment – requiring two-thirds support in both congressional chambers, combined with state ratification – has only happened twenty-seven times in U.S. history. Likewise, the odds of achieving UCMJ reform given executive veto power are negligible. Furthermore, even if checks on war crime interventions were agreed upon, questions would arise about implementation. As law professor Charles J. Dunlap has pointed out, despite the common usage of the phrase "war crimes," none of the U.S. servicemembers granted clemency by Trump were actually prosecuted for war crimes. Rather, they are charged with breaches of the UCMJ.[79] Therefore, a statute preventing clemencies for war crimes might rarely, if ever, technically apply.

Even if politics were no barrier and lawmakers could agree on a pragmatic definition of "war crimes," other objections may abound. Future military cases, for example, could arise where a defendant's rights were legitimately violated. Military, as well as civilian, courts

---

[78] Maurer, Dan. Dec. 3, 2019. "Should There Be a War Crime Pardon Exception?" *Lawfare*. www.lawfareblog.com/should-there-be-war-crime-pardon-exception

[79] Dunlap, Jr. Charles J. Dec. 16, 2019. "Reasonable People Can Differ on Trump's Military Justice Actions." *Small Wars Journal*. https://smallwarsjournal.com/jrnl/art/reasonable-people-can-differ-trumps-military-justice-actions

are not foolproof against prosecutorial indiscretion or judicial errors. It may be unfair to single out U.S. servicemembers as a special class ineligible for clemencies, especially as presidents routinely pardon political associates or the well-connected. An additional concern relates to "slippery slopes." If war crime pardons were forbidden, it could trigger calls for further narrowing clemency powers. This might extend to civilian contexts, such as for nonviolent offenses, where commutations might be more justified.

Executive Order

Besides a war crime carveout, an executive order could also curb presidential power over military clemencies. In a future administration after Trump, the idea would be to reform how petitions for war crime clemencies are vetted and arrive at the president's desk. A common critique is that evaluations are often done on an extemporary or political basis. A case in point involved Trump's war crime interventions, which were spotlighted on Fox News and championed by Republican Congress members. By technically binding future presidents to a formal clemency review procedure, circumventing it would raise political risks. It would not only require that a president grant a controversial clemency. It would also require overturning an executive order that sought more impartiality in the process.

One widely discussed idea, proposed by legal scholars Rachel E. Barkow and Mark Osler, is to form a federal "clemency commission" operating outside of the Justice Department's purview that would review clemency requests.[80] The solution would apply to all potential clemencies, meaning that the effect on war crime cases would be indirect. The idea, however, has direct roots in President Gerald Ford's "Presidential Clemency Board," which made recommendations for conditional pardons related to misconduct in the Vietnam War.[81] Reforming military clemencies via broader clemency reform would remove the optics of servicemembers being singled out as less likely to receive commutations, thereby reducing political hurdles.

---

[80] Barkow, Rachel E. and Mark Oslett. 2015. "Restructuring Clemency: The Cost of Ignoring Clemency and a Plan for Renewal." *University of Chicago Law Review* 82(1): 1–26.

[81] Presidential Clemency Board. 1975. "Report to the President."

6.2 Can Anything Stop Impunity at the Source?

An executive order such as the one described earlier could plausibly be taken up by a reform-minded president. Yet because the act would not be passed as a law through Congress, presidents could overturn it unilaterally, albeit with political challenges. To the degree that presidents most likely to abuse clemency powers generally might also be the most likely to hand down unjust war crime clemencies, the commission might not survive executive transitions. Indeed, the Trump White House considered a presidential clemency commission in 2018, but rejected it.[82] Although several Democrats have expressed interest in broad-based clemency reform, including through the proposed Abuse of the Pardon Prevention Act,[83] the Biden White House took no concrete actions on the issue.

Accession to ICC Jurisdiction

Legislation acceding to ICC jurisdiction over the U.S. could theoretically improve accountability for alleged war crimes. One reason why war crime clemencies have an effect is because there is no "backstop" institution to prosecute U.S. servicemembers besides military courts. In 2002, President George W. Bush signed into law the American Service-Members' Protection Act (ASMPA), often called the "Hague Invasion" Act, which grants authority to the president to "by all means necessary" shield U.S. troops from ICC prosecutions.[84] Revoking this law could lessen the incentive for federal commutations, since U.S. combatants would still be subject to global prosecution. At the very least, it would lessen the impacts of such interventions if U.S. servicemembers could still be held criminally liable by the ICC.

Future legislation acceding to ICC jurisdiction, however, would likely be dead on arrival, even with a progressive in the White House. First, there was general bipartisan agreement in favor of the ASMPA when it originally became law. When Congress enacted it as an

---

[82] Osler, Mark. 2022. "The Trump Clemencies: Celebrities, Chaos, and Lost Opportunity" *William & Mary Bill of Rights Journal* 487.
[83] www.congress.gov/bill/116th-congress/house-bill/1627/cosponsors?s=1&r=88&overview=closed
[84] 2002. "American Servicemembers Protection Act of 2002." Public Law 107–206. www.govinfo.gov/content/pkg/COMPS-3074/pdf/COMPS-3074.pdf

amendment in the wake of 9/11, it did so with large majorities, 280-138 in the House and 75-19[85] in the Senate.[86] The justification by George W. Bush and others was that the ICC could disproportionately target American combatants. In 2001, former U.S. Secretary of State Henry Kissinger warned that the ICC could be used as an "instrument of political warfare."[87] While empirical evidence has casted doubt on this claim,[88] fears of the ICC detaining U.S. servicemembers for political reasons persist among both parties.

In 2022, the Repeal Hague Invasion Act was introduced by Democrat Rep. Ilhan Omar of Minnesota, one of the most liberal members of the House of Representatives, and cosponsored by other leftist "squad" members Rep. Rashida Taleb of Michigan and Rep. Alexandria Ocasio-Cortez of New York. It did not pass.[89] Although recently Republicans have been more hostile to the ICC, even many Democrats remain wary of extending ICC jurisdiction to the U.S. For example, in 2021, the Biden White House declared that it "continues to object to the ICC's assertions of jurisdiction over personnel of such non-States Parties as the United States ... and will vigorously protect current and former United States personnel from any attempts to exercise such jurisdiction."[90]

Impeachment

Impeachment could serve as a penalty for presidents who overtly transgress IHL. Numerous critics, for example, have argued that Trump's war crime clemencies constituted an abuse of power that rose to the

---

[85] https://clerk.house.gov/Votes/2002206
[86] www.senate.gov/legislative/LIS/roll_call_votes/vote1072/vote_107_2_00145.htm?congress=107&session=2&vote=00145
[87] Kissinger, Henry A. 2001. "The Pitfalls of Universal Jurisdiction." *Foreign Affairs* 80(4): 86–96.
[88] Krcmaric, Daniel. 2022. "Does the International Criminal Court Target the American Military?" *American Political Science Review* 117(1): 325–331.
[89] www.congress.gov/bill/117th-congress/house-bill/7523
[90] Apr. 1, 2021. "Executive Order on the Termination of Emergency with Respect to the International Criminal Court." The White House. https://bidenwhitehouse.archives.gov/briefing-room/presidential-actions/2021/04/01/executive-order-on-the-termination-of-emergency-with-respect-to-the-international-criminal-court/#:~:text=BIDEN%20JR.%2C%20President%20of%20the,referral%20by%20the%20United%20Nations

level of "high crimes and misdemeanors."[91] Likewise, in reference to Trump's threats to use disproportionate force in war, one journalist suggested that "Congress may have no other choice but to redeploy the ultimate check [impeachment] against a rogue president bent on committing atrocities [in war]."[92] There is some precedent for this maneuver. In 2008, Democrat Rep. Dennis Kucinich proposed thirty-five articles of impeachment against George W. Bush, including those pertaining to war crimes, although none ultimately reached a full House vote.[93]

Practically, however, impeachment carries limitations. First, it would almost invariably not result in a president's conviction and removal from office. As evidenced by Trump's two impeachment trials, meeting the Senate's two-thirds threshold of voting members is virtually impossible.[94] Impeachment may also reify existing partisan divides. To the extent that impeachment is more a political tool than one rooted in criminal law,[95] it is likely to be viewed through a partisan lens, blunting the impact on public opinion. Especially when it involves controversial charges related to the military, impeachment could even backfire. Voters may perceive it as a power grab or "weaponization" against the commander-in-chief,[96] helping the president's support.[97]

---

[91] Blumenthal, Paul. Dec. 3, 2019. "The Impeachable Offenses Trump Won't Be Impeached For." *HuffPost*. www.huffpost.com/entry/trump-impeachment-impeachable-act_n_5de6edb3e4b0913e6f872731 / Chait, Jonathan. May 21, 2019. "Just This Week, Trump Has Already Committed 5 More Impeachable Acts." *New York Magazine*. https://nymag.com/intelligencer/2019/05/5-more-impeachable-acts-trump-barr-cohen-mcgahn-war-crimes-deutschebank.html

[92] Ford, Matt. Jan. 6, 2020. "Trump's Next Impeachable Offense is Nigh." *The New Republic*. https://newrepublic.com/article/156136/trumps-next-impeachable-offense-nigh

[93] Bresnahan, John. June 9, 2008. "Kucinich Offers Impeachment Articles against Bush." *POLITICO*. www.politico.com/blogs/politico-now/2008/06/kucinich-offers-impeachment-articles-against-bush-009581

[94] Drew, Elizabeth. Dec. 15, 2019. "The Impeachment Process Is Barely Functioning." *New York Times*. www.nytimes.com/2019/12/15/opinion/impeachment-trump.html

[95] Ginsburg, Tom, Aziz Huq, and David Landau. 2020. "The Uses and Abuses of Presidential Impeachment." University of Chicago. Public Law and Legal Theory Working Paper No. 731.

[96] Dershowitz, Alan. 2019. *The Case against Impeaching Trump*. New York: Skyhorse. Melton, Buckner F. Dec. 3, 2019. The Weaponization of Impeachment. *Atlantic*. www.theatlantic.com/ideas/archive/2019/12/weaponization-impeachment/602872/

[97] Murray, Mark and Alexandra Marquez. July 27, 2023. "Trump and Clinton Saw Higher Approval Ratings during Their Impeachments." *NBC News*. www.nbcnews.com/meet-the-press/meetthepressblog/trump-clinton-saw-higher-approval-ratings-impeachments-rcna96689

Broader concerns may also augur against using impeachment to rein in a president's overt strains on IHL. One is the precedent that it sets of Congress encroaching on enumerated executive powers. With war crime pardons, for example, sanctioning a president for exercising a clearly specified constitutional right might itself be construed as an abuse of legislative oversight. Another worry is "normalizing" impeachment regarding military decision-making.[98] This might creep into areas of legitimate policy disagreement, such as use-of-force questions. Finally, if a president were impeached over IHL, it would almost certainly be over a concrete act of noncompliance. It would not cover the kinds of verbal threats that defined many of Trump's public attacks on IHL.

Domestic Prosecution

Domestic prosecution by a federal court could theoretically hold a president accountable for war crimes, or deter such actions. In a normal scenario, the U.S. Justice Department has a longstanding norm of not prosecuting a sitting president.[99] However, as David Scheffer, former U.S. Ambassador at Large for War Crimes Issues, has argued, this norm could potentially be discarded for a president accused of committing "atrocity crimes of the worst character" that inflict "deaths and injury of thousands." "Imagine," Scheffer says, "trying to explain the 'not while president' position to any of our allies, most of which, unlike the United States, joined the International Criminal Court and waived any rationale to immunize top leaders from accountability."[100]

Setting aside the remoteness of the hypothetical, and that none of Trump's acts would have risen to the "atrocities" threshold, even grievous war crimes might not result in a domestic prosecution. Practically,

---

[98] Marcus, David. Jan. 21, 2020. "Impeachment Has Become a Dangerous New Normal." *The Federalist.* https://thefederalist.com/2020/01/21/impeachment-has-become-a-dangerous-new-normal/

[99] Jansen, Bart and Kevin Johnson. May 29, 2019. "Robert Mueller, in First Public Remarks, Says Charging Trump Was 'Not An Option We Could Consider'." *USA Today.* www.usatoday.com/story/news/politics/2019/05/29/robert-mueller-speak-russia-investigation-and-2016-election/1269060001/

[100] Scheffer, David. Dept. 3, 2019. "What If a President Committed Genocide or Other Atrocity Crimes?" *Just Security.* www.justsecurity.org/66025/what-if-a-president-committed-genocide-or-other-atrocity-crimes/

6.2 Can Anything Stop Impunity at the Source?

a president facing a federal indictment for war crimes could, in effect, unilaterally terminate the charges. Although the U.S. Department of Justice (DOJ) enjoys quasi-independence, it sits within the executive branch. Therefore, the president could install an attorney general to end criminal proceedings. A comparable possibility was floated during the Mueller probe into Trump's alleged Russian collusion in the 2016 election. President Richard Nixon also pressured the resignation of several DOJ officials to end his special counsel investigation during Watergate.[101] Trump's election in 2024 also led to the vacating of all federal charges against him.[102]

Even without this option, the DOJ's norm against prosecuting a president could still hold in a war crime case. The Constitution does not explicitly bar prosecutors from charging presidents with crimes. Yet deference to precedent means that the DOJ's norms would likely take priority. The DOJ's Office of Legal Counsel has concluded that indicting a sitting president "would unduly interfere with the ability of the executive branch to perform its constitutionally assigned duties."[103] Moreover, a 2024 Supreme Court ruling involving Trump suggests a wide scope of presidential immunity.[104] Upon leaving office, a president could plausibly claim immunity for actions taken pertaining to executive duties. Consequently, any indictments might only fall on lower-level planners and executors who were complicit in the alleged war crime.[105]

---

[101] Nussbaum, Matthew. June 13, 2017. "Can Trump Fire Mueller? Yup, and in More Ways Than One." *POLITICO*. www.politico.com/story/2017/06/13/can-trump-fire-special-counsel-robert-mueller-239500

[102] Reid, Paula, Tierney Sneed, and Devan Cole. Nov. 25, 2024. "Special Counsel Jack Smith Drops Election Subversion and Classified Documents Cases against Donald Trump." *CNN*. https://edition.cnn.com/2024/11/25/politics/trump-special-counsel-jack-smith/index.html

[103] Office of Legal Counsel. "A Sitting President's Amenability to Indictment and Criminal Prosecution." U.S. Department of Justice. www.justice.gov/olc/opinion/sitting-president's-amenability-indictment-and-criminal-prosecution

[104] Kruzel, John and Andrew Chung. July 2, 2024. "US Supreme Court Rules Trump Has Broad Immunity from Prosecution." *Reuters*. www.reuters.com/legal/us-supreme-court-due-rule-trumps-immunity-bid-blockbuster-case-2024-07-01/

[105] Colangelo, Anthony J. Feb. 12, 2018. "Can the President Be Prosecuted for War Crimes in the Event of a Nuclear Strike?" *Dallas News*. www.dallasnews.com/opinion/commentary/2018/02/12/can-the-president-be-prosecuted-for-war-crimes-in-the-event-of-a-nuclear-strike/

Global Prosecution

Global criminal prosecution is another mechanism that might hold presidents accountable for openly challenging IHL. Even if under domestic law executives may take actions like unjustifiably pardoning American troops, they may still breach international law by doing so. As described earlier, several experts have claimed that at least some of Trump's war crime clemencies likely violated the "command responsibility" principle of IHL.[106] Liability requires that leaders have purview over an armed group, be aware of actual or potential criminal activity, and fail to intervene or punish guilty parties. These requirements, however, presuppose a judicial body with extradition power and regimes willing to cooperate in handing over an accused party. Neither would be the case with a U.S. president and the ICC.

Although not unprecedented, prosecutions of world leaders have normally been reserved for the most heinous of crimes.[107] Notorious examples include former Liberian president Charles Taylor, found guilty in 2012 of aiding and abetting rebel combatants in Sierra Leone; former Côte d'Ivoire president Laurent Gbagbo, acquitted in 2019 at the Hague on charges of fomenting post-election violence; and former Serbian president Slobodan Milosevic, who died in 2006 during a multi-year trial at the Hague over his role in the Balkans conflict that ended in 200,000 fatalities.[108] Perceived lesser acts have generally not triggered foreign tribunals. As stated before, there has been no documented case of an executive facing trial for war crimes due solely to issuing a pardon.[109]

The ICC's lack of effort to investigate, much less prosecute, Trump for his war crime clemencies suggests that future leaders who committed a similar act would likely encounter the same fate. George W. Bush also did not face any attempt by the ICC to hold him

---

[106] Ford, Stuart. 2020. "Has President Trump Committed a War Crime by Pardoning War Criminals?" *American University International Law Review* 35(4): 757–820.

[107] Krcmaric, Daniel. 2020. *The Justice Dilemma: Leaders and Exile in an Era of Accountability*. Ithaca: Cornell University Press.

[108] CBS News. Apr. 26, 2012. "Modern Leaders Accused of War Crimes." *CBS News*. www.cbsnews.com/media/modern-leaders-accused-of-war-crimes/

[109] Ford, Stuart. 2020. "Has President Trump Committed a War Crime by Pardoning War Criminals?" *American University International Law Review* 35(4): 757–820.

accountable for alleged war crimes. Practically, hauling American leaders before the ICC poses immense political and logistical hurdles.[110] Although the UN Security Council has the power to make referrals to the ICC, America's status as a permanent member makes this moot. An alternative is to arrest U.S. perpetrators upon foreign travel, but this also has little precedent. While controversial, current leaders could also petition for head of state immunity in the unlikely scenario of a prosecution.[111]

Reforming the Insurrectionist Act

Narrowing the ability of U.S. presidents to deploy the military domestically, namely through reform of the Insurrectionist Act, is a final mechanism that could help to curb the impunity movement. Although only indirectly bearing on IHL, Trump's record suggests that any efforts to thwart the impunity agenda require combating abuse of the military within America's borders. Trump, for example, threatened to invoke the Insurrectionist Act to quell unrest in the U.S. and to get even with his political adversaries.[112] Calls for reform have been broad-based. The *Washington Post Editorial* board has described the Insurrectionist Act as a "ticking time bomb ripe for abuse."[113] In 2024, a bipartisan group proposed a legal blueprint to address such concerns.[114]

Reform, however, is unlikely even after Trump leaves office. One reason concerns the federal separation of powers. Although the Posse Comitatus Act generally prevents American presidents from summoning the military as an instrument of law enforcement,

---

[110] Mansfield, Michael. Mar. 19, 2013. "Why Bush, Blair Should Be Charged with War Crimes over Iraq Invasion." *CNN*. www.cnn.com/2013/03/19/opinion/iraq-war-bush-blair/index.html

[111] Akande, Dapo. 2018. "The Immunity of Heads of States of Nonparties in the Early Years of the ICC." *AJIL Unbound* 112: 172–176.

[112] Nunn, Joseph. Nov. 17, 2023. "Trump Wants to Use the Military Against His Enemies. Congress Must Act." *Slate*. https://slate.com/news-and-politics/2023/11/trump-second-term-military-nightmare-congress.html

[113] Editorial Board. May 5, 2024. "There's Still Time for Congress to Trump-proof the Insurrection Act." *Washington Post*. www.washingtonpost.com/opinions/2024/05/05/insurrection-act-trump-abuse-reforms/

[114] Apr. 8, 2024. "Principles for Insurrection Act Reform." www.ali.org/media/filer_public/32/a4/32a425d8-d80a-44e5-af39-7ff00ebf809d/principles-insurrection-act-reform.pdf

the Insurrectionist Act offers a sweeping exception with few constraints.[115] According to Supreme Court precedent, the president has sole discretion to determine when the act can be invoked. Only Congress can limit it by passing new legislation, which, if vetoed, would require a supermajority to override. Consequently, presidents enjoy a near "blank check" on calling up the military – a power that has been used thirty times since the law's inception and one that some presidents may not want to relinquish.[116]

A second obstacle stems from partisan politics. Even if some Republicans and Democrats agree on a reform bill to the Insurrectionist Act, and even if a new law would equally apply to a future president of either party, it would inevitably be seen as an effort to "Trump proof" the military. As previously noted, reports suggest that some of Trump's advisers urged him to invoke the Insurrectionist Act on January 6 to delay or prevent the peaceful transfer of power.[117] While Congress did pass the bipartisan Electoral Count Reform Act in 2022 with similar attachments to Trump,[118] the Insurrectionist Act could prove more sensitive because of concerns about politicizing the military. MAGA Republicans might balk at reforms that limit the powers of a future, Trumpist commander-in-chief.

6.3 The End of IHL?

When Trump first took over as commander-in-chief in 2017, many experts predicted that his most controversial pledges to openly challenge the law of war would be stifled. The logic was that governing was different than campaigning, and that attacking IHL would fade

---

[115] Nunn, Joseph. Oct. 14, 2021. "The Posse Comitatus Act Explained." Brennan Center. www.brennancenter.org/our-work/research-reports/posse-comitatus-act-explained#:~:text=The%20law%20generally%20prevents%20the,as%20a%20domestic%20police%20force.&text=The%20Posse%20Comitatus%20Act%20bars,when%20expressly%20authorized%20by%20law.
[116] Nunn, Jospeh and Elizabeth Gooitein. Apr. 25, 2022. "Guide to Invocations of the Insurrection Act." Brennan Center. www.brennancenter.org/our-work/research-reports/guide-invocations-insurrection-act
[117] Alschuler, Albert W. Aug. 16, 2022. "Trump and the Insurrection Act: The Legal Framework." *Just Security*. www.justsecurity.org/82696/trump-and-the-insurrection-act-the-true-legal-framework/
[118] Bauer, Bob and Jack Goldsmith. Dec. 27, 2023. "Trump Is Not the Only Reason to Fix This Uniquely Dangerous Law." *New York Times*. www.nytimes.com/2023/12/27/opinion/insurrection-act-congress-trump.html

6.3 The End of IHL?

into the backdrop. While some of Trump's promises turned out to be hollow, others clearly did not. What Trump did prove was that it was not impossible for an American executive to put the Geneva Conventions in the crosshairs. He also proved it was not disqualifying of a second term. Whether Trump's excesses marked the start of a new trend, or were simply the byproduct of an anomalous presidency, remains unclear. What seems inevitable is that the political dividends paid to the impunity coalition will not be lost on other leaders.

Skeptics may doubt the transformative impact of Trump's ongoing record on IHL. Their case is that Trump's war crime clemencies, despite being widely condemned, were still isolated events. Moreover, despite his bellicose language, absent from Trump's resume are some of the most reckless military misadventures that marred his predecessors. Before Trump, every American president since Jimmy Carter had embroiled the U.S. in a new foreign war.[119] Trump's Pentagon, at least so far, has not been marked by a full-scale return to torture or stained by acts of prisoner abuse. There has been no broad, official pullback from within the military in fulfilling combat ethics. Trump has crowed about carrying a big stick and taking a cocked-and-loaded gun to the Geneva Conventions. But his words have frequently ended in bluffs.

Certain observers still see Trump as operating within conventional parameters of international law, albeit with a marked aversion to the global, laws-based system. For example, political scientists Daniel Deudney and John Ikenberry have claimed that Trump is simply one component of "an ongoing and necessary, if sometimes ugly, equilibration of the arrangements underlying the institutions of the liberal world order."[120] Yet even as prior U.S. leaders may have gone further in obvious noncompliance, Trump's undermining of the existential need for IHL has culminated in an important set of "firsts." Trump is the first U.S. commander-in-chief to openly attack the value of the Geneva Conventions. He is also the first to offer a stark, opposing vision of how the rule of law should apply, if at all, to military justice.

---

[119] Cole, Brendan. Nov. 25, 2020. "Donald Trump Is First President Since Jimmy Carter Not to Enter U.S. Troops into New Conflict." *Newsweek*. www.newsweek.com/donald-trump-first-president-since-jimmy-carter-not-enter-us-troops-new-conflict-1549037

[120] Deudney, Daniel and John G. Ikenberry. 2018. "Liberal World: The Resilient Order." *Foreign Affairs* 97(4): 16–24.

These firsts diverge fundamentally from past American leaders who flouted the laws of war, but always in private or with rationalizations. Trump favors overturning IHL to reforming it from within. He disregards not only specific legal statutes, but the very concept of IHL as a dispensable anachronism. This is why many experts see Trump as a much more radical saboteur of international law. For instance, barrister Stefan Talmon has dubbed Trump a "gravedigger of international law" and accused him of ushering in a new era of "international law nihilism."[121] Law professor Oona Hathaway has claimed that "the Trump administration ... waged an assault on international law unparalleled in the post-war era"[122] and that IHL now faces an "existential challenge."[123]

While an intellectual defense of Trump on IHL might emphasize the layers of restrictions the U.S. has placed on combatants that exceed those required by the Geneva Convention, such arguments are rarely made with nuance. Instead, the administration's tendency has been to attack the foundations of IHL. Pete Hegseth, for instance, summed up the Trump view of IHL as follows: "what an America-first national security policy is not going to do ... is hand its prerogatives over to international bodies that make decisions about how our men and women make decisions on the battlefield."[124] If Trump was trying to send a signal about his approach toward IHL in a second term, his pick of Hegseth could not have made a more emphatic declaration.

If Trump does represent a new prototype of Western leader averse to paying outward deference to the Geneva Conventions, this still does not mean that respect for IHL is careening toward inevitable, or even

---

[121] Talmon, Stefan. 2019. "The United States under President Trump: Gravedigger of International Law." *Chinese Journal of International Law* 18(3): 645–668.

[122] Hathaway, Oona A. Oct. 2, 2020. "Reengaging on Treaties and Other International Agreements (Part I): President Donald Trump's Rejection of International Law." *Just Security*. www.justsecurity.org/72656/reengaging-on-treaties-and-other-international-agreements-part-i-president-donald-trumps-rejection-of-international-law/

[123] Hathaway, Oona. Apr. 23. 2024. "War Unbound Gaza, Ukraine, and the Breakdown of International Law." *Foreign Affairs*. www.foreignaffairs.com/ukraine/war-unbound-gaza-hathaway

[124] Bump, Philip. Jan. 14, 2025. "Pete Hegseth Seems Open to Ordering Soldiers to Shoot Protesters." *Washington Post*. www.washingtonpost.com/politics/2025/01/14/hegseth-seems-open-to-ordering-protesters-shot/

6.3 The End of IHL?

likely, collapse. Public deference to the law of war may be less sturdy than supposed. But it is not anchored in shifting sand. Democratic leaders, including in America, have historically paid lip service to IHL not because of the law's overriding enforcement power, but because of perceived constraints that other executives, unlike Trump, may still be hesitant to challenge. In most Western countries, respect for IHL remains intact. Yet even if high costs of deviation promote public deference to the Geneva Conventions, Trump proves that this status quo is not absolute, even in the West.

Trump's second election offers reason to think that public respect for IHL is tenuous. This is true within America. It looks even truer in conflict zones abroad. Nowhere has this been more visible than with Israel and Russia in their respective wars against Hamas and Ukraine. While the wars themselves are enormously different, and neither involves Western democracies, clear parallels to Trump's impunity agenda can be seen in each. Both Israeli Prime Minister Benjamin Netanyahu and Russian President Vladimir Putin have made statements inimical to IHL. Like Trump, they have also relied on state and media actors to press their agenda, with military support. The cases are particularly relevant given America's close alliance with Israel and Trump's past rapport with Putin.

With Israel, debates continue to rage over whether the Israel Defense Forces (IDF) have perpetrated war crimes as part of retaliating against Hamas following the October 7, 2023, terrorist attacks.[125] Despite disagreements over casualty numbers, estimated death tolls in the tens of thousands in Gaza have intensified accusations of genocide.[126] The ICC has alleged crimes against Netanyahu including "starvation of civilians," "willfully causing great suffering," "intentionally directing attacks against a civilian population," and "other inhumane acts as crimes against humanity."[127]

---

[125] McGreal, Chris. Oct. 31, 2023. "Have War Crimes Been Committed in Israel and Gaza and What International Laws Apply?" *Guardian*. www.theguardian.com/world/2023/oct/31/have-war-crimes-been-committed-in-israel-and-gaza-and-what-international-laws-apply

[126] Roberts, Les. Mar. 15, 2024. "The Science Is Clear. Over 30,000 People Have Died in Gaza." *TIME*. https://time.com/6909636/gaza-death-toll/

[127] May 20, 2024. "Statement of ICC Prosecutor Karim A.A. Khan KC: Applications for Arrest Warrants in the Situation in the State of Palestine." International Criminal Court.

One UN spokesperson cited Israel's "impunity."[128] Yet regardless of opinions on Israel's compliance with the law, it is undeniable that many of the nation's leaders have publicly diminished the significance of IHL.

As leader, Netanyahu has made several explicit statements calling into question military norms of restraint. Reportedly, he told Joe Biden that alleged disproportionate bombings in Gaza were justified because the U.S. "carpet-bombed Germany" and "dropped the atom bomb" during World War II where "[a] lot of civilians died."[129] In a now-deleted comment on X, Netanyahu claimed that Israel's fight was against "the children of darkness" who followed "the law of the jungle."[130] In a TV address referencing Palestine, Netanyahu alluded to the "Amalekites," a group in the Bible whom God commanded to be annihilated, including women, children, and infants. According to a journalist, "Amalek is a code word ... for a ruthless enemy that must be crushed without mercy."[131]

Inside government, public statements by several Israeli officials have shown even greater disregard for IHL. For example, Israeli President Isaac Herzog suggested that the Palestinian people could be militarily targeted because "[i]t's an entire nation out there that is responsible [for terrorism]," including "civilians."[132] More explicit was Tzipi Hotovely, Israel's ambassador to the UK, who pronounced that "'every school, every mosque, every second house' in Gaza is a

---

[128] Ahmatović, Šejla. Apr. 5, 2024. "Israeli Military Admits 'Serious Mistake' in Killing of 7 Food Aid Workers." *POLITICO Europe*. www.politico.eu/article/israeli-military-forces-admit-serious-mistake-killing-7-food-aid-world-central-kitchen-workers/

[129] Egan, Lauren. Dec. 12, 2023. "Biden Says Netanyahu 'Has to Change,' Accuses Israel of 'Indiscriminate Bombing.'" *POLITICO*. www.politico.com/news/2023/12/12/biden-says-netanyahu-has-to-change-00131399

[130] Sheth, Sonam. Oct. 17, 2023. "Netanyahu Deleted a Post on X about a Struggle against 'Children of Darkness' around the Time of a Tragic Hospital explosion in Gaza." *Business Insider*. www.businessinsider.com/netanyahu-deleted-children-of-darkness-post-gaza-hospital-attack-2023-10

[131] Kristof, Nicholas. Nov. 1, 2023. "The Words in the Middle East That Are Breaking My Heart." *New York Times*. www.nytimes.com/2023/11/01/opinion/israel-hamas-gaza-children.html

[132] McGreal, Chris. Oct. 16, 2023. "The Language Being Used to Describe Palestinians Is Genocidal." *Guardian*. www.theguardian.com/commentisfree/2023/oct/16/the-language-being-used-to-describe-palestinians-is-genocidal

legitimate target for the Israeli military."[133] Israeli Heritage Minister Amichay Eliyahu further advocated detonating a nuclear bomb in Gaza because "no uninvolved" civilians lived there.[134] Agriculture Minister Avi Dichter said that Israel had no option except to foment a "Gaza Nakba," meaning "catastrophe."[135]

Outside of government, Israeli leadership has relied on the media to bolster public favorability for its conduct. For example, a writer for a left-leaning British newspaper claimed that "[t]he far right infiltration of Israel's media is blinding the public to the truth about Gaza."[136] Another journalist accused Israeli news outlets of serving as a "propaganda arm" that is "completely ignoring Palestinian casualties."[137] As part of its information campaign, Israel passed legislation enabling it to shutter any global media network that it deemed biased against the war effort. Authorities banned the Al Jazeera network from operating inside the country[138] and seized video equipment from the Associated Press.[139] Experts have also raised concerns about Israeli media self-censorship in light of government crackdowns.[140]

---

[133] Brawn, Steph. Jan. 4, 2024. "LBC: Israeli Ambassador to UK Says EVERY Gaza Building Is a Target." *The National*. www.thenational.scot/news/24026946.lbc-israeli-ambassador-uk-says-every-gaza-building-target/

[134] Goldenberg, Tia. Jan. 18, 2023. "Harsh Israeli Rhetoric against Palestinians Becomes Central to South Africa's Genocide Case." *Associated Press*. apnews.com/article/israel-palestinians-south-africa-genocide-hate-speech-97a9e4a84a3a6bebeddfb80f8a030724

[135] Da Silva, Chantal. 2023. Nov. 13. "'Nakba 2023': Israel Right-wing Ministers' Comments Add Fuel to Palestinian Fears." *NBC News*. www.nbcnews.com/news/world/gaza-nakba-israels-far-right-palestinian-fears-hamas-war-rcna123909

[136] Nechin, Etan. Jan. 9, 2024. "The Far Right Infiltration of Israel's Media Is Blinding the Public to the Truth about Gaza." *Guardian*. www.theguardian.com/commentisfree/2024/jan/09/israel-media-gaza-benjamin-netanyahu-settler-movement

[137] Cohen, Ido David. Dec. 25, 2023. "How Israeli Media Became a Wartime Government Propaganda Arm." *Haaretz*. www.haaretz.com/israel-news/2023-12-25/ty-article-magazine/.premium/how-israeli-media-became-a-wartime-government-propaganda-arm/0000018c-a0d3-d957-a98f-aed3ea5e0000

[138] June 6, 2024. "Israeli Government Seeks to Extend Controversial Al Jazeera Ban as High Court Hears Arguments against Media Law." *CNN*. www.cnn.com/2024/06/06/media/israel-al-jazeera-ban-media-law/index.html

[139] Fischer, Sara and Barak Ravid. May 21, 2024. "'Act of Madness': Israeli Officials Seize AP Equipment, Cut Live Feed of Gaza." *Axios*. www.axios.com/2024/05/21/israel-ap-equipment-seized-al-jazeera

[140] May 30, 2024. "As Press Freedoms Decline in Israel, People There See the War Differently from the Rest of the World." *CBC*. www.cbc.ca/news/world/israel-gaza-war-press-freedom-1.7218365

Inside Israel's military, language directly contrary to IHL has spread among high-ranking officials. For example, IDF spokesperson Daniel Hagari avowed that Israel's primary military focus was on inflicting "what causes maximum damage" in Gaza.[141] Israeli Defense Minister Yoav Gallant disparaged Palestinians as a "beastly people" while bragging about executing "a complete siege of the Gaza Strip," where there would be "no electricity, no food, no fuel." He added that "[w]e are fighting human animals, and we act accordingly."[142] The words prompted a rebuke from the UN's top human rights officer, who affirmed that "sieges that endanger the lives of civilians by depriving them of goods essential for their survival [are] ... prohibited under international humanitarian law."[143]

On the battlefield, IDF combatants have sparked international outrage for gloating about exploits against noncombatants. This includes using TikTok and other social media platforms to broadcast the destruction of civilian sites in Gaza. A *New York Times* analysis, for instance, found evidence of more than fifty videos of the IDF using "bulldozers, excavators and explosives to destroy what appear to be houses, schools and other civilian buildings." In one video, an IDF reservist overlaid clips of a destroyed Gaza house while playing a parody of the popular Israeli tune "This Was My Home."[144] A *Wall Street Journal* report discovered social media posts revealing "stripped and blindfolded Palestinian prisoners and troops inside homes in Gaza boasting about looting property."[145]

---

[141] McKernan, Bethan and Quique Kierzenbaum. Oct. 10, 2023. "'We're Focused on Maximum Damage': Ground Offensive into Gaza Seems Imminent. *Guardian*. www.theguardian.com/world/2023/oct/10/right-now-it-is-one-day-at-a-time-life-on-israels-frontline-with-gaza

[142] Speri, Alice. Oct. 9, 2023. "Israel Responds to Hamas Crimes by Ordering Mass War Crimes in Gaza." *Intercept*. https://theintercept.com/2023/10/09/israel-hamas-war-crimes-palestinians/

[143] Oct. 12, 2023. "Is Israeli Bombing of Gaza a Violation of International Laws?" *Al Jazeera*. www.aljazeera.com/features/2023/10/12/is-israeli-bombing-of-gaza-a-violation-of-international-laws

[144] Toler, Aric, Sarah Kerr, Adam Sella, Arijeta Lajka and Chevaz Clarke. Feb. 6, 2024. "What Israeli Soldiers' Videos Reveal: Cheering Destruction and Mocking Gazans." *New York Times*. www.nytimes.com/2024/02/06/world/middleeast/israel-idf-soldiers-war-social-media-video.html

[145] Cloud, David S. Feb. 21, "Israel Military Investigates Soldiers for Criminal Offenses in Gaza War." *Wall Street Journal*. www.wsj.com/world/middle-east/israel-military-investigates-soldiers-for-criminal-offenses-in-gaza-war-8fe2d947

6.3 The End of IHL?

As evidence of the overtness with which IHL has been challenged in Israel, one group of well-known Israeli lawmakers, scientists, and scholars penned an open, eleven-page letter in January 2024 lamenting what they called "the discourse of annihilation, expulsion and revenge" that had become rife among public and military officials, media figures, and others. The letter stated that "[f]or the first time that we can remember, the explicit calls to commit atrocious crimes … against millions of civilians have turned into a legitimate and regular part of Israeli discourse." It further raised concerns about the potential military impact, noting that "[n]ormalised discourse which calls for annihilation, erasure, devastation and the like is liable to impact the manner by which soldiers conduct themselves."[146]

Trump, according to one analysis, has mostly responded to the Gaza conflict by "not publicly call[ing] for Israel to show restraint or try to limit civilian casualties."[147] One of Trump's key GOP allies, Sen. Lindsey Graham of South Carolina, said on Fox News that Israel should "level" Gaza.[148] Notable is that Trump worked with Netanyahu in 2020 as part of an attempt to sanction the ICC. While the effort was largely aimed at forestalling prosecutions against U.S. forces, the ICC's scrutiny of Israel also played a role.[149] Echoing Trumpian language, Netanyahu called the court "obsessed with carrying out a witch-hunt against Israel and the United States."[150]

---

[146] Graham-Harrison, Emma and Quique Kierszenbaum. Jan 3, 2024. "Israeli Public Figures Accuse Judiciary of Ignoring Incitement to Genocide in Gaza." *Guardian*. www.theguardian.com/world/2024/jan/03/israeli-public-figures-accuse-judiciary-of-ignoring-incitement-to-genocide-in-gaza#:~:text="For%20the%20first%20time%20that,an%20everyday%20matter%20in%20Israel."

[147] Samuels, Brett. Nov. 28, 2023. 'Trump Gives Mixed Messages on How He'd Handle Israel-Hamas War." *The Hill*. https://thehill.com/homenews/administration/4331958-trump-mixed-messages-on-how-hed-handle-israel-hamas-war/

[148] McGreal, Chris. Oct. 16, 2023. "The Language Being Used to Describe Palestinians is Genocidal." *Guardian*. www.theguardian.com/commentisfree/2023/oct/16/the-language-being-used-to-describe-palestinians-is-genocidal

[149] Ravid, Barak. Jun 11, 2020. "Trump Administration Coordinated ICC Sanctions with Israel." *Axios*. www.axios.com/2020/06/11/international-criminal-court-trump-israel

[150] Borger, Julian. Jun 11, 2020. "Trump Targets ICC with Sanctions after Court Opens War Crimes Investigation." *Guardian*. www.theguardian.com/us-news/2020/jun/11/trump-icc-us-war-crimes-investigation-sanctions

Later, he urged the Biden White House to maintain sanctions on the ICC following a judgment that its jurisdiction included occupied Palestinian land.[151]

The Trump–Netanyahu relationship shows how foreign policy interactions can advance the impunity agenda across borders. For example, in the 2024 U.S. election, the broad consensus was that Netanyahu clearly preferred Trump over Vice President Kamala Harris, with one expert noting, "If Netanyahu were able to vote, he would have gladly cast it for Trump ... because he believes a Trump administration would be far more deferential toward Israel."[152] According to polling, Netanyahu's military aggression in Gaza arguably made it more difficult for Harris to win over Arab-American and pro-Palestinian voters, a key demographic in swing states like Michigan. Simultaneously, Trump's win made it more probable that Netanyahu could carry out military actions with limited regard for IHL.

Trump's rhetoric concerning the war in Gaza only hardened after his 2024 election, strengthening the perception that he was willing to give a "green light" to Netanyahu's military plans. In a tweet before his inauguration and in advance of the cease-fire brokered in January 2025, Trump demanded that unless Hamas released Israeli prisoners, there would be "ALL HELL TO PAY in the Middle East." Trump further declared that "[t]hose responsible will be hit harder than anybody has been hit in the long and storied History of the United States of America."[153] One expert noted that "Trump's victory in the U.S. presidential election could not have come at a better time for ... Netanyahu" as the Israeli leader pursued a Middle Eastern realignment that included a decisive Israeli victory and the stymieing of Iran's proxies in Iraq, Syria, and Yemen.

Shortly after entering office, Trump again provoked widespread denunciation in February 2025 after he declared from the White House that the U.S. might "take over" Gaza and "own it," turning it

---

[151] Feb. 25, 2021. "Israel Asked US Not to Lift Trump-era ICC Sanctions: Report." *Al Jazeera*. www.aljazeera.com/news/2021/2/25/israel-asked-us-not-to-lift-trump-era-icc-sanctions-report

[152] DePetris, Daniel. Nov. 7, 2024. "Trump's Win Means Benjamin Netanyahu Has a Freer Hand to Do What He Wants." *MSNBC*. www.msnbc.com/opinion/msnbc-opinion/netanyahu-trump-election-win-israel-gaza-rcna178956

[153] Lipner, Shalom. Nov. 25, 2024. "Israel's Trump Delusion." *Foreign Affairs*. www.foreignaffairs.com/israel/israels-trump-delusion

6.3 The End of IHL?

into the "Riviera of the Middle East."[154] Trump's comments led UN Secretary-General António Guterres to warn against "ethnic cleansing" in Gaza.[155] They also led some to accuse Trump of sounding "more like a real estate developer than an American president."[156, 157] The remarks came on the heels of earlier comments by Trump that Gaza was essentially a "demolition site" and that the U.S. may have to "clean out the whole thing" while resettling Palestinians.[158] The threat, if carried out, would almost certainly violate international law prohibiting the forced transfer of populations.[159]

Apart from Israel, Russian leadership has also been condemned for openly disregarding IHL. Specifically, Putin has been accused of committing numerous war crimes, including genocide, as part of his 2022 invasion of Ukraine.[160] In March 2023, the ICC charged Putin with the IHL violation of abducting and deporting Ukrainian children.[161]

---

[154] Feb. 5, 2025. "What Donald Trump Said about His Plans to 'Take Over' Gaza." *Al Jazeera*. www.aljazeera.com/news/2025/2/5/what-donald-trump-said-about-his-plans-to-take-over-gaza

[155] Graham-Harrison, Emma. Feb. 5, 2025. "UN Chief Warns against 'Ethnic Cleansing' after Trump's Gaza Proposal." *Guardian*. www.theguardian.com/world/2025/feb/05/un-chief-warns-against-ethnic-cleansing-after-donald-trump-gaza-proposal

[156] Liptak, Kevin, Alayna Treene, and Jeff Zeleny. Feb. 5, 2025. "How Trump Arrived at His Stunning Idea to 'Take Over' the Gaza Strip." *CNN*. https://edition.cnn.com/2025/02/05/politics/how-trump-decided-gaza-strip-take-over/index.html

[157] Liptak, Kevin, Alayna Treene, and Jeff Zeleny. Feb. 5, 2025. "How Trump Arrived at His Stunning Idea to 'Take Over' the Gaza Strip." *CNN*. https://edition.cnn.com/2025/02/05/politics/how-trump-decided-gaza-strip-take-over/index.html

[158] Klein, Betsy and Lex Harvey. Jan. 26, 2025. "Trump Suggests His Plan for Gaza Strip Is to 'Clean Out the Whole Thing'." *CNN*. https://edition.cnn.com/2025/01/25/politics/trump-gaza-strip-jordan-egypt/index.html

[159] Bateman, Tom. Feb. 5, 2025. "Trump's Gaza Plan Will be Seen as Flying in Face of International Law." *BBC*. www.bbc.co.uk/news/articles/c9w5q8qn59yo

[160] Hook, Kristina. July 29, 2022. "Why Russia's War in Ukraine Is a Genocide." *Foreign Affairs*. www.foreignaffairs.com/ukraine/why-russias-war-ukraine-genocide

[161] ICC. Mar. 17, 2023. "Situation in Ukraine: ICC Judges Issue Arrest Warrants against Vladimir Vladimirovich Putin and Maria Alekseyevna Lvova-Belova." International Criminal Court. www.icc-cpi.int/news/situation-ukraine-icc-judges-issue-arrest-warrants-against-vladimir-vladimirovich-putin-and#:~:text=Mr%20Vladimir%20Vladimirovich%20Putin%2C%20born,articles%208(2)(a

Reports have documented Russian strikes on civilian centers, including hospitals, schools, and playgrounds.[162] As one analyst observed, "[Russia] is not ... waging war according to the laws of war and the Geneva Convention.... We are revisiting the rules we thought were a given."[163] Another expert insisted that Putin's war crimes "are part and parcel of what Russia is trying to achieve in Ukraine ... they are a feature, not a bug."[164]

Putin has consistently used rhetoric against Ukraine that overtly dismisses global laws guaranteeing national sovereignty. As a rationale for Russia's invasion, he explicitly attacked the idea of Ukrainian nationhood and self-determination.[165] Putin has also pushed zealously for what he labels "denazification" in Ukraine, which, as one journalist notes, implies "the elimination of people" and is used as a "justification for endless war and cleansing."[166] In undercutting the principle of proportionality, Putin declared that if any nations tried to stop Russia from occupying Ukraine, they would trigger "consequences that you have never faced in your history."[167] According to one journalist, Russia's messaging on Ukraine has turned "fully genocidal."[168]

---

[162] Nov. 9, 2023. "'Tanks on the Playground': Attacks on Schools and Military Use of Schools in Ukraine." Human Rights Watch. www.hrw.org/report/2023/11/09/tanks-playground/attacks-schools-and-military-use-schools-ukraine

[163] Nolen, Stephanie. Oct. 21, 2023. "In Global Conflict Zones, Hospitals and Doctors Are No Longer Spared." *New York Times*. www.nytimes.com/2023/10/21/health/gaza-ukraine-hospitals-doctors.html#:~:text="This%20is%20not%20a%20situation,Kovtoniuk%20said.

[164] Wesslau, Fredrik. Feb. 20, 2024. "There Must Be a Reckoning for Russian War Crimes." *Foreign Policy*. https://foreignpolicy.com/2024/02/20/russia-war-crimes-justice-ukraine-putin-children-deportation-torture/

[165] Dickinson, Peter. July 15, 2021. "Putin's New Ukraine Essay Reveals Imperial Ambitions." Atlantic Council. www.atlanticcouncil.org/blogs/ukrainealert/putins-new-ukraine-essay-reflects-imperial-ambitions/

[166] Snyder, Timothy. Mar. 3, 2022. "Putin Has Long Fantasized about a World without Ukrainians. Now We See What That Means." *Washington Post*. www.washingtonpost.com/opinions/2022/03/23/putin-genocide-language-ukraine-wipe-out-state-identity/

[167] Borger, Julian and Angelique Chrisafis. Feb. 24, 2022. "Decision to Invade Ukraine Raises Questions over Putin's 'Sense of Reality.'" *Guardian*. www.theguardian.com/world/2022/feb/24/putin-russian-president-ukraine-invasion-mental-fitness

[168] Kolalev, Alexey. Apr. 9, 2022. "Russia's Ukraine Propaganda Has Turned Fully Genocidal." *Foreign Policy*. https://foreignpolicy.com/2022/04/09/russia-putin-propaganda-ukraine-war-crimes-atrocities/

6.3 The End of IHL?

Inside government, prominent Russian officials have intensified such rhetoric. A 2024 article for *Just Security* published a comprehensive collection of "eliminationist rhetoric against Ukraine"[169] featuring numerous inflammatory quotes by Russian state leaders. Among them, Putin ally and deputy chairman of Russia's Security Council Dmitri Medvedev disparaged "pseudo-Ukrainian rabid mongrels with Russian surnames, choking on their toxic saliva." Boris Chernyshov, a state Duma member, said that Russia's war in Ukraine was "an expression of our hatred, our holy hatred" and called for Ukrainians to "freeze and rot."[170] State Duma deputy Aleksey Zhuravlyov advocated "re-installing" the brains of Ukrainians, asserting that "a maximum of 5% are incurable" and should be "destroyed."[171]

Outside of government, Russian state media has played a significant role in justifying violence against civilians. A UN Human Rights Council official observed that "rhetoric transmitted in Russian state and other media may constitute incitement to genocide."[172] For example, Pavel Gubarev, a public figure, said on Russian television, "We will kill as many ... [Ukrainians] as we have to. We will kill 1 million or 5 million, we can exterminate all of you."[173] Anton Krasovskyi, former broadcasting director of Russia's RT network, declared that the proper response to Russia's opponents is to "[s]hove them right into those huts and burn them up ... [because Ukraine] is not supposed to exist at all."[174] RT host Vladimir Solovyov compared Russia's war in Ukraine to the "deworming" of a cat.[175]

---

[169] Apt, Clara. Apr. 18, 2024. "Russia's Eliminationist Rhetoric Against Ukraine: A Collection." *Just Security*. www.justsecurity.org/81789/russias-eliminationist-rhetoric-against-ukraine-a-collection/

[170] Apt, Clara. Apr. 18, 2024. "Russia's Eliminationist Rhetoric Against Ukraine: A Collection." *Just Security*. www.justsecurity.org/81789/russias-eliminationist-rhetoric-against-ukraine-a-collection/

[171] Davis, Julia. Mar. 13, 2023. "'Morality Shouldn't Get in the Way' – Russia's Genocidal State Media." Center for European Policy Analysis. https://cepa.org/article/morality-shouldnt-get-in-the-way-russias-genocidal-state-media/

[172] Sept. 25, 2023. "Russian Media Rhetoric Could be 'Incitement to Genocide in Ukraine': UN." *Al Jazeera*. www.aljazeera.com/news/2023/9/25/russian-media-rhetoric-could-be-incitement-to-genocide-in-ukraine-un

[173] Davis, Julia. Mar. 13, 2023. "'Morality Shouldn't Get in the Way' – Russia's Genocidal State Media." Center for European Policy Analysis. https://cepa.org/article/morality-shouldnt-get-in-the-way-russias-genocidal-state-media/

[174] https://x.com/JuliaDavisNews/status/1584054018145685504

[175] https://x.com/JuliaDavisNews/status/1549381189336711169/

Within the Russian Armed Forces, high-ranking leaders have also used genocidal language targeted at Ukrainian civilians. For instance, Apti Alaudinov, a commander of the Akhmat Special Forces, demanded that Russia "purge ... itself of this filth [Ukrainians] that permeates our society."[176] Vasily Fatigarov, a retired officer in Russia's military, called Ukraine a "cancerous tumor" that needs to be "purif[ied] ... very precisely, very severely, ... [to] ensure that that fascist infection doesn't grow anywhere else."[177] One Russian soldier said that his orders from the top were to "[k]ill everyone," and that "[i]t does not matter whether they're civilians or not."[178] Ukrainian civilians have reportedly been told that they could be victimized by bioweapons.[179]

On the conflict's front lines, graphic content depicting war crimes, including executions and acts of sexual violence, has become common among pro-Russian groups.[180] In a particularly grisly case of rewarding such behavior, Putin granted an honorary military title to a unit implicated in a massacre resulting in mass civilian graves.[181] One analysis reported that the Ukraine war has so inured the Russian population to barbarity that "methods of torture once only spoken about in witness testimonials are now being promoted online by the perpetrators ... for bragging rights."[182] Another account described

---

[176] Apt, Clara. Apr. 18, 2024. "Russia's Eliminationist Rhetoric Against Ukraine: A Collection." *Just Security*. www.justsecurity.org/81789/russias-eliminationist-rhetoric-against-ukraine-a-collection/

[177] Apt, Clara. Apr. 18, 2024. "Russia's Eliminationist Rhetoric Against Ukraine: A Collection." *Just Security*. www.justsecurity.org/81789/russias-eliminationist-rhetoric-against-ukraine-a-collection/

[178] Kinetz, Erika. Oct. 26, 2022. "'Kill Everyone': Russian Violence in Ukraine Was Strategic." PBS. www.pbs.org/wgbh/frontline/article/russian-general-troops-killed-civilians-ukraine/

[179] Roth, Andrew. Apr. 7, 2022. "Fears Genocidal Language in Russian Media May Prompt More War Crimes." *Guardian*. www.theguardian.com/world/2022/apr/07/russian-media-coverage-ukraine-genocidal-streak

[180] Aug. 5, 2022. "Tracking the Faceless Killers Who Mutilated and Executed a Ukrainian POW." *Bellingcat*. www.bellingcat.com/news/2022/08/05/tracking-the-faceless-killers-who-mutilated-and-executed-a-ukrainian-pow/

[181] Pleitgen, Fred, Claudia Otto, and Ivana Kottasová. Dec. 14, 2022. "'There Are Maniacs Who Enjoy Killing,' Russian Defector Says of His Former Unit Accused of War Crimes in Bucha." *CNN*.

[182] Roth, Andrew and Pjotr Sauer. Mar. 25, 2024. "Russia Lauding Torture Was Unthinkable – Now It Is Proud to Do So." *Guardian*. www.theguardian.com/world/2024/mar/25/russian-officials-lauding-torture-was-unthinkable-now-it-is-proud-to-do-so

6.3 The End of IHL?   241

"no attempt [by Russia] to hide a desire to target ordinary people."[183] One scholar remarked that Russian authorities are now "almost advertising genocide" by the military.[184]

According to some analysis, Russia's overt assaults on IHL in Ukraine had their precursors in the Trump years. For example, in late 2019, coinciding closely with Trump handing down his war crime clemencies, Putin made Russia the first country to formally revoke its commitment to Additional Protocol 1 of the Geneva Conventions, aimed at protecting noncombatants.[185] Legal scholar David M. Crane referred to the edict as part of a broader "movement away from a global approach to the rule of law" that, in a tie-in to Trump, had become apparent in the "Age of the Strongman."[186] Later in 2023, Putin followed this act by de-ratifying the 1996 Comprehensive Test Ban Treaty, which makes it illegal to participate in nuclear weapons explosions and testing.[187]

Critics have accused Trump of emboldening Putin to commit atrocities. This included for failing to condemn Russia's targeting of Ukrainian civilians, for calling Putin a "genius" and "savvy" for his incursion into Eastern Europe,[188] and even for saying that he might "encourage" Russia to attack NATO allies.[189] In refusing to expressly condemn Putin, Trump remarked, "If you say [Putin]'s a war criminal, it's going to be a lot tougher to make a deal to make ...

---

[183] Kirillova, Kseniya. Nov. 7, 2022. "Russia Fears Return of a Criminal Army." CEPA. https://cepa.org/article/russia-fears-the-return-of-a-criminal-army/

[184] Beauchamp, Zack. Apr. 13, 2022. "Is Russia Committing Genocide in Ukraine?" *Vox.* www.vox.com/23020696/ukraine-russia-genocide-allegations

[185] Oct. 17, 2019. "Russia's Putin Revokes Geneva Convention Protocol on War Crimes Victims." *Reuters.* www.reuters.com/article/us-russia-warcrimes-convention-idUSKBN1WW2IN/

[186] Crane, David M. Oct. 20, 2019. "Russia's Snub of Geneva Convention Protocol Sets Dangerous Precedent." *The Hill.* https://thehill.com/opinion/international/466531-russias-snub-of-geneva-convention-protocol-sets-dangerous-precedent/

[187] Richard, Ted. Feb. 16, 2024. "An Assessment of Russia's Withdrawal from the Comprehensive Test Ban Treat." https://lieber.westpoint.edu/assessment-russias-withdrawal-comprehensive-test-ban-treaty/

[188] Gedeon, Joseph. Feb. 23, 2022. "Trump Calls Putin 'Genius' and 'Savvy' for Ukraine Invasion." *POLITICO.* www.politico.com/news/2022/02/23/trump-putin-ukraine-invasion-00010923

[189] Gold, Michael. Feb. 10, 2024. "Trump Says He Gave NATO Allies Warning: Pay in or He'd Urge Russian Aggression." *New York Times.* www.nytimes.com/2024/02/10/us/politics/trump-nato-russia.html

[the war in Ukraine] stopped." He further lamented, "If he's going to be a war criminal, people are going to grab him and execute him."[190] Later, Putin defended Trump against his own alleged criminality in an act described by one journalist as "Trump get[ting] a sympathetic shout-out from his favorite war criminal."[191]

Like with Netanyahu, Trump's rapport with Putin arguably contributed to Trump's 2024 election win, while simultaneously fueling the impunity agenda in Russia. Despite Putin jokingly expressing a preference for Kamala Harris,[192] the conventional wisdom held that Trump's agenda for Russia's war better served Putin's interest. As one writer put it, "the biggest attraction for the Kremlin when it comes to Trump, of course, is his stance on Ukraine."[193] Polling showed that Trump's promise to end the war "in one day" and his running mate JD Vance's sharp criticism of aid to Kiev appealed to war-weary American voters.[194] At the same time, it signaled to the Kremlin that Ukrainian land concessions and limited accountability for Putin would be the price to pay for any cease-fire.

In the cases of Netanyahu and Putin, the narrative is not merely one of the impunity agenda gaining traction in ways that parallel Trump. Instead, they demonstrate how this agenda can penetrate even more deeply in settings where formal and informal pushback against IHL violations is minimal. As established earlier, the U.S. should be a hard case in which to overtly challenge IHL because it has

---

[190] Forredst, Jack. May 11, 2023. "Trump Won't Commit to Backing Ukraine in War with Russia." *CNN*. https://edition.cnn.com/2023/05/10/politics/ukraine-russia-putin-trump-town-hall/index.html

[191] Levin, Bess. Sept. 13, 2023. "Donald Trump Gets a Sympathetic Shout-Out from His Favorite War Criminal: Vladimir Putin." *Vanity Fair*. www.vanityfair.com/news/2023/09/donald-trump-gets-a-sympathetic-shout-out-from-vladimir-putin

[192] Haner, Joanne. Sept. 21, 2024. "Russian Official Stresses Putin Was 'Joking' about Support for Harris." *The Hill*. https://thehill.com/policy/international/4892273-putin-jokes-harris-election/

[193] Hartog, Eva. Nov. 5, 2024. "What Putin Really Wants from the US Election." *POLITICO*. www.politico.eu/article/donald-trump-kamala-harris-vladimir-putin-wants-from-the-us-election/

[194] "Watch: Trump Says as President He'd Settle Ukraine War Within 24 Hours." *Wall Street Journal*. www.wsj.com/video/watch-trump-says-as-president-hed-settle-ukraine-war-within-24-hours/0BCA9F18-D3BF-43DA-9220-C13587EAEDF2?embed=true&gsid=06b6eb06-fa0b-424c-b128-fe9ab0a75798

6.3 The End of IHL?

established guardrails and norms that protect against such behavior. Those constraints, however, are mostly weaker or absent elsewhere, allowing "strongman"-type leaders to make statements and to take military actions that openly flout the law of war. Where leaders want to enact an impunity agenda, clearing the path by removing executive constraints may be a first step for Trump imitators.

Nowhere are executive constraints more limited than in many fledgling nondemocracies. Beyond the Gaza and Ukraine wars, an important case comes from the civil conflict in Myanmar, where, according to political scientist Brian Klaas, Trump gave military leaders "fresh rhetorical ammunition" to carry out a coup in 2021, just weeks after he first left office.[195] After the siege, UN experts reported on a "dramatic increase in war crimes and crimes against humanity" that grew "increasingly frequent and brazen."[196] In describing the junta's violent overthrow, one writer observed "parallels" with Trump that were "striking."[197] Former Trump national security adviser Michael Flynn later said that there was "no reason" a Myanmar-style coup should not happen in the U.S.[198]

As these examples portend, Trump's open disregard of IHL could have far-reaching consequences beyond the U.S., and even the West. Historian Anne Applebaum, for example, has observed that, in the aftermath of Trump's first term, "We are heading into an era when there is no order, rules-based or otherwise, at all," adding that "like the equally outdated Pax Americana that accompanied the rules-based world order – the expectation that the U.S. plays some role in the resolution of every conflict – we might miss the Geneva Conventions

---

[195] Haltiwanger, John. Feb. 1, 2021. "Trump's Baseless Claims of Election Fraud Gave 'Fresh Rhetorical Ammunition' to Despots Like Myanmar's Generals, Who Just Staged a Coup." *Business Insider*. www.businessinsider.com/trump-gave-rhetorical-ammunition-to-myanmar-generals-prior-to-coup-2021-2?r=US&IR=T

[196] Aug. 8, 2023. "'Dramatic Increase' in Myanmar War Crimes, UN Probe Finds." *Al Jazeera*. www.aljazeera.com/news/2023/8/8/dramatic-increase-in-myanmar-war-crimes-un-probe-finds

[197] Shepp, Jonah. Feb. 2, 2021. "Myanmar's Military Pulled Off the Coup Trump Couldn't." *New York Magazine*. https://nymag.com/intelligencer/article/myanmar-military-coup-trump.html

[198] Astor, Maggie. June 1, 2021. "Michael Flynn Suggested at a QAnon-affiliated Event That a Coup Should Happen in the U.S." *New York Times*. www.nytimes.com/2021/06/01/us/politics/flynn-coup-gohmert-qanon.html

when they are gone."[199] The dystopian notion of the U.S. entering a world of no rules-based order at all may be too strong. Yet what seems evident is that Trump has severely hampered global efforts to advance respect for IHL.

The Trump case reinforces the importance of individual leadership in shaping both national and global cultures around IHL. Although nation-states can be held accountable for violating the law of war, the Nuremberg trials emphasized an enduring lesson: "Crimes against international law are committed by men, not abstract entities ... [I]ndividuals have international duties which transcend the national obligations of obedience imposed by the individual state."[200] These men (and women) include combatants expected to abide by international regimes that restrain the use of force. However, they also include leaders who maintain responsibilities to protect laws both *ad bellum* (laws governing the right to go to war) and *in bello* (laws governing conduct in war).

To be clear, there is no evidence that Trump has, implicitly or explicitly, endorsed the actual execution of grievous war crimes such as civilian targeting, rape, or torture. However, his incendiary remarks about the value of IHL, his insistence that rules of war be remade or expunged, and his handpicking of advisers who have not been shy about their desire to roll back the protections of the Geneva Conventions could erode respect for the law of war. Moreover, Trump's turning a blind eye to war crimes by U.S. combatants, and downplaying their significance, increases the chance that a new precedent is being set – that following the law of war is voluntary. More war crime clemencies by Trump during his second term would only increase these concerns.

Almost certainly, Trump's overt challenges to IHL have the potential to inspire more reneging from international law, both in Washington and globally. A grim reality is that even before Trump, the U.S. was already trending toward the adoption of policies that placed fewer restrictions on the use of military force – similar policies of which had been adopted by several of its allies and foes alike.

[199] Applebaum, Anne. Oct. 9, 2023. "There Are No Rules." *Atlantic.* www.theatlantic.com/international/archive/2023/10/israel-war-hamas-terrorism-ukraine-russia/675590/

[200] 1946. "Affirmation of the Principles of International Law recognized by the Charter of the Nürnberg Tribunal General Assembly resolution 95 (I)." UN. https://legal.un.org/avl/ha/ga_95-i/ga_95-i.html

6.3 The End of IHL? 245

Consider U.S. policies since 9/11 that have broadened the definitions of self-defense, as well as enabled fewer restrictions on strikes against "dual-use" targets, which serve both civilian and military purposes. The impunity agenda's successes only make it more likely that future leaders will push for loosened interpretations of the law of war, without the need to publicly justify them.

Meanwhile, the normalization of an anti-IHL agenda in the US risks further hobbling efforts at both domestic and global accountability for alleged war crimes. Legal expert Michael N. Schmitt, for example, has warned of "attention deficit disorder" and "outrage fatigue" regarding the law of armed conflict, leading to desensitization to its breaches.[201] Similarly, the head of the ICRC has talked about the "increasing elasticity" in how militaries apply IHL, reducing the likelihood of prosecuting violations.[202] Some of these challenges may be attributable not just to doctrinaire debates over the interpretation of the Geneva Conventions – what is and is not permissible in combat – but how IHL as a general concept is treated and respected by leaders.

Such problems are only likely to intensify as technological advancements and more complex forms of combat, including cyberwarfare, become standard practice.[203] In areas where there is even less legal precedent and more ambiguity in how IHL applies, new norms may reflect the priorities of leaders. The U.S. government has declared that cyber operations can constitute an illegal use of force, comparable to dropping a bomb or carrying out a drone strike, though the determination is ultimately "effects-based."[204] An open question is how states carry out their own modern fighting tactics in the context of IHL, such as potentially deadly computer network attacks and government-sponsored

---

[201] Schmitt, Michael N. Sept. 12, 2024. "Regaining Perspective on the Law of Armed Conflict." Lieber Institute West Point. https://lieber.westpoint.edu/regaining-perspective-law-armed-conflict/
[202] July 18, 2024. "Could America Fight Its Enemies Without Breaking the Law?" *Economist*. www.economist.com/international/2024/07/18/could-america-fight-its-enemies-without-breaking-the-law
[203] Delerue, Francois. 2020. *Cyber Operations and International Law*. Cambridge: Cambridge University Press. Ohlin, Jens Davic, Claire Finkelstein, and Kevin Govern, eds. 2015. *Cyberwar: Law and Ethics for Virtual Conflicts*. Oxford: Oxford University Press.
[204] Hodgkinson, Sandra. 2018. "Crossing the Line: The Law of War and Cyber Engagement – Applying the Existing Body of Law to This New National Security Threat." *International Lawyer* 51(3): 613–628.

hacks. The second Trump White House may be the first U.S. administration to tackle these questions on a broad scale.

Related is how the Trump administration is likely to approach AI-enabled warfare. American software firm Palantir, for example, has been at the forefront in using algorithms, powered by satellite and sensor data, to increase battlefield lethality. This work involves executing so-called "kill chains" to automate the process of finding and eliminating adversaries. However, major questions loom over the protocols encoded into these algorithms, such as when controls shift from AI to humans and how civilian casualties are assessed. Palantir CEO Alex Karp has acknowledged that "one thing … that's not quite understood is that there's an ethics to AI in the military," and that, for now, "you can't just have … the algorithm decide when to engage … [and] what distance from a hospital or a school can a target be taken."[205] Such questions will be left up to Trump's DoD.

Also unclear is how far Washington will go in trying to prevent IHL violations from being carried out with American dollars and weaponry.[206] While U.S. domestic law prohibits military and intelligence support that could be deployed to breach IHL, critics argue that some U.S. aid has done exactly that. In 2024, for example, Amnesty International accused the U.S. of "complicity" in alleged Israeli war crimes.[207] Another report found that U.S. officials in Israel "have gone to great lengths to preserve continued access to US weapons for the units responsible for … alleged violations," fostering what it called a "sense of impunity."[208] Compared to the Biden White House, the Trump team, marked by an indifference to IHL, may place even less emphasis on ensuring accountability for U.S. aid.

---

[205] Mar. 8, 2023. "Operational AI for Critical Institutions | Palantir CEO Alex Karp at CERAWeek." Palantir. www.youtube.com/watch?v=hkeohWt6rGA

[206] Finucane, Brian. Nov. 17, 2023. "Is Washington Responsible for What Israel Does with American Weapons?" *Foreign Affairs*. www.foreignaffairs.com/israel/washington-responsible-what-israel-does-american-weapons

[207] July 23, 2024. "USA: Fresh Warning over Complicity in Israeli War Crimes as Netanyahu Visits Washington." Amnesty International. www.amnesty.org.uk/press-releases/usa-fresh-warning-over-complicity-israeli-war-crimes-netanyahu-visits-washington

[208] Kirchgaessner, Stephanie. Jan. 18, 2024. "'Different Rules': Special Policies Keep US Supplying Weapons to Israel Despite Alleged Abuses." *Guardian*. www.theguardian.com/world/2024/jan/18/us-supply-weapons-israel-alleged-abuses-human-rights

Ultimately, Trump's "America First" agenda accords with a broader, inward-looking approach to the law of war. Its neo-sovereigntist critique – which views international law, including IHL, as robbing countries of their own abilities to govern – rejects counter-party rules as a basis for foreign policy.[209] In its place, Trump's agenda supports "go-it-alone" pursuits where countries become solo arbiters of the law. Such belligerent isolationism could lead to the gratuitous discounting of IHL because it fails to recognize the centrality of binding constraints. This includes constitutional checks regarding when and how the president wields force abroad. Law professor Tess Bridgeman, for example, has stated that Trump will be remembered for his "expansive – and sometimes lawless – claims of authority to take military action."[210]

At stake, therefore, may not just be America's posture toward IHL specifically, international law generally, or even the particular foreign policies of a president or sequence of presidents. In the worst case, it may be respect for the transnational, Kantian order.[211] The hard-earned victories achieved by diplomats, world leaders, and military attachés that resulted in the signing of the Geneva Conventions did not spontaneously emerge. Instead, they were the product of labor to curb centuries of unspeakable tragedies in war. America has played a central role in this project, even if it has been imperfect in complying. Conceivably, in the long run, Trump's overt denigration of IHL could prove destabilizing. Dents to IHL may not lead to its wholesale fracturing. However, the risk is that more cracks will.

The fact that some of these overt challenges to the norms of restraint could spill over into the U.S. military's use domestically only deepens the stakes. January 6 showed the damage that could be wrought by a sizable military population with a leader's prodding. A concerning prospect is a U.S. president formally summoning the military against American civilians. Trump has threatened that, if given the chance again, he is "not waiting" to deploy the military to quell turbulences

---

[209] Hathaway, Oona A. "International Delegation and State Sovereignty." *Law and Contemporary Problems* 71(1): 115–149.
[210] Brideman, Tess. Feb. 23, 2021. "Trump's War Powers Legacy and Questions for Biden." *Just Security*. www.justsecurity.org/74903/trumps-war-powers-legacy-and-questions-for-biden/
[211] Koh, Harold. 2017. "The Trump Administration and International Law." *Washburn Law Journal* 56: 413–469.

at home.[212] He has also talked ominously of purging the "enemy from within."[213] While the picture of "tanks rolling down Main Street,"[214] as suggested by one writer, remains highly unlikely, even its suggestion could erode expectations for what constitutes an appropriate use of force by the U.S. military.

Adding to this scenario is Pete Hegseth, the man tapped by Trump to lead the Defense Department. Hegseth has issued his own call to arms for MAGA supporters, urging them to prepare for violence domestically: "If you don't own a gun, buy one. Train to use it. Then buy more." The reason, Hegseth says, is the inevitability of "some form of civil war."[215] Although much of his attention has been on loosening U.S. rules of engagement in war,[216] Hegseth has also been preoccupied by a cadre of liberal radicals at home that he says have infiltrated its institutions. To confront this threat, Hegseth has declared, America must "mock, humiliate, intimidate, and crush our leftist opponents."[217] Hegseth has also kept open the possibility of using the military to shoot U.S. civilians.[218]

---

[212] Fields, Gary. Nov. 27, 2023. "Trump Hints at Expanded Role for the Military within the US. A Legacy Law Gives Him Few Guardrails." *Associated Press*. https://apnews.com/article/trump-military-insurrection-act-2024-election-03858b6291e4721991b5a18c2dfb3c36

[213] Tait, Robert. Oct. 24. "Trump Sparks Outrage after Calling for Army to Handle Enemies on Election Day." *Guardian*. www.theguardian.com/us-news/2024/oct/14/trump-military-enemy-within-armed-forces-election-day

[214] Tandanpolie, Tatyana. Nov. 28, 2023. "'Tanks Rolling Down Main Street': Experts Warn Law Won't Stop Trump from Deploying Military in US." *Salon*. www.salon.com/2023/11/28/tanks-rolling-down-main-street-experts-warn-law-wont-stop-from-deploying-military-in-us/

[215] Will, George F. Jan. 25, 2025. "There Were Ample Reasons, Not about His Personal Life, for Rejecting Hegseth." *Washington Post*. www.washingtonpost.com/opinions/2025/01/24/pete-hegseth-defense-department-unqualified/

[216] Press release. Jan. 7, 2025. "Warren Lays Out Detailed List of Concerns, Questions in Advance of Senate Armed Services Committee Hearing on Defense Secretary-Nominee Pete Hegseth." www.warren.senate.gov/newsroom/press-releases/warren-lays-out-detailed-list-of-concerns-questions-in-advance-of-senate-armed-services-committee-hearing-on-defense-secretary-nominee-pete-hegseth

[217] Wilson, Jason. Nov. 22, 2024. "Trump's Pentagon Pick Hegseth Wrote of US Military Taking Sides in 'Civil War'." *Guardian*. www.theguardian.com/us-news/2024/nov/22/trump-defense-secretary-pete-hegseth-book

[218] Bum, Philip. Jan. 14, 2025. "Pete Hegseth Seems Open to Ordering Soldiers to Shoot Protesters." *Washington Post*. www.washingtonpost.com/politics/2025/01/14/hegseth-seems-open-to-ordering-protesters-shot/

6.4 Why Trump 2.0 Could Be Worse for IHL

Against this backdrop, there are several reasons to believe that a second Trump term could prove even more detrimental to IHL than the first. One, which bears emphasizing, is Trump's decision to put Pete Hegseth at the helm of the Pentagon, the figure central to every consequential decision that Trump has made regarding the U.S. military justice system. By selecting the former Fox News anchor to reestablish what he calls a "warrior culture" at the DoD,[219] elevating him to sixth in line to the presidency, Trump offers little equivocation about his intent for more impunity.[220] While some of Hegeth's controversial views on IHL faced scrutiny during his Senate confirmation hearing, Trump almost certainly chose him because of, not despite, his overtly hostile stance to the laws of war.

On this point, Hegseth could be well-poised to advance his aim of reducing the role of international law in constraining U.S. military conduct. Hegseth has been criticized as the least-credentialed modern Defense Secretary, having never led a large organization despite being tasked to oversee 1.3 million active-duty servicemembers and a budget of $849 billion.[221] However, Hegseth brings several personal attributes uniquely suited to advancing the impunity agenda. His media-savvy persona, honed at Fox News, on which he continues to appear, is chief among them. Hegseth's celebrity among conservative rank-and-file servicemembers and deep connections with organizations that have lobbied for jailed U.S. servicemembers position him to reshape the military's ethos of accountability.

Another likely contributor to military impunity during Trump's second term is the composition of his administration beyond Pete Hegseth. During his first term, Trump filled high-level military and

---

[219] Jan. 14, 2025. "Pete Hegseth Vows to Foster a 'Warrior Culture' at the Pentagon and Be a Change Agent for Trump." *Associated Press.* https://newsroom.ap.org/editorial-photos-videos/detail?itemid=05bad5a6dbb24603aaf81b43e258c18e

[220] Shuham, Matt. Nov. 26, 2024. "Trump Defense Secretary Pick Thinks 'Marxists Are Our Enemies'." *HuffPost.* www.huffpost.com/entry/pete-hegseth-war-on-warriors-defense-department-nominee_n_674624e2e4b0733bf01de02a

[221] Cooper, Helene and Eric Schmitt. Jan. 25, 2025. "Hegseth's Views May Clash with Reality at the Pentagon." *New York Times.* www.nytimes.com/2025/01/25/us/politics/pete-hegseth-new-defense-secretary.html

nonmilitary posts with longstanding public servants. By contrast, the main criterion on which Trump has chosen his second-term picks is loyalty.[222] Military leaders who were previously moderating influences on Trump, such as Mark Esper, Jim Mattis, and Mark Milley, are gone and may be replaced with loyalists. If so, advocates of the impunity movement will no longer need to fight from the outside against the "Washington insiders." They will be the insiders. Trump's trust in figures under Hegseth is likely to grant them considerable latitude in both crafting and executing IHL-related policy.

Trump has already made several aggressive moves on this front. Shortly after re-entering office, as part of a purge of six senior Pentagon officials, Trump fired Gen. Charles Q. "C.Q." Brown, Jr. as Chairman of the Joint Chiefs of Staff, replacing him with a lesser-known retired three-star officer, Lt. Gen. Dan "Razin" Caine. Pete Hegseth had previously criticized Brown, who is black, for being preoccupied with DEI and "woke" initiatives, saying "Either you're in for warfighting, and that's it."[223] Alongside Brown, Trump also fired Adm. Lisa Franchetti, the first female chief of operations of the Navy; Gen. James Slife, the vice chief of the Air Force; and three high-ranking military lawyers from the Army, Navy, and Air Force. One expert described the purge as "praetorianism, pure and simple."[224]

Perhaps even more than Brown's termination, the firings of the three top military lawyers – judge advocate generals (JAGs) – provide the clearest indication of how Hegseth intends to approach the law of war as Secretary of Defense. One report, for example, said that the firings represented "an opening salvo in [Hegseth's] push to remake the military into a force that is more aggressive on the battlefield and potentially less hindered by the laws of armed conflict."[225]

---

[222] Bump, Philip. Nov. 13, 2024. "The Hegseth Nomination Is a Multilayered Trump Loyalty Test." *Washington Post*. www.washingtonpost.com/politics/2024/11/13/hegseth-trump-cabinet-nomination-military-pentagon/
[223] Schmitt, Helene Cooper, and Jonathan Swan. Feb. 21, 2025. "Trump Fires Joint Chiefs Chairman Amid Flurry of Dismissals at Pentagon." *New York Times*. www.nytimes.com/2025/02/21/us/politics/trump-fires-cq-brown-pentagon.html
[224] https://x.com/RadioFreeTom/status/1893139290047074631
[225] Jaffe, Greg. Feb. 22, 2025. "In Pursuit of a 'Warrior Ethos,' Hegseth Targets Military's Top Lawyers." *New York Times*. www.nytimes.com/2025/02/22/us/politics/hegseth-firings-military-lawyers-jag.html

6.4 Why Trump 2.0 Could Be Worse for IHL

There was no evidence that the JAG terminations reflected a specific confrontation with Hegseth. However, Hegseth in his book *War on Warriors* had mocked military attorneys as "jagoffs,"[226] and many experts have commented that Hegseth's goal is to lessen the role of lawyers in constraining battlefield conduct.

Along these lines, Trump has also made efforts to lessen oversight at the Pentagon, which could provide room for rolling back norms of restraint. After taking office in 2025, Trump terminated the contracts of more than a dozen independent inspectors general, including at DoD.[227] The terminations were targeted at government "watchdogs" charged with minimizing waste and abuse. Trump refused to provide the Senate with the required thirty-day notice of the firings, leading to questions about their legality. More importantly, however, the firings were decried for sharply departing from executive norms, as inspectors general typically stay in place during presidential transitions.[228] The moves could be a harbinger of Trump's broader intent to sideline independent accountability agents in the military, including over IHL.

In tandem with these actions, Trump has made clear that internal dissent will not be tolerated at the DoD. In January 2025, Trump signed an executive order revoking the security clearances of forty-nine former national security agents related to their alleged "misleading and inappropriate political coordination with the 2020 Biden presidential campaign."[229] One expert called the moves "the most politically saturated security action since the [J. Robert]

---

[226] Kelly, Kate. Jan. 14, 2025. "Hegseth Spars with Senator Over What He Meant by Slang Term." *New York Times*. www.nytimes.com/2025/01/14/us/politics/hegseth-jagoff-confirmation-hearing.html

[227] Nakamura, David, Lisa Rein, and Matt Viser. Jan. 26, 2025. "Trump Defends Ousting at Least 15 Independent Inspectors General in Late-night Purge." *Washington Post*. www.washingtonpost.com/politics/2025/01/24/trump-fire-inspectors-general-federal-agencies/

[228] May 22, 2024. "Removal of Inspectors General: Rules, Practice, and Considerations for Congress." Congressional Research Service. https://crsreports.congress.gov/product/pdf/IF/IF11546

[229] Jan. 20, 2025. "Holding Former Government Officials Accountable for Election Interference and Improper Disclosure of Sensitive Governmental Information." The White House. www.whitehouse.gov/presidential-actions/2025/01/holding-former-government-officials-accountablefor-election-interference-and-improper-disclosure-of-sensitive-governmental-information/

Oppenheimer case in the 1950s."[230] Pete Hegseth also ordered an inspector general probe into Ret. Gen. Mark Milley's tenure as chairman of the Joint Chiefs of Staff, which critics condemned as political retribution.[231] While not relating specifically to IHL, the actions could prove a warning for U.S. military personnel inclined to oppose Trump's stance on the law of war.

Another factor militating against IHL in the Trump 2.0 presidency stems from the actions of Trump's predecessor. Even more than his preemptive pardons of Gen. Mark Milley and members of the January 6 House committee,[232] Joe Biden's pardon of his son, Hunter Biden, for tax evasion and gun charges sparked bipartisan criticism.[233] Some experts suggest that Biden's pardon could establish a precedent for Trump to exploit, which might include more crime clemencies. Political scientist Sean J. Westwood has warned, "Democratic erosion is an iterative game. Biden just gave Trump an excuse to further abuse presidential pardons."[234] According to one columnist, "Biden ... by his nepotistic act adds to the pile of rancid pardons…, including Trump's first-term grants to … war criminals."[235]

Trump's pardon spree for January 6 rioters is the clearest example of his readiness to deliver on a campaign pledge to aid those with military backgrounds who had violently broken the law. Altogether, Trump granted clemencies for more than 200 current or ex-U.S. servicemembers, including 21 members of the Oath Keepers and

[230] De Luce, Dan. Jan. 25, 2025. "Trump's Canceling of 50 Security Clearances Is Unprecedented and Partisan, Experts Say." *NBC News*. www.nbcnews.com/politics/national-security/trumps-canceling-scores-security-clearances-unprecedented-rcna189245

[231] Liebermann, Oren. Jan. 29, 2025. "Defense Secretary Revokes Security Detail and Clearance for Trump Critic Gen. Mark Milley, Orders Investigation." *CNN*. https://edition.cnn.com/2025/01/28/politics/mark-milley-security-detail-pulled/index.html

[232] Sentner, Irie, Kyle Cheney, and Nicholas Wu. Jan. 20, 2025. "Biden Issues Preemptive Pardons for Fauci, Milley, Jan. 6 Committee and others." *POLITICO*. www.politico.com/news/2025/01/20/biden-pardons-fauci-milley-jan-6-committee-00199244

[233] Lee, Carol E. and Sarah Fitzpatrick. Dec. 2, 2024. "President Biden Pardons His Son Hunter Biden." *NBC News*. www.nbcnews.com/politics/joe-biden/joe-biden-issue-pardon-son-hunter-biden-rcna182369

[234] https://twitter.com/seanjwestwood/status/1863390724382666972

[235] Calmes, Jackie. Dec. 6, 2024. "Column: The Backlash on the Backlash against the Hunter Biden Pardon." *Los Angeles Times*. www.latimes.com/opinion/story/2024-12-06/pardon-hunter-joe-biden

27 members of the Proud Boys.[236] While Republicans largely defended the moves, Democrat Rep. Jamie Raskin of Maryland pilloried the decisions by asking whether the Capitol rioters were "being released as a reserve army of political foot soldiers to act on behalf of MAGA and Donald Trump."[237] Under Trump, the DoD has also not foreclosed the possibility that active-duty and National Guard servicemembers granted pardons could continue their military careers.[238]

A further concern for IHL in Trump's second administration is that the strategy for the impunity coalition has already been written. Given a full term behind him, Trump has a deeper understanding of the mechanisms of power within the Pentagon and the military – not only how to navigate them but also how to remove checks on his agenda. As one expert notes, "Trump has certainly learned from his first term in office and is stepping into this second term with an eye toward removing every guardrail that stood in the way of his lawless impulses before."[239] After his first inauguration, more than two years elapsed before Trump issued a war crime pardon. This time, Trump could start the process earlier, meaning more opportunities for clemencies and other acts that openly flout IHL.

Also heightening the likelihood of Trump openly defying IHL is the perceived strength of his electoral mandate, which could embolden him to further advance the impunity agenda. Although debatable, political scientist Francis Fukuyama referred to Trump's 2024 win as a "blowout victory,"[240] while one former adviser for Bill Clinton said

---

[236] Wentling, Nikki. Jan. 21, 2025. "Convicted Veterans among Jan. 6 Rioters Granted Pardons, Commutations." *Military Times*. www.militarytimes.com/flashpoints/extremism-disinformation/2025/01/21/convicted-veterans-among-jan-6-rioters-granted-pardons-commutations/

[237] Fields, Ashleigh. Jan. 22, 2025. "Raskin: Pardoned Jan. 6 Rioters 'A Reserve Army of Political Foot Soldiers'." *The Hill*. https://thehill.com/homenews/house/5100075-raskin-pardoned-jan-6-rioters-reserve-army-political-foot-soldiers/

[238] Toropin, Konstantin, Thomas Novelly, and Drew F. Lawrence. Jan. 17, 2025. "Troop Pardons Set to Complicate Military's Muddled Response to Jan. 6." Military.com. www.military.com/daily-news/2025/01/17/will-troops-pardoned-jan-6-have-place-military-they-already-do.html

[239] Velshi, Ali. Dec. 2, 2024. "Trump Learned Some Lessons from His First Term. But So Did We." *MSNBC*. www.msnbc.com/top-stories/latest/lessons-learned-trump-term-guardrails-rcna181868

[240] Fukuyama, Francis. Nov. 8, 2024. "Francis Fukuyama: What Trump Unleashed Means for America." *Financial Times*. www.ft.com/content/f4dbc0df-ab0d-431e-9886-44acd4236922

that "[t]he 2024 election marks the biggest shift to the right in our country since Ronald Reagan's victory in 1980."[241] Unlike in 2016, when Trump lost the popular vote but won the Electoral College, his sweep of every swing state in 2024 means that Trump will likely interpret the victory as a sign that America is four-square behind the impunity agenda. As noted earlier, most relevant for the functioning of the Pentagon is that 65 percent of U.S. veterans supported Trump over Kamala Harris, according to 2024 exit polls.[242]

Beyond the mandate itself, Trump 2.0 has already demonstrated a bold governance style, which could play into Trump's plans for the military.[243] By shattering norms at a breakneck speed and inundating the media with relentless policy proposals, the odds are greater that any isolated transgressions, including overt challenges to IHL, go unnoticed or unchallenged. Consider that, in his first several weeks in office, Trump signed more than fifty executive orders and floated radical proposals, including ending birthright citizenship, seizing Greenland, making Canada the fifty-first state, retaking the Panama Canal, enacting tariffs on a scale not seen since the 1930s, shuttering the U.S. Agency for International Development, and carrying out the largest migrant deportation in history.

The constant chaos appears to be a feature, not a bug of Trump 2.0. Any semblance of the Trump "resistance" may be unable to keep pace, creating political cover for Trump to push controversial agendas like overtly challenging IHL. As former Trump strategist Steve Bannon put it, Trump's goal is to "Attack! Attack! Attack! Keep driving it. Flood the zone. Overwhelm 'em."[244] Trump's former White House lawyer, Ty Cobb, echoed this idea, saying that Trump 2.0 is pursuing "a naked power grab" intended to "flood the zone with as much unconstitutional activity as possible, with the hope that they

---

[241] Brownstein, Ronald. Nov. 7, 2024. "What Swayed Trump Voters Was Bidenomics." *Atlantic*. www.theatlantic.com/politics/archive/2024/11/uncertain-future-vs-unacceptable-present/680577/

[242] Guskin, Emily, Chris Alcantara, and Janice Kai Chen. Dec. 2, 2024. "Exit Polls from the 2024 Presidential Election." *Washington Post*. www.washingtonpost.com/elections/interactive/2024/exit-polls-2024-election/

[243] Bailey, Phillip M. and Sudiksha Kochi. "Blitz! President Trump Returns to Familiar Strategy That Exhausts Foes, Delights Friends." *USA Today*. https://eu.usatoday.com/story/news/politics/elections/2025/02/02/trump-blitz-white-house/78051061007/

[244] https://x.com/GBNAmerica/status/1887267459826393128

6.4 Why Trump 2.0 Could Be Worse for IHL

get away with some or all of it."[245] Against this political backdrop, Trump's open challenges to the law of war may receive less pushback, bolstering incentives to press forward.

Finally, and maybe most important, Trump's second term could be more harmful for IHL because Trump has nothing to lose politically. Although Trump has mused about amending the Constitution to serve more than eight years, he is unconstrained by future elections due to term limits. As one writer put it, Trump's second administration might best be described with a simple phrase: "You ain't seen nothing yet."[246] A Trump White House unburdened by elections could pursue war crime clemencies regardless of whether they are politically beneficial, potentially opening a wider set of war crime cases that could prove controversial even in the eyes of some conservative voters. Additionally, without the added pressure of courting public opinion, Trump could use the bully pulpit and commander-in-chief powers to more radically attack IHL with few repercussions.

Although the future of military impunity in the U.S. post-Trump is uncertain, Trump's 2024 staging of the most significant comeback in modern American politics underscores his persistent appeal with the GOP base. While much of Trump's success owes to domestic issues like inflation and immigration, his approach to foreign policy and the military also deserves credit. Central to this agenda is an unabashed disregard for IHL. Looking ahead to 2028 or beyond, a question is whether Trump's Republican heir will continue his direct challenges to IHL, or escalate them. The degree to which America drifts from the once-unassailable consensus that IHL should be given public deference may hinge on how much Trump disregards this principle during his last four years in office.

Within the U.S , the idea that support for publicly challenging IHL could actually increase in a future devoid of Trump is consistent with him being both a symptom and a cause of the impunity agenda. To

---

[245] Diamond, Dan, Lauren Kaori Gurley, Lena H. Sun, Hannah Knowles, and Emily Davies. Feb. 6, 2025. "DOGE Broadens Sweep of Federal Agencies, Gains Access to Health Payment Systems." *Washington Post*. www.washingtonpost.com/health/2025/02/05/doge-health-agencies-labor/

[246] Freedland, Jonathan. Nov. 8, 2024. "Think You Know How Bad Trump Unleashed Will Be? Look at the Evidence: It Will be Even Worse." *Guardian*. www.theguardian.com/commentisfree/2024/nov/08/donald-trump-evidence-public-health-crisis-nato

the extent that Trump has gone beyond any modern U.S. president in overtly rejecting the validity of IHL, he has tapped into preexisting demands from the conservative electorate and openness to the agenda from the military community. If support for the impunity agenda has gained a self-perpetuating momentum, it may no longer require Trump. Future presidents willing to carry Trump's mantle, with help from allies in the media and on Capitol Hill, could become more extreme, given clear backing from right-leaning voters with flimsier commitments to the laws of war.

6.5 Where to Go from Here

This book raises a number of questions for future research. Among the most pressing is how the Trump case generalizes to other Western democracies. Put differently, do "means, motives, and opportunity" typically exist for overtly challenging IHL, waiting for leaders to exploit? Or are they relatively rare conditions? When it comes to means, the essential element of the impunity agenda has been Trump's partnership with Fox News and Republican Congress members. Yet it is unclear whether analogous enablers can be found in most Western democracies or whether the political landscape Trump inherited, marked by a twenty-four-hour right-wing news cycle and polarization on Capitol Hill, is distinct. It is also unclear whether other Western leaders hold the same kinds of authority as U.S. presidents to attack IHL.

In the U.S., seminal work on the "two faces" of the presidency suggests that executives wield more power over foreign policy and the military than domestic policy.[247] However, given the robustness of "checks and balances" in America's federal system, one could argue that Trump's overt challenges to IHL were unlikely to stem from idiosyncratic weaknesses of executive constraints. Fundamentally, this may underscore how authority over civilian and military concerns determines whether leaders are poised to attack IHL. In the U.S., one salient, if not unique, tension is the competing, enumerated responsibilities of the president: first, to ensure the faithful execution of laws; and second, to preside over the military as commander-in-chief.[248]

---

[247] Wildavsky, Aaron. 1998. "The Two Presidencies." *Society* 35: 23–31.
[248] Maurer, Dan. "War Crime Clemency: The President's Self-(Defeating) Pardon." *Maryland Law Review* 82(3): 581–669.

This dual role places U.S. presidents in a position where enforcing the laws can inherently conflict with combat-level management of troops, both of which may be influenced by politics. While this tension may be irresolvable in the U.S., where Article 2 powers of the president are firmly delimited in the Constitution, it provides a point of comparison for thinking about whether leaders are able to strain IHL in different settings (e.g., in Western democracies that meaningfully divide the roles of heads of government and state, or where executives have differing responsibilities over military justice). It is plausible that more diffuse executive powers could reduce, if not eliminate, the capacity of democratic leaders to directly challenge IHL.

In terms of motive, it is equally unclear whether the Trump era has been a particularly propitious moment to score political points by openly attacking the law of war, or whether Trump is simply the first U.S. president willing to take such a chance. One possibility is that Trump has been singularly prescient in activating the Republican base through brazenly attacking IHL, even as he is less concerned by its ethics or the risks of alienating moderate voters. In terms of opportunity, it is also a question whether all militaries are prone to deep-seated, ideological subcultures that can be persuaded to abandon norms of restraint. The extent and pervasiveness of these subcultures could vary across settings, making some militaries more susceptible to activation than others.

Future studies in these areas could analyze historical cases. An example might be to contrast support for the U.S. troops granted clemency by Trump with that for William Calley, Jr., who, as noted earlier, was implicated in the 1968 "My Lai" massacre in Vietnam. After Calley's court-martial and sentencing, Democratic Sen. Adlai Stevenson reportedly had his mailbox filled with letters from Americans registering 200 to 1 in his defense. A poll also showed that approximately two-thirds of citizens viewed Calley as a "scapegoat," and one local VFW post fundraised on his behalf.[249] His story shows the groundswell of support that has previously existed for a convicted American war criminal, but without an ironclad effort by a president to herald his case.

Researchers could also analyze responses to war crime controversies outside the U.S. One approach might compare how leaders in non-Western contexts have explicitly undermined IHL, such as above with

[249] https://twitter.com/GregoryDaddis/status/1401666450473979905

Israel and Russia. Another might probe how other advanced democracies have grappled with war crime cases differently than Trump. Consider Australia. Shortly after Trump lost his election in 2020, the inspector general of the Australian Defence Force published the "Brereton Report," a 500-plus page document detailing the alleged killings of thirty-nine noncombatants in Afghanistan at the hands of its special forces from 2005 to 2016.[250] Unlike the impunity agenda in the U.S., however, there were no widespread efforts by Australian politicians to exonerate the implicated ADF servicemembers.

Concerning the U.S. case, one priority for research is to unpack further the Trump-Fox News "feedback loop."[251] A central part of the impunity movement's success is that Fox News does not just defend the impunity agenda. It also helps to create it. This shift, from partisan media as a sponsor of government activities to its progenitor, is worthy of more inquiry. Although analyses have identified elements of this change in other areas,[252] most remain observational. For example, a recent journalistic study coded more than a year's worth of transcripts from "Fox and Friends" to document how Fox News cultivated two audiences: the American public and Trump himself.[253] These dynamics are consistent with the impunity movement. Trump takes cues from Fox News, and vice versa.

A related question is the extent to which Trump's other main ally in openly challenging IHL, congressional Republicans, initiated or has simply perpetuated the impunity agenda. One interpretation is that GOP lawmakers were already pursuing a nascent impunity agenda pre-2016, and Trump proved useful for leading on these policies. In this way, Trump ramped up an existing trend. However, another reading is that, after Trump proved his willingness to attack the validity of IHL, Republican allies forced him to go further. Trump may have even

---

[250] Inspector-General of the Australian Defence Force Afghanistan Inquiry Report. 2020. www.defence.gov.au/sites/default/files/2021-10/IGADF-Afghanistan-Inquiry-Public-Release-Version.pdf

[251] Gertz, Matthew. Jan. 5, 2018. "I've Studied the Trump-Fox Feedback Loop for Months. It's Crazier Than You Think." *POLITICO*. www.politico.com/magazine/story/2018/01/05/trump-media-feedback-loop-216248

[252] Stelter, Brian. 2020. *Hoax: Donald Trump, Fox News, and the Dangerous Distortion of Truth*. New York: One Signal Publishers/Atria.

[253] Chang, Alvin. Feb. 9, 2018. "We Analyzed 17 Months of Fox & Friends Transcripts. It's Far Weirder than State-run Media." *Vox*. www.vox.com/2017/8/7/16083122/breakfast-club-fox-and-friends

6.5 Where to Go from Here

become subordinate to the impunity movement that he created, giving him less room to maneuver if he wanted to retain support on Capitol Hill. Under this scenario, Trump instigated the impunity agenda, and GOP lawmakers accelerated it.

A final question regards the long-term impacts of the impunity agenda on the actual behavior of U.S. servicemembers in battle. Even if combatant attitudes toward IHL have become laxer under Trump, understanding whether this translates into more crimes in war requires on-the-ground conflict data. Capturing IHL violations and measuring effect sizes both pre- and post-Trump would be instructive. Skeptics have questioned whether negative effects materialize. Eddie Gallagher even sarcastically asked critics to "preach to me again the dangers of moral hazards," referring to the apparent incentive his clemency could have in inducing combatants to disregard IHL.[254] Yet many experts have argued that excusing the bad behavior by U.S. troops degrades order and discipline.[255]

In the end, Trump will, for good reason, be remembered for his blistering attacks on domestic institutions, such as Congress, the free press, and the U.S. electoral system. Yet as this book has shown, he also has another, ongoing legacy of impunity: one tied to the military. Trump has not only redefined norms for undermining IHL. He has discarded even the pretense of valuing the law of war. That legacy is a critical part of the Trump era and will define his final four years in office. This book calls for revisiting the consensus that, once established, public respect for IHL is self-sustaining. The seeds for openly challenging IHL may be embedded in Western democracies. If overt affronts to the law of war can materialize in the U.S., which has long supported the Geneva Conventions, they could plausibly happen in other regimes.

---

[254] Rosas, Julio. Nov. 27, 2019. "Eddie Gallagher's Family Speaks Out: We Will Vote for Those Who 'Actually Support Our Warfighters.'" *Townhall*. https://townhall.com/tipsheet/juliorosas/2019/11/27/eddie-gallaghers-family-speaks-out-we-will-vote-for-those-who-actually-support-our-warfighters-n2557174

[255] Ioanes, Ellen. Nov. 27, 2019. "Trump's Pardons Erode Good Order and Discipline and Could Shatter the Military's Reputation, Veterans Say." *Insider*. www.businessinsider.com/veterans-respond-to-trumps-pardons-for-alleged-war-crimes-2019-11

Index

Locators in bold indicate information in tables, and those in italics indicate information in figures.

9/11 terrorist attacks, 25
   ASMPA 2002, 222
   discourse of fear, 30
   self-defense concept, 245
   Trump's anti-Muslim narrative, 81
   war on terror, 4

Abuse of the Pardon Prevention Act (proposed), 221
accountability
   accountability mechanisms, lack of, 15, 178
   domestic prosecutions for war crimes, 224
   global criminal prosecutions for war crimes, 226
   global violations of IHL, 206, 221
   ICC jurisdiction, 221. *See also* International Criminal Court (ICC)
   impunity coalition, impact of, 37, 249
   individual leadership, 216, 244, 251
      prevention/penalization of war crimes, 17
   nation-states, 244
   noncombatant casualties, 61–62
      Israel-Hamas war, 234
      Russo-Ukrainian War, 241, 242
   normalization of an anti-IHL agenda, impact of, 245
   Russo-Ukrainian War, 241, 242
   unrestrained legal authority, 85
Afghanistan, 2, 29, 139, 148, 179, 190, 258
AI-enabled warfare, 246
algorithms
   AI-enabled warfare, 246

America First agenda, 247
American Civil Liberties Union (ACLU), 68
American Enterprise Institute (AEI), 211
American Service-Members' Protection Act (2002), 221
Amnesty International, 246
Anti-Defamation League's Center on Extremism, 146
Antifa, 159
Anti-Personnel Mine Ban Treaty (1997), 23
Applebaum, Anne, 243
Army Times, 139
Article 2 powers, 22, 31, 73, 203, 257
Austin, Lloyd, 145, 205
Australia
   noncombatant casualties, 258
authority, 82
   accountability, 85
   anarchy and the "deep state," 85–87
   "by all means necessary," 221
   limiting authority, 203
   superior orders defense, 162
   unfettered legal domestically, 84–86

Babbitt, Ashli, 157
Baker, Peter, 44
Bales, Robert, 179, 180
Bannon, Steve, 196, 254
Barr, William, 85, 88
Behenna, Michael, 2, 37, 180
Bembenek, Christina, 163
Benedict, Helen, 136
Best, Mat, 135
Biden, Joe and the Biden Administration, 55, 163

Index 261

Biden–Netanyahu relationship, 232
Biden–Putin relationship, 216
Blackwater prosecutions, 38, 44, 45, 58
 criminal charges within the military, 205
 ICC, relationship with, 24, 222
 military votes, 131
 presidential pardons
  Hunter Biden and precedent for abuse, 252
  January 6th House committee, 252
  Trump's derogatory language about, 95
Biggs, Joseph, 163
Bilah, Jededia, 41
Billingslea, Marshall, 58
birthright citizenship, 254
Black Lives Matter, 83
Blackwater Memorial Alumni Association, 191
Blackwater pardons, 37, 38, 43–45, 50, 54, 58, 88, 91, 182, 189, 191–192
Boot, Max, 164
Bradley, Curtis, 26
Bream, Shannon, 41
Breitbart, 171
Brereton Report (Australia 2020), 258
Brock, Larry, 156
Brooks, Mo, 158, 159
Brooks, Rosa, 26, 213
Brown, Charles Q. (C.Q.), 250
Burkina Faso, 14
Bush, George W., 4, 24, 25, 29, 211, 226
 ICC, relationship with, 221–222
 impeachment attempts, 223
 torture memos, 26, 212
Butler, Jeremey, 162

Cabinet resistance
 rejection of the impunity agenda from within, 214–216
Cain, Will, 193
Caine, Dan (Razin), 250
Caldwell, Thomas Edward, 161
Calley, Jr, William, 24, 257
Canada
 Trump's annexation proposals, 254

Carlson, Tucker, 153
Carter, Jimmy, 229
Cawthorn, Madison, 158
"central casting" narrative, 78–79
Certo, Peter, 90
Chansley, Jacob Anthony, 14, 164
checks and balances in the U.S. federal system, 204, 247, 256
 Trump's navigation of, 253
Cheney, Liz, 160
Chernyshov, Boris, 239
CIA black sites, 8, 24, 68
civil war threat, 248
 January 6th, 155
Civilian Harm Mitigation and Response Action Plan, 205
Civilian Protection Center of Excellence (CPCoE), 205
Clinton, Hillary, 55
 military votes, 131
 Trump's derogatory language about, 95
CNN, 171, 172, 174
Cobb, Ty, 254
Cohen, Andrew, 80
collective mobilization, 5, 31
Combat Clemency Project (CCP), 180–181
command responsibility principle, 16–18, 226
commander-in-chief. *See* Article 2 powers
commitment to IHL, 10, 14, 22, 25, 32. *See also* disregard for IHL; opportunity to upend commitments to IHL
Comprehensive Test Ban Treaty 1996
 Putin, 241
Concha, Joe, 197
Congressional Justice for Warriors Caucus (CJWC)
 impunity agenda, 138–140, 175–176
 media presence, 173
 pardons for war crime convictions
  defending war crime clemencies, 55–58
  lobbying, 50–55
 reinforcement of the impunity agenda from within, 175–176
 storming of the U.S. Capitol, 159

congressional oversight, 177
conservative intellectual circles
    impunity agenda, influence over, 211–212
consolidation of power and disregard for the law of war, 6, 31, 35. *See also* cronyism; impunity coalition
conspiracy theories, 86, 157, 174
Convention on the Prohibition of the Use, Stockpiling, Production and Transfer of Anti-Personnel Mines and on their Destruction. *See* Anti-Personnel Mine Ban Treaty (1997)
Coomer, Micah, 155
Cooper, Anderson, 162
Cotton, Tom, 62, 65, 68
COVID-19 vaccine, 87
Cramer, Kevin, 194
Crane, David M., 241
Crenshaw, Dan, 140
criminal investigations
    charges against military personnel, 140, 205
    extremism within the U.S. military, 145
    ICC investigations
        Trump's war crime clemencies, 226
        U.S. military personnel, 62
cronyism, 130, 204, 205
    Biden's nepotistic pardons, 252
    Fox News and Hegseth, 192–199
Crow, Jason, 146
Cruz, Ted, 60, 62, 68, 69
Cunningham, James, 148
cyberwarfare, 245

Daily Caller, 171
"deep state" anti-Trump resistance, 49, 85–87, 213
    false perception of 2020 election, 163, 214
    Hegseth's nomination, 195
democracy and the law of war, 4, 6, 8, 11–12, 16, 36, 231, 256–259
democratic backsliding, 6, 203–204
Dempsey, Martin, 208
detentions, 25
Deudney, Daniel, 229

Dichter, Avi, 233
discourse of fear, 30
    immigrants, 81
disproportionate force, 65
    Israel-Hamas war, 232
    restraints on the use of force, 59, 104, 244
disregard for IHL, 14, 32
    Geneva Conventions, 104–106, **106**, *107*, *108*, *109*, **123**
    Israel-Hamas war, 231–237
        criticisms of, 235
        Israel Defense Forces, 231
        Israeli government, 232
        Israeli media, 233
        Israeli military, 234
        Netanyahu, 231
    moral foundations theory, 104–106
        by ideology, **106**, *107*, *108*
        by MFT values, *109*, **123**
    Netanyahu, 231–232
    Putin, 231, 241
    Russo-Ukrainian War
        government, 239
        Putin, 237–238
        Russian Armed Forces, 240
        state media, 239
    U.S. military, 104–108, 200
diversity, equity, and inclusion (DEI)
    purging of "DEI hires," 150, 250
domestic audience cost theories, 6, 20, 74
domestic prosecutions
    rejection of the impunity agenda from within, 224–225
domestic terrorist plots and attacks
    U.S. service members, 145
Doocey, Peter, 41
drone strikes, 8, 59, 64, 245

Earhardt, Ainsley, 41, 66
Electoral Count Reform Act (2022), 228
electoral integrity, 16, 159
Eliyahu, Amichay, 233
enhanced interrogation program, 26, 212
Ernst, Joni, 195, 209
Esper, Mark, 42, 165, 250
ethical aversion to contravening IHL, 6, 200, 202

Index 263

executive constraints safeguarding the law of war, 5, 243, 256
executive orders
  rejection of the impunity agenda from within, 220–221
executive oversight, 178
executive powers
  rejection of the impunity agenda from within, 219–220
exploitation of political openings, 7
extremism (far-right) in the military, 142–144
  9/11 terrorist attacks, impact of, 144
  Ku Klux Klan membership, 144
  Oklahoma City bombing, 144
  Trump's impact, 144–151
  white supremacist infiltration, 144

Facebook, 155, 164. *See also* social media
  CJWC, 54, 58
  Free Raven 23, 192
  SOH, 181
  UAP, 180
Feaver, Peter, 146
Flores, Bill, 58
Flynn, Michael, 88, 165, 243
forcible transfer of persons, 237
Ford, Gerald, 220
Ford, Stuart, 17
Fox & Friends, 39, 41, 59
  Blackwater pardons, 43–44, 50
  Hegseth's appointment, 62, 170
  pardons for war crime convictions, 43–44, 46, 50, 51, 191
Fox News, 31, 32, 258
  defense of clemencies, 45–50, 55
  disproportionate force, 66
  Hegseth, support for, 192–194, 198
  ICC, 62
  pro-military slant, 134–138
  relationship with military, 134–138
  Republican lawmakers, relationship with, 173–175
  Soleimani strike, 65
  state sovereignty, 63
  storming of the U.S. Capitol, 158
  torture, 67–69
Fracker, Jacob, 155

Franchetti, Lisa, 250
Free Press, 171
French, David, 45
Fukuyama, Francis, 253

Gaetz, Matt, 58, 141, 159
Gallagher, Eddie, 1, 18, 37, 86, 200
  moral purity arguments, 91, 94–96
  overzealous prosecutors narrative, 87–89
  pardon for war crime conviction, 37, 51
  CJWC, 51–54, 140
  Fox News, 41, 45–50, 136
  lobbying organizations, 181–182
  Republican lawmakers and conservative media, 172–173
  social media, 183
  right-wing influencer, as, 184–188
  Trumpian hero, as, 90–91, 168
  us/them binary, 77–79
Garcia, Gabriel, 161
Gaza. *See* Israel-Hamas war
Gbagbo, Laurent, 226
  ICC investigation, 226
Geneva Call, 206
Geneva Conventions, 9, 23, 200–202
  Additional Protocol I, 23, 241
  denunciations of, 2
  disregard for, 104–106, 106, 107, 108, 109, 123
genocide
  Israel-Hamas war, 231
  Russo-Ukrainian War, 238, 239, 241
German, Michael, 153
Giuliani, Rudolph, 89, 156
global criminal prosecution
  rejection of the impunity agenda from within, 226–227
Gohmert, Louie, 57, 58, 139. *See also* Congressional Justice for Warriors Caucus (CJWC)
  Blackwater pardons, 44, 91
  National Defense Authorization Act, 176
  storming of the U.S. Capitol, 160
Goldgeier, James M., 177
Goldsmith, Jack, 26
Goldsmith, Kristofer, 147

Golsteyn, Mathew, 200
  celebrity, as, 190–191
  moral purity arguments, 91
  overzealous prosecutors narrative, 87–89
  pardon for war crime conviction, 2, 4, 17, 37
    CJWC, 53
    Fox News, 39, 46
    lobbyist organizations, 180
  Trumpian hero, as, 90
GOP. *See* Republican lawmakers
Gorka, Sebastian, 198
Gosar, Paul, 55, 56, 58, 159
Graham, Lindsey, 63, 65, 142, 235
Grant, Rebecca, 49
Greene, Matthew, 156
Greene Taylor, Marjorie, 159
Greenland
  Trump's annexation proposals, 254
Griffin, Couy, 93
Guantanamo Bay, 69
"guerrilla sabotage" in government
  rejection of the impunity agenda from within, 213–214
Gurfein, David, 184, 199
Gutfield, Greg, 69

habeas corpus violations, 25
Hagari, Daniel, 234
Hague Invasion Act (2002), 221
Hannity, Sean, 59, 63
  Blackwater pardons, 43
  Hegseth, support for, 47, 171, 197
  pardons for war crimes convictions, 48
  rules of engagement, 61
  Soleimani, 65
  torture, support for, 67
Hanson, Victor Davis
  us/them binary, 77
Harris, Kamala
  Israel-Hamas war, 236
  military votes, 131, 254
  Russo-Ukrainian War, 242
Haspel, Gina, 68
Hathaway, Oona, 230
Hatley, John, 57, 180
Heard, Dustin, 38, 191

Hegseth, Pete, 4, 30, 67, 149
  Blackwater pardons, 44
  Defense Secretary, 169–171, 193–198
  furthering the impunity agenda, 249–250
  moral purity arguments, 91, 94
  Navy prosecutions, 88
  us/them binary, 76
Hemmer, Nicole, 89
Henry, Ed, 41
Heritage Foundation, 194
Herzog, Isaac, 232
Higbie, Carl, 197
The Hill, 171
Hodges, Eric, 160
Hotovely, Tzipi, 232
HuffPost, 171
Human Rights First, 163
Hunter, Duncan, 139. *See also* Congressional Justice for Warriors Caucus (CJWC)
  corruption charges, 175
  pardons for war crime convictions, 52, 139, 140
  us/them binary, 76, 86

Ikenberry, John, 229
illegal interrogation techniques, 67–69
illegality of military conduct, 15
impeachment
  rejection of the impunity agenda from within, 222–224
impunity agenda, 13–15
  behavior of service members in battle, 259
  future of, 249–256
  individual troops granted clemency, impact of, 184–192
  lobbyist organizations, 179–184
  remedies
    binding methods, 219–228
    nonbinding methods, 207–218
  Republican lawmakers' advocacy, 175–178, 258
  right-wing media's aggressive advocacy, 169–175
impunity coalition, 31, 34–37, 70, 74
  citizens activation and rejection of IHL, 108–118
  military, influence over

Index 265

Fox News, 134–138, 258
Republican lawmakers, 138–142
Trump, 130–134, 192–199
survey of attitudes toward war crimes, 96–97
incentive to disrespect IHL, 6
Ingraham, Laura, 149, 158
in-group status and loyalty, 75–82, 118, **120**, **121**, **123**, **125**
  MFT values, 96–97, **100**, *105*, *109*, *113*
  patriotism and/or white nationalism narrative, 160–162
inhumane acts as crimes against humanity
  Israel-Hamas war, 231
Insurrectionist Act (1807), 165
  reform
    rejection of the impunity agenda from within, 227–228
intentionally directing attacks against a civilian population
  Israel-Hamas war, 231
International Committee of the Red Cross (ICRC), 201, 206
International Criminal Court (ICC), 11
  criminal prosecutions, 226–227
  Gbagbo, 226
  investigations of U.S. servicemembers, 62
  Netanyahu, 231, 235
  rejection of the impunity agenda from within, 221–222
  war crimes threshold, 18
International Criminal Tribunal for Rwanda (ICTR), 18
International Criminal Tribunal for the Former Yugoslavia (ICTFY), 18
  Slobodan Milosevic, 226
Iran Nuclear Deal, 23
Iraq, 1, 29, 53, 139, 148, 180, 211. *See also* Blackwater pardons; Raven 23 convoy
  violations of Iraq's sovereignty, 25
  pillaging threat, 63
  Iraq and Afghanistan Veterans of America, 78
Israel
  public respect for IHL, tenuous nature, 231

Israel-Hamas war, 13, 33
  disregard for IHL, 231–237
  criticisms of, 235
  Israel Defense Forces, 231
  Israeli government, 232
  Israeli media, 233
  Israeli military, 234
  Netanyahu, 231
  impunity agenda, 231–237
  public respect for IHL, tenuous nature, 231
  Trump–Netanyahu relationship, 235–237

Jaffer, Jameel, 68
Japan's strike on Pearl Harbor, 30
Joint Chiefs of Staff, 85
Jordan, Jim, 174
Justice for Victims of War Crimes Act (2022), 205

Karp, Alex, 246
Kennard, Matthew, 148
Khan, Humayun, 133
Kilmeade, Sean, 41
King, Steve, 88
Kirk, Charlie, 195
Kissinger, Henry, 222
Klaas, Brian, 243
Kolditz, Thomas, 146
Korean War, 23
Kucinich, Dennis, 223

language
  dehumanizing language, 79
  derogatory labels to undermine adversaries, 95
  inflammatory, racially charged, 81
Lantis, Jeffrey S., 178
law of war, U.S. presidents' relationship with, 25–30
lawyers, attacks on, 47, 52, 58, 87–88, 173, 205, 250–251
leadership transitions, 16
Lee, Mike, 65, 197
legislative oversight, 224
Lepper, Steven J., 132
Liberty, Evan, 38, 191
Libya, 29
limiting authority, 203

Lincoln Project, 137
lobbyist organizations
  advocacy for war crime interventions, 179–184
Lohmeier, Matthew, 150
Lorance, Clint, 200
  application to American Bar Association, 190
  moral purity arguments, 91
  overzealous prosecutors narrative, 88
  pardon for war crime conviction, 2, 37, 41, 139, 188–190
    CJWC, 53–54
    Fox News, 45–48
    lobbyist organizations, 179–181

MacCallum, Martha, 158
Manafort, Paul, 89
Manigault-Newman, Omarosa, 80
Marquez, Tommy, 197
Marsh, Kevin, 178
Mast, Brian, 140
Matthews, Earl, 166
Mattis, James, 60, 78, 250
  resignation, 214–215
McCabe, Neil, 173
McCaffrey, Barry R., 63
McCain, John, 69, 133, 142
McCallum, Martha, 41
McCausland, Jeff, 146
McConnell, Mitch, 66
McCormick, David, 148
McEnany, Kayleigh, 83
McInerney, Tom, 69
McVeigh, Timothy, 144
means to challenge IHL, 31, 34–37
  storming of the U.S. Capitol, 156–160
  war crime clemencies, 37–38
    Fox News' defense of, 45–50
    Fox News' influence, 38–45
    public reactions, 96–97
    public reactions (impunity coalition), 108–125
    public reactions (support for challenges to IHL), 101–108
    public reactions (support for exonerating crimes), 98–100
    Republican lawmakers' defense of, 55–58
    Republican lawmakers' influence, 50–55
media rotation program, 171
Mele, Jillian, 41
Meritt, Tyler, 182
migrant deportations, 254. *See also* noncombatant immunity
military advantage, 6
military impunity agenda. *See* impunity agenda
military lawyers, attacks on, 47, 52, 58, 87–88, 173, 205, 250–251
military voices speaking out, 207–209
Military.com, 188
Miller, Craig, 95
Miller, Derrick, 57, 141, 175, 197
Milley, Mark, 42, 85, 159, 165, 200, 209, 250, 252
Milosevic, Slobodan, 226
mockery of military service by Trump, 132–134
moderate Republicans
  impunity agenda, influence over, 209–211, 217
moral foundations theory (MFT), 72
  disregard for Geneva Conventions, 104–106
    by ideology, **106**, *107*, *108*
    by MFT values, *109*, **123**
  distributions of MFT values, by ideology, *98*
  MFT values, 97
  support for exoneration from the law, 98–99
    by ideology, **100**
    by MFT values, *100*, **120**
  support for using maximum firepower
    by ideology, 103, *104*
    by MFT values, *105*, **121**
U.S. military actions that challenge IHL
  disregard for Geneva Conventions, 104–108, 200
  rules of engagement, 101–104
waterboarding
  support for use, by ideology, **112**, *113*
  support for use, by MFT values, *113*, *114*, **115**, **125**

moral purity
 IHL violations, 32, 92
 moral purity in the law, 89
 us/them binary, 92–96
 war crime clemencies, 90
motive to publicly challenge IHL, 31–32, 71–75
 storming of the U.S. Capitol, 160–164
MSNBC, 172, 174
Mulligan, Katrina, 153
Mullin, Markwayne, 194, 197
My Lai Massacre (1968), 24, 257
Myanmar, 14, 243

National Defense Authorization Act, 176, 205
National Public Radio, 171
national sovereignty. *See* state sovereignty
Navarro, Peter, 85
Navy SEALs Fund (NSF), 181–183
NBC News, 171
Netanyahu, Benjamin, 13. *See also* Israel-Hamas war
 disregard for IHL, 231–232
 ICC investigation, 231, 235
New York Post, 171
New York Times, 1, 39, 139, 150, 171
 Gallagher, 182, 185
 Hegseth, 196
 Israel-Hamas war, 234
 Lorance, 188
Newbold, Adam, 157
Newbold, Kevin, 156
Newsmax, 171–173, 194, 198
 Republican lawmakers, relationship with, 173–175
Nichols, Terry Lynn, 144
Nichols, Tom, 136
Niehoff, Leonard M., 162
Nine Line Apparel, 182
 Gallagher-themed merchandise, 185
Nisour Square Massacre (2007), 37
Nixon, Richard, 24, 29, 225
noncombatant immunity, 59–60
 accountability for noncombatant casualties, 61–62
  Israel-Hamas war, 234
  Russo-Ukrainian war, 241

Nordean, Ethan, 163
normalization of anti-IHL agenda
 Netanyahu, 232, 235–236
 US, 13, 245
North Atlantic Treaty Organization (NATO)
 Trump's attacks on, 22, 217, 241

Oath Keepers, 143, 154, 157, 252
Obama, Barack, 56, 60, 61
 torture, condemnation of, 110
Ocasio-Cortez, Alexandria, 222
Omar, Ilhan, 222
One America News Network (OAN), 171, 172
 Republican lawmakers, relationship with, 173–175
O'Neill, Rob, 135, 187
Operation Iraqi Freedom, 152
opportunity to upend commitments to IHL, 32, 127–129
 military subcultures and norm socialization, 129
 storming of the U.S. Capitol, 164–167
Ornstein, Norman, 45
Ottawa Convention. *See* Anti-Personnel Mine Ban Treaty (1997)
oversight at the Pentagon, 205, 250–252
overtness of Trump's challenges to IHL, 5, 8, 22–30
 normalization of an anti-IHL agenda, 244–248
"ownership" of military, 132, 134

Palantir
 AI-enabled warfare, 246
Palestine. *See* Israel-Hamas war
Palmer, James, 24
Panama Canal
 USA seizure of, 254
Panetta, Leon, 85
pardons for war crime convictions, 1–2, 13, 30, 31
 Blackwater pardons, 37, 38, 43–45, 50, 54, 58, 88, 91, 182, 189, 191–192
 CJWC, 55–58
 Fox & Friends, 43–44, 46, 50, 51, 191

pardons for war crime (cont.)
  Fox News, 45–50, 55
    defense of pardons, 45–50
    influence, 38–45
  Gohmert, 44, 91
  Hannity, 43, 48
  Hegseth, 44
  Hunter, 52, 139, 140
  ICC investigations, 226
  individual troops granted clemency, impact of, 184–192
  means to challenge IHL, 37–38
  moral purity, 90
  public reactions, 96–97
    impunity coalition, 108–125
    support for challenges to IHL, 101–108
    support for exonerating crimes, 98–100
  Republican lawmakers' defense of, 55–58
  Republican lawmakers' influence, 50–55
Parlatore, Timothy, 94, 198
partisan conflicts in Congress, 177
Paul, Rand, 65
Payne, Charles, 63
Pelosi, Nancy, 81, 166
Pence, Mike, 78
Pentagon
  oversight and accountability, 205, 250–252
  political purges, 250
Perry, Mark, 133
Peters, Ralph, 135
Petraeus, David, 208
pillaging, 3, 34, 63, 209
Pipe Hitter Foundation, 197
Pirro, Jeanine, 41
Pitcavage, Mark, 146
political entrepreneurs, 6, 31, 70, 156
politicization of the military, 73, 165–167
Pompeo, Mike, 62
Porch, Douglas, 90
Posse Comitatus Act (1878), 227, 248
pressures from U.S. military voices
  rejection of the impunity agenda from within, 207–209
prohibitions on torture, 59

pro-Kremlin rhetoric, 177. *See also* Putin, Vladimir; Russo-Ukrainian War
proportionality principle, 65
  Russo-Ukrainian War, 238
prosecutorial deterrence
  rejection of the impunity agenda from within, 216–217
Proud Boys, 143, 154, 157, 185, 253
public gatherings
  advocacy for war crime interventions, 183
public opinion toward war crimes, 96–97, 231
  Israel, 231
  Russia, 231
  waterboarding, 108–118
purging of Pentagon officials, 250
Putin, Vladimir. *See also* Russia; Russo-Ukrainian War
  disregard for IHL, 231, 241

QAnon, 14, 158, 174
  storming of the U.S. Capitol, 163

racebaiting, 8, 81
Rainey, Emily, 155
Raskin, Jamie, 253
Raven 23 convoy, 37, 43, 45, 55, 182, 191–92. *See also* Blackwater pardons
Reagan, Ronald, 254
reinforcement of the impunity agenda from within
  CJWC, 175–176
  polarization in Congress, 176–178
Repeal Hague Invasion Act (2022), 222
Republican lawmakers
  disproportionate force, 66
  noncombatant immunity, 62
  relationship with military, 138–142
  right-wing media, relationship with, 173–175
  state sovereignty, 65
  storming of the U.S. Capitol, 158–160
  torture, 67–69
Reschenthaler, Guy, 56
restraining the impunity agenda from within

Cabinet resistance, 214–216
critiques from conservative intellectual circles, 211–212
domestic prosecution, 224–225
executive orders, 220–221
global criminal prosecution, 226–227
"guerrilla sabotage" in government, 213–214
ICC jurisdiction, 221–222
impeachment, 222–224
limiting executive powers, 219–220
pressures from U.S. military voices, 207–209
pushback from moderate Republicans, 209–211
reform of the Insurrectionist Act, 227–228
social deterrence and prosecutorial deterrence, 216–217
UN resolutions, 217–218
restraints on the use of force, 59, 104, 244
Rhodes, Stewart, 154
Richmond, Edward, 152
Riddle, Jason, 155
Rieckhoff, Paul, 78
Robertson, Thomas, 155
Rogers, Mike, 149
Rome Statute of ICC, 18
Rounds, Mike, 194
Rubio, Marco, 62, 65, 69
rule of law, 160, 241
  military justice, 229
rules of engagement. *See* U.S. military rules of engagement (ROE)
Russia. *See also* Russo-Ukrainian War
  public respect for IHL, tenuous nature, 231
Russo-Ukrainian War, 33
  abducting and deporting Ukrainian children, 237
  disregard for IHL
    government, 239
    Putin, 237–238
    Russian Armed Forces, 240
    state media, 239
  genocide, 238, 239, 241
  Harris, 242
  impunity agenda, 237–242

nationhood and self-determination, 238
noncombatant casualties, 241
public respect for IHL, tenuous nature, 231
Trump–Putin relationship, 241–243

Sasse, Ben, 65
Saunders, Elizabeth N., 177
Save Our Heroes (SOH), 181
Scalise, Steve, 56, 85
Schumer, Chuck, 81
Scott, Rick, 194
screening of recruits and training of commanders, 203
self-governing norms and regulations, 32
Senate Armed Services Committee, 30
Sessions, Jeff, 85
Slatten, Nicholas, 38, 43, 191
Slife, James, 250
Slotkin, Elissa, 146
Slough, Paul, 38, 43, 192
Smith, Rob, 149
Smith, Sandra, 41
social deterrence
  rejection of the impunity agenda from within, 216–217
social media, 175. *See also* Facebook; X (formerly Twitter)
  advocacy for war crime interventions, 183
  CJWC, 54, 56, 58
  Gallagher, 78, 183
  IDF and noncombatant immunity, 234
  Lorance, 189
socialization theories, 7, 21, 128, 129–130
Soleimani, Qasem, 64–65, 81
Special Court for Sierra Leone, 18
  Charles Taylor's trial, 226
Spencer, Richard, 49, 57, 213
Springer, Drew, 58
starvation of civilians. *See also* noncombatant immunity
  Israel-Hamas war, 231
state sovereignty
  Fox News, 63
  Iraq War, 25
  legality of foreign assassinations, 64–67

state sovereignty (cont.)
  Putin's rhetoric against Ukraine, 13, 238
  Republican lawmakers, 65
  Trump's contempt for international law, 3, 59, 62–64
Stevenson, Adlai, 257
Stone, Roger, 88
storming of the U.S. Capitol, 151–152
  delayed military response, 164–167
  means to incite violence, 152, 156–158
    Fox News' role, 158
    Republican lawmakers' role, 158–160
  military service members, role of, 152–156
  motive to court right-wing military community, 152, 160–164
  opportunity to inflict damage, 152, 164–167
strikes on civilian centers, 24, 198, 238, 245. *See also* noncombatant immunity
structural reforms and criminal charges, 205
structuralism, 5, 19
Sudan, 14
superior orders defense
  storming of the U.S. Capitol, 162
Swalwell, Eric, 137
Syria, 14, 29, 214
  drone strikes, 59
  rules of engagement, 61
  violations of Syrian sovereignty pillaging threat, 63

Taleb, Rashida, 222
Talmon, Stefan, 230
Tankel, Stephen, 83
Taylor, Charles, 226
technological advancements, 245
Thornberry, Mac, 61
Tirman, John, 23
torture, 25, 67–69
  Bush torture memos, 26, 212
  Fox News' support for, 67–69
  Hannity's support for, 67
  Obama's condemnation of, 110
  Republican lawmakers, 67–69

Trump's support for, 31, 59
trade tariffs, 254
Trump's contempt for international law, 1–9, 22–30, 200
  policy and governance, importance for, 12–15
  scholarship and research, importance for, 9–12
Trump's relationship with military, 130–134
Turning Point USA, 195
Twitter. *See* X (formerly Twitter)

Ukraine. *See* Russo-Ukrainian War
UN Human Rights Council, 23
UN resolutions
  rejection of the impunity agenda from within, 217–218
Uniform Code of Military Justice (UCMJ), 31
United American Patriots (UAP), 179–180
United Nations (UN) High Commissioner for Human Rights, 13
upholding the law of war as an ethical and strategic imperative, 6, 200, 202–203
Urben, Heidi, 208
U.S. Agency for International Development, 254
U.S. Capitol, assault of January 6th, 2023, 13, 32
U.S. military
  agents of death, as, 200
  disregard for Geneva Conventions, 104–108, 200
  Fox News, relationship with, 134–138
  illegality of military conduct, 15
  Law of War Manual, 22
  military lawyers, 47, 52, 58, 87–88, 173, 205, 250–251
  military subcultures and norm socialization, 129
    right-wing extremism, 142–151
  military votes, 131
  ownership of military, 132, 134
  politicization of the military, 73
  recruitment, 147–149

Republican lawmakers, relationship with, 138–142
support for Trump, 130–134
Trump's relationship with, 130–134
violations of IHL, 1–3, 8
U.S. military rules of engagement (ROE), 57, 60, 101–104, 198
U.S.–Mexico border wall, 81
us/them binary, 75–82
moral purity, 92–96

Vance, J.D., 242
Vietnam War, 30
Vindman, Alexander, 214
Vriens, Joshua, 95

Waltz, Michael, 56, 61, 198
war crime clemencies. *See* pardons for war crime convictions
war crime interventions. *See* pardons for war crime convictions
War Crimes Act (1996), 206
war criminal, Trump as, 15–18
war on terror, 4, 25
Warrior Boards, 150
Washington Post, 84, 139, 158, 171, 213, 227
waterboarding
moral foundations theory
support for use, by ideology, 112, *113*
support for use, by MFT values, *113*, *114*, 115, 125

Obama's disapproval, 110
public opinion toward war crimes, 108–118
Trump's endorsement, 2, 67–68, 79, 92, 108–110
Waters, Jesse, 68
Watkins, Jessica, 155
Webster, Daniel, 58
white supremacy
military service members, 146, 161
Whiton, Christian, 62
willfully causing great suffering
Israel-Hamas war, 231
witness intimidation, 196, 214
wokeness
purging of "woke" hires, 150, 250

X (formerly Twitter), 67, 78, 190, 197. *See also* social media
CJWC, 56, 58
Free Raven 23, 192
Trump, 49
xenophobia, 8, 81

Yoo, John, 47, 212

Zelensky, Volodymyr, 87. *See also* Russo-Ukrainian War
Zhuravlyov, Aleksey, 239
Zinke, Ryan
pardons for war crime convictions, 139

For EU product safety concerns, contact us at Calle de José Abascal, 56–1°, 28003 Madrid, Spain or eugpsr@cambridge.org.

www.ingramcontent.com/pod-product-compliance
Lightning Source LLC
LaVergne TN
LVHW020342260326
834688LV00045B/1490